THE ROAD NOT TAKEN

THE ROAD NOT TAKEN

A History of Radical Social Work in the United States

Michael Reisch, Ph.D.
University of Michigan

Janice Andrews, Ph.D.
*University of St. Thomas
and College of St. Catherine*

USA	Publishing Office:	BRUNNER-ROUTLEDGE
		A member of the Taylor & Francis Group
		325 Chestnut Street
		Philadelphia, PA 19106
		Tel: (215) 625-8900
		Fax: (215) 625-2940
	Distribution Center:	BRUNNER-ROUTLEDGE
		A member of the Taylor & Francis Group
		7625 Empire Drive
		Florence, KY 41042
		Tel: 1-800-634-7064
		Fax: 1-800-248-4724
UK		BRUNNER-ROUTLEDGE
		A member of the Taylor & Francis Group
		27 Church Road
		Hove
		E. Sussex, BN3 2FA
		Tel: +44 (0) 1273 207411
		Fax: +44 (0) 1273 205612

THE ROAD NOT TAKEN: A History of Radical Social Work in the United States

1 2 3 4 5 6 7 8 9 0

Printed by Sheridan Books, Ann Arbor, MI, 2001
Cover design by Ellen Seguin

A CIP catalog record for this book is available from the British Library.
 The paper in this publication meets the requirements of the ANSI Standard
Z39.48-1984 (Permanence of Paper)

Library of Congress Cataloging-in-Publication Data
Reisch, Michael, 1948-
 The road not taken : a history of radical social work in the United States / Michael Reisch, Janice Andrews.
  p. cm.
 Includes index.
 ISBN 1-58391-025-5
  1. Social service--United States--History--20th century. 2. Radicalism--United States--History--20th century. I. Andrews, Janice. II. Title.

HV91 .R455 2001
361.3'2'0973--dc21   2001025363

Contents

Preface

Part of the [current] political struggle in social work is . . . how to remember its past.
—Robert Fisher and Jacob Karger,
Social Work and Community in a Private World

This book examines the evolution of the profession of social work in the United States through a radical lens, a lens seldom utilized in such explorations of social work's past. Beginning with the origins of modern social work in the Progressive Era and ending with a view of the potential of radical social work in the twenty-first century, we offer an analysis that provides an alternative to most histories of social work. Generally, the development of social work in the United States is discussed in terms of the roles played by major institutional and organizational forces, the individuals who led them, and the dominant ideas they produced. Consequently, there is little attention paid in most histories to the influence of radicals *within the profession* or of external radical ideas and groups *on the profession* in shaping social work's ideology or the social policies, programs, and modes of intervention proposed and implemented by the field.

We sought to go beyond this traditional analysis, giving voice to the effects of nonmainstream social service and social work organizations on the creation of U.S. social welfare and the emergence of social work theories and methods. The sources of this history are varied. They include oral histories we conducted, interviews with contemporary social workers ranging in age from their twenties to their eighties, a survey of current social work radicals, archival and other primary source materials, and secondary works produced by scholars inside and outside the social work field.

We believe that the data we compiled alter the prevailing conception of social work. We are called upon to reflect on the roads not taken and the journeys abandoned by the profession during its first hundred years. This also requires us to examine more closely the response of mainstream institutions, political leaders, and the media to radical ideas in social welfare and social work.

These responses, which ranged from accommodation, co-optation, and incorporation to harsh repression, often have been unreported in histories of social work.

Consequently, many contemporary social workers, students, and even faculty are ignorant of the ways in which social workers with radical ideas have been attacked by politicians and the press, harassed by government agencies like the FBI and the House Un-American Activities Committee, and fired or blacklisted from gainful employment in both the public and private sectors. Conversely, today's social workers are also unaware of how many formerly radical concepts and proposals are now accepted as "givens" by the profession and the society as a whole. In a climate in which the values of social welfare and social work are under unprecedented challenge by powerful forces in U.S. society, it would be useful to recognize why radical social work ideas were and continue to be regarded as threatening by economic and political elites. This knowledge could help social workers and their allies develop effective responses to their opponents and critics now and in the future.

This book, therefore, is intended for several audiences. Undergraduate and graduate students of social work may find it a useful alternative to traditional histories of the profession, one that better illustrates the long-standing struggle to translate its values into action. The book could provoke social work faculty and practitioners in the community to examine more closely the relationship between rhetoric and reality in contemporary theory, policy, and methods. The book also may be of interest to faculty and students in the fields of American social history, women's studies, and the history or sociology of the professions. Finally, the book may appeal to individuals who lived through or are interested in the tumultuous periods it covers. As social work in many ways embodies or challenges persistent American beliefs about people's problems and society's responsibility to address them, exploring the ways in which these beliefs evolved casts an interesting light on contemporary political debates.

We began our collaboration in the mid-1990s to study the impact of McCarthyism on the social work profession. This focus emerged out of our long-standing interest in the history of the field and was further stimulated by our growing awareness of the personal experiences of older colleagues that were largely omitted from historical accounts of the profession. Not surprisingly, we discovered that anti-Communism in the post–World War II era had a long-lasting influence on domestic social policies and the development of social work in the United States. We were particularly moved by the deep psychological scars McCarthyism left on many radical social workers of that era and the impact it had on their careers. Fortunately, we were able to interview in person or through correspondence many of these individuals late in their lives.

Through such conversations and correspondence, we came to understand that the repression of social work radicals and their ideas—sometimes overt, more often subtle—was not entirely external. The organized forces of the profession itself, along with many individual social workers, engaged in repressive activities against radical colleagues, often out of fear or professional insecurity, sometimes out of deeply held ideological differences. Our growing awareness of these events and their legacy also shed new light on the arguments of social work scholars and activists that the process and dictates of professionalism itself were impediments to the acceptance of radical ideas (Fisher, 1994; Specht & Courtney, 1994; Wagner, 1990; Walkowitz, 1999; Wenocur & Reisch, 1989).

This led us to expand the breadth of our research to include the entire twentieth century to obtain a fuller picture of the history of social work radicalism. We found incidents of remarkable courage as well as stories of fear and reprisal, which help explain some of the current anti-social welfare attitudes and actions in the nation, and the resistance to radical ideas within government and the social work profession itself. Some of these events are already well known; others have received little or no attention in books. We realized early that we could never hear all the silenced voices or read the unrecorded testimony of many unheralded radical social workers of the past. Our study, therefore, has been limited by the sources available to us as well as our own abilities.

Acknowledgments

Many people were of enormous help to us as we engaged in our research and writing. Clarke Chambers, professor emeritus at the University of Minnesota and a distinguished historian of social work, and Harold Lewis, dean emeritus of Hunter College School of Social Work and a distinguished radical social work scholar, met with us in the early stages of our project, helped us find important materials and key sources of information, and encouraged us in our work. Dr. Lewis also provided essential background information on the McCarthy period from the perspective of a survivor of its worst aspects.

Stanley Wenocur of the University of Maryland, colleague, mentor, and friend, provided us with source materials on the Social Welfare Workers Movement (SWWM) in which he was integrally involved in the late 1960s and early 1970s. Joel Blau of the State University of New York at Stony Brook, an original member of the Catalyst Collective and a cofounder of the Radical Alliance of Social Service Workers (RASSW) in the 1970s, and Paul Stuart of the University of Alabama read a draft of the manuscript and provided valuable suggestions. Faculty colleagues like Stanley Ofsevit, now retired from San Francisco State University, Paul Ephross of the University of Maryland, Louis Levitt of the Wurzweiler School of Social Work at Yeshiva University, and Charles Garvin of the University of Michigan encouraged us to pursue this work, as did other colleagues in the Association of Community Organization and Social Administration (ACOSA), the Association for the Advancement of Social Work with Groups (AASWG), and the Bertha Capen Reynolds Society (BCRS, now the Social Welfare Action Alliance). A special posthumous thanks must also go to Norman Goroff, Susan Kinoy, and Nancy Cook von Bretzel for their constant inspiration, ideas, good humor, and support.

In addition, we appreciate the assistance of the National Association of Social Workers (NASW), the Council on Social Work Education (CSWE), ACOSA, AASWG, and the BCRS in helping us locate contemporary radical social workers. David Klaassen, archivist of the Social Welfare History Archives at the University of Minnesota, met with us several times and enabled us to find essential and previously unused materials. The staff at the Evelyn Butler Archive at the University of Pennsylvania, the manuscript collection of the New York Public Library, the Columbia University Library, the Verne Weed Collection at Hunter College School of Social Work, the Sophia Smith Collection at Smith College, and the Marion Hathway Collection at the University of Pittsburgh were also particularly helpful. Special thanks go to Professor Edward Sites of the University of Pittsburgh for helping us to gain access to the latter. Ursula Bischoff and Fiona Patterson were dedicated, hardworking, and understanding research assistants. Our respective universities provided research support, including a sabbatical leave for one of us. Above all, we thank our families and friends for their ongoing support and indulgence. Any omissions or errors of fact or judgment in our work are, of course, entirely our responsibility.

Finally, the heroes of our story are the people we met during our own journey of discovery, those whose words came to life in various archival sources, oral histories, diaries, letters, interviews, and written surveys. We believe their experiences can provide important lessons for their professional descendants, now and in the years ahead. We thank them most of all and hope this book honors their lives and their memories.

1

Social Work—
A Radical Profession?

> *The profession of social work has never been able to rid itself of the ambiguity of hovering between an archaic individualism and a possibly radical collectivism.*
> —Marvin Gettleman, "Charity and Social Classes in the U.S., 1874–1900, I," *American Journal of Economics and Society*

RADICAL RHETORIC AND REALITY

These days social workers often refer to social justice and overcoming oppression, particularly in the official documents of their leading organizations. The Curriculum Policy Statement of the Council on Social Work Education (CSWE, 2001), the accrediting body of all bachelor's and master's social work degree programs in the United States, requires all social work programs to teach students how to promote economic and social justice. The revised *Code of Ethics* (1996) of the National Association of Social Workers proclaims the pursuit of social justice one of the profession's core values and establishes as an ethical imperative "Social workers challenge social injustice" (p. 5). The *Code's* ethical standards, in fact, are explicit:

> Social workers should engage in social and political action that seeks to ensure that all people have equal access to the resources, employment, services, and opportunities they require to meet their basic human needs and to develop fully. Social workers should . . . advocate for changes in policy and legislation to improve social conditions in order to meet basic human needs and promote social justice . . . with special regard for vulnerable, disadvantaged, oppressed, and exploited people and groups . . . [In this regard], social workers should act to prevent and eliminate domination of, exploitation of, and discrimination

against any person, group, or class on the basis of race, ethnicity, national origin, sex, sexual orientation, age, marital status, political belief, religion, or mental or physical disability (p. 27).

At first glance, these statements give the appearance that social work in the United States at the end of the twentieth century had taken a distinctly dramatic turn. The rhetoric in the *Code of Ethics* articulates what some might consider a radical vision for the profession. In today's context, however, the *Code* actually may be patronizing and not at all empowerment focused because it continues to assume that social workers work *for* rather than *with* people. What, then, do its statements really signify?

For nearly a decade, pundits have regularly proclaimed the bankruptcy of socialist ideas, the triumph of the free market and liberal democracy, the so-called end of history (Fukuyama, 1992). Feminist ideas have become increasingly disparaged as irrelevant even by women (Faludi, 1991), and modestly redistributive programs like Affirmative Action have been rolled back by state governments, the courts, and even new public referenda. Proposals to privatize Social Security—the cornerstone of the limited U.S. welfare state—have gained credibility and popularity, even a sense of inevitability. In the chorus of voices praising global capitalism (Friedman, 2000), words like justice and oppression sound increasingly out of tune and out of touch with policymakers and the public. They seem to hark back to another, distant time when radicalism in society and in the field of social work was more vital and more viable.

Besides, most social workers today are hardly radicals; few engage in social and political action even of a reformist nature. In 1996, when President Bill Clinton signed legislation that "end[ed] welfare as we know it," there was little organized protest from the social work profession. Although the act terminated a 60-year-old entitlement to assistance for low-income children and their caretakers that social workers had helped to create and had defended vigorously for decades, NASW endorsed Clinton for reelection with little reference to the issue. In marked contrast to past generations, the protests of radical social workers received scant attention inside and outside the profession.

Some writers regard this gap between rhetoric and reality as a betrayal of the profession's original mission (Specht & Courtney, 1994). Others argue that social work has never been a radical profession (Iglehart & Becerra, 1995; Stoesz, 1999; Wagner, 1990). In fact, there has been a persistent question in the field, among both conservatives and radicals, of whether radicalism—or even social activism—is compatible with professionalism at all (Burghardt & Fabricant, 1992; Leonard, 1995; Newdom, 1997; Reamer, 1993; Reeser & Epstein, 1990; Wenocur & Reisch, 1989; Withorn, 1984).

If issues of social justice and overcoming oppression are increasingly irrelevant to the nation's political agenda and if social workers have only marginal impact today on shaping this agenda, do such debates really matter? To paraphrase an oft-quoted question from another era (Rein, 1970): Is contemporary social work a (potentially) radical profession? Has it ever been and could it ever be?

It is our contention that such issues are still relevant—for society and for social work—and that such questions are important to address even if organized social work never pursues explicitly radical goals. The mere act of asking the questions creates the opportunity to examine the potential role of social work in the rapidly changing global society of the twenty-first century. Yet asking such questions involves considerable risk, because a question that probes beneath the surface meaning of things is dangerous in a society (and a profession) that survives by accepting certain historical "givens" unquestioningly. We believe that the rewards involved in the exploration of how radical ideas, individuals, and groups influenced American social policies and the formation of the social work profession are worth such risks. They can provide fresh insights into contemporary dilemmas and broaden our strategic options for the future.

NEGLECT OF THE RADICAL TRADITION IN AMERICAN SOCIAL WORK

As George Orwell vividly portrayed in his classic novel *1984*, one way a society shapes the future is by controlling the images of its past. The denial of the radical tradition in American society and of the social conflict it both reflected and produced has reinforced the aura of inevitability that surrounds mythic portrayals of the nation's history—from the Manifest Destiny of the midnineteenth century to the so-called triumph of capitalism and democracy today. Differences between the United States and other industrialized nations in the development of their social welfare systems are usually explained by "American exceptionalism" (Gilbert, 1983; Jansson, 1997). The various roads not taken are rarely mentioned, nor are the ways these unrealized alternative choices shaped our institutions, values, and policies up to the present. In an increasingly ahistorical culture, we are ignorant of those elements of our past that challenged the status quo and deny the roles that radical actors and ideas played in bettering the lives of people. This views "the present through a distorted prism of the past . . . [and] subtly encourage[s us] to dissociate present problems and [their] solutions from their historical antecedents" (Reisch, 1988, p. 4). It is important, therefore, that we introduce alternative sources of information to acquire fresh perspectives on contemporary issues.

This historical amnesia afflicts the field of social work as well. Most histories of U.S. social work and social welfare focus on the ways dominant culture organizations shaped the society's conceptions of need and helping. They largely ignore the influence of radical ideas, individuals, and groups on the development of U.S. social policies and the formation of the profession of social work. They do this by discussing the evolution of the profession in terms of the roles played by those organizations and leaders that reflected the mainstream ideas and political currents of their eras (Axinn & Stern, 2000; Ehrenreich, 1985; Jansson, 1997; Katz, 1986; Lubove, 1965; Trattner, 1995). With few exceptions (Abramovitz, 1999; Day, 2000; Iglehart & Becerra, 1995; Popple & Leighninger, 1998; Rivera & Erlich, 1998), social work texts pay scant attention to the impact of "outsiders"—communities of color, women, Jews, trade unionists, and radicals—on the development of the field and the policies that shaped it.

These so-called "Whig histories" (Gettleman, 1974), therefore, ignore the conscious or compelled choices the profession made about its ideology, goals, methods of intervention, and public policy positions. They obscure the role that radical social work played in shaping many of the concepts that the profession and the society now take for granted, such as legal entitlements to social benefits, client self-determination and empowerment, the role of the environment in creating personal problems, and the essential dignity of all human beings. Consequently, as many of these concepts have been assimilated into mainstream institutions they have been largely stripped of their radical origins, content, and intent. This makes it difficult to imagine how American society or American social work would have evolved without their influence. It also makes alternative visions of the future harder to imagine.

USES OF A RADICAL HISTORY OF SOCIAL WORK

In writing this history, however, we assume that U.S. social welfare and social work evolved through more dynamic and complex processes than are usually depicted. This evolution involved an ongoing synthesis of ideas and actions that emerged both from hegemonic institutions and organizations created by disadvantaged and marginalized populations and their allies. Radical individuals and groups played a critical role in forging this synthesis.

To understand this dynamic process we also need to examine how mainstream institutions responded to the radical challenge, particularly in repressive ways that are often overlooked (Gordon, 1990; Wenocur & Reisch, 1989). Just as many Americans are unaware of the "darker side" of our nation's history (the true nature of slavery, the genocide of American Indians, the suppression of organized labor and left-wing movements), many social workers today are ignorant of the ways in which politicians, the media, and colleagues attacked their radical predecessors. They are unaware that government agencies harassed radical social workers, often leading to their dismissal, blacklisting, and imprisonment. Nor do today's social workers know how their radical ancestors and their principled supporters resisted such attacks, individually and collectively. In today's climate, in which powerful political and cultural forces condemn even the liberal values of social work, knowledge of such historical antecedents could help social workers create more effective responses.

Recognition of how radical ideas influenced or were repressed by the dominant societal and professional cultures would, therefore, be helpful in overcoming students' ahistorical conception of social work's development and in countering contemporary anti–social work rhetoric (Reisch, 1988). By viewing social work's history as a dynamic process, today's practitioners and students can acquire a better appreciation of the potential roles of their clients and constituents in shaping the future environment of practice and policy formation. This will provide them with a stronger conceptual foundation upon which to apply empowerment- or strengths-based perspectives in their daily work and clarify the significance of the curricular and ethical imperatives established by CSWE and NASW regarding economic and social justice (Gutierrez, Parsons, & Cox, 1998; Saleeby, 1997; Simon, 1994).

DEFINITIONS OF RADICAL SOCIAL WORK

One reason the history of radicalism in social work has been neglected is the persistent confusion over the meaning of radicalism within the field. During the past century, the term "radical" has been defined in various ways both inside and outside the profession. William De Maria (1992) captures this difficulty succinctly:

> The social work radical is someone who has a philosophical leaning towards the importance of discovering first causes of oppression (or injustice or disadvantage). That, however, is only half the story and many social workers who are called radical end here. The next stage is to transform the insights gleaned from the foundation material into immediate social action . . . to move from structural analysis to structural practice . . . with the sobering awareness that the latter is far more difficult to achieve than the former." (p. 237)

Jansson (1994) also remarks on the diversity of radical positions within social work. He asserts that although all radical social workers are united in a focus on equality, the failings of capitalism, and a belief "that the social and economic problems of subgroups stem from their oppression by the broader society and corporate interests," there are considerable differences of emphasis and shading. "Some radicals, such as socialists, want to transform capitalist institutions into publicly run industries or favor worker ownership of corporations." Short of this difficult goal, "radicals favor the major redistribution of wealth through tax policies [and extensive] government programs" that although universal in scope provide special benefits to the most needy segments of society. For example, some radicals propose policies that target specific groups such as persons of color. Feminists promote policies that "equalize conditions between women and men" and that promote equal rights. Although "radicals have fewer inhibitions about far-reaching government interventions, [they] are often critical of existing social programs, which, they argue, reflect the interests of corporate and conservative groups" (p. 7). Some radicals, in fact, adopt a conspiratorial analysis of government programs regarding them as means to divert attention from long-term, structural change in society and its institutions.

Reamer (1995) agrees that radical perspectives in social work are "less clear cut" than those of liberals and conservatives. Although many radicals share the concerns of conservatives about excessive government interference into people's lives, they often promote an expanded role for government "to correct imperfections of free enterprise and to promote social justice" (p. 130). They are critical, however, of the ways in which government promotes the economic interests of capitalists while ignoring the needs of ordinary people. Radical social workers focus on people's rights rather than on their needs (Blau, 1989; Reamer, 1993; Reisch, 1998). They often link these rights to dramatic changes in socioeconomic conditions, overcoming political subjugation, support for unionization over professionalization, and anti-corporate policies.

Longres (1996) argues that the underlying principles of radical social work have remained constant. They include: (1) a belief that the institutional structure of society is the primary source of the personal problems of clients; (2) a focus on economic inequality as a central concern and cause of other social and individual problems; (3) a critical view of social service agencies as instruments of social control, co-optation, or stigmatization; (4) a focus on both structural and internalized oppression; and (5) a linkage of cause and function and private troubles and public issues.

Radical social workers in his view may differ, however, in their understanding of capitalism and the degree to which they espouse some form of socialism—from a set of ideals that guide practice to concrete rules for social policies. Like Mullaly and Keating (1991), Longres characterizes these different radical groups as revolutionary Marxists, evolutionary Marxists, and social democrats. Reflecting ideas found in the work of Bertha Capen Reynolds, an icon among many contemporary radical social workers, Longres asserts that "social work[ers] as . . . profession[als] cannot lead working- and lower-middle-class people, our natural constituencies, back into the fold (i.e., pro-social welfare)," nor can they be "neutral mediators." At a time when conservative ideas are ascendant, "there is no immediate hope for a return to liberal, let alone radical, ideas." Therefore, although the special contribution of U.S. progressives is their analysis of multicultural issues, "progressive social workers in the U.S. need to refocus on economic class conflict. The struggle for material equality must be the glue that holds us together as a profession" (pp. 236–238).

Wagner offers another narrower definition of social work radicalism as consisting of those "social workers who have labeled themselves [radical] by joining left-wing organizations or visibly supporting leftist causes" (Wagner, 1989a, p. 281). Here are included social workers who joined or were affiliated with the Communist or Socialist Parties, the more radical civil rights and antiwar organizations of the 1960s, local and national welfare rights organizations, and various support groups for revolutionary movements in Central America and South Africa. Also included in this category are radical social workers who do not necessarily identify with a particular ideology, political organization, or theory of social change, yet espouse a dramatic transformation of society, its institutions, and of social relationships.

This confusion over the meaning of radicalism in social work has had two important consequences. First, the radical roots of social work are obscured or overlooked in this jumble of definitions. The radical origins of now widely accepted values are forgotten because these values (and the policies they produce) are often taken for granted. In an environment in which young workers question the importance of labor unions, young women take abortion rights for granted, and even some African Americans challenge the necessity of maintaining civil rights laws, it should not be surprising that contemporary social workers show little cognizance of the battles fought by their social worker ancestors. Despite their inclusion of the standard rhetoric of social justice, empowerment, and multiculturalism, few contemporary texts on social work practice incorporate a consciously radical perspective on practice (Gutierrez, Parsons, & Cox, 1998; Simon, 1994).

Second, the absence of a historical perspective leads some observers to criticize the radicals of the past for not living up to twenty-first-century standards of political correctness. Jane Addams is chastised for not being a feminist (Lacerte, 1976); Florence Kelley is criticized for opposing the Equal Rights Amendment in the 1920s (Sklar, 1995); and the Rank and File Movement of the 1930s is attacked for failing to address adequately the needs of African Americans (Iglehart & Becerra, 1995; Lasch-Quinn, 1993). It is ironic that such criticisms have emerged in a profession that places so much importance in recognizing how context shapes individual and group behavior. It is also a distortion of history to apply universal meanings to complex concepts like radicalism and contemporary standards to the conduct of individuals and groups in very different eras.

Consequently, one of the themes of this book is that the definition of a "radical social worker" or a radical conception of social work practice evolved both in substance and significance as a result of changes in the sociopolitical climate of the United States, the status of the profession, and the ideology of its practitioners. The application of a single definition of social work radicalism, therefore, does not capture the profession's rich history or reflect accurately the degree of risk taking among social workers in distinctive historical periods, including the present. Judging radicals of previous generations by contemporary standards or contemporary radicals by past standards obscures the impact and significance of their ideas and actions.

EMERGENCE OF RADICAL SOCIAL WORK

The earliest generations of social workers were either, like Florence Kelley, Lillian Wald, and Ellen Gates Starr, radicals before they became social workers, or became radicalized, like Robert Hunter and Jane Addams, as a consequence of their work in the field. Yet, a self-conscious vision of radical social work practice, as opposed to a radical vision of society or a radical analysis of its problems, did not emerge until *after* social work had become established as an organized occupation and aspiring profession. This occurred during the New Deal, largely through the Rank and File Movement and its organizational allies (Fisher, 1936, 1990). Thus, although there were radicals within the social welfare field prior to the 1930s, there were few radical *social workers* and no radical movements within the social services, per se, before the mid-1930s (Fisher, 1980; Spano, 1982; Wenocur & Reisch, 1989).

This is not to suggest, however, that the actions of such diverse figures as Hunter, Kelley, Addams, Wald, Starr, and Jeanette Rankin were not radical. It took enormous courage for Addams and Wald to actively oppose U.S. intervention in World War I and for Rankin to be the only member of Congress to vote against a declaration of war in both 1917 and 1941. The socialist vision that inspired Hunter, Kelley, Wald, Starr, and others was certainly well outside the political mainstream, even during a period when Eugene V. Debs and other socialists openly ran for and were elected to public office.

After the demise of the Rank and File Movement in the early 1940s, there was little reference to radical social work for several decades, for reasons we will explore in subsequent chapters. Ironically, most of the literature on radical social work practice and education has appeared during the past thirty years as radical movements in the field declined in scope and influence. During these years, the official rhetoric of professional organizations like NASW and CSWE have paradoxically reflected radical influences even as their activities have focused primarily on the pursuit and maintenance of professional prerogatives (Austin, 1997; Specht & Courtney, 1994). This illustrates the ongoing and inherent tensions between radicalism and professionalism—a persistent theme of this book.

REPRESSION OF SOCIAL WORK RADICALISM

A fuller picture of the influence of social work radicals over the past century also requires an examination of the persistent repression of radical individuals and ideas within the field. This occurred in several ways. Radical social work leaders, such as Addams, Kelley, Wald, Bertha Capen Reynolds, Mary van Kleeck, and many others of lesser renown, have been investigated by legislative committees; denounced as subversives by political, civic, and corporate leaders; and hounded by the press. On occasion, radical social workers have been prosecuted and organizations to which they belonged have been attacked in the courts and the media. Many ordinary social workers were fired or blacklisted from government posts, nonprofit agencies, and universities for their political views. These are merely the most dramatic and visible aspects of the repression of social work radicals and radicalism during the past century. They are by no means the most significant.

Often, the repression of social work radicals and their ideas occurred through more subtle means than a legislative investigation or well-publicized trial and was initiated by forces within the profession itself. Radical solutions to social problems have been diluted through their incorporation into liberal reforms and radical analyses of social issues have been ignored. The pursuit of professionalism often precluded the introduction of radical theories and methods into social work education and agency practice (Reisch, 1998; Wenocur & Reisch, 1989). Individual radicals have also sometimes been coopted by status, power, and public acclaim.

Probably the prime example of this co-optation was the creation of the myth of "Saint Jane" out of the social criticism and radical activism of Jane Addams, the cofounder of Hull House. Placing Addams on a public pedestal weakened the force of her criticism of U.S. society and hastened her fall from grace when she opposed U.S. entry into World War I (Lasch, 1965). It also obscured the fundamental questions she raised about the direction of U.S. society, such as, "Is industrialism compatible with humanity?" It masked the radicalism behind her vocal opposition to American imperialism in the Philippines; her defense of the anarchist, Abraham Isaak (who had been arrested after the assassination of President McKinley); and her delivery of a passionate eulogy for Illinois Governor John Altgeld, who had been vilified for his pardon of the Haymarket riot defendants and his support for prolabor legislation (Symes & Clement, 1972).

In the post–World War I era, for the first time, radical ideas were repressed through the legal instruments of government at the federal and state levels. U.S. Attorney General A. Mitchell Palmer tried and deported hundreds of suspected radicals. Legislative bodies, like the Lusk Committee in New York, in cooperation with the press, stirred up a well-orchestrated postwar red scare. Attacks on radicals also appeared in the form of quasi-institutional propaganda such as the widely promoted "spider web conspiracy," and through the influence of corporate-dominated federated fund-raising in large and mid-sized cities.

Although social workers were not the primary targets of these repressive activities, they often were singled out and accused of unpatriotic or "Bolshevik" sympathies. The explicit attacks on social work leaders like Addams, Kelley, and Wald have been well-documented recently by historians, yet the broader significance of these events for the history of social work receives scant attention in the profession's literature. While some scholars have noted their impact on the social action orientation of the settlement movement (Chambers, 1963; Trolander, 1975), the long-term implications of labeling social work leaders subversives have not been fully explored.

Beginning in the mid-1930s and for several decades thereafter, many ordinary social workers lost their jobs because they espoused radical ideas, supported clients' demands for services, backed left-wing political candidates, opposed U.S. overseas intervention, or joined and organized left-leaning social work unions. Dismissals and blacklisting did not end, however, with the demise of the post–World War II phenomenon known as McCarthyism. Based on interviews we conducted with contemporary social work radicals, there is evidence that such practices continue in both social service agencies and universities.

To a considerable extent, the repression of social work radicalism mirrored developments in the larger society. Between World War I and the New Deal, radical social workers were a major target of government, industry, and media attacks because they were among the leading spokespersons for structural changes in U.S. society and social policies. Since the 1930s, however, the repression of radical social workers has been a secondary and rarely visible component of more sweeping efforts to suppress radical views. This reflected the diminished role that social workers played as advocates for controversial views and the effects of professionalization on the radical and activist impulses within the field (Ehrenreich, 1985; Specht & Courtney, 1994; Wenocur & Reisch, 1989). Unlike Addams and Kelley, the radical social workers of these eras posed little threat to the status quo.

Although no social workers endured vitriolic public attacks on the same scale as those of the post–World War I era, after World War II and well into the 1960s they suffered through their own private hells nonetheless. Their experiences reveal another form of repression that was (and, some maintain, still is) more subtle, insidious, and difficult to confront: the suppression of radical ideas and the radical tradition within the social work profession itself (Schrecker, 1998). This self-censorship—whether the inevitable by-product of the pursuit of professional status, capitulation to powerful political-economic forces, the pervasive influence of conservative American values, or the antiradical nature of social work practice itself—continues to have dramatic effects on the policies of the nation and the well-being of the populations that social workers are ethically obligated to serve.

AN OVERVIEW

No book can cover adequately all the radical currents in American social work during the past century. What we have attempted to do, instead, is write an alternate history of social work, to describe and analyze the diverse forms that radical social work took and the different ways it influenced the profession and society. We also have tried to illuminate some of the more distressing incidents in the profession's history, when forces inside and outside the field attempted to repress the expression of radical ideas. In part, we hope to do this by allowing the voices of radical social workers to tell the story themselves throughout the book. In Chapter 10, we give these voices center stage.

Although the book is organized largely in chronological format, the chapters focus on specific themes and events that we regard as particularly dramatic or significant. Naturally, our choices of what to include or exclude reflect our own biases, as well as the availability of resource materials. Wherever possible, we focused on events that utilized previously untapped primary sources or that had been given little attention in standard histories. Our omission of certain developments, organizations, or personalities is not intended to deny their importance; it was merely a matter of judgment and space limitations.

Chapter 2, "Radical Social Work in the Progressive Era," describes how a wide range of intellectual and political currents influenced radical social workers in the earliest days of the profession. The major ideological sources of social work radicalism during this period included religious and secular utopian philosophies of the nineteenth century such as transcendentalism, Marxism, and socialism. At the turn of the twentieth century, social work radicals were closely involved with the diverse social movements of the period, such as radical trade unionism—both domestic and foreign, "first wave" feminism, and religiously based pacifism. Social work radicals worked with well-known counterparts outside of social work, such as Emma Goldman and Crystal Eastman, defended labor militants and anarchists, and were outspoken in their defense of civil liberties. These interactions helped shape their political agendas, their conceptions of social work practice, and their definitions of professional and personal roles. Prior to World War I, social work radicals made distinctive contributions to the development of U.S. social policies, to the formulation of social work values, and to the structure of the emerging field.

During and after World War I, social work radicals were the subjects of fierce attacks by patriotic organizations and conservative politicians because of these views, in particular, their opposition to American entry into the war and their advocacy of ground-breaking social legislation like the Sheppard–Towner Act that established federally funded maternal and child health centers around the country. The repression of radicalism within social work in the 1920s culminated in attacks on the "spider web conspiracy" and the campaign to repeal Sheppard–Towner. These are discussed in Chapter 3, "The 'Spider Web Conspiracy' and the Death of Progressivism." It covers the broader implications of this repressive campaign as part of a general attack on the radical and reformist principles of social work and assesses the effects of these attacks during an era when the professionalizing impulse in the field became particularly powerful.

Chapter 4, "The Rank and File Movement and the Precursors to McCarthyism," summarizes the resurgence of radicalism in the social work field during the Great Depression of the 1930s and the emergence of the first radical social work movement. It discusses the creation of left-wing social work unions, the linkage of radical social workers to the Socialist and Communist Parties, and the emergence of radical concepts of social work practice, through the influence of individuals like Bertha Capen Reynolds and Mary van Kleeck. It also assesses the complex relationship between radical social workers and the New Deal, the appearance of splits among radicals over U.S. intervention in World War II, and the beginnings of attacks on radicals inside and outside the social work profession that foreshadowed the postwar McCarthy era.

Chapters 5 and 6 focus on the impact of McCarthyism on well-known social work radicals like Reynolds, Jacob Fisher, and Marion Hathway, as well as many of their lesser-known colleagues, and the broader implications of the anti-Communist purges for social work and social welfare in the United States. For nearly two decades, from the mid-1940s to the mid-1960s, radical social workers were investigated by the FBI and Congressional committees, blacklisted by professional colleagues, and fired or forced to resign from jobs because of their political views. The Justice Department listed organizations of radical social workers as subversive, and anti-Communists in the labor movement destroyed radical social work unions. At the same time, the field of social work retreated from its advocacy for social reform and focused most of its energies on theory building and enhancing its professional status. Based on little-used archival sources and interviews with social workers who survived the period, these chapters attempt to bring to light how these developments were interrelated. They also discuss the short- and long-term effects of McCarthyism on the profession.

Radicalism in social work revived during the tumultuous 1960s. Chapter 7 explores the different forms it took—from alternative forms of social service such as Mobilization for Youth, to alliances with grassroots social movements like the National Welfare Rights Organization, to the formation of the short-lived Social Welfare Workers Movement. It examines the lingering impact of McCarthyism, the mainstream reaction to social work radicalism, and the new directions radicalism began to take by the early 1970s.

The final chapters analyze the evolution of social work radicalism in the late twentieth century when social work radicalism took new and often confusing directions. Chapters 8 and 9, "The Redefinition of Social Work Radicalism, 1970–1999, I and II" attempt to capture both the richness and fragmentation of social work radicalism during this period. They examine the development of alternative radical social work theories and describe efforts to apply these theories in community projects, social work education, and through locally based radical social work organizations, such as the Radical Alliance of Social Service Workers (RASSW).

Chapter 10, "Social Work Radicalism at the End of the Twentieth Century," is based largely on interviews conducted with more than 100 contemporary social work radicals and an analysis of current radical social work literature and organizations. It attempts to provide an interpretive snapshot of recent trends among social work radicals in both professional practice and academic settings. It also places these developments in the context of sweeping changes in the nation's economy, politics, and culture.

In Chapter 11, "Conclusion—The Future of Radical Social Work in the United States," we briefly summarize the major themes presented in the previous chapters and assess the overall impact of radicalism on the field. We return to the questions raised at the beginning of this chapter and address whether the term "radical profession" is an oxymoron. Finally, we try to peek into the future and assess whether social work radicalism has any potential usefulness for the field and in society or whether, as some critics assert, social work radicals, like radicals in general, should be consigned to the dustbin of history.

2

Radical Social Work in the Progressive Era

It was not a crank who said that Jane Addams ought to be hanged to the nearest lamp post: it was a solid citizen who, like other solid citizens, regarded any legislation aimed at the protection of children in factories as an attack on his right, as a citizen of a free country, to do as he pleased. And it was not an irresponsible newspaper which hounded her as a radical: it was a newspaper most of the responsible people of the city read.

—Archibald MacLeish, "Jane Addams and the Future, " *Social Service Review*, 1991

ROOTS OF RADICAL SOCIAL WORK

*I*n the decade prior to World War I, Jane Addams was a true American heroine. Her work with immigrants in Chicago's famous settlement, Hull House, had captured the public's imagination and heart. She was lionized in the press and celebrated by politicians and corporate magnates. If *Time Magazine* had existed at the turn of the twentieth century, she probably would have been a regular on its famous covers.

The good works for which Addams had become famous masked the radical nature of her criticisms of American society and the even more radical views of other settlement workers whom she had trained and supported. Images of happy immigrant children cavorting in settlement playgrounds and learning useful skills generated enormous sympathy for Addams and the settlement movement as a whole. When Addams and her colleagues used this political capital, however, to speak out against U.S. entry into World War I, the public reacted to this betrayal with unprecedented anger.

Although Addams' pacifism flowed from the same ideological source as the humanism that inspired her settlement work and was strongly influenced by religious beliefs, it was regarded as no less than treason by patriotic organizations and the pro-war press. Just as she had been universally acclaimed prior to the war, she was now universally scorned and ridiculed. Vilified by politicians and editorialists, labeled a subversive and a traitor by legislative committees, Addams experienced a fall from grace unparalleled among public figures in American history. She was not rehabilitated in the public's eye until late in her life, when she received the Nobel Peace Prize for her work (Lundblad, 1995). Today, she is remembered largely for her good deeds and noble intentions. The radical nature of some of her ideas, the influence she had on the careers of other radical social workers and the social work profession itself and, above all, the enormous risks she and others took on behalf of their beliefs are often ignored.

Although Addams is often celebrated today as one of the foremost ancestors of modern social work, most contemporary social workers are either unaware of the radical roots of their profession or overlook how radical some of the ideas and actions of their professional ancestors were considered to be at the time. This historical amnesia is no accident. The absence of more than passing emphasis to the radical tradition and radical influences on social work and social welfare in the United States is a by-product of what Gettleman (1974) referred to as the "Whig interpretation of social welfare history." This interpretation—somewhat modified in recent years by the growth of feminist scholarship and studies that analyze the influence of people and organizations of color (Abramovitz, 1999; Carlton & Laney, 2001; Carlton-Laney & Burwell, 1995; Iglehart & Becerra, 1995; van den Bergh, 1995)—has led to an avoidance of a class analysis of social work and ignorance of the relationship among conservative social and political forces, reform movements, and the suppression or co-optation of radical movements and ideas. In an era when dramatic rhetoric about social justice and overcoming oppression often masks the profession's lack of social activism, "raising this historical legacy to the level of consciousness is a necessary precondition to the struggle to overcome it" (Gettleman, 1974, p. 155). It also reveals how social work continues to have the potential to work with others to transform society.

Historians have presented different views of social work radicalism, particularly within the settlement house movement where most radicals were located. One view holds that their emphasis on democracy (Addams, 1893, 1902) distinguished the settlements from the Charities Organization Societies (COS), which were "the embodiment of inequality in theory and in practice" (Trattner, 1995, p. 167). Another view maintains that although Addams, Graham Taylor, Lillian Wald, Florence Kelley, and others were radical in their political and social orientation, most settlement workers held negative views of the people with whom they worked, but did so by subtler means than the COS (Austin & Betten, 1990; Boyer, 1978; Crocker, 1992; Fisher, 1994; Mohl, 1988).

Social work radicalism during the Progressive Era was real and significant, however, and both its roots and impact were deep, complex, and often misunderstood, particularly by modern scholars and critics. The principle sources of radicalism for early social workers included the secular and religious utopian philosophies of the nineteenth century, early feminist thinkers like Elizabeth Cady Stanton, radical trade unionism (domestic and foreign), and radical organizations, such as anarchist groups, the Industrial Workers of the World (IWW), and the Socialist and Communist Parties. For many early social work radicals, religious ideas from the militant Social Gospel movement helped form their political and social ideologies, particularly through the movement's focus on issues of poverty and social justice and its sympathy for the working classes, comparable to that of liberation theology today.

As the ministry was closed to women, social work allowed women drawn to such values to practice a form of secular ministry. American born philosophers like Thoreau, Emerson, James, and Dewey, social scientists like Lester Ward, foreign born radicals like Laurence Gronlund and Emma Goldman, and domestic radicals like Henry George, Eugene Debs, Edward Bellamy, and William Demarest Lloyd all shaped the thinking of radical social workers. Young women and men, who came primarily from middle- and upper-class Protestant families, were also influenced by the new post–Civil War scholarship that began to diverge from the moralistic and rigid patterns of thought of the previous 150 years. Initially, they turned to history, political economy, psychology, and a new form of sociology for ideas and inspiration. Eventually, they sought to translate these new ideas into actions for both personal and idealogical reasons (Addams, 1910; Harkavy & Puckett, 1994; Sklar, 1995; Wald, 1915a, b).

From contemporary radicals like Henry George (1884) they became aware of the widening gap between rich and poor, even in times of prosperity. From Edward Bellamy, whose work, *Looking Backward*, was considered by John Dewey in 1935 to be second in importance only to Marx's *Das Kapital* among the most important books of the past half century, they derived a passionate critique of the prevailing ethos of Social Darwinism and a conception of socialism that was rooted in American rather than European history and culture. Middle-class authors like Henry Demarest Lloyd, whose background and sensibilities closely resembled their own, provided radical social workers with a sympathetic perspective on the working class and an accessible bridge to the ideas of European socialists. Lloyd was particularly influential on Jane Addams and Florence Kelley, with whom he had a long-standing personal friendship (Speizman, 1968). And in radical activists, like socialist and labor leader Eugene V. Debs, they found a role model who linked radical ideas to the social problems they observed daily in their communities.

From these diverse sources, radical social workers developed a multilayered analysis of social inequality and the breakdown of the community, in which economic, cultural, and social causes played an important role (Gordon, 1988, p. 73). Poverty, rather than immorality, became the primary explanation of antisocial behavior (Fitzpatrick, 1990). As critics of the settlement movement often noted this perspective had radical implications for American society at the turn of the twentieth century.

Strongly influenced by their parents' backgrounds in politics and socially concerned religion, such as the Social Gospel movement, radical social workers, largely women, projected a public image of social and cultural radicalism through a combination of social science and social activism. They were independent, economically autonomous, and socially responsible. Although the first radical social workers came primarily from upper-class families, the generation of social work radicals they recruited and that succeeded them increasingly came from the same ethnic and class backgrounds as their clients and constituents. This second generation of social work radicals reflected a stronger influence of European ideas about socialism and trade unionism (Andrews, 1993a; Wagner, 1989a; Wenocur & Reisch, 1989).

Christianity provided women like Jane Addams with both an ethical purpose and powerful symbols (Stebner, 1997). Addams was strongly influenced by her father, whose Quaker beliefs and attraction to European political movements, including Christian Socialism, molded her thinking about the world. At the Rockford Female Seminary, her ideas regarding social change were further shaped by writers like Thomas Carlyle and John Ruskin, from whom she learned the importance of social responsibility, the moral aspects of economics, and the potential role of government in ameliorating the effects of capitalism (Kayser, 1996).

The Social Gospel movement in the United States provided her with a religious basis for her ethics and actions. These beliefs enabled women like Addams to go beyond "abstract obedience to a formal model of moral conduct" (Elshtain, 1988, p. 260). At Toynbee Hall in London's East End, Addams saw these religious ideas put into practice in both social activism and day-to-day communal living. They became the model for her subsequent work at Hull House in Chicago (Kayser, 1996). From such sources, Addams developed a philosophy based on the solidarity of the human race (Addams, 1902, 1893).

Addams's Chicago colleague, Graham Taylor, was also strongly influenced by religious beliefs. A minister's son, Taylor started the Chicago Federation of Settlements in 1894, a forerunner of the National Federation, along with Addams and Mary McDowell. Two years later, he launched the influential magazine, *The Commons*. At Chicago Commons, which he founded in 1894, Taylor promoted a radical vision of human cooperation across barriers of class, race, and culture (Plotkin, 1996). He also played an active role in integrating social science research into community practice.

Even radical secularists like Florence Kelley were influenced by religious ideas, in Kelley's case her Quaker upbringing. Kelley was born in 1859, the daughter of William Kelley, a prominent Republican member of Congress from Pennsylvania from 1860 to 1890. She was one of the few women of her era to be admitted to the Bar and the first woman State Factory Inspector in the United States. Kelley was influenced by abolitionist friends of her family and her father's support for Radical Reconstruction after the Civil War (Sklar, 1995). Thus, while Kelley's politics were not specifically rooted in orthodox or evangelical Christianity, her powerful sense of social justice was guided by moral sensibilities (Sklar, 1995).

The work of John Dewey and, to a lesser extent, William James also had a profound influence on the radical social workers of the Progressive Era. Their writings shaped new concepts of science, of women's role in society, and of the nature of the helping process itself, emphasizing community or mutual aid rather than charity (Dewey, 1935; Harkavy & Puckett, 1994). These views about helping, which were later combined with ideas gleaned from anarchist literature, the social ethics of the Jewish community and African American churches, and the labor movement, differed substantially from the prevailing Christian concept of charity. Instead of seeing the poor as "other"—who could be helped by "good works" (according to the Catholic Church) or the state (the Protestant view), radical social workers saw the poor as part of humanity. Here, they reintroduced the concept of fraternity or "fellowship," the long-neglected third of the revolutionary trinity, to the field of social welfare (Konopka, 1958, p. 90). Thus, they "attempted to move the field away from a paternalistic focus on charity to an emphasis on social justice, working with not for people" (Lovejoy, 1912, p. 394). Dewey's ideas continued to guide the settlement movement, shaped the development of group work in the 1930s, and reemerged in the 1960s among social work radicals and activists. His influence persists to this day—in different forms—in the fields of community organization, social work education, and the currently popular concept of service learning in universities (Harkavy & Puckett, 1994; Lowe & Reisch, 1998).

The role of philosophers like Dewey and their social work disciples in articulating and modeling the changing role of women in industrial society was particularly critical. "This revolution was not just a reversal of roles; . . . it meant a completely new family constellation. It raised the questions of democratic human relations, of freedom and limitation, of equality and its deeper meaning" (Konopka, 1958, p. 99).

Thus, most early social work radicals were influenced in their upbringing by a combination of religious ideals, secular philosophy, and political action (Coss, 1989; Daniels, 1989; Davis, 1973; Diliberto, 1997; Kalberg, 1975; Levine, 1971; Sklar, 1995). Settlement workers like Addams and Grace Abbott also drew inspiration from the mutual aid efforts of the immigrants with whom they worked (Abbott, 1909). These diverse intellectual origins contributed to the widespread failure among the general public to understand the complex and evolving nature of social work itself.

Even the cofounder of Hull House, Ellen Gates Starr, whose radicalism far surpassed that of her former partner Addams, synthesized spiritual and social justice perspectives in her work. Her Christianity lead to her socialism (Starr, n.d.). One way in which she attempted to do this was through the use of art, which provided the means for people to express their material and spiritual aspirations (Stebner, 1997).

The movement from charity to justice Starr and others embodied emerged out of a growing sense of urgency over the effects of economic inequality and the breakdown of community (Reisch, 1998). "[I]t put forth as its chief principle of action that in any attempt to solve the problem of economic poverty, the stress should be laid upon justice rather than upon charity" (Tucker, 1903, p. 290). By contrast, the stated function of organized charity, particularly the COS, was to exorcise "the specter of a Europeanized, class-ridden America." Like their corporate sponsors, COS workers "were eager to avoid any kind of class analysis; they spoke instead of reconciling class differences and reuniting American society" (Kusmer, 1973, pp. 663, 674). Although some settlement workers such as Addams expressed similar sentiments for different reasons (Addams, 1910), others explicitly or implicitly highlighted the nature and significance of class distinctions, even as they argued for the importance of universal themes and universal social welfare programs (Sklar, 1995; Wald, 1915a).

INFLUENCE OF SOCIALISM ON RADICAL SOCIAL WORK

One way in which radical social workers expressed their growing class consciousness was by embracing socialism. Yet socialism played a complex role in shaping the views of radical social workers, best exemplified by Florence Kelley's relationship with the socialist movement and the Socialist Party (Sklar, 1995). Shortly after returning to the United States in 1886 with her Polish socialist husband, Lazare Wischnewetzky, and child (with two more soon on the way), Kelley joined the Socialist Labor Party. She soon produced the first English translations of Friedrich Engels's classic study, *The Condition of the Working Class in England in 1844*, and Marx's *Free Trade* speech. A year later, she and her husband were expelled from the party, which was dominated by European-born men, and she maintained an ambivalent attitude toward U.S. socialists for the rest of her life. Some observers have argued that her absorption in the day-to-day issues of industrialization diluted her Marxist philosophy, although she maintained her allegiance to socialism throughout her career (Ryan, 1979). In hindsight it appears that her connection to socialism was based more upon the appeal of its values than a specific program (Sklar, 1995; Woloch, 1984).

Nevertheless, these values led Kelley and other radical social workers to embrace a radical vision of society and attempt to influence the settlement movement in the direction of structural change. Kelley began her socialist activism in the 1880s, influenced by her correspondence with Engels. A letter he wrote her in the late 1880s helps explain the particular character of her socialism: "Our theory [Marxian socialism] is a theory of development, not of dogma to be learned by heart and repeated mechanically. The less it is hammered into the Americans from the outside and the more they test it through their own experience . . . the more it will become a part of their flesh and blood" (quoted in Symes & Clement, 1972, p. 209).

In 1893, she wrote to Engels that although she would continue to advance socialist ideals through articles, pamphlets, and reports, "she could accomplish more for workingwomen through her work in Hull House than in the Socialist movement" (Florence Kelley Papers, Sophia Smith Collection, Smith College Library). Similarly, Jane Addams saw her role as "socializing democracy" through her settlement and political work, rather than creating a democratic form of socialism (Ryan, 1979). Conservative opponents inside and outside the field, however, rarely respected these distinctions.

Whereas some early radical social workers were socialists, few were influenced by Marxism. They acknowledged the existence of classes, but they did not endorse the idea of class conflict. Most, like Charlotte Perkins Gilman, who worked at Hull House in 1895, expressed a combination of evolutionary socialist and early feminist ideas. Linda Gordon (1995) calls them "socialists of the heart," who disdained greed and exploitation and sought a higher form of community (p. 75). The very imprecision of their vocabulary shaped the response to radical social workers inside and outside the field. Both the general public and other professionals often confused "social work, sociology, and socialism," a confusion that persists today (Brackett, 1909; Shoemaker, 1998).

To understand the source of this confusion, it is important to recognize how influential the Socialist Party and socialist ideas were in the United States before World War I. Public lectures by socialist speakers were well attended. The Socialist Party grew from fewer than 5,000 members in 1900 to nearly 120,000 in 1912. Its leader, Eugene V. Debs, had near mythic status among working people and social activists (Salvatore, 1982). In the 1912 election, he received 6% of the popular vote for president, while more than 1,000 socialists were elected to state and local offices. Intellectuals like Dewey, Gilman, Frederick Douglass, and W.E.B. DuBois were all attracted to socialist ideas. They, in turn, worked with and influenced the ideas of social work radicals.

CONTEXT OF RADICAL SOCIAL WORK

Radical social work would not have developed, however, unless the times were right. Fertile ideas needed fertile soil to grow and bear fruit. The economic crisis of the 1890s provided the necessary environment for radical ideas to take root in the emerging field of social work. It stimulated a reappraisal of prevailing attitudes and solutions toward what politicians and the press euphemistically called the "social question."

Old-style charity ignored the consequences of industrialization, urbanization, and class conflict. It was designed to enforce the work ethic and was based upon a personal relationship between benefactor and recipient. It appeared to have little impact on the "new poor," whose poverty was largely the product of environmental conditions and was exacerbated by racial and cultural differences. Unwilling to confront the structural roots of poverty and inequality, both defenders and mainstream critics of the status quo embraced "technology" as the means to harness the forces of change and social disruption (Kasson, 1976, p. 186). This integration of a technological approach to the field of social welfare enabled reformers to obtain the support of political and economic elites who were applying technology in an analogous manner to industrial and political processes to strengthen their control over the direction of society.

Many of the recipients of these new programs and services, however, particularly poor Jewish and Catholic immigrants and African Americans, regarded the new institutional forms of charity as alien and preferred self-help organizations such as the Irish Emigrant Aid Society, the Hebrew Benevolent Society, and the White Rose Home for Girls. Despite their limited resources, these organizations provided the majority of social services to such populations throughout the late nineteenth century (Carlton-Laney, 1999). In addition to delivering concrete services such as employment counseling, material relief, education, and social supports, these agencies served as institutional means for urban immigrants to resist the attacks on their heritage by dominant culture institutions, such as public schools, child welfare agencies, Charities Organization Societies, and churches (Wenocur & Reisch, 1989).

In this context, settlement houses attempted to create an institutionalized form of self-help for the urban poor, to meet their economic and social needs while socializing them into the new industrial order. Some settlement leaders, such as Florence Kelley and Lillian Wald, simultaneously pushed for structural changes in society through collaboration with trade unions and radical political groups, and the creation of advocacy organizations like the National Consumers League. Although they often reflected the paternalistic attitudes of their upper-class origins, by focusing on the relationship between economic and social change and the needs of poor and working-class families, settlement house leaders laid the foundation for the development of the limited U.S. welfare state in the 1930s and 1960s. During the Progressive Era, these ideas had, or were perceived to have, radical implications for the country (Coss, 1989; Daniels, 1989; Sklar, 1995).

In the development of social policies, the settlements and their reform allies in the Progressive Movement combined the scientific method's emphasis on explanation and prediction with the corporate focus on efficiency. Although this synthesis facilitated radicals' efforts to acquire the backing of powerful economic and political forces for their proposals, it abounded in contradictions, which were reflected in the policies the reforms produced. These policies tried to provide services and to restructure existing institutions while preserving class-based ideals and prejudices. They sought to establish an alternative sense of justice and democracy through the support and sponsorship of the very classes that benefited most from maintaining the status quo. These contradictions had profound consequences for the future of U.S. social welfare.

One way in which these contradictions appeared was in the divisions between reformers and radicals about the direction of social policies targeted at urban conditions. Although liberal reformers accepted the reality of urbanization, they often harbored powerful prejudices against urban populations, particularly non-Protestant immigrants and African Americans. Some radical social workers like Kelley professed socialist sympathies, but most favored redistributive efforts through an increase in the overall national wealth, prefiguring modern Keynesian policies. Some reformers focused on specific improvements in housing, public welfare, public health, and education, whereas others emphasized shaping public opinion and promoting cooperation among social classes. Most reformers promoted the idea of a "community of interest" as a counterweight to growing class antagonisms (Bender, 1982).

Given the social background of its proponents, it is not surprising that this community of interest contained many of the values of the dominant culture. These included the focus on individual achievement and self-help, the assimilation of immigrants into the dominant American culture, and the importance of education as the basis for expanding economic opportunity. Given the self-interest of even the most altruistic of the Progressives, it is also not surprising that they proposed solutions to the problems of industrialization and urbanization, which required the utilization of specialists and professionals like themselves. The social policies that emerged from this web of contradictions (between 1900–1930) therefore were characterized by a focus on dependent populations (such as widows and children), limited scope, state initiation and control, and the beginnings of the acceptance of the insurance concept (Axinn & Stern, 2000).

By the outbreak of World War I, however, the broad Progressive coalition of reformers and radicals began to disintegrate in an increasingly conservative political environment. The repression of dissent that occurred in the war's aftermath strengthened the professionalizing impulse among social workers. It also had profound implications for social work radicals and for the field as a whole.

REVOLUTION IN CHARITABLE METHODS

As early as the mid-1880s, the potential for political and social upheaval in the new formulation of charitable thought was widely recognized. The political power of the working class as expressed through unions, organized labor's participation in electoral politics, and the growing popularity of Socialist Parties could scarcely be ignored. The influence of British and French ideas and experiences on both legislation and practice in charitable organizations often was cited by social observers as part of a feared "Europeanization" of U.S. society (Gettleman, 1963). The Charities Organization movement signified an attempt by elites to avoid class conflict, in part through discouraging the indiscriminate distribution of relief. The friendly visiting it adopted was the "secular successor" to Christian Socialism and contained none of its radicalism. It was strongly influenced by the Social Darwinist ideas of the period, in sharp contrast to the more egalitarian philosophic and social scientific influences on radical social workers in the settlements.

Yet the intellectual forces behind both reformist and radical progressivism and the radical ideology of the Social Gospel movement—Dewey, Marx, Henry George, Lester Ward, and, later, Sigmund Freud—shared aspects of the socialist utopian vision. They believed in the ultimate goodness of humanity and in the power of education and science to create a just and perfect society (Keith-Lucas, 1967, pp. 9–10). Like other members of their class, reformers and middle-class radicals during the Progressive Era were haunted by the twin specters of "the word" (Marxism) and "the deed" (the Paris Commune of 1870–1871 and other revolutionary events of the late nineteenth century). In other words, they feared "the consequences if the masses of the needy were not paid heed" (Mendes, 1964, p. 7).

The tensions that emerged in this period between these perspectives permanently shaped the development of the social work profession and were already noted before the turn of the twentieth century. In contrast to the leaders of organized charity who avoided any references to class analysis in their work, opposed "careless meddling with the social question," and equated indiscriminate almsgiving with socialism or anarchism, radical social workers were among the first to point out the significance of class distinctions (Gettleman, 1963; Kusmer, 1973). As for their COS colleagues in the late nineteenth and early twentieth centuries, "feminist impulses coincided with class interests" (Rauch, 1975, p. 256).

Conservatives and upper-class reformers recognized the implications of these distinctions as early as the 1870s and regarded the organized charity movement as "the real answer to the socialistic and communistic theories now being energetically taught to the people" (Kellogg, 1880, p. 719). Other observers promoted organized charities as a means of eliminating the threat of communism and anarchism or as "the only tolerable alternative to socialism" (Agnew, 1880, p. 10). Two years before the founding of Hull House in 1889, John Glenn of the New York COS wrote to Daniel Coit Gilman, President of Johns Hopkins University, that the friendly visiting promoted by the COS was the "true antidote to socialism" (Glenn, 1887, quoted in Gettleman, 1975, p. 58). Seven years later, John Graham Brooks, a Unitarian clergyman, suggested that "the root passion of this [varied and growing social justice movement] is the longing for larger equality of opportunity, and the thing which seems to me of extreme practical significance is that a multitude of those who have won intellectual influence of high order are already won to the belief that this which the demos demands is essentially just and should be listened to. The more socialistic view of charity and the unemployed is no longer confined to the proletariat" (Brooks, 1894, p. 13). The growth of radical social work reflected, therefore, what one contemporary of Brooks called "The Progress of the Social Conscience," "to resist the encroachments of monopolistic wealth upon the liberties of the people" (Tucker, 1903, p. 290).

Professionalism seemed to offer the antidote to growing radical influences on the field. At the 1896 meeting of the National Conference of Charities and Corrections, COS leader Mary Richmond articulated an emerging view that regarded professionalization as a means to create necessary changes in social service work without promoting a dramatic restructuring of society and its institutions. She referred to the professionalism of charity work as the route "between the charitable Scylla of an old fogy conservatism, and the charitable Charybdis of . . . socialism" (1896, p. 59). Twelve years later, Edward Devine, the head of the New York COS and later Director of the New York School of Social Work, repeated this sentiment in an article in the *Atlantic Monthly*, "The

New View in Charity." He referred to professionalism and reform as the only viable alternatives to socialism (1908, p. 741). Thus, from its earliest days, "professionalism operat[ed] as a brake on radicalism within social work and as an assurance to the business elite that their hegemony would never be seriously challenged by the growing corps of social workers" (Gettleman, 1975, p. 59).

Unlike mainstream charity workers, who focused on the individual moral deficiencies of the new urban poor, radical social workers during the Progressive Era were acutely aware of the social context of poverty. They used cities as laboratories to discover the causes and cures of social and economic ills (Reisch, 1996; Rothman, 1978). The career of Josephine Shaw Lowell, which abounded in contradictions, exemplifies one unusual path in this regard.

Immediately after the Civil War, Lowell served as the chief fundraiser for the National Freedman's Relief Association in New York and the first woman member of the New York State Board of Charities, where she investigated allegations of fraud among outdoor relief organizations. She led efforts to eliminate outdoor relief in Brooklyn in the late 1870s and again in the early 1880s, as founder of the New York COS. By 1889, however, "she had become convinced that it was more important to prevent poverty than to try to cure it" (Bolin, 1973, p. 6). She soon left the Board of Charities and helped found the Consumers League of New York, which worked closely with the National Consumers League headed by Florence Kelley. By the early twentieth century, she had joined the Socialist Party (Katz, 1986).

Like Lowell, "many of the most prominent . . . women settlement house workers established an impressive socialist and feminist agenda" (Chambers, 1986; Walkowitz, 1988, pp. 6–7). They investigated such issues as the problems of low-income immigrant households, the lives of African Americans, the prevalence and consequences of child labor, and tenement housing conditions in cities like New York and Chicago. For example, workers at Greenwich House, under the direction of Mary Simkhovitch, researched the family economy of the poor in New York in a half dozen studies before World War I. In the first decade of the twentieth century, under the supervision of Florence Kelley, Mary van Kleeck began her ground-breaking studies of factory conditions for women and girls.

The pursuit of social justice during these years among radical social workers was closely connected to the movement known as social feminism (Conway, 1971–1972; O'Neill, 1969). Jane Addams "felt that women had distinctive interests that could no more be served by men than the interests of the proletariat could be served by the bourgeoisie" (Bolin, 1973, pp. 10–11). This view inspired a "maternalist" approach to the problems of women and children, even among socialists like Florence Kelley (Perkins, 1954; Sklar, 1995).

EMERGENCE OF RADICAL SOCIAL WORK METHODS

Radicalism, therefore, took several forms within the social work field during the formative years of the profession. Through the application of social science methods rather than Social Darwinist ideas it presented an alternative set of explanations for the burgeoning social crisis that preoccupied economic and political elites between the Civil War and World War I. With striking parallels to the present day, social work radicals analyzed poverty and the breakdown of community as the consequences of industrialization, slum housing, and the rapid changes in social relations they produced, instead of individual moral deficiency (Gordon, 1988). The focus of their efforts was a dramatic alteration of U.S. society through intergroup interaction, research, analysis, and debate.

In addition to an alternative vision of society, radical social workers developed innovative practices. For the first time, they applied social science to the analysis of the problem of poverty *with the specific intention* of ameliorating the plight of economically disadvantaged populations, thus creating what is now "termed action research." They became directly involved in the political arena, a particularly treacherous field for women and radicals in the late nineteenth century. They took substantial risks by making direct and indirect attacks on urban political bosses and fighting to integrate female suffrage into the Progressives' agenda (Chambers, 1963; Davis, 1964).

Radical social workers also supported the unionization of workers and their right to strike. They contributed to unions' strike funds, provided space for union meetings, and participated in the public defense of radical trade unionists when they were prosecuted. They organized the National Women's Trade Union League (WTUL) and the Women's Clerk Benefit Association and served as officers in both groups. To broaden the base of their social change efforts, Florence Kelley linked support for the elimination of child labor to the improvement of conditions for adult workers. All this occurred during an era when support for unions was considered radical and un-American (Rothman, 1978, p. 119). Radical social workers nevertheless believed that their work involved more than the amelioration of urban poverty and misery, that it could "be the expression of great convictions; the conviction of the new order" (Vida Scudder, quoted in Rothman, 1978, p. 114).

By the beginning of the twentieth century, radical social workers were also actively involved in the formation of modern methods and philosophies of social science. Although some modern critics have criticized their efforts to "instigate and guide reform" as subjective journalism rather than objective science (Zimbalist, 1977), there is no doubt that the efforts of individuals like Graham Taylor, Sophinisba Breckinridge, and the Abbott sisters expanded the scope of social science research and enhanced its impact on the formation of public policy (Kahn, 1998).

Social observers of the period noted how the efforts of radical social workers reinforced the increasing political power of the working class. The influence of European ideas and experiences on their goals and strategies was also apparent. These political and ideological forces shaped both social change efforts and daily practice in social service agencies. The spread of this influence into unions and college settlements, John Graham Brooks argued, "seem[s] . . . not without threatening possibilities" (1894, p. 214).

The potential to forge a social movement that reconciled class differences and reunited American society was not lost on settlement leaders like Jane Addams. In fact, Addams considered the educational component of her work, which she defined in its broadest sense as both mutual and multifaceted, as its most radical aspect. The intellectual climate at places like Hull House in Chicago and the Henry Street Settlement in New York, in which radical intellectuals and activists mingled, nurtured the development of radical ideas, including feminism, and created an opportunity for women to expand their intellectual and political horizons (Lundblad, 1995). Networks of academics and social work activists such as Kelley, Lillian Wald, and Mary Simkhovitch, presaged the formation of national coalitions of a similar nature that emerged during the Progressive Era, the New Deal, and the War on Poverty. Leading social work radicals like Florence Kelley, whom Sophinisba Breckinridge described as "the embodiment of the public conscience on the subject of child labor and its attendant evils," played a critical role in transforming informal local groups into national alliances (quoted in Fitzpatrick, 1990, pp. 188–189).

Inspired by this atmosphere of dissent and debate, research by settlement workers like Robert Hunter (1904) and university-based social scientists such as Grace and Edith Abbott (1917) and Sophinisba Breckinridge challenged the prevailing wisdom that linked poverty and individual morality. Hunter, like many of his radical social work contemporaries, came from an upper-middle-class family. While working at Hull House from 1899 to 1902, he chaired the Investigating Committee of the City Homes Association and published a monograph, *Tenement Conditions in Chicago* (1901). He then moved to New York to head the University Settlement. There, he headed the state's Child Labor Committee, established by Wald and Kelley, and led the fight to pass the state's landmark child labor law of 1903.

In 1904, Hunter published his influential work, *Poverty* (1904), which contained the startling revelation that one out of eight Americans was poor. The book was widely read and made an impact on Kelley and others. Until World War I, when his political philosophy turned to the right, Hunter was an active member of the nonrevolutionary American Socialist Party and ran for political office as a socialist in New York and Connecticut. He also traveled abroad and met European socialists and communists, like Lenin and Keir Hardie (Edwards-Orr, 1986, pp. 413–415).

In their writings, Hunter and the Abbotts argued that poverty, rather than bad morals or incorrigible behavior, was the cause of social problems like truancy and child abuse (Fitzpatrick, 1990). Other radical social workers differed with the mainstream idea that mass immigration and cultural diversity imperiled American civilization (Association for the Improvement of the Condition of the Poor [AICP], 1880; Strong, 1898). In opposition to the prevailing Social Darwinist ethos of the day, Jane Addams "believed that the fundamental problem created by immigration was that of finding a new basis for unity in a heterogeneous society and of conserving old world traits that would bring elements of strength and beauty to American life" (White, 1959, p. 56).

She also differed from many of her contemporaries, who feared the creation of an American "melting pot" and who claimed that U.S. civilization was imperiled by the flood of immigrants from Southern and Eastern Europe. Long before the concept of multiculturalism was introduced, Addams argued that a new sense of community would not be based on homogeneity, but on "a respect for variety" and the potential contributions of new immigrants. It was the function of the settlement "to forward this process of discovery," by building on the strong sense of democracy, idealism, and mutuality found among immigrants (White, 1959, p. 57).

Yet the diversity Addams heralded did not include African Americans, Latinos, American Indians, or immigrants from Asia and the Pacific Islands. Few settlements, even those directed by radicals like Wald, served people of color at the time, and participation by African Americans in the National Federation of Settlements was minimal. The concept of the melting pot was never intended to refer to any groups other than White ethnics from Europe (Iglehart & Becerra, 1995; Lasch-Quinn, 1993).

Nevertheless, despite its inability to overcome the racism of U.S. society, through its radical leaders and ground-breaking research, the settlement movement influenced the development of social work values regarding the receipt of help, the impact of helping, the meaning of equality, the importance of fellowship, and the value of cultural pluralism (what we refer to today as multiculturalism). At the 1897 National Conference of Charities and Corrections, Addams underscored these contradictions when she remarked, "I have not the great fear of pauperizing people which many of you seem to have. We have all accepted bread from someone, at least until we were fourteen" (quoted in Bruno, 1957, p. 114).

Radical social workers thus challenged both the values and the practices of their social work colleagues. Although they formed alliances with COS leaders on specific issues, they attacked the way in which charity visitors behaved toward the poor:

> A most striking incongruity, at once apparent, is the difference between the emotional kindness with which relief is given by one poor neighbor to another poor neighbor, and the guarded care with which relief is given by a charity visitor to a charity recipient. The neighborhood mind is at once confronted not only by the difference of method, *but by an absolute clashing of two ethical standards.* (Addams, 1902, pp. 19–20, emphasis added)

Addams's address to the 1910 National Conference of Social Work as its first woman president on "charity and social justice" highlighted the distinctions between the two major branches of social work. The innovations she introduced at Hull House similarly marked a shift in public priorities from charitable relief to the development of recreational and cultural programs based on the concept of health, rather than pathology, with the aim being to ennoble and empower poor and working-class people, particularly immigrants. These ideas helped shape the public health movement of the period and presaged the social health movement of today (Lowe, 1997).

Despite the differences in their analysis, the goal of most radical social workers during the Progressive Era was neither to narrow class divisions nor to promote or exploit existing class conflict. Addams consistently sought to find common ground among the classes. Her famous statement, "The things that make men alike are fine and better than the things that keep them apart," expressed her preference for class reconciliation and the reconstruction of an "organic community" over class warfare (Addams, 1910, pp. 111–112).

The settlements' focus on education complemented these efforts to build bridges across class lines. It was also another area in which Addams, Kelley, and others stood out from more moderate reformers. They promoted education not only to assimilate the immigrant masses into U.S. society but also as a means to break the sweatshop and child labor systems, forge an intelligent electorate, and through the democratization of education, democratize society by making the nation's newest citizens a force for change (Rothman, 1978). Their attitudes and methods in educational and cultural work, and their linkage of both to efforts to combat poverty, inspired the progressive education movement and marked the first example of an attempt to create a multicultural society in the United States (Lundblad, 1995).

Even a sympathetic reformer like Mary Richmond felt that the settlements' orientation had dangerous implications for the field of social work (Boyer, 1978; Chambers, 1963). Perhaps this was because they were not engaged in social service in the traditional sense. In a manner reflected in the late twentieth century by proponents of empowerment theory and practice, radical social workers did not work for their clients and constituents, but with them (Fisher, 1994; Simon, 1994). They recognized the strengths of low-income groups and the potential to establish mutual interests and mutual goals. This clearly represented a threat to traditional conceptions of charity. A 1901 editorial, in the COS organ, *Charities*, pondered, "Is there any stopping place in following out [such] principle[s], short of socialism?" (*Charities*, 1901, pp. 420–421).

To rebuild U.S. society, radical social workers and their allies emphasized the relationships between community participation, social services, and abstract concepts like democracy, equality, and social justice (Wenocur & Reisch, 1989). This emphasis led to their involvement in social change activities, including union and political organizing; the promotion of women's suffrage and reproductive rights; support for racial justice; advocacy for improvements in public health, occupational health and safety, education, housing, and child welfare; and opposition to war and militarism (Addams, 1895; Bombyk, 1995; Wald, 1915a). In addition, their "social feminism" (O'Neill, 1971) fostered alliances among settlement leaders like Addams, Kelley, and Wald and radicals outside of social work, such as socialist and feminist attorney Crystal Eastman and the anarchist Emma Goldman, around such women's issues as prostitution and White slavery (Cook, 1978).

RADICAL SOCIAL WORK
AND THE LABOR MOVEMENT

A major arena of radical social work activity occurred through support of the labor movement (Fisher, 1994; Karger, 1988). In cities like New York, Chicago, Detroit, Philadelphia, and Boston, the larger settlement houses provided a place for unions to meet, took an active part in strikes, and helped organize unions, particularly among working girls and women. Hull House workers, such as "Fighting Mary" McDowell, assisted in the organization of four unions: the Women Shirt Makers, the Women Cloak Makers, the Dorcas Federal Labor Union, and the Chicago Women's Trade Union League.

Despite their initial class and ethnic prejudices, radical social workers had greater trust in the working class than their professional counterparts and even other radicals of the period. They differed among themselves, however, in their ideological justifications for cooperating with unions. Kelley saw trade unionism as one strategy to achieve socialism. Addams's perspective was more in line with the British Fabians, who promoted social democratic solutions to the problems of economic and social inequality. She regarded "the task of the labor movement [as] the interpretation of democracy into industrial affairs" (Addams, 1895, p. 191). Before the outbreak of World War I they found common cause in the 1912 "Social Standards for Industry," produced by the National Conference on Social Work's Committee on Standards of Living and Labor, which "established the ideal of community or public responsibility for the welfare of the disadvantaged and disinherited" (Chambers, 1956, p. 162).

Above all, the words and deeds of Kelley, Wald, and Addams contrasted sharply with those of other reformers like Mary Richmond and even liberal child welfare advocates like Homer Folks. Richmond maintained a sharp distinction in her views between the deserving and undeserving poor and appealed to business interests through support of antitramp legislation (Richmond, 1906). Although a long-time champion of reforms in child welfare—he lived from 1867 until 1963—Folks possessed a distrust and fear of the working class. At the turn of the century, he stated, "The uneducated masses have the most exalted ideas of individual rights and spurred on by socialistic orators and by a vicious foreign element have become the most destructive factors of good government" (Folks, 1898, p. 2).

In addition to working for labor and social welfare legislation, the larger settlement houses—Hull House, and the Chicago Commons in Chicago, the Henry and University Street Settlements in New York, and Denison House and South End House in Boston—provided day-to-day support for the labor movement, particularly for women. Hull House opened its doors regularly to the Chicago Working Women's Association, which had been founded two years before the settlement appeared. "While there was inevitably some patronizing of working-class women by the upper- and middle-class settlement workers, the relationship, in the main, was of benefit to the female workers. . . . In fact, most of the women's unions that existed at the beginning of the twentieth century had been organized by militant women workers often . . . with the help of a social settlement" (Foner, 1982, pp. 105, 123). Bucking popular opinion, settlement house workers in New York even supported boycotts organized by women garment workers (Foner, 1982, pp. 124–125).

In their support for women laborers, settlement house workers were, in some ways, more advanced than male trade union activists, who often felt that organizing women was a waste of time and precious resources. An exception was William Walling, son of a well-known physician and a millionaire resident of University Settlement, who became interested in trade unions through Hull House and eventually became a prominent member of the Socialist Party. Supported by Kelley in his concern over the plight of poor women, Walling went to England in 1903 to learn more about the British Women's Trade Union League. Upon his return, he worked with Kelley, Wald, and other residents of University Settlement and Hull House to organize the WTUL modeled after its British counterpart. Addams served as its first vice president and Mary McDowell, Lillian Wald, and Leonora O'Reilly were named to its executive board (Foner, 1982). For decades, the WTUL provided an organizational base for union leaders and radical women, such as Rose Scheiderman, to carry on their work.

Although most social workers who worked with unions rejected the idea of class conflict and the utopian ideals of socialism, their more radical allies— inside and outside the field—acknowledged the effectiveness of working-class groups and the saliency of the ideas that molded them. Kelley believed that trade unions were needed "to establish the right to leisure, to transmute the unemployed time of the full season . . . into regular daily leisure" (Kelley, 1905, p. 162). She, Mary van Kleeck, and Mary Simkovitch of Greenwich House were charter members of the American Association for Labor Legislation's (AALL) Committee on Constitution Convention in 1906. Although Kelley does not appear on the list two years later, van Kleeck remained active and wrote a report for the AALL in 1911 on the prospects for minimum wage legislation (Kerber, Kessler-Harris, & Sklar, 1995).

Through their work with unions, radical social workers demonstrated the linkages between radical social work ideas and social action. In 1892, Kelley began speaking before working-class audiences at antisweatshop demonstrations (Sklar, 1995). In her first published research on the wages of unskilled laborers, Edith Abbott (1905) quoted Marx's *Communist Manifesto* and attempted to demonstrate some of his propositions about the relationship between wages and the nature of work. These efforts must be understood in the wider context of labor conflict in the United States during the period. Radical social workers, largely women, provided an alternative, but no less radical solution to the violent class warfare that was sweeping the country (Sklar, 1993).

Almost from its foundation, settlement workers at Hull House linked their efforts to improve working conditions and wages with broader themes of social change. The staff at Hull House provided advice and support to the Chicago Working Women's Improvement Association. The constitution of the University Settlement in New York declared as one of its fundamental purposes "to bring men and women of education into closer relations with the laboring classes for their mutual benefit" (quoted in Foner, 1982, p. 105). According to Alice Hamilton, a pioneer in industrial medicine, these settlement workers "got into the labor movement as a matter of course without realizing how or when" (quoted in Foner, 1982, p. 105).

Such collaboration was made possible, in part, by labor's willingness to work with others who did not share all their views on tactics such as the use of strikes. The approach appeared to be successful. Writing to Friedrich Engels in May 1893, Kelley compared the impact of settlement work favorably with that of many socialists, who while "active," were often "practically unorganized and very few at best." Although she would continue to advance socialist ideals through articles, pamphlets, reports, and papers, she "found that she could accomplish more for workingwomen through her work in Hull House than in the Socialist movement" (Kelley letter of May 27, 1893, quoted in Foner, 1982, p. 122).

Not surprisingly, radical social workers in the settlements were more successful in forming coalitions with women workers and unions than with their male counterparts in the labor movement, who often saw settlement workers as more interested in gathering data than improving the lives of the working class. Overcoming initial distrust, Jane Addams connected labor organizers like Mary Kenney with sympathizers such as William Demarest Lloyd (author of *Wealth against Commonwealth*) and labor lawyer Clarence Darrow, helped Kenney start a women's cooperative factory, and provided her with shelter at Hull House during organizing drives. Florence Kelley successfully lobbied with Kenney and Elizabeth Morgan, whom Addams had helped organize unions in Chicago, on behalf of the Factory and Workshop Inspection Act of 1893 (Foner, 1982). In an era when the New York City Young Women's Christian Association (YWCA) claimed that at least $9/week in wages was needed to pay room and board alone, and the median wage was $10/week, support for labor unions was more than merely an altruistic gesture (Tentler, 1979).

As early as 1905, with the support of the Russell Sage Foundation and the YWCA, radical social workers like Mary van Kleeck began investigating child labor and the working conditions of women in New York factories. Van Kleeck's research demonstrated "that the problems women encountered in employment were related to the industrial and social conditions which affected both men and women" (Hagen, 1986, p. 725). This was similar to the conclusions of Edith Abbott's studies (1909) on women in industry and Florence Kelley's efforts to utilize gender-specific approaches to social problems instead of a class-based analysis (Sklar, 1995).

Inspired by events like the 1911 Triangle Shirtwaist Fire, Abbott and van Kleeck, assisted by future Secretary of Labor Frances Perkins, conducted ground-breaking research to prevent such tragedies from recurring. They fought for minimum wage laws and factory health and safety codes. Kelley and Lillian Wald played major roles in developing the case for labor protection in *Muller v. Oregon* (1908) and persuaded National Consumers League Board member, Josephine Goldmark, to convince her brother-in-law, Louis Brandeis, to argue the case before the Supreme Court (Rosenberg, 1992). van Kleeck disseminated her findings widely through monographs published by the Russell Sage Foundation. In October 1915, she prepared instructional materials, "Facts about Wage-Earners in the United States Census," to be used in a course on industrial conditions by the New York School of Philanthropy (van Kleeck, 1915).

In March 1919, van Kleeck joined with Mary Anderson of the Woman-in-Industry Service and many women from the WTUL to support a well-publicized employment discrimination case in Cleveland. In October of that year, Lillian Wald and Ida Tarbell were the two women represented among the public group of 25 members at an industrial conference convened by President Wilson to discuss postwar reconstruction. Their particular concern was the impact of peacetime on women's economic well-being (Foner, 1982; Groneman & Norton, 1987; Tentler, 1979; Woloch, 1984).

Florence Kelley incisively articulated the two opposing motives for the promotion of protective legislation for women workers: men's fear of losing their jobs to women and men's desire to improve their own working conditions through the indirect strategy of improving conditions for those who worked with them (Goldin, 1990). In the 1920s, this belief in women's exceptionalism placed some radical social workers like Kelley at odds with allies in the feminist movement over such issues as the Equal Rights Amendment. (See Chapter 3.)

In addition to their alliances with women trade unionists, radical social workers maintained close relations to Jewish radical and trade union leaders in cities like Chicago and New York. Among the Jewish radicals who worked closely with Hull House residents were Philip Davis and Abraham Bisno, the president of the Chicago Cloakmakers Union, who helped in the investigation of sweatshops and was nominated to be a factory inspector by Florence Kelley. Ellen Gates Starr, who remained a radical activist in the labor movement and lived at Hull House for most of her life despite her "breakup" with Jane Addams, established close ties with Sidney Hillman of the Amalgamated Clothing Workers Union. Addams also worked with Jewish socialists on both domestic and foreign issues. Similarly, Italian leftists in Chicago established close connections with Hull House through one of their intellectual leaders, Alessandro Mastro-Valerio. In 1906–1907, the radical and anticlerical Giordano Bruno Club met at Hull House and Italian socialists and unionists used Hull House for occasional meetings (Lissak, 1989).

The connections between Hull House and Italian radicalism inspired the Catholic Church and its press to attack Addams for alleged anti-Catholic bigotry. Even in 1908, after the Giordano Bruno Club was no longer permitted to hold its meetings at Hull House, the Catholic hierarchy continued to deride Addams as part of its anti-anarchist campaign. The Church's newspaper, *The New World*, referred to her as "the . . . patron saint of anti-Catholic bigotry in this city." Ironically, at the same time, Italian American socialists attacked Addams for refusing to allow the Giordano Bruno Club to meet at Hull House (Lissak, 1989, p. 98).

During this period, radicals in social work also defended labor leaders like

James McNamara, who had been accused of bombing the *Los Angeles Times* building. The head of the University of Chicago's Settlement House wrote in *The Survey* that while "the machinery of the state must stop violence, . . . [it] must also put peaceful weapons in the hands of labor" so that they could "secure a living wage" (*The Survey*, December 30, 1911, pp. 1417–1418). Florence Kelley also defended labor unrest by stating that desperate acts were a by-product of the "wrath and despair of baffled effort and vain struggle" (quoted in Weinstein, 1968, p. 181). This support for militant trade unionism gave settlements like Hull House the appearance of being radical strongholds and laid the foundation for future attacks on their leaders (Sklar, 1989). It also contributed to the antagonism expressed toward social work radicals in the postwar decade.

CREATING NEW ROLES FOR WOMEN

In 1889, when Hull House was founded, fewer than 3% of COS and settlement workers were women. At the end of the nineteenth century, cultural barriers discouraged even well-educated, upper-class women from pursuing their career and life goals (Chafe, 1977). By 1910, however, women were a majority within the social work field and more women college graduates were entering social work than any other profession besides teaching (Rosenberg, 1992). The assertion of new roles for women, therefore, represented another way in which social work radicals had an impact on the social work profession and U.S. society. They promoted feminist causes in their advocacy efforts and demanded new roles for women in the occupational and political spheres. In addition to their positions in the National Conference of Charities and Corrections and the National Federation of Settlements, Addams, Kelley, and Wald played leadership roles in "an extensive interlocking directorate of women leaders" of feminist, labor, and pacifist organizations. These included the National Consumers League, the WTUL, the National Federation of Women's Clubs, the Women's Peace Party, the Women's International League for Peace and Freedom, the National American Women's Suffrage Association, and the Mothers' Congress, which later became the Parent Teachers Associations (Rosenberg, 1992, p. 56).

Through collaborative efforts on issues like suffrage, child labor, and industrial working conditions, women developed a common political vocabulary. Settlement houses hosted radicals and socialists in an "atmosphere that encouraged new ways of thinking and acting" (Evans, 1989, p. 149). This produced interclass coalitions like the Illinois Women's Alliance that worked for protective labor legislation and the Jane Clubs, that provided a residence for working-class women associated with Hull House. These developments paved the way even during the conservative 1920s for future New Deal reforms (Ware, 1981).

The assertion of new roles for women in the domestic sphere was of equal importance, particularly in its long-term impact. A significant proportion of radical social workers were not merely activist women, they also were women who rejected the traditional concepts of marriage and family in the private sphere and of rigid gender roles in the public arena. In a sense, these women created their own kind of families. Although there were many reasons they did not marry, high on the list was the preservation of their independence to achieve their human potential (Muncy, 1991; Ryan, 1979; Woloch, 1984).

In places like Hull House, which had the environment of a cooperative, communal salon, they pioneered new forms of relationships with other women. Sometimes, these relationships were romantic, as between Ellen Gates Starr and Mary Runyon and Jane Addams and Mary Rozet Smith (Woloch, 1984). Like many other settlement activists, Lillian Wald was a lesbian and had several long-term relationships with professional women (Coss, 1989).

Whether all such bonds were lesbian relationships or simply lifelong intimate friendships, the radical implications of these women's behavior cannot be understated. The sexual nature of these relationships was not even the core issue. It was the existence of the relationships themselves and what they implied about women's social roles that was unprecedented (Rosenberg, 1992). Settlements offered such women a radical role in society: independence from families and marriage, unique and socially useful employment, communal living, and the opportunity to aspire to leadership positions (Muncy, 1991; Woloch, 1984). They also enabled strong, even angry, women like Kelley and Starr to apply their considerable intellectual and interpersonal skills freed from the constraints of submissive Victorian womanhood.

Political activism was also part of a broader transformation of women's roles and clearly implied "a completely new family constellation. It raised the questions of democratic human relations, of freedom and limitation, of equality and its deeper meaning. . . . It changed the relation of parents to children and children to parents. . . . It changed the composition of the labor market" (Konopka, 1958, p. 99). The impact of this transformation was certainly radical in consequence, if not always in design. The political enemies of these radical women understood this all too well. In fact, many of the attacks upon the policies and programs they promoted, such as the Sheppard–Towner Act, focused on the subversive nature of their sexuality. (See Chapter 3.)

SOCIAL WORK RADICALISM AND RACIAL JUSTICE

Despite the presence of institutional racism within the settlement movement, some early radical social workers were far more willing than their mainstream counterparts to work cooperatively with people of color and to participate in inter-racial organizations or multiracial coalitions. Spurred by the efforts of African American women, they worked through such organizations as the YWCA's Committee on InterRacial Cooperation, the Methodist Women's Missionary Societies, and the Association of Southern Women for the Prevention of Lynching to combat lynching in the South and racial oppression throughout the nation (Chafe, 1977). In the face of great popular opposition and the growing influence of the Ku Klux Klan—to which one of eight White male Americans belonged at its peak—they fought for racial equality and the elimination of racial discrimination (Day, 2000). They helped create the National Association for the Advancement of Colored People (NAACP) in 1909 and the National Urban League (1911) and served as delegates to the 1921 Pan-African Congress held in London, Brussels, and Paris under the leadership of W.E.B. DuBois. These alliances persisted throughout the more conservative postwar era and bore fruit in modest social progress during the New Deal. Yet, although some settlement house workers helped African Americans expand their rights, improve their economic well-being, and affirm their cultural heritage, nearly all settlement houses continued to be segregated. This led African Americans to establish their own settlement houses in New York, Atlanta, and throughout smaller cities in the South. (Carlton-Laney & Burwell, 1995; Iglehart & Becerra, 1995).

Although their views on racial justice drew criticism from reformers and even radical feminists during the Progressive Era, radical social workers were more inclined to be concerned about racial oppression than either their feminist allies or male supporters in the trade union and socialist movements. Among women and communities of color, the focus tended to be on obtaining long-denied rights (e.g., to vote, organize, be educated) rather than universal needs. In combination with the failure of radical groups dominated by White men to address the needs of women and minorities, or even to allow them participation in their organizations, this focus planted the seeds of separatist political activity, which flourished in the 1920s and again in the 1960s. Like today, ethnic, gender, and racial divisions inhibited the development of broad, class-based coalitions (Jansson, 1994, p. 362).

Jane Addams's ideas about race and relations were well outside the political mainstream. Along with Wald and Kelley, she worked with African American scholar and radical W.E.B. DuBois to establish the NAACP. Although a strong supporter of Theodore Roosevelt's presidential candidacy at the Progressive Party Convention in 1912, where Addams seconded his nomination, she nevertheless expressed her discomfort over his failure to seat African American delegates from Southern states (Rosenberg, 1992). Other social work radicals shared her views.

Lillian Wald's unequivocal support for civil rights was reflected in nearly all aspects of her work. Although racially integrated public meetings were illegal in New York, she opened the Henry Street Settlement to the National Negro Conference in 1909 that led to the formation of the NAACP. She also worked with NAACP leader Mary White Ovington to bring a production of a controversial play about racism and lynching, *Rachel*, to the Neighborhood Playhouse. This "was the first time a theater in the United States presented a play by a black author with a black cast before a white audience" (Coss, 1989, p. 12).

Wald was very active in anti–Ku Klux Klan organizations, the American League to Abolish Capital Punishment, and the American Anti-Imperialist League for Independence of the Philippines. At the same time, research conducted at Hull House by Louise de Koven Bowen detailed the extent of institutional discrimination against African Americans in Chicago (Lundblad, 1995).

As a member of the Executive Committee of the National Women's Party (NWP), Florence Kelley voiced her concerns that the NWP had failed to adequately support the needs of African American women (Cott, 1987). These racial splits continue to plague the feminist movement today.

WERE SETTLEMENT WORKERS REALLY RADICAL?

In hindsight, few radical social workers during the Progressive Era had consciously revolutionary goals in their daily work. A hundred years later, their achievements seem far more reformist than radical. Yet their emphasis on social justice, their analysis of socioeconomic conditions in structural or systemic terms, their focus on issues of social class, their links to movements organized by feminists and African Americans, and their ties to radical trade unionists and left-wing political parties represented a threat to the established order that contemporaries could not ignore. Radical social workers like Kelley, McDowell, and Wald also got their hands dirty by engaging in local political struggles around issues such as transportation planning and garbage collection (Davis, 1964). Paul Kellogg, the founder of *The Survey* and editor of *The Commons*, recognized both this radical potential and the contradictory position held by radical social workers (Chambers & Hinding, 1968).

Radical social workers like Wald and Kelley inadvertently contributed to this ambiguity by often downplaying their politics for the sake of social reform. This strategy helped produce advances such as the White House Conference on Dependent Children, the Children's Bureau, the National Child Labor Committee, and other liberal reforms like those embodied in the Progressive Party platform of 1912. Yet, by soft-pedaling their radicalism, social workers obscured the role of such ideas in transforming the nation's social agenda.

Wald's career perhaps best typifies the combination of activist reform with more radical views on domestic and international issues. She founded the field of public health nursing by creating the Visiting Nurses Service, the school nurse program, and special education courses for the disabled. She also helped organize unions for women and led the fight to reform the New York State Labor Code after the disastrous Triangle Fire of 1911. She fought against tuberculosis and for date stamping of milk containers, and with Florence Kelley set up the New York Child Labor Committee. At the same time, Wald was also an outspoken defender of civil liberties and a long-time activist against militarism and U.S. overseas intervention, serving as president of the radical American Union Against Militarism during the critical early years of World War I (Coss, 1989; Daniels, 1989).

Just as some analysts have challenged the radicalism of early radical social workers, late twentieth century feminist historians and feminist activists have also questioned their commitment to feminism (Fitzpatrick, 1990; Gordon, 1990; Lacerte, 1976). Certainly, the language they employed reflected the values of a different era with different cultural and political sensibilities. Yet these critics fail to acknowledge the different influences on women like Addams and her contemporaries—influences that enabled them to be transitional figures between Victorian ideals of femininity and more modern conceptions of women's complex roles in industrial society. During the Progressive Era, in their writings and political work, radical social workers began to express this new vision of women. For example, according to Grace Abbott, Addams was instrumental in persuading Theodore Roosevelt, as presidential candidate on the Progressive Party ticket, to endorse women's suffrage at the 1912 "Bull Moose" Convention (Rosenberg, 1992).

At other times, radical social workers appeared to vacillate between maternalist and universal perspectives in promoting their policy agenda. Sometimes, they linked their support for feminist causes, such as suffrage, to broad, universal rights. For example, they supported women's suffrage as a necessary step to protect women workers and women in their homes (Rosenberg, 1992). "Poor women," Addams argued, "should vote for the same reason that poor men should vote—they need the franchise for their own protection" (quoted in Levine, 1971, p. 171). Kelley regarded suffrage for women as "indispensable to the solution of the child labor problem" (quoted in Cott, 1987, p. 100). Thus, despite the moral appeal of socialist values, it was the suffrage movement, and not the socialist movement, that helped forge alliances between feminists and socialists (Woloch, 1984).

Although radicals like Kelley and Starr reflected a leftward tilt within the feminist movement, they focused their effects on the distinctive needs of women rather than gender equality. This created splits among feminists in the 1920s over such issues as the Equal Rights Amendment. (See Chapter 3.) Kelley, Addams, and their supporters favored women's equality, but wanted that equality accompanied by protection from the dangers of economic exploitation and domestic abuse. They believed that such protection should take precedence over other aspects of equality which, at the time, they regarded as little more than an abstraction (Cook, 1978). Whether this maternalist strategy, which focused on women's exceptionalism, undermined the long-term cause of feminism continues to be the subject of much historical debate among feminists.

Neither Addams, Kelley, nor their radical social work colleagues, however, engaged in direct attacks on societal values about gender. "They were *de facto* radicals whose actions spelled rejection of the sexual and political status quo, but whose words were consistent with, or at least within the framework of, prevailing norms" (Chafe, 1977, p. 38). Even among women, they consistently sought to bridge the gap between social classes.

Ironically, settlement houses that supported radical activities could not have survived without the financial backing of a few wealthy supporters. In Chicago, Jane Addams depended on the help of Mary Rozet Smith, who later became her life partner, Bertha Palmer, wife of a Chicago millionaire and an active member of the Chicago Woman's Club, and a close friend, Louise deKoven Bowen, to help pay Hull House's bills. Smith alone contributed more than $116,000 to the settlement between 1906–1934. Bowen's assistance brought

Hull House respectability at a time when the agency's support of organized labor in the frequently bloody conflicts of the period gave the settlement the appearance of being a radical stronghold. Her donations of more than $300,000 lent credibility to the organization and provided it with financial stability (Sklar, 1989; Woloch, 1984).

The Chicago Women's Club paid Florence Kelley's salary as director of the Hull House Bureau of Labor in 1892 (Sklar, 1989). In return, Kelley headed the Industrial Division of the General Federation of Women's Clubs while directing the National Consumers League and living at the Henry Street Settlement for nearly three decades. Kelley's host at Henry Street, Lillian Wald, also benefited from the assistance of wealthy benefactors, in her case, Jacob Schiff, a German Jewish financier, whose family later founded the New York Evening Post, which for many years was the leading liberal-labor daily in New York (Coss, 1989; Daniels, 1989; Wald, 1915a).

The influence of radicals in the otherwise liberal settlement movement peaked between 1911–1920, when they were well represented on the Executive Committee of the National Federation of Settlements and held the organization's presidency for six years (National Federation of Settlements, papers 1911–1920, Lillian Wald Papers, New York Public Library). During the progressive era, they helped shape the careers of "Second Generation" radical social workers as well as radicals in other fields (Andrews, 1993). Historian Charles Beard, educator Elizabeth Irwin, and public health physician Alice Hamilton, all cite the powerful role the radical social workers played in their lives. Hamilton wrote, "I should never have taken up the cause of the working class had I not lived at Hull House and learned much from Jane Addams, Florence Kelley, Julia Lathrop, and others" (National Federation of Settlements, 1946).

This influence was severely constrained, however, by the drive that emerged around the turn of the century to professionalize the field of social work. Even before Abraham Flexner's famous speech (1915), professionalism would "override any impulse to bring about radical social change" (Gettleman, 1975, p. 59). Shortly after Flexner's address, in which he asserted that social work was not yet a profession, the dictates of professionalism combined with overt political repression produced by wartime hysteria to reduce dramatically the influence of radical social workers in the field and the nation (Walkowitz, 1999).

Although radical social workers often drew scorn and political fire for their views on domestic issues, their opposition to American militarism and jingoism, particularly U.S. entry into World War I, produced the greatest public outcry and had the longest-lasting consequences on the social work profession. These attacks undermined radical social workers' influence on public opinion, divided the feminist and radical movements, marginalized radicals within the emerging social work profession, and weakened the nation's prospects for even modest social reforms. Among the first salvos in a decade-long attack was the investigation of Addams and Wald by the Lusk Committee of the New York State Legislature in 1919. A more insidious form of repression began two years later in the seemingly innocent surroundings of the War Department library.

3

The Spider Web Conspiracy and the Death of Progressivism

> *As for the Communists, they are*
> *logically letting the Gold Dust Twins,*
> *Feminism and Pacifism do their work. . . .*
> *The pinks are all red sisters under the skin.*
> —Woman Patriot (1927)

SPIDER WEB PAMPHLET

In 1922, Lucia Maxwell, a librarian on the staff of Brigadier General Amos Fries director of the War Department's Chemical Warfare Service, drafted a pamphlet that would have a dramatic effect on the development of American social work and social policy in the post–World War I era. She drew up a "spider web chart" depicting an interlocking network of 15 women's organizations, including the Young Women's Christian Association (YWCA), Women's Trade Union League (WRUL), and Women's International League for Peace and Freedom (WILPF), and 29 women leaders, including Jane Addams, Julia Lathrop, and Florence Kelley, all joined by their membership in the National Council for the Prevention of War and the Women's Joint Congressional Committee.

The pamphlet accused these pacifist and feminist groups, which promoted peace and a variety of progressive social welfare and anti–child labor legislation, of being agents of "international communism." Quoting from the report of the Lusk Committee established by the New York Legislature, which labeled Jane Addams a "dangerous red," the pamphlet attempted to demonstrate how a network of women's organizations sought to disarm the United States and abet a Bolshevik coup through the subversion of American institutions. Addams and Kelley were often placed at the center of the web because of their opposition to

39

World War I, their defense of the civil liberties of domestic radicals, and their outspoken advocacy of progressive social legislation.

This was no crank publication written by an obscure bureaucrat. Maxwell was also chair of the Patriotic Committee of the League of American Penwomen. She had a sympathetic boss in General Fries and access to influential groups in government and the private sector. The spider web pamphlet was soon widely distributed by powerful organizations like the National Association of Manufacturers, the Daughters of the American Revolution (DAR), and the American Medical Association (AMA), and influential politicians like Senator Thomas Bayard of Delaware, to serve their own political ends (Lemons, 1975; Rosenberg, 1992).

The pamphlet was, in fact, part of a widespread attack on pacifist organizations such as WILPF, launched in the aftermath of the war by military officers such as General Fries. Fries himself falsely alleged that WILPF had committed an act "nothing short of treason" by circulating an oath of wartime noncooperation among its members. In the mid-1920s, with the assistance of new FBI director J. Edgar Hoover and industrialist Henry Ford, who had ironically attempted to end World War I before U.S. involvement, the spider web chart circulated widely among patriotic organizations and drew the attention of the general public. Although denounced by women's organizations, it soon led to similar, larger charts from other hyperpatriotic individuals and groups, presaging the blacklists circulated a quarter of a century later during the height of McCarthyism.

The national press quickly picked up the pamphlet's message in its reports on the activities of pacifist, feminist, and labor groups. In January 1923, the publication *Industrial Progress* charged that the First Conference on Women in Industry, in which Kelley, Lathrop, Sophonisba Breckinridge, Mary McDowell, and Mary van Kleeck played important roles, was controlled by communists. A reporter for the Associated Press, R. M. Whitney, similarly commented that the 1923 WILPF conference "was dominated by the spirit of Russian Communism" (quoted in Lemons, 1975, pp. 213–214).

Over the next few years, the DAR expanded the spider web theme to attack 90 progressive organizations, including social welfare and civil rights groups such as the YWCA, Young Men's Christian Association (YMCA), National Association for the Advancement of Colored People (NAACP), and the Federal Council of Churches, whose advocacy efforts tied them to domestic radicals. Leaders of such organizations were barred from addressing DAR functions and state and local chapters developed a blacklist. The DAR singled out Addams, Kelley, Lathrop, and W.E.B. DuBois for personal attacks. Anticipating the political climate created a generation later by McCarthyism, Carrie Chapman Catt remarked that the DAR "were unable to find any Bolsheviks [and] therefore turned their fear and hatred on other citizens, charging that those interested in reform were . . . secretly allied to the dread *Bolsheviki*." In response, Hermine Schwed, field secretary of the National Association for Constitutional Government, attacked Catt as a communist, alleged that Kelley "was the chief promoter of communism in the United States," and that Addams was aiding the communist cause (quoted in Lemons, 1975, p. 224).

The climate of repression symbolized by the spider web pamphlet continued throughout the 1920s. In 1927, the DAR again denounced Addams and other social work leaders and placed them on a list of "doubtful speakers" circulated to its local chapters, along with other so-called internationalists, pro-Soviet, and feminist activists (termed "pinks, reds, and yellows" in some of the literature). Lieutenant Colonel Lee Alexander Stone, speaking before an Illinois women's club, accused Florence Kelley of being a "Leninist" (Cott, 1987, p. 259).

These denunciations were without foundation, but they affected the progress of pending social welfare legislation such as the child labor amendment. They also contributed significantly to the retreat of the social work profession from its prewar advocacy on behalf of social reform into a self-serving pursuit of professional status and individually oriented method. By the end of the decade, the landmark Milford Conference wrestled with matters of practice theory and technique, rather than social change. That same year, 1929, Porter Lee, president of the National Conference of Social Work (NCSW), declared the passing of the "cause" phase of social work's development. The inward-looking drive for professionalism that shaped social work during these years was, however, not merely the logical consequence of its development within the American occupational hierarchy (Wenocur & Reisch, 1989). Social work chose the path of professionalism because the alternative—the pursuit of radical change—was too fraught with political danger.

THE GREAT WAR AND THE ATTACK ON SOCIAL WORK RADICALS

The spider web pamphlet and its consequences raise several important questions about the history of social work. Why were women like Addams, Kelley, Wald, and Lathrop considered such threats to national security? Why didn't the organized social work profession come to their active defense? Why did the ludicrous charges against them "stick" and influence the course of social legislation? And, why haven't social workers been considered important enough to attack with such vehemence since? The answers lie in the close relationship between domestic and military policy during the period, the hysteria generated by the Russian Revolution, and a backlash against the rapid social changes that had occurred since the turn of the century. The extraordinary influence of radical social workers—well outside traditional or contemporary professional boundaries—also played an important role.

Like the radical/reform wing of the social work profession itself, the antiwar views of radical social workers emerged from two different sources: Quaker religious values and socialist ideals (Addams, 1907; Sklar, 1995; Wald, 1915a). The feminism of social work radicals also led naturally to their expression of antiwar and pacifist sentiments when World War I started in 1914. They were instrumental in creating peace divisions in many women's organizations such as the National American Woman Suffrage Association and the National Women's Party (NWP). Despite the different philosophical sources of their pacifism and somewhat differing explanations of the war's causes, Addams, Kelley, and Wald found themselves in active alliance with radicals from a variety of left-wing groups.

Lillian Wald's controversial peace activities spanned two decades. The founder of both the Henry Street Settlement and the Visiting Nurses Service in 1893, Wald had single-handedly raised the funds for both organizations and essentially created the field of public health nursing. In her tireless efforts to improve working conditions for women, she tried to define a common ground for middle-class reformers and working-class women. Given her feminist and socialist views, her broad definition of public health and well-being, and her support for the working class, it is not surprising that she held strong convictions about war and militarism. At the outbreak of World War I, she stated that "a spirit of militarism has invaded us [and] threatens the great constructive upbuilding, life-saving social work" (quoted in Coss, 1989, p. 93). The Henry Street Settlement that she directed served as a focal point for pacifist activity and the linchpin between religious pacifists, antiwar intellectuals, upper-class reformers, and radical opponents of an "imperialist war."

In December 1914, Wald discussed her antiwar philosophy in an interview in the *New York Evening Post*: "In its broadest conceptions, [social] work is teaching the sanctity of human life and . . . the doctrine of the brotherhood of man. . . . The social workers of our time are dreaming a great dream, and seeing a great vision of democracy, of a real brotherhood among men. . . . War is the doom of all that has taken years to build up" (Committee for the Election of Lillian D. Wald to the Hall of Fame for Great Americans at New York University, 1960, p. 18, Evelyn Butler Archive, University of Pennsylvania).

Two months later in a speech at Cooper Union, she asked women to take the lead in opposing the war. Soon after, along with Paul Kellogg, editor of *The Survey*, Roger Baldwin, future director of the American Civil Liberties Union, Crystal Eastman and her brother, Max, editor of the left-wing publication, *The Masses*, Wald cofounded the American Union Against Militarism (AUAM) out of the Henry Street Group that she, Addams, and Kellogg formed at the outbreak of the war. Wald was elected its president, a post she held until September 1917, and Crystal Eastman served as its executive director. Wald was also active during these years in the Women's Peace Party, the antecedent of the WILPF, and in other antiwar efforts.

The AUAM lobbied Congress against intervention and was active coast to coast through 22 local chapters. The Union's focus went beyond U.S. involvement in World War I to include opposition to imperialist intervention in Latin America and the Caribbean. It helped thwart attempts to invade Mexico in 1916 and became the source of the American Civil Liberties Union, which Baldwin founded and headed for many years, and the Foreign Policy Association.

Wald and Kellogg did not approve, however, of the group's confrontational tactics. Out of fear of being seen as "antiwar agitators," they took a more cautious, internationalist approach (Cook, 1978). In a letter to Emily Balch, written June 14, 1917, two months after the U.S. entered the war, Eastman suggested that Kellogg, "is more interested in the international aspect of our work, in hastening a liberal peace and proceeding to organize the world for democracy, than in the struggle to hold the fort for democracy against militarism at home. He disagrees with the establishment of a Conscientious Objectors Bureau by the American Union Against Militarism" (quoted in Cook, 1978, pp. 254–257). As a result of this split over tactics, Kellogg and Wald wanted to leave the Union but Eastman, who felt their presence was important, convinced them to stay. On her death, Kellogg noted how Wald "risked much to take the chairmanship of the AUAM" (*New York Times*, September 3, 1940).

Wald was fully aware of the risks she took in opposing the war. Corporate leaders had warned her that her reputation was at stake and philanthropic sponsors, like J. Horace Harding, Chairman of the Board of the American Railway Express, sharply attacked her politics (letter of August 4, 1917). Nevertheless, Wald scoffed at the charges, which she found "foolish since after all, . . . I am at least one insurance against unreasonable revolution in New York" (quoted in Coss, 1989, p. 13).

In contrast to Wald's socialist internationalism, Jane Addams's pacifism reflected an "affirmation of the humanitarian and democratic ideals she associated with the United States" (Kendall, 1989, p. 2). The international arena, especially regarding international peace and cooperation, was one sphere of activity that flowed out of the multicultural environment of settlements like Hull House and the Henry Street Settlement. Addams was less prepared, therefore, for the vehemence of the attacks upon her by politicians and in the press when she opposed American intervention.

Addams's antiwar activities began in 1893 when she chaired the Chicago committee of the American Peace Society Congress. In 1904, she was a delegate to the International Peace Congress, and three years later she published her philosophy of peace in a book, *Newer Ideals of Peace* (1907). Influenced by her Quaker father's religious ideals, the philosophy of William James, and contemporary maternalistic views of women's role, Addams "found hope for the prevention of war in the peaceful instincts of the working class" (Lundblad, 1996, p. 1). Following the outbreak of World War I, she organized a temporary peace group at Hull House, similar to the one established at the Henry Street Settlement in New York (Addams, 1922).

Once the war started, Addams became a leader in the movement to stop the hostilities and prevent U.S. entry in the conflict. Although she was opposed to direct action such as draft resistance, in January 1915 she endorsed a national peace conference of several thousand women in Washington. Later that year, she played a leading role in founding the Women's Peace Party, became its first chair, and persuaded Sophonisba Breckinridge to serve as its treasurer. In the spring of 1915 in The Hague, she presided over an international peace congress of women, also attended by Grace Abbott, Kelley, Wald, and Alice Hamilton, which sought unsuccessfully to end the war. Although some militant representatives viewed Addams as being too willing to compromise in the face of conflict, the conference ultimately led to the creation of the WILPF (Costin, 1989; Fitzpatrick, 1990).

Frustrated in these antiwar efforts, Addams joined Wald and other peace activists in Henry Ford's ill-fated and occasionally ridiculed peace expedition to Europe to organize a conference of neutrals (Kraft, 1978). In early 1917, she advocated a public referendum as a precondition for a U.S. declaration of war. Unlike other radicals, however, once Congress declared war she did not speak out against mobilization, but focused on postwar aims such as the establishment of a League of Nations and the promulgation of Wilson's 14 points (Lundblad, 1995).

Despite her tempered advocacy of nonintervention, as early as 1915 Addams's views produced a wave of vilification, anger, and scorn among patriotic groups, politicians, and respectable newspapers. By the end of the war, the press often labeled her a traitor (Lundblad, 1995; Sanders, 1989). As Archibald MacLeish stated in paying tribute to Addams twenty-five years after her death,

> It was not a crank who said that Jane Addams ought to be hanged to the nearest lamp post: it was a solid citizen who, like other solid citizens, regarded any legislation aimed at the protection of children in factories as an attack on his right, as a citizen of a free country, to do as he pleased. And it was not an irresponsible newspaper which hounded her as a radical; it was a newspaper [the *Chicago Tribune*] most of the responsible people of the city read. (MacLeish, 1961, p. 3)

Opposition to the war among social workers was not confined to White radical feminists. Chandler Owen, a socialist African American, who coedited the activist newspaper, *The Messenger*, with labor leader A. Philip Randolph, also spoke out against intervention. As a young man, Owen had received one of the first social work fellowships, sponsored by the National Urban League to study at the New York School of Philanthropy. His studies led him into radical philosophy and instilled a deep commitment to socialism as the solution to the problems confronting African Americans.

In 1915, Randolph's wife, Lucille, introduced Owen to her husband, who taught him about Marxism while Owen instructed Randolph in Lester Ward's sociological theories on the importance of the environment (Andersen, 1986). Soon, they integrated their views and concluded that men could only find freedom when released from economic bondage. They formed a life-long relationship despite the fact that when Owen left *The Messenger* in the early 1920s they went their separate ways professionally.

Owen looked to the working class to bring forth a new society (*The Messenger*, October 1920, pp. 2–3). He believed that capitalism was fundamentally racist and indicted as bourgeois both those Whites and Blacks who rejected radicalism. Owen was also critical of other Black leaders, whom he portrayed as ignorant. In an article called "The Failure of the Negro Leaders" he provocatively declared that most prominent African American leaders were "a discredit to Negroes and a laughing stock among whites" (*The Messenger*, January 1918, p. 23).

Both Owen and Randolph supported feminist issues and their organization, the Political Council, was the only African American political group to support women's suffrage. They appealed both to suffragettes and their supporters, who they called the "New Crowd Negroes," to embrace socialism. In a newspaper editorial, Owen urged African Americans to join with the socialists:

> The Socialist Party is your party, because you are the victim of every injustice which it opposes. . . . [It is] controlled by the working class, the class to which you belong, and consequently, it is from this party alone that you can expect a square deal. (Owen, *The Messenger*, January 1918, pp. 24–25)

E. Franklin Frazier, future director of the Atlanta School of Social Work, also spoke out openly against the war and American racism and endured strong denunciations because of his views. In his autobiography, Frazier reflected on how he felt about the war when he graduated from Howard University in 1916: "I resented being drafted in a war which, in my opinion, was essentially a conflict between imperialistic powers, and in view of the treatment of the Negro in the United States, the avowed aim, to make the world safe for democracy, represented hypocrisy on the part of America" (quoted in Chandler, 1995, p. 498).

Like Kelley and Wald, the opposition of Randolph, Owen, and Frazier to the war was based less on pacifist humanitarian principles, than on a socialist analysis of the war's causes and purposes. They also applied this analysis to race relations in the United States. Owen and Randolph linked capitalism and racism and were strong advocates for the unionization of African American laborers. This set them apart from African American social work leaders like George Edmund Haynes and reformist groups like the National Urban League, whose written policies were deliberately vague on such issues as strike breaking, a major barrier to interracial cooperation within organized labor (Carlton-Laney, 1993). In *The Messenger*, Owen and Randolph went so far as to attack the league's policies in this area as "completely dominated by capital" (quoted in Chandler, 1996, pp. 8, 19).

Frazier's radicalism focused more on the structural and psychological aspects of institutional racism than it did on the relationship between capitalism and race prejudice. He advocated the creation of self-help organizations and cooperatives among African Americans, such as the Neighborhood Union in Atlanta. Frazier also promoted self-defense measures among African Americans in response to urban race riots and rural lynchings. In this regard, his work distinguished him from moderate civil rights leaders of the period and anticipated the radical thought of the 1960s. As director of the Atlanta School of Social Work in the mid-1920s, Frazier never tempered his militant views. His attack on the pathology of White racism, published in 1927, provoked a scathing editorial in the *Atlanta Constitution* and led to his forced resignation as director of the Atlanta School (Platt & Chandler, 1988).

AFTERMATH OF WAR AND THE BEGINNINGS OF THE "RED SCARE"

After World War I, the fear of communist-inspired revolution spurred the growth of the federal intelligence establishment in the United States. African American radicalism was particularly feared because of the belief that Bolshevik revolutionaries were targeting African Americans by supporting issues that would attract them to the Communist cause (Kornweibel, 1998). Consequently, all African American activists were suspect and likely to be branded a communist, Bolshevik, or anarchist. These attacks placed both Owen and Randolph, who openly embraced social and economic revolution, in great personal and professional jeopardy. Their newspaper was considered the most dangerous of all Black publications because of its emphasis on radical themes, including the right of Blacks to arm themselves in self-defense against lynch mobs and White rioters; a demand for total social equality, including racial intermarriage; support for the revolutionary Industrial Workers of the World (IWW); and hostility toward the South, the Wilson Administration, the Versailles Treaty, and the League of Nations (Kornweibel, 1975). The Justice Department so feared their political organization that they "offered the press various, so-called "news" stories about radicalism already engraved on plates and ready for printing. Government documents were leaked to influential, large circulation magazines with Attorney General Palmer's personal suggestion that they use them to expose the Bolshevik menace" (Kornweibel, 1998, p. 22).

Similarly, the antiwar efforts of radical social workers like Addams, Kelley, and Wald intensified the antipathy and distrust they had incurred among conservatives because of their advocacy for domestic reforms and the protection of civil liberties. Addams's "activities on behalf of the welfare state and the cause of peace won her the hatred of the American Legion and the Daughters of the American Revolution, who stigmatized her as a factor in a movement to destroy civilization and Christianity" (Lundblad, 1995, p. 667). As early as 1918, women's agitation for peace was linked to Bolshevism. Both the tone and the impact of this antiradical crusade presaged more sweeping repressive developments 30 years later and had similar consequences within the social work profession.

What seemed to be threatening was not merely the promotion of pacifism, but also the effort it produced to organize women into a political class. This was, in the *New York Times's* view, an un-American, Bolshevik notion (Cott, 1987). As Clarke Chambers pointed out (1986), these women were also threatening because they were not dependent on men financially or emotionally. For the most part, they lived outside of a traditional family and created their own family forms and intimate relationships.

Addams sacrificed her health and enormous national prestige on behalf of the peace movement, because she regarded war as undermining efforts at domestic reform. When her efforts to stop the war in Europe failed, she and other social workers with pacifist inclinations turned their attention to opposing U.S. entry into the war and confronted the growing tide of militarism and ultrapatriotism sweeping the nation. As a result, Addams, who had once been acclaimed "The Only Saint America Has Produced" (Woloch, 1984), suffered the wrath of right-wing and ultrapatriotic organizations for most of the remainder of her career.

After the armistice, Addams played a leading role in creating the WILPF out of the Women's Peace Party. She was elected its first president, a post she held until 1934 and for which she was later awarded the Nobel Peace Prize. In line with her continuing focus on the domestic impact of war, Addams's work with WILPF emphasized the elimination of the causes of future wars (Bussey, 1965). In 1922, she stated, "We believed that war seeking its end through coercion, not only interrupted but fatally reversed this process of cooperating good will [which had been initiated by the Settlement Movement]" (Addams, 1922, p. 4).

Addams's principled positions, however, made her and other social work radicals like Wald and Kelley the subject of strident attacks and overt political repression. Wald's antiwar activities put her in "Who's Who in Pacifism," the first red scare list, which was drafted by the U.S. Military Intelligence Bureau and circulated to the press and the Senate Judiciary Committee. In 1919, Addams and Wald were labeled "undesirable citizens" by the Overman Committee of the U.S. Congress, an ancestor of the House Un-American Activities Committee, and accused of leading pro-German pacifist movements prior to U.S. entry into the war. Two years later, the Lusk Committee of the New York State legislature, charged with the investigation of radicalism in the state's settlement houses and schools, identified both Wald and Addams as "anxious to bring about the overthrow of the government and establish in this country a soviet government on the same lines as in Russia" (quoted in Coss, 1989, p. 13). Wald's support of efforts to get the United States to recognize the newly formed Soviet Union undoubtedly provided further ammunition for the committee (Fisher, 1943).

In 1919–1920, under Attorney General A. Mitchell Palmer, the Justice Department orchestrated a massive red scare that resulted in the imprisonment and deportation of hundreds of trade unionists and pacifists as suspected subversives and the overall chilling of the political climate. State legislative committees, such as the Lusk Committee in New York (which labeled Addams a "dangerous red"), conservative organizations like the National Association of Manufacturers, patriotic and veterans groups, and the press abetted Palmer's efforts. The fear of Bolshevik revolution served as the justification for the suppression of domestic radicalism and reform, on a scale unmatched since the Alien and Sedition Acts of the late eighteenth century. No one seemed immune. African American radicals like Owen, Randolph, and Dubois were particularly regarded as political threats: "[E]ven men and women of liberal views who traced their ancestry back to the Mayflower hesitated before appearing on the street with a copy of *The Nation* or *New Republic* under their arms" (Muncy, 1991, p. 332).

While initially dismissed by social work leaders like Grace Abbott, these attacks led wealthy benefactors to withdraw financial support from many settlement houses (Trolander, 1975). Only the continued backing of the wealthy Schiff family enabled the Henry Street Settlement to survive and allow Wald to pursue radical causes (Coss, 1989; Trolander, 1987; Wald, 1915a, b). Portents of more serious repression to come, the attacks even ensnared Abbott and other proponents of reformist federal legislation like the Sheppard–Towner Act. Backers of this legislation, which was designed to meet the health needs of low-income women and children, were charged with socialist or communist sympathies because of their connections to Addams, Wald, and Kelley and the antiwar causes they championed (Costin, 1989). The attacks also undermined radical social workers' influence on public opinion, divided the feminist and radical movements, marginalized radicals within the emerging social work profession, and weakened the nation's prospects for even modest social reforms. The repercussions of this repressive climate continued to be felt even when radicalism reemerged in the social work field at the height of the Great Depression.

The antiwar activities of radical social workers widened the gap between them and their liberal colleagues inside and outside social work. In 1922, a report on the prospects of the settlement movement, published by the Russell Sage Foundation, referred to the "misunderstanding" of radicalism by settlement workers (Woods & Kennedy, 1922, p. 420). At the 1923 National Conference of Social Work (NCSW) meeting, a series of resolutions on peace, child labor, the minimum wage, and amnesty for political prisoners presented by Julia Lathrop were virtually ignored (Chambers, 1963). This split was so wide that today even prominent historians distinguish between social workers and settlement workers in their classification of welfare reform leaders of the postwar period (Gordon, 1995).

THE RED SCARE AND THE SHEPPARD-TOWNER ACT

In 1921 and 1922, in the aftermath of the red scare, organizations such as the Woman Patriots began linking supporters of the Sheppard–Towner Act and other protective legislation with Bolshevism. The first legislation produced directly by the Children's Bureau's research on maternal and infant mortality, Sheppard–Towner created maternal and child health centers around the country, particularly in rural areas. Drafted by Julia Lathrop in 1918, the bill was introduced into the House of Representatives that year by social worker and pacifist Jeanette Rankin, the only member of Congress who voted against U.S. entry into both World War I and World War II. "During the campaign for its enactment, the epithets of socialism, communism, and nationalization of the nation's youth, hurled earlier against the Children's Bureau and other pieces of social legislation, were again heard, this time even more often because of the recent Bolshevik Revolution" (Trattner, 1995, p. 221).

For two years, in the face of considerable opposition and without support from the Wilson administration, Sheppard–Towner made little progress. Opponents of the bill, which included the "leading physicians and medical societies of the country, manufacturers' associations and alliances" attacked it as "vicious, unnecessary, and unwarranted . . . [as] not even half-way honest socialism" (Volk, 1921). In 1920, however, a revised bill, endorsed by a broad and unusual coalition, including the Socialist, Prohibition, and Farmer–Labor Parties and the DAR, passed after extensive lobbying by the Women's Joint Congressional Committee. In testimony before Congress, Florence Kelley proclaimed, "What answer can be given to the women in a myriad of organizations, who are . . . asking 'Why does Congress wish women and children to die? Why does it neglect women and children in the full light of knowledge?'" (Kelley, 1920).

Kelley, as chair of the subcommittee of the Women's Joint Congressional Committee (WJCC), played a leadership role in the lobbying campaign for the bill as she had in the anti–child labor movement. Although opponents decried it as a "foreign experiment in communism," the bill eventually passed by overwhelming majorities in both houses. Supporters and opponents recognized that the implications of the act were enormous as it involved the first allocation of federal funds for social welfare purposes since the establishment of the Freedmen's Bureau after the Civil War.

Shortly after Sheppard–Towner's passage, however, pamphlets distributed by the Woman Patriots alleged that the U.S. Women's Bureau and other proponents of the act were part of a conspiracy to "Bolshevize America" by destroying the family. The attacks focused on individuals like Addams and Kelley and organizations in which they played leadership roles, such as the WILPF, the WTUL, and the Children's Bureau. In the *Woman Patriot*, they depicted the latter as a "radical federal bureau of social workers" acting under the orders of the Soviet Union to promote communistic programs like Sheppard–Towner (Muncy, 1991, pp. 128–129; Ryan, 1979). The Woman Patriots also linked the WTUL with the socialist Amsterdam International, "an organization so radical that it has been repeatedly denounced by the AFL [American Federation of Labor]" (quoted in Lemons, 1975, p. 212).

The efforts of the Woman Patriots complemented those promoting the spider web conspiracy. As a result, the broad-based coalition that had supported legislation like the Sheppard–Towner Act began to collapse almost as soon as the legislation was enacted into law in 1921. Reflecting the conservative climate of the 1920s, critics charged that the act undermined individualism, weakened the role of sovereign states, and eroded civil liberties. The DAR withdrew its support after 1923 and circulated the spider web pamphlet throughout the country. The AMA termed Sheppard–Towner an "imported socialist scheme" and, as early as 1922, its national board approved a strategy of attacking the program at the state level (Rosenberg, 1992, p. 77). Senator James Reed added an element of misogynism to this chorus when he declared that Sheppard–Towner invaded the private lives of families because of the influence of the "female celibates" who ran the Children's Bureau (Muncy, 1991, p. 132).

When the act came up for reauthorization, these charges were repeated with greater ferocity. In October 1925, Lilla Day Monroe, editor of the *Kansas Woman's Journal*, wrote that the purpose of the spider web was to attack big business and thereby "do the bidding of the communist knave" (quoted in Lemons, 1975, p. 218). Although Monroe also considered Lathrop and Grace Abbott as threats, she singled out Addams as a dangerous subversive because she worked under the guise of promoting welfare causes. At first, social work radicals did not bother to refute the charges, failing to realize the seriousness of the situation. Yet the attacks persisted and contributed to the defeat of the child labor amendment in 1925 (*The Survey*, October 1925).

The next year, right-wing forces expanded the scope of their attacks. The head of the National Association of Manufacturers, John Edgerton, blasted the Second Conference on Women in Industry as communist dominated, singling out such leaders as Lathrop, Kelley, Breckinridge, Mary McDowell, and Mary van Kleeck. A state officer in the South Dakota PTA also denounced Kelley, Addams, and Lathrop. Kelley's ideas, she claimed, were "red from start to finish" and Hull House provided "a meeting place for Communists" (Lemons, 1975).

This round of attacks culminated when Senator Thomas Bayard of Delaware read into the *Congressional Record* a 36-page petition and a letter from the Woman Patriots that went far beyond the misogynistic attacks of his colleague, Senator James Reed. The petition claimed that not only Sheppard–Towner but also an entire range of social welfare programs (including child labor laws) had Bolshevik origins. These programs, the petition alleged, were part of "a conspiracy to Sovietize the U.S. . . . [They are] a feminist-socialist-communist plot under the leadership of Florence Kelley Wishniewski—the ablest general communism had produced." The letter charged the Children's Bureau with falsifying its statistics in the interests of establishing a "nationalized, standardized care of children." Even the concept of the grant-in-aid, hardly novel to Sheppard–Towner, was denounced as a "Bolshevik gimmick to subvert the states" (*Congressional Record*, October 1926).

Although some social work leaders like Grace Abbott laughed off these attacks, there is little doubt that they contributed to the marginalization of domestic radicals, particularly women. As a result of the vicious red-baiting of its leader, Florence Kelley, the National Consumers League (NCL) experienced a significant drop in membership and income. The WTUL lost influence and was generally ignored by the conservative AFL. Further evidence of the repressive climate these attacks produced can be found in the reluctance of Lathrop and Abbott to ally themselves with Margaret Sanger and use the clinics established by Sheppard–Towner to promote birth control education. Fear of incurring further attacks by the AMA lay at the heart of this decision (Rosenberg, 1992). On a broader scale, the repressive political climate and a slew of reactionary lawsuits combined with the promotion of a consumer culture and sexual freedom by mass advertising to channel the energies of many women away from social justice issues toward self-liberation and sexual freedom, a trend with re-markable similarities to contemporary events (Addams, 1935; Faludi, 1991; Ryan, 1979).

EQUAL RIGHTS AMENDMENT (ERA)

While they were defending themselves against the persistent attacks of right-wing groups, leading social work radicals became embroiled in a protracted conflict with feminist allies over the Lucretia Mott or Equal Rights Amend-ment (ERA) that had been proposed by the NWP. The key issue was "whether the strategy of so sweeping an assertion of sexual equality would nullify all gen-der-specific legislation that women reformers and women's organizations had fought so hard to implement between 1890 and 1920" (Sklar, 1993, p. 47). Al-though Florence Kelley held a leadership position in the NWP that proposed the amendment as part of its overall feminist agenda, she feared that recent legislative victories, including protective labor legislation, mothers' pensions, and the newly passed Sheppard–Towner Act, would be jeopardized by its pas-sage (Cott, 1987). Crystal Eastman described Kelley in an essay, "Equality or Protection," (1924) as someone "known the world over as a passionate advocate of protective laws for women and children in industry, an exceedingly forceful, almost violent personality, a born fighter, and a [devoted and able] leader" (quoted in Cook, 1978, pp. 158–159).

Nevertheless, Kelley split with NWP president Alice Paul over both racial issues and the ERA. In her eyes, "the NWP leadership was more wedded to equal rights than to labor laws" (Cott, 1987, p. 123). Rather than abstract egali-tarian rights, Kelley sought to establish the right to explicit forms of social pro-tection based on social justice principles, rather than charity. At the NWP's 1921 convention, and the following year in a pamphlet, "Twenty Questions about the Proposed Equal Rights Amendment" (1922), she reiterated her opposition to the amendment on so-called maternalist grounds. With the support of Mary Anderson, head of the Women's Bureau, and Ethel Smith, leader of the WTUL, she argued that the ERA would invalidate protective labor and social legislation that women's groups had struggled to pass since the turn of the century.

Earlier evidence of such splits among feminist activists appeared over the issue of birth control. Despite their support of many issues concerning women and their promotion of alternative social roles for women, most social work radicals were not involved in promoting birth control efforts until after the pas-sage of the Sheppard–Towner Act in the 1920s. Even the staff at Hull House distanced themselves from the work of birth control advocate Margaret Sanger when she asked them for their support. Julia Lathrop, president of the NCSW, was a notable exception (Gordon, 1990). Modern critics of social work activists in the Progressive Era frequently cite their opposition to birth control reform and child care as reflections of their "maternalist" perspective, which restrained the progress of feminism in the pre–World War I period (Gordon, 1995).

The split between Kelley and Paul revealed serious differences over their conception of women as a social group and over how public policy could best support women's rights. Reflecting a quarter century of experience battling for protective legislation, Kelley declared in 1922:

> So long as men cannot be mothers, so long as legislation adequate for them can never be adequate for wage-earning women; and the cry Equality, Equality, where Nature has created Inequality, is as stupid and deadly as the cry Peace, Peace, where there is no Peace. (quoted in Cott, 1987, p. 138)

Jane Addams agreed with Kelley. She chastised the NWP for its "legalistic" approach to the issue of women's equality, an approach that was ignorant of history, society, and life: "Protective legislation for women and children is necessary to overcome nature's handicap, has always preceded better legislation for men, and equalizes for all in the end" (quoted in Cott, 1987, p. 140; Rosenberg, 1992).

In opposing the ERA, Kelley and Mary van Kleeck were allied with trade union activists like Melinda Scott, Rose Schneiderman, Agnes Nestor, and Nellie Swartz. Reflecting the class differences that had divided the feminist movement between pro- and anti-ERA forces, Scott told the Senate Judiciary Committee in February 1923:

> What if it should take longer to secure equal rights for women by dealing with discrimination separately? Would it not be better to take a little longer than to inflict upon millions of working women the sufferings that would be involved by destruction of the laws which now give them decent hours and working conditions? The working women are not much concerned with property rights—they have no property. The National Women's Party does not know what it is to work 10 or 12 hours a day in a factory; so they do not know what it means to lose an eight-hour-day or a nine-hour-day law. The working women do know, and that's why they are unanimously opposing this amendment. (quoted in Foner, 1982, p. 286)

Other groups, including the YWCA and the NCL also opposed the ERA, believing it would do more harm than good. They maintained this position through World War II, along with the New York Branch of the WTUL, Secretary of Labor Frances Perkins, African American leader Mary MacLeod Bethune, and others. Jane Addams also feared that the postsuffrage political climate would lead to the "masculinization" of women and their adoption of men's political values, rather than unleashing women's unique revolutionary potential (Addams, 1914). Ironically, modern feminists who have criticized Addams for her failure to support feminist principles have made remarkably similar arguments in recent years (Gilligan, 1982; LaCerte, 1976).

NETWORKS FOR SOCIAL JUSTICE

The divisions over the ERA reflected broader ideological and political schisms within the feminist movement, among women in general, and among social work radicals. Attacks by some women's groups on communists in public schools illustrated Jane Addams's anxieties about the growing conservatism of some feminists and their separation of gender issues from those of race and class. Throughout the 1920s, social work radicals felt increasingly distanced from their former feminist allies and from supporters in the religious community, especially among Protestants. Although adherence to vague Social Gospel ideals had forged some common ground between radical secularists and churchgoers, in the postwar decade "new forms of fundamentalism among poor Protestants and a business-promoting positivism among middle-class Protestants . . . discouraged commitments to social justice" (Sklar, 1993, p. 76).

At the same time, social work radicals disagreed over their relationship to the labor movement and working people. Roger Baldwin and Mary van Kleeck urged closer ties, including the formation of a political alliance with "the producing classes" (Baldwin, 1924, pp. 376–377). Kelley and Kellogg disagreed, arguing that social work would be more effective if it maintained its autonomy (Kellogg, 1924). Most social workers had little interest in the issue at all (Walker, 1924).

Consequently, social work radicals were ostracized, inside and outside the profession, because of their support for social justice causes that seemed to more conservative colleagues only tangential to the interests of the field. Changing patterns of fundraising after World War I reinforced this tendency. Only those settlements in non-Community Chest cities that had independent sources of financial support maintained strong social action agendas in the postwar period (Trolander, 1975). The new generation of social workers also focused less on the mission of the profession than on upward mobility within the era's culture of consumption (Walkowitz, 1999; Wenocur & Reisch, 1989). The broad networks they had established within other social movements, however, helped support radical social workers in the face of professional rejection and frequent legislative and judicial setbacks.

On a cultural level, these networks sheltered intimate, personal relationships among women and created the foundation for the lesbian subculture that flourished in the 1950s and after. Although many historians have suggested that the attacks on radical social workers in the 1920s reduced their influence on public policy and social science research (particularly around ideas of peace and feminism) through the New Deal, others suggest that women's authority continued to grow at the state and local level. This helped lay the foundation for postwar advances and the growth of the modern feminist movement (Andrews, 1990; Freedman, 1995).

For example, the Abbott sisters and Sophonisba Breckinridge continued to write about unpopular issues, such as immigration, and to advocate for an expansion of the nation's welfare system along the lines of the British model. In the early 1930s, when the Hoover administration failed to respond adequately to the social consequences of the Depression, Grace Abbott attacked the President and his cabinet in successive essays in *The New Republic*. Well in advance of other reformers, Abbott and Breckinridge also championed the idea of a permanent, well-funded national relief program (Fitzpatrick, 1990).

In a more radical vein, Lillian Wald served in the late 1920s on the Committee to Free Sacco and Vanzetti, two Boston anarchists convicted of murder in a sensational antired trial. Earlier in 1923 with the support of colleagues at the Henry Street Settlement, she wrote President Harding opposing U.S. intervention in Nicaragua. Her language was remarkably similar to that of opponents of U.S. intervention in Central America in the 1980s (Lillian Wald Papers, New York Public Library).

In an era in which the Ku Klux Klan reached unprecedented levels of political influence, Wald was active in anti-Klan organizations. An early proponent of official recognition of the U.S.S.R., Wald traveled to the Soviet Union in the mid-1920s to assist the government in establishing public health nursing and nursing education programs. Although she was often vilified for her political views and personal lifestyle, Wald's nomination to the Hall of Fame for Great Americans in the 1960s was endorsed by such scions of American capitalism as Governor Nelson Rockefeller of New York (Committee for the election of William D. Wald to the Hall of Fame for Great Americans, 1965).

CIVIL RIGHTS

The legacy of separate personal and professional networks among radical social workers that had emerged during the Progressive Era continued in the 1920s in new ways. For the first time, it provided the foundation for extensive interracial cooperation through such organizations as the NCL and the YWCA. It also fostered linkages with government bodies that addressed issues of women and children. Sometimes the two networks overlapped, as in the Inter-Racial Committee of Philadelphia, which included among its members Abraham Epstein, the Executive Secretary of the Old Age Assistance Commission, and Hanna Clothier Hull, a board member of the WILPF (The Inter-Racial Committee of Philadelphia, 1922). Another example of this cooperation is found in the civil rights work of Florence Kelley.

Like Addams, Kelley joined with W.E.B. DuBois in founding the NAACP in 1909. Yet although Addams adopted a liberal/reformist position on issues of race relations, Kelley remained true to her egalitarian socialist ideas. She served as a delegate to the 1921 Pan-African Congress in Europe organized by DuBois. On her death, he paid glowing tribute to her lifelong dedication to the battle against jim crowism.

Unlike most social workers—including her colleagues in the NCL—DuBois declared, who failed "to see the plight of the American Negro as an integral part of the problem of American democracy" Kelley "opposed every single attempt to perpetuate in new law the old discrimination against American Negroes" (quoted in Aptheker, 1966, pp. 99–100). Kelley paid a high price for her antiracist stance. At her memorial service, DuBois recalled:

> For the handing on of that lesson she paid—she paid in bitter dislike, in determined misunderstanding, and in the loss of nearly every reward that smug respectability and calculating conformity bring to their legion of devotees. And of all [her] sins against convention, none—not even her socialism and pacifism, her championing of sex equality and religious freedom, her fight for children and democracy—none cost her more fair-weather friends than her demand for the rights of twelve million Americans who are black. (quoted in Aptheker, 1966, p. 100)

Like Kelley, leaders of the YWCA had initiated efforts at interracial cooperation long before World War I in the South and in northern industrial cities like Baltimore, based on "the bond of common womanhood, deeper than all racial separateness" (Hammond, 1917, p. 18). A 1917 paper concluded, "We must lay aside the mental attitude of the past—the attitude of a people toward a slave race—and face the present with a forward look. To accomplish this is the task of women, and by all the token they are accepting it as theirs" (Hammond, 1917, p. 32). For many leaders of the YWCA, interracial cooperation was part of a broader "collective human endeavor" that applied to the economic arena as well (Fox, 1920). It was closely linked to the organization's ongoing efforts to improve the working conditions of women laborers (Groneman & Norton, 1987).

In the 1920s, when the Ku Klux Klan reached its peak membership of more than three million members and exercised powerful influence in the Democratic Party and the press, the YWCA and prominent African American social workers like E. Franklin Frazier spoke out repeatedly against racial segregation and lynchings in the South. In an alliance with major Protestant churches and the National Federation of Colored Woman's Clubs, the YWCA Commission on Interracial Cooperation published a powerful statement, "Southern White Women on Lynching and Mob Violence" (1920), which "deplore[d] the failure of State Governments to handle this, the most conspicuous enemy to justice and righteousness, and the most flagrant violation of the Constitution of our great nation" (YWCA Commission on Inter-Racial Cooperation, 1920).

This courageous position was in sharp contrast with the de facto segregation that had existed for decades within the YMCA. Although the YWCA promoted interracial cooperation and supported activism among African Americans, particularly around issues like lynching, the individualistically oriented moralism of the YMCA, coupled with its segregationist practices, drew the wrath of African American radicals like DuBois. In his words, the YMCA's policies "clearly sought to deaden every strong move on the part of [African Americans] toward freedom" and race and class consciousness (Chandler, 1995, p. 511).

Another social work champion of civil rights was Eduard Lindeman, one of the few male social work radicals in the 1920s. Raised in poverty, despite the aristocratic background of his Danish mother, Lindeman's ideas were influenced by socialism and the philosophy of the Federal Council of Churches of Christ. After World War I, as director of the Sociology Department at the North Carolina College for Women in Greensboro, he angered local newspapers and Ku Klux Klan (KKK) chapters with his ideas on racial equality and was forced to leave in 1921.

Later that year, Lindeman published *The Community*, which attracted the attention of liberal and radical intellectuals, like Mary Parker Follett, Walter Lippman, and John Dewey. In 1924, he joined the faculty of the New York School of Social Work where, often against the prevailing trend for over a quarter of a century, he addressed the social context of social work. Lindeman's political influence peaked during the 1930s when he served as an adviser to Harry Hopkins, as consulting director of the Division of Recreation of the Works Progress Administration, and as chair of the National Sharecroppers Fund. During the postwar McCarthy era, Lindeman focused his writing on civil liberties and civil rights issues and was himself the target of attacks by conservatives within both political and professional circles. (See Chapter 6.)

IMPACT OF SOCIAL WORK RADICALISM IN THE POSTWAR ERA

The persecution of social work radicals, particularly Jane Addams and Florence Kelley, for their antiwar stance during World War I continued throughout the 1920s. In the spring of 1928, less than two years after President Coolidge had acknowledged her work at an awards ceremony in Washington, a DAR document linked Addams with "other notorious Reds, pinks, and yellows" for her endorsement of a Russian war relief program sponsored by the American Friends Service Committee. In May 1931, an article in the American Legion's newspaper linked the WILPF, which Addams founded, with communism and accused her of greater participation "in more pink and red affairs than any other person in the United States" (Foster, 1995, p. 181).

Although she voted for Herbert Hoover for president in 1932, Addams recognized the growing danger to peace portended by the rise of fascism in Europe. Up to her death in 1935 she consistently articulated antiwar and internationalist perspectives and took controversial public positions on behalf of these ideas. Three weeks before she died, she participated in an international radio broadcast on the fascist threat to world peace along with Lenin's widow, Krupskaya (Lundblad, 1995).

Because radicals within social work were attacked throughout the postwar era, their impact would not be felt until the 1930s when the seeds of ideas and alliances sown in the 1920s would begin to bear fruit. Their class, gender, and race-bridging efforts provided the foundation for the future emergence of the

U.S. welfare state by "serv[ing] as a surrogate for working class social-welfare activism" and "an entering wedge for the extension of state responsibility to wage-earning men and to other aspects of women's lives" (Sklar, 1993, pp. 44, 50). They shaped the American form of social democracy that appeared in full flower during the New Deal, largely through the establishment of minimum standards for living and working conditions and protections against the exploitive aspects of capitalism.

For example, Molly Dewson, a former social worker, was Florence Kelley's chief assistant in the NCL, where she earned the nickname "minimum wage Dewson" for her leadership in the campaign for state minimum wage laws for women and children. Dewson began her career as the superintendent of the Parole Department of the Massachusetts State Industrial School for Girls, where she helped draft the state's model minimum wage law in 1912 and was active in the suffrage movement before joining the NCL as research secretary under Kelley. Judicial setbacks in the 1920s persuaded her to pursue changes through the Democratic Party, where she became director of the party's women's division and later Eleanor Roosevelt's closest political associate and a member of the Social Security Board in 1937–1938 (Muncy, 1991; Ware, 1981). Thus, although often indirect and diluted, the social work radicals of the 1920s made their impact felt on the important social legislation of the New Deal.

Title IV of the Social Security Act of 1935, which established the Aid to Dependent Children program (ADC, later AFDC, or "welfare") was essentially the work of Grace Abbott and her successor as chief of the Children's Bureau, Katherine Lenroot. In the aftermath of the attacks on the maternal and child health centers established under the Sheppard–Towner Act, they tried to develop legislation that would revive the health programs lost when Congress failed to reauthorize the program in 1929. This effort reflected a broader definition of aid to children than state-sponsored widows' pensions. As Julia Lathrop remarked as early as 1919 to the NCSW, "Let us not deceive ourselves: the power to maintain a decent family living standard is the primary essential of child welfare. This means a living wage and a wholesome working life for the man, a good and skillful mother at home to keep the house and comfort all within it" (quoted in Muncy, 1991, p. 162; NCSW, 1919). Not surprisingly, during Congressional hearings on the Social Security Act, such provisions, which today would appear sexist, were attacked as socialism and as subversive of the American way of life (Abramovitz, 1999).

During this period, radical social workers acquired a common political vocabulary through joint efforts on feminist, peace, and social welfare causes. They also strengthened their political and social networks with other radicals in trade unions, and male and female reformers. Throughout the hostile 1920s, the WTUL, Survey Associates, the American Association for Labor Legislation (AALL), and the National Consumers League, in particular, "laid the groundwork . . . for the New Deal's social welfare legislation" (Ware, 1981, pp. 142–143). Grace Abbott was active in both the WTUL and AALL while head of the Children's Bureau (1921–1934), where she incurred the wrath of conservatives because she had primary responsibility for the enforcement of the Sheppard–Towner Act.

Despite earning the enmity of conservatives, Abbott was so highly regarded that she was elected president of the NCSW (1923–1924) and mentioned as Herbert Hoover's next Secretary of Labor in 1928. Although Hoover did not name a woman to his Cabinet, in part because of the opposition of the conservative, male-dominated American Federation of Labor, activist women lobbied hard to ensure that his successor, Franklin Roosevelt, would. They rallied around the candidacy of Frances Perkins and developed a well-orchestrated campaign on her behalf (Muncy, 1991; Ware, 1981).

Perkins's supporters included leading social work radicals and reformers such as Jane Addams, Lillian Wald, Sophonisba Breckinridge, Graham Taylor, Helen Hall, Paul Kellogg, and Florence Kelley. In many ways, Perkins was a natural candidate for high office. As a young woman, she had worked at both Hull House and the Chicago Commons. In 1910, she completed a study of the Hell's Kitchen neighborhood in New York with the support of a Russell Sage Foundation fellowship. She lobbied with Kelley on behalf of the 54-hour bill for women and investigated the 1911 Triangle Shirtwaist fire. On hearing of Perkins's appointment as Secretary of Labor, Kelley exclaimed, "I never thought I would live to see the day when someone we had trained, who knew about industrial conditions, cared about women, cared to have things right, would have the chance to be an administrative officer" (quoted in Martin, 1976, pp. 143–144).

During the 1930s, Perkins gathered talented women around her in the Labor Department, women who had been trained by radicals in the NCL and who had worked with Kelley, Wald, and Mary van Kleeck. These women were also appointed to influential posts in the Federal Emergency Relief Administration (FERA), the Works Progress Administration (WPA; both directed by social worker Harry Hopkins), the National Youth Administration (a frequent target of antiradical attacks in the 1930s), the Treasury Department, and the Bureau of Public Assistance within the Social Security Administration.

Mary McLeod Bethune, head of the Negro Affairs Department at the National Youth Administration during the New Deal, led the fight of Black women in the YWCA to establish racial equality within the organization and to direct it toward national issues. Despite her efforts and the protests of the WTUL, National Consumers League, and YWCA, the labor codes established by the National Recovery Administration (NRA) allowed for lower wages for women and specified lower wages for workers in the South.

Other influential women shaped by social work radicalism in the postwar period included Mary Anderson, who had been associated with the WTUL since 1905 and became head of the newly created Women's Bureau in 1920; Jane Hoey, who became Director of the Bureau of Public Assistance from 1936 to 1953; Mary Ladame, who had worked with Mary van Kleeck on industrial research for the Russell Sage Foundation and later served as Special Assistant to Secretary of Labor Perkins from 1938 to 1945; Josephine Aspinwall Roche,

Assistant Secretary of the Treasury in charge of health service and welfare work, overseeing the U.S. Public Health Service; and Hilda Worthington Smith, future Director of the Workers Service Program in the FERA and the WPA from 1933 to 1943, where she focused on workers' education (Muncy, 1991; Ware, 1981). Thus, many of the women who occupied leading posts in the New Deal came from radical backgrounds (Woloch, 1984). Through their influence, many of the formerly radical ideas of the Progressive Era were woven into the basic fabric of U.S. society and became further institutionalized during the New Deal (Kolko, 1963). Yet their radicalism was often masked by their pragmatism. They had learned, like Perkins and Kelley in Illinois, to take "half a loaf" in dealing with more conservative male politicians.

By the mid- and late 1920s, long before the onset of the Great Depression, a handful of radical and reformist social workers began to warn of the danger of ignoring issues of unemployment. In 1924, the National Unemployment League, in which Kelley played a key role, published *Unemployment and the Stabilization of Business: A Problem for Industry,* placing the problem in the broader economic context. Helen Hall's study of unemployment in 1928, commissioned by the Unemployment Committee of the National Federation of Settlements, whose members included Mary van Kleeck, dispelled the myth of full employment and underscored the precarious nature of the Roaring Twenties prosperity by focusing on the social consequences of unemployment (Andrews, 1993b). This study became the basis of a well-publicized book, *Some Folks Won't Work* (Calkins, 1930), which was widely circulated by the radical Rank and File Movement in the 1930s. Like her future husband, Paul Kellogg, Hall's views were more radical than those of most other settlement leaders, particularly on issues like unemployment and the need for economic planning and public sector jobs (Helen Hall papers).

These messages went largely unheeded, however, even within the social work profession. Echoing sentiments expressed by President Hoover in April 1929 that the nation was close to eliminating poverty for all time, Porter Lee (1937), President of the NCSW, pronounced in a famous lecture that the era of social work activism (its "cause") was past. Fortunately for the profession and the nation, radical social workers thought otherwise.

PRELUDE TO THE RANK AND FILE MOVEMENT

The conservative climate of the post–World War I years, therefore, did not entirely suppress radicalism or activism within the social service field. During the 1920s, efforts to promote social insurance continued, ultimately culminating in a series of public welfare proposals that formed the nucleus of the 1935 Social Security Act (Chambers, 1956; Lubove, 1968). Meanwhile, the implementation of the Sheppard–Towner Act, although short-lived, gave renewed impetus to advocacy on behalf of women and children.

During these years, the introduction of Freudian psychology reflected a radical challenge to prevailing theories of human behavior. Although Freudian ideas have since been severely criticized by contemporary radicals within social work, especially feminists, they were particularly attractive to social workers on the left from the early 1920s through at least the 1950s. Yet, despite this appeal, as early as 1924, Bertha Capen Reynolds, associate director of the psychiatrically oriented Smith College School of Social Work and an early convert to Freudian ideas, criticized the power differential and the authoritarian assumptions upon which the new psychiatric social work was based.

Unlike many of her colleagues who embraced new theories of personality, Reynolds "could not bring herself to embrace the disease model of practice inherent in the adoption of psychoanalytic techniques" (Reynolds, 1924). At the time, Reynolds's views were influenced by deep religious beliefs and the ideas of W.E.B. DuBois, whom she had met during a brief tenure at Atlanta University. Her emphasis, rooted in both humanitarian concerns and a growing impulse toward social reform, remained on the psychological adjustment, not the cure, of mental patients (Reisch, 1993b). Shortly, she would integrate Marxist philosophy and elements of Rankian psychology into her thinking and create a revolutionary model of social work practice. The foundations of what became radical social work theory and practice in the 1970s and 1980s thus began to emerge even prior to the tumult of the 1930s.

Signs of what Wagner (1989a) termed "an incipient radicalism" began to reappear among social service workers even before the stock market crashed in October 1929 (Fisher, 1936; Spano, 1982). The Depression rapidly intensified this activity because it threatened the economic well-being of social workers in private sector agencies and brought them into closer contact with the consequences of growing poverty and unemployment, particularly in the nation's cities. The emergence of Workers' Councils and the Association of Federation Workers (AFW), particularly within Jewish agencies, reflected the growth of trade union ideals within the social work profession (Karger, 1988). Although they did not reach their peak influence until 1931, these councils set the stage for the appearance of the first grassroots radical movement in the profession's history: the Rank and File Movement of 1931–1942 (Fisher, 1936; Walkowitz, 1999).

4

The Rank and File Movement and the Precursors to McCarthyism

As a professional group, we are in general tied up with the reactionary rather than with the advancing forces of social change.
— Harry Lurie, "The Dilemma of the Case Worker,"
Social Work Today

THE NEW DEAL AND THE RANK AND FILE MOVEMENT

In May 1934, the first phase of the New Deal was in full flower. In the four-teen months since Franklin Roosevelt took office, the Federal Emergency Relief Administration (FERA), organized and directed by social worker and presidential advisor, Harry Hopkins, had distributed an unprecedented sum of $500 million in federal relief payments to unemployed workers. A host of so-called alphabet agencies had been created to address some of the consequences of the Depression, particularly industrial unemployment.

For the most part, organized social work, speaking through the leadership of the American Association of Social Work (AASW) and the National Confer-ence of Social Work (NCSW), endorsed the goals and proposals of the New Deal, despite some trepidation about the effects of untrammeled public sector growth on social work professionalism. In this context, at the May 1934 NCSW conference in Kansas City, Mary van Kleeck, Director of the Department of Industrial Studies at the Russell Sage Foundation and author of several ground-breaking monographs on labor conditions in factories, rose to challenge the profession's uncritical support of New Deal policies in one of three papers she presented, "Our Illusions Regarding Government" (1934b). In many ways, her speech was the defining moment of what became known in social work as the Rank and File Movement.

Van Kleeck was about 50 years old at the NCSW conference. Like many other female radicals and reformers of her generation, she was the daughter of a Protestant minister and the child of a wealthy family (Wenocur & Reisch, 1989). Although she embraced Marxism by the 1930s, religious values continued to inspire her work and she remained a member of the Society of the Companions of the Holy Cross (Freedman, 1995).

Van Kleeck was first exposed to the problems of industrialization at the College Settlement Association on the Lower East Side of New York, where she conducted research on the problems of women and children in local factories and tenements. In 1908, after completing a postgraduate fellowship at the New York College Settlement, she began a long association with the Russell Sage Foundation, which funded her studies of industrial and living conditions. She was trained by Florence Kelley and in 1913–1914 established her reputation with the publication of three research projects on the working conditions of women in factories. In 1916, the Russell Sage Foundation made her director of its Department of Industrial Studies.

Although her politics evolved from reform to radicalism, van Kleeck's abilities led to her appointment to prestigious positions at the local and national levels. In 1918, President Wilson named her director of the Department of Labor's Women in Industry Service, the forerunner of the U.S. Women's Bureau. During the conservative postwar decade, she continued to work at the Russell Sage Foundation and became increasingly involved in national activities regarding unemployment and civil rights.

In the 1920s, van Kleeck drifted steadily to the left in her politics. Yet, like her mentor, Kelley, she opposed the Equal Rights Amendment (ERA) and continued to do so into the late 1930s. At the 1924 NCSW conference, she criticized the growing conservatism of the field of social work and advocated unionism rather than professional status enhancement—views that were not received warmly by the audience (Fisher, 1980a). In 1928, she chaired the National Interracial Conference sponsored by the Young Women's Christian Association (YWCA).

Although part of Eleanor Roosevelt's network of social activists, she refused to support Roosevelt for president in 1932. Nevertheless, in 1933 she was persuaded to accept an appointment to the Federal Advisory Council of the U.S. Employment Service within the National Recovery Administration. She resigned after one day, however, because the President eliminated its labor protection provisions. This marked her formal split with the Roosevelt administration and emergence as a staunch critic of its policies and the larger economic and political structure of the nation (Brenden, 1993).

van Kleek arrived at the 1934 NCSW conference, therefore, with a national reputation as a researcher, theoretician, and outspoken activist. An avowed socialist and leading spokesperson for the growing Rank and File Movement within the field, she previously had expressed enthusiasm for Soviet efforts to create a planned economy. Through her research and international contacts, she had "concluded that to prevent poverty and to raise the standard of living, both the economic and political structure of the United States must be changed" and replaced by a democratic socialist society (Hagen, 1986, p. 726; van Kleeck, 1936, 1934). Her support of labor and a planned economy thus went beyond advocacy for the social standards of industry that an earlier generation of activists had promoted (van Kleeck, 1934a).

Speaking before an overflow crowd at the NCSW conference, van Kleeck charged the New Deal with preserving the property rights and profits of the corporate elite under the guise of improving the living standards of the common people. The unparalleled increase in federal programs and funding, she claimed, had distracted social workers from the real issue at hand. This, she argued, "is not whether [the profession] is changing its base from private to governmental sources, but whether this reliance on government commits social workers to the preservation of the status quo and separates them from their clients" (van Kleeck, 1934b, p. 474). In place of the status quo oriented programs of the New Deal, van Kleeck proposed comprehensive social insurance policies and the development of a full-blown welfare state. She criticized the Roosevelt administration for its support of corporate interests and its failure to back unions' demands for collective bargaining. To a standing ovation, van Kleeck declared that only a more planned economy and greater emphasis on economic redistribution would eradicate prevailing social ills and produce a new economic order.

In harshly criticizing the New Deal for its protection of entrenched economic interests and its sacrifice of workers' rights, van Kleeck risked her reputation with all its potential professional and political advantages. She was convinced, however, that only a radical restructuring of the U.S. economy, in which industry and natural resources would be socialized, would eradicate poverty and reduce the level of inequality in the nation. This clearly placed her at odds with both the Roosevelt administration and mainstream opinion in the social work profession (Hagen, 1986, pp. 725–727).

Although most social workers at the time supported the New Deal, "a radical minority" like van Kleeck and Harry Lurie of the Council of Jewish Federations and Welfare Funds sought "a fundamental reorganization of society—a planned socialist economy." They attacked both the aims and the accomplishments of the New Deal, as well as its racism, political compromises, and ties to big business (Trattner, 1995, p. 287). Lurie felt that his more conservative professional colleagues were equally culpable and "share responsibility with industrial and political leaders for the present catastrophe" for their failure to "throw ourselves into the struggle for a . . . reconstruction of our economic society as zealously as we gave ourselves [over] to the perfection of our technique" (quoted in Trattner, 1995, p. 275). After the relative quiescence of the 1920s, the views of such radical social workers, as well as those of reformers like Paul Kellogg, Helen Hall, and Grace Coyle repoliticized the social work profession

Mary van Kleeck's remarks at the 1934 NCSW conference were astounding less for their substance—she had expressed similar views before in social work journals and at other national conferences (NCSW, 1932)—than for their timing and for the electrifying response they generated. She not only received the Pugsley Award for the outstanding paper at the conference, she was asked to deliver the paper again to accommodate demand. There was widespread clamor among those present at the conference that her remarks be printed and widely disseminated as soon as possible.

This firestorm of approval shook the NCSW leadership and led to a pointed and controversial response from William Hodson, NCSW President, at the organization's annual dinner that evening. Without mentioning van Kleeck by name, the formally attired Hodson sharply criticized her paper's attack on the Roosevelt administration. Disputing both her radical analysis and her call for direct action by social workers, he reiterated the view of the mainstream social work profession that the New Deal, despite its imperfections, was the only viable alternative to economic and social chaos and fascism (Hodson, 1934, pp. 11–12). After Hodson attacked van Kleeck, nearly 1,000 delegates met in an unofficial session to censure him (Fisher, 1934). (Ironically, in a few years the Rank and File Movement would split over this very issue. Some of its leaders would, at that time, profess sentiments remarkably close to those expressed by Hodson that night.)

In spotlighting the "road not taken," this 1934 controversy captures the tensions that existed in social work during the 1930s between an establishment-based and professionally oriented leadership and emerging grassroots radicalism. It underscores the critical choices confronting social workers in the calamitous decade that followed the onset of the Great Depression—choices that persist to this day. It hints at the measures social workers would soon take or be silent about that repressed radical sentiments within their ranks. It reveals how new forces and new leaders on behalf of radical ideas appeared from the "bottom up" as the profession expanded rapidly in the 1930s. Finally, it demonstrates the basic contradiction between the status demands on an aspiring profession and the field's rhetorical commitment to social justice. This contradiction is both more apparent and more pressing at the beginning of the twenty-first century.

RISE OF THE RANK AND FILE MOVEMENT

The social work radicalism of the 1930s exemplified by van Kleeck was rooted in the general economic and political climate of the period, which made anti-capitalist ideologies and calls for radical action increasingly popular and accessible. Younger social workers employed by expanding public sector agencies were especially attracted to such ideas. They focused their energies on unionization within the social services and coalition building with like-minded groups in labor and left-wing organizations. A significant number of social workers joined the Communist or Socialist Parties, including leaders of the Rank and File

Movement such as Jacob Fisher; Bertha Capen Reynolds; Abram Flaxer, who later became head of the State, County and Municipal Workers Association; and Lewis Merrill, president of the left-wing United Office and Professional Workers of America (Wagner, 1989a). Other well-known radicals like van Kleeck were closely affiliated with the Communist Party, but never actually became members (Klehr, Haynes, & Anderson, 1998).

A second source of radicalism among social workers during the 1930s was the influence of long-time radicals within the Jewish welfare field, such as Fisher, Joseph Levy, and Lurie. Prompted by the effects of salary cuts, the frustrations of day-to-day practice, the rage and despair of their clients, and fears about the consequences of work-relief on their already precarious economic situation, social workers in the Jewish communal field organized discussion clubs beginning in New York in early 1931. These became the springboard for the Rank and File Movement (Fisher, 1936; Spano, 1982).

The Rank and File Movement thus arose primarily from the heightened consciousness among social workers of the contradictions between their daily work and the imperatives of the capitalist system. Factors that shaped this new consciousness included impossible working conditions, excessive caseloads, recognition of the inadequacy of the relief system, and personal anguish over their inability to address the plight of increasing numbers of clients. In her autobiography, Bertha Reynolds (1963) linked support of the Rank and File Movement to criticism of the basic structure of social services: "The Community Fund movement has by and large been under the leadership of the oligarchy of wealth. . . . To resist [these conditions] alone is professional suicide. To resist in a strong organization inclusive of all who are employed in a given social service and allied with thousands of others in organized labor and professional workers' unions, is to have real effectiveness in the fight for democracy in the whole community" (pp. 156–157).

In the context of more widespread political and trade union activism, some with revolutionary implications, thousands of social workers—particularly in public sector agencies and the Jewish center field—were, therefore, radicalized out of a desire to improve their own working conditions and change the structure of U.S. society. Social work radicalism in the 1930s was also shaped by the spread of fascism, both native and foreign, and, ultimately, by the outbreak of World War II (Fisher, 1936; Spano, 1982; Wenocur & Reisch, 1989). As it grew throughout the decade, it changed its character and its focus.

The strength of the Rank and File Movement, the major vehicle of this radicalism, lay not in its theoretical analysis of the general economic and political climate of the period, in which critiques of capitalism were increasingly acceptable and radical political ideologies, such as Marxism, had growing appeal. Instead, it lay in the power of the personal experiences of its members. Nothing could drive home the mutuality of the situation of workers and clients more vividly than day-to-day practice in underfunded welfare agencies. This raw awareness, stripped of the protective cover of a class-based ideology of professionalism, led to the recognition that nothing short of major institutional changes could "preserve the human spirit . . . provide social protection and [promote] a decent way of life" (Wenocur & Reisch, 1989, p. 187). Social work radicals adopted a Marxist analysis, therefore, not because of its theoretical elegance, but because it appeared to offer the most cogent and comprehensive explanation of the conditions they observed daily in their agencies and communities (Reynolds, 1963).

The new movement first appeared in the spring of 1931 in social workers' discussion clubs in New York City (Fisher, 1936). In some ways these resembled the consciousness-raising groups of the feminist movement in the 1960s. Within a year, workers from both public and private agencies at all levels of practice experience formed similar groups, where they debated such issues as the function of public welfare, unionization versus professionalism, clinical versus community practice, and race relations. In three years, the discussion clubs spread quickly to most major cities, including Chicago, Philadelphia, Boston, St. Louis, Cleveland, Pittsburgh, Kansas City, Los Angeles, and San Francisco.

The growth of new groups increased dramatically in 1934–1935. Of the 51 groups organized between 1931 and 1935, approximately 75% appeared in those years (Fisher, 1936). By November 1935, the directory of Rank and File organizations compiled in *Social Work Today* included groups in 29 cities and two states. By the end of 1935, the movement had more than 15,000 members, nearly twice that of the AASW (Fisher, 1980).

Most of these clubs focused primarily on educational activities and were nonsectarian in a political sense, although they did link radical social workers to broader social and political movements. Whereas they often organized short-term "actions," supported labor and hunger strikes, and advocated on behalf of policy issues such as unemployment insurance and birth control, they did not promote a particular program in their early phases (Fisher, 1936; Levy, 1934; Spano, 1982). Clubs in St. Louis, Chicago, and Los Angeles, however, actually became protective associations, drawing members attracted equally by idealism and workplace concerns.

In cities like Chicago, New York, Cleveland, Seattle, and Los Angeles, the clubs had closer connections to the Communist Party, which many newly unionized public sector workers had joined (Fisher, 1980). Yet it was not until 1934–1935, when the Rank and File convention in Cleveland united many previously separate groups and the journal *Social Work Today* appeared for the first time, that the movement adopted a specifically anticapitalist perspective as its platform. Shortly thereafter, the National Coordinating Committee (NCC) of Rank and File Groups in Social Work NCC joined with the communists to create the Farmer-Labor Party in Minnesota (Fisher, 1936).

In February 1936, Jacob Fisher asserted that the Rank and File Movement "appealed to the more progressive relief workers as the only bulwark against low wages, the lack of job tenure and the primitive working conditions . . . in the great majority of relief agencies" (Fisher, 1936, p. 5). Fisher was both the first editor of *Social Work Today* and the President of the Social Service Employees Union in New York and was active in such Popular Front organizations as the American Youth Congress and the American League Against War and Fascism (Fisher, 1980a). To Fisher, the Social Workers Discussion Clubs "symbolized . . . the dissatisfaction among . . . younger workers with what seemed to be the failure of the profession to adjust its thinking to the crisis facing America." The Rank and File Movement they inspired was "a [permanent] force that is bringing social work nearer its real function of serving truly and vitally the great mass of the American people" (Fisher, 1936, p. 6).

The development of radical discussion clubs drew strength from the formation of the Emergency Home Relief Bureau Association, which appeared in 1933 shortly after the establishment of the FERA. The association soon evolved into the Association of Workers in Public Relief Agencies (AWPRA), a militant rank and file public workers union with ties to the Communist Party. The Rank and File Movement allied itself with the Socialist and Communist Parties in criticizing the early programs and policies of the New Deal. It regarded Roosevelt's efforts as inadequate, even as obstacles to more significant social change (Jansson, 1997, p. 193). Thus, from the outset, the Rank and File Movement drew strength from several sources: radical trade unionism, left-wing political parties, and the incipient working-class radicalism of its members.

Organization at the national level and the creation of a medium of expression and communication clarified the movement's analysis and strengthened the impact of the Rank and Filers' efforts. Edited by movement leader Jacob Fisher, the Rank and File publication *Social Work Today* contained regular contributions from many prominent social workers such as Bertha Capen Reynolds, Mary van Kleeck, Eduard Lindeman, Grace Coyle, and Forrester Washington. Its circulation soon reached about 6,000 (half that of *The Survey*). Allies such as American Civil Liberties Union (ACLU) executive director Roger Baldwin and future Senator (then economist) Paul Douglas also wrote articles for the journal. Editorials regularly criticized the New Deal, supported civil rights legislation, promoted greater activism both inside and outside the profession, and drew attention to the dangers of the "slow fascization of American economic life" (Fisher, 1934).

In the mid-1930s, the Rank and File Movement mounted a well-organized campaign against the decision of the Roosevelt administration to terminate the federal relief program operated through the FERA and replace it entirely with the public works programs of the Public Works Administration (PWA) and the Works Progress Administration (WPA). Movement spokespersons denounced the decision as a capitulation to corporate interests and as implementing a "work or starve" policy. They argued that "the work program should be speeded up, should pay union wages, and should emphasize socially useful projects" (Boyer, 1935, pp. 7–8; *Social Work Today*, December 1935, pp. 3–4). They backed protests by the Mothers' Pension Movements against the moral requirements for receipt of welfare grants. These alliances presaged the development of the modern welfare rights movement in the 1960s (Bell, 1965; Blawle, 1970).

After 1936, the Popular Front strategy developed by the Communist Party to combat the worldwide growth of fascism led Rank and Filers to support

Roosevelt and his New Deal policies (Klehr, 1984). In the 1936 election, the National Coordinating Committee of Rank and File Groups in Social Work, established in 1933, had provided only lukewarm support for the President (Fisher, 1936a, 1980a). It preferred to support the American Labor Party in New York and Farmer-Labor coalitions in the Midwest (*Social Work Today*, November 1936, p. 25). After the election, *Social Work Today* declared in an editorial, "Government action during the coming year will be determined however not by [popular opinion in support of liberal and progressive policies] but by the inner logic of an administration that wants to maintain economic life upon a capitalist basis" (*Social Work Today*, December 1936, p. 3).

In the late 1930s, however, *Social Work Today* published more articles that were supportive of New Deal programs. In large part, this strategy reflected the increasingly defensive posture of the left in the United States and abroad, especially after the fall of the Spanish Republic and the rise of fascist influence. The Communist Party shifted from a popular front to a united front approach, allying itself with former adversaries on the left (Klehr, 1984; Klehr, Haynes, & Anderson, 1998; Naison, 1983; Ottanelli, 1991). According to some conservative analysts, the close association of the Rank and File Movement with the shifting positions of the Communist Party may have weakened its broader impact on the social work profession and other reform movements (Glazer, 1961; Haynes, 1975).

Yet, while it lasted, the Popular Front strategy also helped to diminish the adversarial relationship between the Rank and File Movement and mainstream social work organizations. The movement began to cooperate with such organizations, to focus on practice issues, and to identify increasingly with the functionalist school based at the University of Pennsylvania (Fisher, 1980b; Spano, 1982; Wagner, 1989). The impact of this shift on the social work profession included growing acceptance of public welfare as an arena of practice, acknowledging group work and community organization as legitimate methods, and developing a broader view of direct practice that incorporated client-related goals (Iglehart & Becerra, 1995). In turn, as radical social workers embraced professional standards, the AASW adopted a more activist stance in defense of New Deal social legislation.

The influence of the Rank and File Movement on public policy was, therefore, probably greater than its numbers might imply, in part because of the central role of unemployment policy in shaping the political and economic climate. In California, Rank and Filers played a critical role in several issues: the elimination of single men's camps after 1936; the campaign against local, rather than state, control of relief; and the defense of relief workers' civil rights. After 1936, however, the Rank and File Movement had more difficulty maintaining its position as an outsider in the political arena. Many of its ideas had been incorporated—with modifications—into New Deal programs. The Rank and Filers now had more of a stake in the preservation of the policy status quo and the movement's militancy diminished somewhat (Spano, 1982).

RADICAL UNIONS IN SOCIAL WORK

The Rank and File Movement's organizational strength made it particularly attractive to social workers in the burgeoning public sector, beginning with the Home Relief Employees Association, created in late 1933. For the first time, social work trade unions emerged on a large scale, initially in Chicago and, later, in far greater numbers and militancy in New York with the formation of the Association of Workers in Public Relief Agencies (AWPRA). Private sector workers had organized even earlier. Serious efforts to organize social workers into unions had begun in 1926 with the formation of the Association of Federation Social Workers (AFSW) among staff members in Jewish agencies in New York. A larger union, the Association of Federation Workers (AFW), which included other nonprofessional workers, emerged in the early 1930s in response to salary cuts imposed by the Jewish Federation in New York. Social workers at the Jewish Federation in New York formed a union as early as 1931 and called the first strike in social work history soon thereafter (Day, 2000). This paved the way for the establishment of other social work trade unions such as the Home Relief Employees Association in December 1933 when newly hired workers in the Home Relief Bureaus to organize the Emergency Home Relief Bureau Association. This union quickly became one of the most radical public worker unions with strong ties to the Communist Party.

The growth of radical social work unions in the 1930s reflected "the recognition that only through organized concerted action could workers protect their own interests" (Rittenhouse, 1937). The New York Discussion Club, the most radical of all, focused on both workers' issues and broader topics such as fascism, civil rights, and social welfare. Lack of experience and limited public support, however, hampered the AFW's initial organizing efforts (Jacob Fisher Papers, Social Welfare History Archives, University of Minnesota). Eventually, its limited success in combating further salary cuts through labor militancy boosted the union's profile and, despite management lockouts and firings, by 1934 its membership had increased to more than 700 workers in 30 agencies.

Similar unions were then organized in Philadelphia, Boston, and Detroit. Public sector workers affiliated with the Rank and File Movement allied briefly with the American Federation of Labor (AFL) in 1935 through the American Federation of State, County, and Municipal Employees (AFSCME) but joined the Congress of Industrial Organizations (CIO) in 1937. By mid-1938, *Social Work Today* listed 28 public welfare locals and nine private sector locals (*Social Work Today*, June 1936, p. 24). By 1942, there were locals in 16 cities with over 4,000 members.

Most locals, however, with the exception of those in New York and Chicago, had fewer than 50 members. By the late 1940s, the New York local was the largest within the Union of Office and Professional Workers of America (UOPWA). The success of unionization, however, can be measured less in terms of the overall numbers of unionized social workers than in the ways union development made social workers a political force on the local and national stage. "A more significant measure of its power and influence can be derived from the agitation and anxiety precipitated in those quarters that felt the pressure (Alexander & Speizman, 1979; Shlakman, 1950, p. 214). In 1936, the AFW became the Social Service Employees Union (SSEU) and affiliated with the CIO. These developments in the private social service sector complemented larger movements among public welfare workers in New York and Chicago.

In 1933, public sector workers in the Emergency Relief Administration in New York organized and successfully opposed salary cuts. In 1934, the group won dramatic salary increases and changed its name to the AWPRA. That year, AWPRA locals were established in other large cities such as Philadelphia, Cleveland, Cincinnati, Minneapolis, Newark, and Pittsburgh. In 1935, they were organized in other major urban areas across the country, along with statewide groups in Michigan, Ohio, and Pennsylvania. That year the AWPRA drew 15,000 workers to a rally at Madison Square Garden, New York to protest proposed layoffs (Radical Alliance of Social Service Workers [RASSW], April 1981).

It was not surprising that the earliest support for militant trade unions within social work came from the Jewish center field in New York and Chicago and among Jewish radicals in public welfare departments. Working-class Jewish neighborhoods in both cities overflowed with left-wing intellectual and political activities. Beginning in 1929, groups like the United Council of Working Class Women (UCWCW), built on the informal networks established by Jewish service organizations, forged close ties with the Socialist and Communist Parties and left-wing unions in the garment industries. Within two years, 48 neighborhoods in New York alone had local councils. These groups cooperated with the unemployed councils, which communists began to organize in 1930 (Piven & Cloward, 1977).

By the mid-1930s, similar groups appeared in large cities across the country in Jewish neighborhoods, among other immigrants, and in African American communities. In 1937, renamed the Progressive Women's Council, the UCWCW had 75 affiliates in the New York Metropolitan area alone. These organizations supported antieviction efforts and local boycotts and were closely allied with radical unions. Among their leaders was a communist activist, Rose Chernin, sister of Milton Chernin, the future dean of the University of California-Berkeley School of Social Welfare (Chernin, 1983; Orleck, 1987). (See Chapter 7.)

The emergence of loosely organized pressure groups of the unemployed after the election of Roosevelt was one of the most dramatic developments during the Depression era. These groups often allied themselves with sympathetic social workers in the Rank and File Movement (Piven & Cloward, 1977). Thus, although these workers alliances often came into conflict with public welfare workers and officials over the adequacy of relief benefits, wage scales on public works projects, and the unionization of WPA workers,

> their ultimate result was probably to cause the local, state, and national governments to provide more money for relief than would otherwise have

been granted. . . . [T]hey were, therefore, basically allies of the true social workers who also sought to have more adequate relief provided. . . . [In addition] this self-organization on the part of the unemployed helped to prevent them from being used by the extreme right or the extreme left as hired storm troopers of reaction or revolution. (Douglas, in Seymour, 1937, pp. 1–2)

By 1936, 12,000 Rank and Filers were in some form of protective groups. Of these, 90% were public sector workers (Fisher, 1936). Two years later, 14,500 workers belonged to union locals in such cities as Chicago, Cincinnati, Cleveland, Detroit, Minneapolis, Newark, Philadelphia, and Pittsburgh (Galper, 1980). Until 1937, unionized social workers split their loyalties between two unions, both chartered by the CIO: public sector employees affiliated with the State, County, and Municipal Workers of America (SCMWA), particularly in California, whereas private sector workers joined the United Office and Professional Workers of America. By mid-1938, few social workers remained within the conservative AFL. By the late 1930s, with thousands of members coast-to-coast, these unions and the Rank and File Movement in general were subject to intensive red-baiting.

Modeling themselves after the CIO organizing drives of the period among industrial workers, protective associations strove to improve the conditions of social work employment and to demonstrate their solidarity with other trade union and class-based struggles. They cooperated with groups organized by clients, communist-led councils of the unemployed, and other unions in both direct action and legislative advocacy. In the area of social policy, they fought for adequate relief standards, a federal Department of Welfare, and the socialistic policy alternatives embodied in the Frazier–Lundeen bill. Their vision soon expanded to encompass universal, federally funded employment at a living wage, an end to discrimination against African Americans in public sector jobs, opposition to the use of regressive taxes to support public assistance and social service programs, and support for antilynching legislation (Fisher, 1936a, 1980a, b; Rose, 1992).

The New York SSEU local, headed by Jacob Fisher, an employee of the Bureau of Jewish Social Research, was one of the most important unions in social work (Moore, 1949). In the late 1930s, the union's legislative program included expansion of Social Security coverage to workers in the nonprofit fields and the overall liberalization of the Act, protection of labor's right to organize and to other civil liberties, support for the Wagner National Health Bill, and an adequate public welfare program including the creation of at least three million WPA jobs (SSEU, 1939).

In addition to the expansion of the welfare state, the SSEU fought throughout the 1930s for higher salaries and benefits and enhanced job security for social workers. It also advocated for greater participation by workers in formulating agency policy and community action projects (Fitch, 1938; SSEU, 1938). A persistent issue was the right of social workers to engage in collective bargaining (SSEU, July 1938). Need for such continuing efforts is illustrated by the struggle of the staff of the Jewish Welfare Society, who belonged to Local 21 of the UOPWA, to obtain collective bargaining rights from the agency's board (SSEU, 1941). In January 1940, New York Local 19 made affirmation of this right the first item in its contract with the National Council of Jewish Women (SSEU, 1940).

The other major social work union affiliated with the CIO was the State, County, and Municipal Workers of America (SCMWA). By mid-1938, SCMWA had organized more than 8,000 public welfare workers (nearly 25%), many of them in New York. Two years later, the union boasted three dozen locals. UOPWA experienced similar growth. By 1939, nearly 4,000 social workers were among its 45,000 members, the bulk of them in New York and Chicago (Alexander, 1977; Fisher, 1980).

The SCMWA organized both relief workers and agricultural laborers in California. This led to allegations by the 1940 "Little Dies Committee" of the California state legislature, chaired by future Los Angeles mayor, Sam Yorty, that the State Relief Administration was infiltrated by communists and that the "SCMWA was engaged in such subversive activities as providing relief to striking farm workers and supporting efforts of the Communist-led organization of the unemployed, the Workers Alliance" (Healey & Isserman, 1993; Hunter, 1999, pp. 3–4). Witnesses, including some social workers, who refused to cooperate with Yorty's committee were arrested and jailed. The hearings also produced an informal precursor of the blacklists that appeared a decade later (Barrett, 1951).

Despite these activities, throughout the 1930s, social workers debated the question of whether unionization was compatible with social work. The basic division among social workers was between the Rank and Filers, who advocated on behalf of greater worker control and role standardization as a means of job protection, and the mainstream AASW, which supported managerial control, bureaucratization, and job protection as a means of guaranteeing professional autonomy (Fabricant & Burghardt, 1992). Support for CIO-type "industrial" unions even in private sector agencies, rather than professional "craft unions," came from social work leaders like Bertha Reynolds, Paul Kellogg, Mary van Kleeck, Marion Hathway, and Robert P. Lane.

Reynolds argued that without such unions "professional workers tend to become ingrown, unrealistic, [and] bureaucratic" (SSEU pamphlet, July 1938, Evelyn Butler Archive, University of Pennsylvania). Van Kleeck and Hathway explicitly linked the trade union movement to the need for national and international democratic social action. Van Kleeck's work in the early 1930s, such as her study of the coal mining industry (1934), supported efforts to expand worker participation in the management of industry. Hathway, then Executive Secretary of the American Association of Schools of Social Work, asserted that unions "could counteract the sinister threat of fascist ideology to American democracy" (Hathway, 1939).

In January and February 1936, *Social Work Today* published a symposium

"Should Social Work Employees Use Labor Tactics?" triggered by a work stoppage in the New York Emergency Relief Bureau in October 1935. Participants included Kellogg, Lurie, van Kleeck, Reynolds, Ewan Clague, and Frank Bancroft. All of them supported unionization, but some did not feel that strikes were justified in all circumstances (*Social Work Today*, January 1936, pp. 5–7; February 1936, pp. 18–19).

Although the passage of the Social Security Act (SSA) in 1935 led to the softening of Rank and File attacks on the social work profession, there were still significant differences remained over what constituted social work skill, what training (if any) was required to be a social worker, how to resolve conflicts of interest between workers and administration in social service agencies and, above all, who should be considered a professional social worker. Even the leaders of the so-called Functional School of Social Work at the University of Pennsylvania disagreed with the Rank and File Movement around these matters (Robinson, 1937). Another important issue was whether direct affiliation with the labor movement would violate standards of professional objectivity and ethics (Rittenhouse, 1937).

The Rank and File Movement and its labor union allies, therefore, challenged both the concept of social work as a profession and prevailing conceptions of social work practice. Unlike the mainstream AASW, it strongly identified with clients, used radical tactics such as strikes and boycotts, and displayed open sympathy for allied left-wing causes and social movements (Karger, 1988). Leaders of the Rank and File Movement played key roles in organized labor and were active in so-called front organizations affiliated with the Communist Party.

These alliances often led government investigators to suspect Communist infiltration into white-collar unions. Nathan Glazer claimed that the UOPWA "may have contained a higher proportion of Communists than any other existing legitimate trade union" (Glazer, 1961, p. 143). Like Glazer, Haynes (1975) asserts that the close relationship between the UOPWA, the Rank and File Movement, and the Communist Party weakened the movement's ability to gain support for its reform proposals and ultimately led to its expulsion from the labor movement. For more than 30 years, this perspective fed the nation's anti-Communist crusade and "wrought long-term and often devastating effects upon both civic and intellectual discourse" (Hunter, 1999, p. 12).

RANK AND FILE MOVEMENT, UNIONS, AND NEW DEAL POLITICS

The impact of unemployment was the major issue of the 1930s for radicals and nonradicals in social work. Publications like the *Survey Graphic* frequently published articles on the socioeconomic effects of plant shutdowns on local communities (Clague & Couper, 1931). A confidential letter to President Roosevelt, drafted in 1934 by activists Paul Kellogg and Helen Hall and supported by intellectuals like John Dewey, called for a more equitable distribution of the nation's wealth through the creation of a Labor Board to safeguard workers' rights, the overhauling of the National Recovery Administration's (NRA) minimum wage provisions, greater influence by consumers in determining NRA pricing policies, the development of expanded and permanent public sector employment programs, and government provision of long-term, low interest loans for housing development (Kellog et al., 1934).

Besides unemployment and the widespread hunger it produced, substandard housing was another major issue in the 1930s. The 1930 census revealed that there were six million nonfarm substandard dwelling units in the United States. In the mid-1930s, government inventories demonstrated that about one sixth of all units needed major repairs, one seventh lacked private indoor toilets, and one fifth lacked bathtubs (Shaffer, 1952). Left-wing unions and political parties seized on this issue and throughout the decade continued to attack the inadequacy of the housing programs developed by the Roosevelt administration (Hill, 1934). Radicals in social work also linked housing development with plans for urban revitalization (Kahn, 1934).

In contrast to the structural changes advocated by radical social workers, liberals focused on issues like measuring and forecasting the impact of unemployment, revitalizing (but not restructuring) the U.S. economy, improving welfare standards and administration, cooperating with churches in relief distribution, advocating for new service approaches, and increased spending on unemployment relief. They promoted fiscal efficiency in social welfare (that is, the superiority of insurance programs over relief), assessing the efficacy and ethics of what later was called "the public use of the private sector," addressing emergencies in small communities, and conducting research on the relief situation around the United States (AASW, 1933, February 1937; American Association of Public Welfare Officials, November 1931; American Association for Social Security, 1933; American Public Welfare Association, 1932; Pray, 1931, 1933, 1937; Russell Sage Foundation, December 1930; Social Work Conference on Federal Action, 1931; Toll, 1934; Tugwell, May 1934). Major social service organizations like the Young Men's Christian Association (YMCA) cooperated with government, industry, and labor to analyze economic security problems and publicize these reports (YMCA, 1934). Yet, in the early 1930s, few professional social workers "kn[e]w little and care[d] less about economic or political theory and practice" or "raise[d] their voices in analyzing and protesting the misery they see every day of their lives" (Guild, 1933). Some reformers regarded the mere introduction of the insurance concept in welfare as "a radical reconstruction of public relief" (Folks, 1934). Others like Jane Hoey, Director of the Bureau of Public Assistance, were instrumental in developing social work's role in this area (Leighninger, 1999). Largely for this reason, although she was not a radical, Hoey became the target of right-wing investigators. (See Chapter 6.)

Radical social workers went beyond advocacy for social insurance and the expansion of public relief. They focused on providing support for welfare clients, particularly councils of the unemployed. They educated WPA workers about their rights and promoted the development of skills in public assistance work among employees. Above all, they fought for more comprehensive work relief legislation such as the Federal Relief and Work Projects Standards Act, introduced by Vito Marcantonio, and the Frazier–Lundeen Workers' Social Insurance Act, which van Kleeck had helped draft (Rubin, Iberg, Silverstein, & Vincent, 1935; National Joint Action Committee for Genuine Social Insurance, 1936; Committee on Public Assistance Skills, n.d.). In this regard, their views were in line with radical labor groups (Kennedy, 1933) and other progressive organizations such as the Unemployment Committee of the Friends General Conference (Willits, 1935). Like these left-wing allies, radical social workers also expressed growing concern over the repression of women's economic rights by private industries, government regulations, and public welfare agencies (American League Against War and Fascism, December 1935). Local activist groups such as the Pennsylvania Security League (1933) and the Women's Trade Union League (WTUL, 1933), with the support of radicals like van Kleeck, fought for minimum wage laws for women and work hour regulations.

By 1936, unemployment had fallen only slightly to eleven million. Even the conservative AFL proposed dramatic measures to address the problem, such as the establishment of the 30-hour week. The arguments they used in support of this idea are remarkably similar to those later marshaled in the 1950s and 1990s (Galbraith, 1958; Green, 1936; Rifkin, 1995).

Although many radical social workers supported the Communist Party because of its long-standing leadership on issues like unemployment, the program of some Rank and Filers in the mid-1930s more closely resembled that of the Socialist Party under Norman Thomas. This included protection of civil liberties and the promotion of workers' rights, redistributive social policies, and an end to racial discrimination (Thomas, 1936). Social work radicals like Eduard Lindeman and Roger Baldwin and liberal reformers like Abraham Epstein presented lectures sponsored by the Socialist League for Industrial Democracy as part of its educational programs on topics related to labor, social welfare, and the spread of fascism (League for Industrial Democracy, 1935). During this period, the YWCA's Commission on Interracial Cooperation continued to press for the complete eradication of lynching and the mob anarchy and barbarism that prompted it (YWCA, 1932).

For most of the 1930s, the battle over the Social Security Act (SSA), the centerpiece of the New Deal, reflected the major political divisions in U.S. society. After years of debate, the legislation ultimately drafted by the Roosevelt administration and approved by Congress was a conservative compromise. Far more radical proposals had been developed by diverse groups and social movements led by Huey Long and Francis Townsend (Edsforth, 2000; Heale, 1999; McElvaine, 1993). One book that was favorably reviewed by progressives was called *Prohibiting Poverty* (Martin, 1934); it proposed the establishment of welfare state policies far beyond those considered by Roosevelt (Rose, 1989).

Shortly after the Act's passage, Abraham Epstein, who through his leadership of the American Association for Labor Legislation (AALL) had been instrumental in its development (Lubove, 1968), strongly criticized its inadequacies and called for immediate, dramatic revisions (Epstein, 1937). The AASW pressed for the inclusion of social workers under the SSA in early 1937 (*Social Work Today*, February 1937). Radicals like Mary van Kleeck, however, took a broader view and framed the debate over Social Security in the context of monopoly control of the economy, the struggle for human freedom, racial exploitation, and international developments such as the Spanish Civil War (van Kleeck, 1936). By 1938, other radicals like Jacob Fisher, who served on the planning committee of a national conference on work and security, expanded the discussion of Social Security to include public housing, health and vocational training programs, flood control projects, and the construction of schools, hospitals, and community centers (National Conference on Work and Security, 1938).

Republicans, however, attacked Social Security as part of their general opposition to the Roosevelt administration's initiatives in all areas from agriculture to youth. They tried to present the New Deal as antidemocratic, subversive of the Bill of Rights, and antithetical to American ideals (Hoover, 1935–1936). Some speakers even alleged that Roosevelt was using the New Deal to establish a dictatorship (Warburg, 1936).

Conservative attacks upon the rights of labor, working-class, and radical movements intensified between 1934–1936, particularly "by employers, vigilantes, mobs, troops, private gunmen and compliant sheriffs and police" (ACLU, 1936, p. 5). They persisted because "despite the absurdity of the reactionary barrage against all reform measures, from those of the New Deal to the child labor amendment, as Communist manoeuvres, the red scare still works" (p. 5). As soon as Roosevelt proposed the idea of social insurance, reformers like Abraham Epstein noted that "opposition to [such proposals] in the United States has been far more vicious and subtle than in other countries" (Epstein, 1934, p. 134). Largely in response to such attacks, many liberal and radical social workers supported Roosevelt over Wilkie in the 1940 election, fearing a return to pre–New Deal social policies (Pray, 1940).

RADICALISM IN SOCIAL WORK PRACTICE

The consequences of the Great Depression underscored the tension between environmental perspectives on practice and individually oriented models of intervention. Radical critics of social work practice in the mid-1930s argued that "there is an appalling gap between promise and performance" (Rogers & Fitzgerald, 1934, p. 266). They attributed this failure to several factors, including capitalist control of the resources that support private sector agencies, the absence of a consistent theoretical basis in social work education, and the confused state of the profession's philosophy and ideology.

Harry Lurie, one of Bertha Reynolds and Mary van Kleeck's allies in the Rank and File Movement, argued that "a sweeping realignment of the whole profession, both in philosophy and in program, . . . would have to precede any effective change" (Lurie, 1935). In the 1930s, this realignment began to appear in several ways, including the development of an alternative theoretical framework for practice and the promotion of more democratic practice methods. Surprisingly, the former emerged in the elite environment of the University of Pennsylvania.

At the Penn School of Social Work, intellectual leaders of the profession, such as Bertha Reynolds from Smith College, met regularly with Penn leaders Jessie Taft and Virginia Robinson to discuss the integration of Freudian and Rankian theories into social work methods. The Functional Approach, developed by Taft and Robinson at the University of Pennsylvania, was not explicitly radical. Yet in sharp contrast to traditional models of practice, including the Diagnostic Approach developed at the New York School, it provided radical social workers, especially those in the public social services, with a practice paradigm that justified social action and the recognition of the mutuality of the worker–client relationship (Lewis, 1966). This was particularly important after 1937, when the mainstream social work leadership defined "professional social work" as requiring a graduate degree, thereby excluding most social workers in public welfare, who formed the bulk of the Rank and File Movement, from professional status (Lowe, 1987).

The Functional School attempted to correct this situation. Although its chief proponents, Taft and Robinson, were not radicals, they made several important contributions to social work practice theory that complemented the efforts of radical colleagues in the Rank and File Movement. First, they acknowledged the role of the agency, the importance of functional definition by the social worker, and client participation as critical components of effective practice. This validated the cooperative efforts between workers and clients promoted by public sector social work unions.

Second, they promoted a view of casework that was incompatible with psychoanalytic therapy and that implicitly embraced the significance of socioeconomic factors in shaping the client's needs. Although not explicitly linked to Marxist ideas, it allowed such analyses to be incorporated into social work practice frameworks. Finally, the Rankian principles at the core of the Functional School rejected Freudian determinism and emphasized the centrality of the human will and social process. This led to a dynamic view of the human condition, society, and the worker-client relationship that was sympathetic to the worldviews of many radical social workers (Dore, 1990; Lewis, 1966; Robinson, 1937; Taft, 1939).

Radical social workers also introduced or reemphasized new practice methods to the field in response to rapidly changing social conditions. Important innovations occurred within the field of community organizing. Major differences emerged between new neighborhood community organizations and traditional settlement houses in the 1930s as the service focused on control by community members, rather than creating agency-directed programs or services (Industrial Areas Foundation, 1940; National Community Center Association, 1931). The Lane Report (1939) issued by the NCSW tried to resolve these differences, but it did so by using terms that were consistent with the ideas of mainstream social work (Cazenave, 1993; Reisch & Wenocur, 1986; Wenocur & Reisch, 1989). Concurrent debates occurred over the qualifications or required training for full-time community organizers (Rabinoff & King, 1940).

Along similar lines, Mary van Kleeck proposed the use of social work research as an action tool to create "a rational and social control of industry for the common welfare" (1932, p. 1). Prompted by the need to support New Deal legislative initiatives, activists in such organizations as the Unemployed Councils, the Women's Trade Union League (WTUL), the National Consumers League (NCL), and the National Child Labor Committee joined with liberal colleagues to legitimize the function of lobbying by social workers (Kirk, 1936). Another popular new idea was the development of self-help cooperatives, promoted both by activists and government organizations like the FERA (Division of Self-Help Cooperatives, 1934). The cooperative ideal drew its inspiration from European antecedents dating back to the nineteenth century and the work of American intellectuals like Mary Parker Follett and Eduard Lindeman (Follett, 1920; Lindeman, 1921).

As the Rank and Filers retreated from their strident antiprofessional stance in the late 1930s, *Social Work Today* began to promote social work methods like group work that were consistent with the values of self-help and mutual aid at the heart of these cooperatives. Group work, the journal argued, could promote cooperative living and collective action to enhance human well-being (Bernstein, Coyle, Hendry, & Kaiser, n.d., Evelyn Butler Archive, University of Pennsylvania). It was no mere coincidence, therefore, that many of the leaders of radical social work organizations throughout the 1930s and into the postwar period were group workers. Consequently, in the repressive climate of McCarthyism, government investigators and conservative critics within the social work profession particularly targeted group workers and the ideals they stressed in their practice. (See Chapters 5 and 6.)

By the mid-1930s, in addition to her theoretical work with Taft and Robinson, Bertha Reynolds strove to incorporate Marxist principles into a practice framework that already included such diverse influences as Calvinism and Freudian psychology (1963). Like many other intellectuals and activists of her generation, Reynolds found in Marxism an explanation of social conditions that complemented the "philosophy of growth" she had expounded as the basis for social work practice since the 1920s. In her words, "A Marxist outlook finally relieved us of the 'Jehovah complex' which had always plagued our profession. It was not we, a handful of social workers, against a sea of human misery. It was humanity itself building dikes, and we were helping in our peculiarly useful way" (Reynolds, 1963, p. 184).

Reynolds's interests were more than theoretical. She sought to expand the role of social welfare by recognizing the relationship between government funded economic support and the social supports provided by agencies through casework. She believed that social workers had to defend the socioeconomic interests of their clients as part of a broader defense of welfare state provisions. This was a radical concept at the time, although it later became incorporated into the mainstream rhetoric of the social work profession as demonstrated by Charlotte Towle's publication *Common Human Needs* (1945) and the National Association of Social Workers (NASW) *Code of Ethics* (1996). In fact, by the late 1930s, liberal reformers like Grace Coyle often agreed with Reynolds's analysis and attacked those who continued "to pick up the pieces without ever attempting to stop the breakage" (1937, p. 138).

In a comment that is remarkably relevant to recent debates over so-called welfare reform, Reynolds reflected, "If public assistance could be destroyed, Labor would be forced to accept wages below subsistence levels, and without recourse. If protests of organized labor could be eliminated, public assistance could be reduced to legalized starvation under controls approximating slavery (1963, p. 271). Reynolds warned that unless New Deal policies moved beyond "offering palliatives to assuage the miseries of poverty and racism," social workers would do little more than "carry out the designs of the ruling class and victimize clients" (quoted in Joseph, 1986, p. 122).

This analysis moved Reynolds toward a more radical vision of society, similar to the ideas proposed by van Kleeck and other leaders of the Rank and File Movement. For the most part, her greatest influence was through her publications and presentations, in which she attempted to integrate Freud, Marx, and Rank into a coherent practice framework. Yet, in her professional activities, she also sought to reconcile the Rank and File Movement's desire for structural change in the economy with the potentially ameliorative role of social casework. Reynolds linked the future of casework to recognition of the roots of the Depression in the increased concentration of wealth and the need to create countermovements for democracy, including the democratization of social services (Reynolds, 1938).

Although she believed that the current social order was fundamentally unjust, she strove to create a practice model that embodied social democratic principles on a daily basis. In effect, decades before most of her colleagues, she recognized the mutuality of worker and client interests in the support of social reforms. Without explicitly using the modern term "empowerment," Reynolds highlighted the political functions of social service work to "free men from the crippling accumulations of fear and hate so that they may have energy to use what intelligence they possess . . . [to work for] . . . a better social order" (Reynolds, 1934, p. 27).

Reynolds's commitment, however, was both to thought and action, as demonstrated by her affiliation with the Socialist and Communist Parties, labor organizations, including the Social Service Employees Union, the Inter-professional Association for Social Insurance, the National Organization of Practitioner Groups in Social Work, and the Rank and File Movement itself. Reynolds's support for the unionization of social service employees also reflected an inclusive view of membership in the profession. Unlike the profession's mainstream leadership, who felt that the rapid expansion of public social welfare threatened their dominance within the field and subverted the status aspirations of the profession, she argued that social work organizations should respect the strengths that new workers possessed and facilitate their entry into the profession (Reynolds, 1932, 1938).

Many of Reynolds's views were not widely shared even among long-standing colleagues. Reynolds's affiliation with the Communist Party and the Rank and File Movement soon made her one of the first and most visible victims of antiradical fervor within the profession. By the late 1930s, social work leaders like Grace Marcus attacked her for her radical ideas. (Ironically, 10 years later Marcus defended Marion Hathway against red-baiting charges at the University of Pittsburgh. See Chapter 5.) Everett Kimball, the Director of the Smith College School of Social Work, openly doubted Reynolds' loyalties and forced her to resign in 1938 after two decades on the faculty.

Despite her acknowledged standing in the field—she was one of the most published authors in social work during the 1930s—no other school would offer Reynolds a position. It seemed "[t]here was no place in institutionalized social work [that would accept her] . . . peculiar mix of democratic principles, Freudian theory, and [activism on behalf of] radical political and social change" (Freedberg, 1986, p. 106). Although she later found employment with the National Maritime Union during World War II and as an independent consultant and trainer throughout the 1940s, Reynolds's forced departure from Smith because of her Marxist ideas and leadership among Rank and Filers marked the first step in her blacklisting within the social work field. Her treatment by the administration of Smith College and the ensuing ostracism by the organized profession foreshadowed the more widespread repression of the McCarthy era that lay ahead.

The blacklisting of Reynolds occurred at the same time as the Rank and File Movement and its publication, *Social Work Today*, disappeared as a force within the social work field. Reynolds wrote in her autobiography that when *Social Work Today* stopped publishing "a light went out of social work which has never been rekindled" (Reynolds, 1963, p. 240).

Despite her status as a pariah and a subject of frequent investigations by federal and state authorities, she remained a member of the Communist Party until her death. In her writings and lectures, she tried to shape social work practice theory and to avoid—particularly in the late 1940s and 1950s—implicating supportive colleagues. Her commitment to radical perspectives and goals never faded, nor did her attempts to synthesize Marxist and Freudian ideas. In her autobiography, *An Uncharted Journey*, Reynolds recalled the primary influences on her professional development as the "depression, which forced new formulations under new conditions; and the Marxist science of society which guided the thinking of some of the leaders of the rank and file movement" (Reynolds, 1963, p. 173).

PRECURSORS TO MCCARTHYISM: REPRESSION OF RADICAL SOCIAL WORKERS IN THE 1930S

Reynolds was one of many social workers, not all of whom were professed radicals, who experienced a backlash against their politics and practice even prior

to the purges of the postwar McCarthy period. Some of this repression occurred through government intervention, primarily the use of investigative committees by state legislatures and the Congress. In the early 1930s, for example,
the Lusk Committee of the New York State Legislature once again labeled Jane
Addams a subversive, although she had voted for Herbert Hoover in 1932. Perhaps this was because in the previous decade she had referred to the Russian
Revolution as "the greatest social experiment in history" or had organized and
served for many years as president of the Women's International League for
Peace and Freedom. During the same period, the Lash Committee of the Illinois State Legislature identified Hull House as a center of subversion (Caute,
1973). A few years later, WPA administrator Victor Ridder promoted red-baiting and police violence against workers who attempted to organize or file grievances (American Civil Liberties Union [ACLU], 1936, p. 56). As early as 1936,
the Rank and File Movement expressed a fear that such political repression
would become more widespread (*Social Work Today*, November 1936, p. 25).

In the late 1930s, the Yorty Committee established by the California State
legislature accused the state branch of the SCMWA of being dominated by
communists. Its investigations led to the dismissal of dozens of county welfare
workers who were SCMWA members in 1940 and the initiation of a purge of
left-wing leaders in public employees' unions. Similar firings occurred among
private sector agencies throughout the state. The committee's hearings also
prompted attacks against radical social workers in unions that had organized
within private sector agencies in Los Angeles such as the Jewish Social Service
Bureau (Caute, 1978; Gellhorn, 1952; Schrecker, 1992). Purges of radical social
workers also took place in Pennsylvania, Illinois, Maryland, Texas, and Michigan (Caute, 1978; *Social Work Today*, February 1942). In fact, five years before
the purges prompted by the Yorty committee, social workers in Michigan, including future University of Michigan professor Henry Meyer had been fired
by the Washtenaw County Relief Commission for union organizing (*Social Work
Today*, December 1935, p. 21).

Around the same time as the Yorty hearings, the Rapp–Coudert Committee of the New York State Legislature began its investigations of college faculty,
other public sector employees, and even radical student groups on college campuses in what Marvin Gettleman termed "a rehearsal for McCarthyism"
(Gettleman, 1982b). The main historical significance of the committee "was to
establish the pattern, develop the legal rationales, train the personnel, and produce the evidence that would resurface in the era of the Cold War" (p. 2). Although no one called before the committee admitted membership in the Communist Party or was found guilty of misconduct, the work of the committee
established a pattern of close cooperation among government officials and administrators of universities and private sector agencies (Gettleman, 1982a;
Schrecker, 1986). It also demonstrated ominously how liberal reformers would
acquiesce to political pressure and abandon their former radical allies in the
New Deal coalition.

Similar patterns emerged in response to anti-Communist investigations at the federal level. In November 1938, Representative Martin Dies, chair of the newly created House Un-American Activities Committee (HUAC), listed among "purveyors of class hatred" (along with Josef Stalin) such influential social workers of the 1930s as Secretary of Labor Frances Perkins and Presidential advisor Harry Hopkins, in addition to other prominent New Dealers (Caute, 1978). Soon, HUAC launched an investigation into the Farmer-Labor Party, the ACLU, and New Deal programs in the arts and youth activities field, such as the Civilian Conservation Corps, the Federal Theatre Project, and the National Youth Administration, where many radical social workers were employed. The committee also investigated Communist influence in unions like the SCMWA, the editorial board of *Social Work Today*, and the Rank and File Movement's National Board of Cooperators, which included radicals like Reynolds and van Kleeck. As a consequence of these hearings, *Social Work Today* acquired the label of a "Communist front publication," prompting HUAC to generate files on Reynolds, van Kleeck, and radical union leaders. These investigations fueled the purges of radical groups during and after the war by anti-Communist labor leaders.

Such actions sparked a growing outcry among social work radicals in the 1930s over the suppression of civil liberties. Of particular concern were the attacks of the Dies Committee on progressive and liberal workers' movements and the Congressional investigation of the political and union affiliations of WPA employees (ACLU, 1939, p. 11). Although it gave lip service to the investigation of fascist groups, the Dies Committee focused most of its energies on the alleged "red menace" and, in the words of the ACLU, "became the voice of that brand of professional patriots whose capital is defense of spurious Americanism against progressive change" (ACLU, 1939, p. 20). The ACLU, whose leadership included Mary van Kleeck, Mary McDowell, Jeanette Rankin, and Vida Scudder, also criticized the Supreme Court for its weak support of civil liberties and for failing to expand the concept of civil rights to allow for the regulation of private forces (ACLU, 1936, 1939; Fraenkel, 1937).

These investigations quickly inspired repressive activities within the social work profession itself. From Philadelphia to Los Angeles, and in states as varied as Michigan, Texas, Illinois, and Maryland, public and private sector employees were dismissed on charges ranging from subversion to inefficiency to association with the Communist Party. Anti-Communist labor leaders urged the expulsion of left-wing unions like the SCMWA and the UOPWA from the CIO. In about five years, organized social work had gone much further than William Hodson, the NCSW President and Commissioner of the New York City Department of Public Welfare, had in 1934 when he singled out Mary van Kleeck for attack and rejected the radical ideas she proffered because of their danger of "destroy[ing] the present economic and industrial order" (Hodson, 1934).

Even radical social work students were vulnerable to such attacks. In 1939, the Dean of the University of California at Berkeley, Harry Cassidy, attacked student radicals in the newly formed School of Social Welfare in a confidential memo. These students, employed at the State Relief Administration, "were committed to mobilizing the working class against its oppressors, focusing attention on social problems and social change, and in general radicalizing social work. They had vocal allies in the California Conference of Social Welfare and, nationally, in those affiliated with *Social Work Today*" (Terrell, 1994, p. 16). Cassidy claimed these radicals were engaged in agitation and propaganda work:

> Several incidents have occurred recently to indicate some degree of unrest among members of the student group. . . . Two or three members of the Communist Party, along with eight or ten who are very active fellow travelers, all work together pretty effectively. They are, in effect, in revolt against the system and are seeking to acquire the [social work] certificate so that they can be in a better position to push their revolutionary objectives in the field. (p. 16)

THE COMING OF WORLD WAR II AND THE DECLINE OF THE RANK AND FILE MOVEMENT

Yet, just as in the previous generation it was foreign affairs and the threat of war, rather than domestic policy, that inspired the bitterest controversies within the profession. For most of the decade, issues of war and peace and the rise of fascism in Europe and its consequences had united liberals and radicals in the social work field. The Non-Sectarian Committee for German Refugee Children, based in New York and an offshoot of the National Coordinating Committee for Aid to Refugees and Emigrants Coming from Germany, received widespread support among social workers and social work unions. Its national committee members included Grace Abbott, Mary Dewson, and Paul Kellogg. Groups like the American Friends Service Committee (AFSC) and the Young Women's Christian Association (YWCA) cooperated with the rescue efforts of Jewish organizations (*AFSC Bulletin*, June 12, 1939). Other social work groups joined the AFSC in its efforts to assist Republican refugees from the Spanish Civil War (Forbes, 1943). Mary van Kleeck played a leadership role in an organization called Hospites, which collected contributions on behalf of European social workers who were the victims of political persecution (letter from J. C. Colcord, *Social Work Today*, February 1937, p. 25).

In the late 1930s and early 1940s, as war clouds gathered over Europe, the editors of *Social Work Today* drafted a statement of principles, "Meeting Social Need: A Program for Peace" (January 1940), articulating the noninterventionist position supported by many left-wing organizations at the time. It was endorsed by the Joint Committee of Trade Unions in Social Work (JCTUSW), signed by 75 national and local leaders in the profession, and circulated widely at the 1940 NCSW conference (JCTUSW, 1940; Fisher, 1980b). In its statement of support, the SSEU local in New York headed by Jacob Fisher came out in favor of strict neutrality and in strong opposition to increases in military spending and the production of war materials, government loans to belligerents, threats to civil liberties generated by war hysteria, and proposals to grant the President "emergency war powers" (SSEU, January 17, 1940). This was a shift from its emphasis on collective security in 1937–1938.

Although the journal's isolationist stance contrasted sharply with the growing support for defense preparedness within the AASW and even among some Rank and Filers, it garnered substantial backing among social workers (*Social Work Today*, November 1940). At the NCSW conference in the spring of 1940, even after the Nazi-Soviet Non-Aggression Pact of August 1939 and the outbreak of World War II one month later, more than 1,000 social workers signed the "Statement of Principles." Such non-Rank and Filers as Paul Kellogg and John Palmer Gavit, editors of the *Survey Midmonthly* and *Survey Graphic*, NCSW President Grace Coyle, and Max Lerner, former editor of *The Nation* and a frequent contributor to the NCSW, supported the radical position as well.

Responding to growing criticism from both inside and outside the social work field that its position echoed the Communist Party line, in February 1941 *Social Work Today* published a special issue entitled "Social Work, Peace and the People's Well-Being" (Van Kleeck, Reynolds, Hetzel, & Bancroft, 1941) which included essays by van Kleeck and Reynolds and an introduction by Marion Hathway. Its purpose was to restate the 1940 Statement of Principles that supported U.S. neutrality and the priority of domestic concerns, and to clarify "the role of the social services in a functioning democracy and to find and hold its roots in the democratic ideology" (Hathway, 1941, p. 2). The essays analyzed the war in the context of the economic crisis, advocated for the defense of civil rights for workers and political activists, protested against the militarization of social services, and promoted the expansion of WPA employment. Particularly after the Nazi-Soviet Pact in 1939, these positions led to the growing marginalization of the Rank and Filers.

Mainstream social work leaders vehemently criticized this neutralist position. It was also bitterly attacked by two unsigned pamphlets distributed by the Committee of Social Work Trade Unionists for Britain and Democracy, organized by John Fitch and Philip Klein, professors at the New York School and former supporters of the Rank and File Movement. At the 1941 NCSW, Fitch, who drafted the pamphlets, accused 46 individuals from social work unions and *Social Work Today* of having Communist affiliations (Social Work Forum, 1941). These attacks reflected the divisions on the left that fragmented the Popular Front coalition of the 1930s, particularly after the Nazi-Soviet Pact, and foreshadowed events of the postwar era.

Fitch lashed out at the Rank and File leaders for allowing social service unions and their journal to be employed by Communists "as channels for propaganda against defense measures, and against aid to the enemies of totalitarianism" (Haynes, 1975; Olson, 1972). Even former leaders of the Rank and File Movement allied themselves with Fitch. Harry Lurie criticized the journal's editorial policies for their dogmatic tendencies and unquestioning support of the Soviet Union. Roger Baldwin voted to expel Communist Elizabeth Gurley Brown from the ACLU's board, a move board member Mary van Kleeck opposed (Harry Lurie Papers, Social Welfare History Archives, University of Minnesota).

Radical social work unions also lost influence after the Nazi-Soviet pact when they attacked intervention as a diversion from pressing domestic concerns. They were accused of following the Communist Party line by promoting neutrality and attacking the "militarization" of New Deal programs like the Civilian Conservation Corps. These positions on intervention reflected deep divisions within the social work field, even among radicals and pacifists. In June 1941, the *Survey Graphic* red baited the editors of *Social Work Today* and radical union officials and began the process of "naming names" that accelerated after the war (Harry Lurie Papers, Social Welfare History Archives, University of Minnesota).

Yet the ideas at the heart of *Social Work Today's* Peace Program remained popular as late as the spring of 1941. In May 1941, radicals appealed in the journal for support for a "People's Program" that placed "democratic social advancement" above military conflict. Within a month, however, Germany invaded the Soviet Union and *Social Work Today* quickly shifted its position on the war. Calling fascism "the annihilation of social work," it now advocated for war preparation to defend democracy (Deutsch, 1941). The international struggle against fascism, rather than persistent domestic problems, became its primary focus. Ironically, this rapid turnaround increased the credibility of the journal's critics.

After Pearl Harbor, *Social Work Today's* prowar position became even stronger. Social mobilization in support of the war effort became, in its own words, the field's "essential task" (*Social Work Today*, January 1942). Radical unions followed suit. By fall 1941, the SCMWA supported aid to Britain and the Soviet Union; the following year both the SCMWA and the UOPWA endorsed the CIO's position on the war including its no strike pledge (*Social Work Today*, November 1941, February 1942).

During the war years, the promotion of national unity, coupled with the partial attainment of the radicals' domestic agenda in New Deal legislation, made it increasingly difficult for social work radicals to take public positions against mainstream institutions or programs. Some socialist social work union leaders acquiesced to wartime no-strike pledges and war production schedules. Nevertheless, social work unions, which had grown considerably in the late 1930s, continued to be attacked for their leftist views, even after the German invasion of the Soviet Union and the formation of the war-time U.S.–U.S.S.R. alliance (Karger, 1988; Wagner, 1989; Wenocur & Reisch, 1989).

Thus, even before World War II and the Cold War that followed, radicals and reformers within social work had cause to fear an assault on their civil liberties because of their advocacy of social justice and their affiliation with left-wing parties. In 1938, Solomon Lowenstein remarked in a keynote address to the NCSW "One cannot fail to be concerned at the serious efforts being manifested in parts of our country to prevent the constitutional guarantees of freedom of assembly. . . . In the last presidential election, various attempts were successfully made to prevent the appearance of candidates of the Socialist and Communist parties" (Lowenstein, 1938, p. 5). In less than ten years, these fears were to be fully realized with dire consequences for the profession and the entire nation.

5

Anti-Communism and the Attack on the New Deal

A country with the strongest economy in the world, first in wealth and per capita income, invulnerable to attack, with military bases and military allies encircling the globe, was haunted by a sense of insecurity, saw ghosts in every closet, phantoms in every dark corner, witches on every broomstick riding over every chimney.
—Jacob Fisher, *The Postwar Purge of Federal Employees*

A FEW SIMPLE QUESTIONS

And so he pulls out this dossier on me . . . [and asks] . . . was I a Communist or had I ever been? I said no, that I had had a very religious background and was brought up in a highly moralistic and religious family, and I could hardly accept the Communist doctrine of a lack of religious values. So for that reason, if no other, I couldn't be a Communist.

"Well, [he continued] did you sign such and such a petition?" I don't know . . . what was it about? It turned out to be the Oklahoma Sedition Cases and when he quoted it by name, that meant nothing to me. When he told me the content, I said yes, I believe that represented humanity and equality and justice to a people or group being abused or mistreated or something.

"Didn't you know that it was Communist dominated?" I said no, I didn't see any proof of that. I saw the injustice being perpetrated against a human being.

"Did I belong to *Social Work Today*?" Yes, I do. "Didn't I think it was Communist dominated?" No, my interpretation and explanation I have of its movement is that because of the expanding nature of social work we've had to take a lot of untrained workers into administering the service and those of us who have some background and training want to help them to do it the right way and we have done everything we could do to supply them with lectures and with literature.

[T]he Cooperative Bookstore over on Connecticut Street, did I attend meetings there? Well, I shop there to get the books at a discount. You know how academic salaries aren't so extravagant that you can pay to go downtown to a regular bookstore and buy a first run book.

And he went on and on like that for a good two hours of my being grilled about being a Communist sympathizer . . . [T]hat was the way they approached getting rid of "dangerous" people. (Lindsay, 1980, pp. 158–159)

Like Inabel Lindsay, dean of the School of Social Work at Howard University, whose recollections of the McCarthy era are excerpted above, many reform-minded social workers in the post–World War II era were investigated by the FBI or the House Un-American Activities Committee (HUAC) or fired by public and private agencies because of their membership in suspect organizations, their previous involvement with the New Deal, their association with the Rank and File Movement, their subscriptions to proscribed journals (like *Social Work Today*), their advocacy of unpopular ideas like civil rights, even for owning "socialist books" or befriending Bertha Reynolds (Withorn, 1984).

Some, like Lindsay, were fortunate. When HUAC pressured the president of Howard University to fire Lindsay, he refused, citing his belief "in humanity to mankind and a religious orientation to social work" (Lindsay, 1980, p. 156), although she had told him to do so if it would protect the university from harm. Never formally named a "fellow traveler," nor publicly assaulted for her political views (such as support for Henry Wallace's 1948 Presidential candidacy), Lindsay remained at the helm of Howard's School of Social Work until the late 1960s. Other social workers, both the prominent and the unknown, were far less fortunate than Lindsay.

In 1947, Jacob Fisher, a leader of the Rank and File Movement and editor of *Social Work Today*, was charged with disloyalty under Executive Order 9835, the Loyalty Program instituted by the Truman administration to weed out Communists and suspected Communists from the federal government. Although he was cleared the following year, Fisher was suspended from his government job in April 1954 under the Security Risk Program. Forced to resign from government service, professionally ruined, and personally embittered, Fisher worked as an analyst for the Surveys and Research Corporation and operated a tree and shrub nursery for the rest of his career.

In Jacob Fisher, the social work profession lost a brilliant practitioner whose contributions were cut short because of this politically imposed ostracism. Although he continued to write into old age, he struggled to find a publisher for his work. His final book, *The Postwar Purge of Federal Employees: The World that Made It and the Government's Loyalty-Security Program Today*, remains an unpublished manuscript. (It is available at the Social Welfare History Archives at the University of Minnesota.)

What had Inabel Lindsay, Jacob Fisher, and hundreds of other social workers like them done to deserve this fate? In the 1970s, through the Freedom of Information Act, Fisher learned that the FBI had maintained an extensive file on his political activities and personal acquaintances since the 1930s, even the kind of neighborhood in which he lived. From the latter, one FBI agent somehow concluded "The fact that [Fisher] lives in a New Deal community with many alleged Communists makes his association with Communists possible if not probable" (Fisher, 1987, p. 60).

Fisher's file not only drew such spurious conclusions, it was quite selective in its contents. For example, it included a list of all "Communist-front" organizations that Fisher had supported in the 1930s and detailed summaries of his more radical writings, but virtually none of the many mainstream articles he had published in professional journals. In fact, the file made no mention of Fisher's work in professional societies. It focused instead on his association with the American Youth Congress and his leadership of a left-wing union, the Social Service Employees Union (SSEU), the Rank and File Movement, and *Social Work Today*, which government investigators had concluded was a Communist-leaning publication by "purchas[ing] a copy of a 1936 issue at the Worker's Bookshop, [a store] located in the very same building occupied exclusively by the national, New York State, and New York County headquarters of the Communist Party–USA and other organizations affiliated with the Communist Party." As Fisher noted in his memoirs, "[If] the FBI bothered to consult the Union List of Serials, . . . it would have learned that copies of the magazine were available in 64 libraries in the country, including the Library of Congress, and that complete sets were on file in 25 public libraries in Washington, Chicago, New York, Boston, and other large cities" (Fisher, 1987, p. 62).

During the postwar assault on the New Deal, social workers like Inabel Lindsay and Jacob Fisher were particularly vulnerable to attacks by antiwelfare politicians who equated the welfare state with communism or socialism. Past membership or assumed membership in the Communist Party or organizations linked to the Communist Party, for whatever period or purpose, aroused the suspicions of government investigators. In this climate, even proponents of modest reforms were subject to vituperative attacks.

The persecution of Fisher and others, therefore, "was part of a deliberate campaign to discredit the very concept of social insurance and social assistance, symbolized by the Social Security Act" (Schreiber, 1990, p. 123). By linking Fisher to radical movements for social justice, the thrust of progressive social work and social reform that he represented could be undermined. Although Lindsay was probably singled out because she was a prominent female African American educator, Fisher was selected because his status as a federal employee made him a prime target of the sweeping repression of dissent that characterized the period, now known as the McCarthy era.

MCCARTHYISM, LOYALTY OATHS, AND THE SUPPRESSION OF POLITICAL DISSENT

Although Senator Joseph McCarthy (R-Wisconsin) held national prominence for less than a decade, his name has come to symbolize the official anti-Communism, in both government and the private sector, that characterized the period of roughly 1945–1960. McCarthyism both emerged from and promoted the political and cultural climate that fueled the Cold War. Even among McCarthy's persistent and recent defenders, the term "McCarthyism" characterizes an atmosphere of personal recrimination and political oppression, in which thousands of workers lost their jobs and millions of others curtailed their political activities out of fear of being labeled a communist or communist sympathizer (Schrecker, 1998).

Despite its grassroots appearances, McCarthyism was hardly a populist movement. Rather, it was "artificially stimulated at the national and local level by competing political elites, and fanned in turn by mass media motivated both by panic and opportunism" (Caute, 1978, p. 320). By the late 1940s, the anti-Communism that fueled McCarthyism had become a "hysterical pandemic. Most Americans accepted its effects quite willingly, believing their nation to be locked in a death struggle with evil communists" (Miller & Nowak, 1975, p. 22).

The roots of this perception lie in the intricate politics of the 1930s and the complex role American Communists and other left-wing activists played in support of the New Deal:

> [The] tendency to associate Communism with American liberalism and progressivism spring[s] from more than self-protective impulses. During the popular front period [of the mid-1930s] American Communists (academics especially) considered themselves with some justification as the left wing of the New Deal coalition. . . . Whether one likes it or not, the Communists . . . were central to the left's activities in this period, whether these were trade union struggles, [civil] rights or the fight against fascism. (Gettleman, 1982, p. 13)

Yet the postwar anti-Communist purges need to be understood also in a broader historical context. As discussed in earlier chapters, there is a long history in the United States of opposition to radical and reformist movements, dating back to the American Revolution itself. Ideologies that challenge cherished beliefs about the sanctity of private property and the free enterprise system, or that even draw attention to their shortcomings, have rarely been tolerated, particularly if the ideas have seemingly foreign origins. In the post–World War II era, the philosophy of the welfare state, even as embodied in the pragmatic policies of the New Deal, was linked with dangerous foreign doctrines like Communism because it focused on rights and not needs and possessed inherently egalitarian tendencies (Reisch, 1998).

Through the vehicle of McCarthyism, anti-communists blended opposition to the New Deal and the growth of the welfare state with fear of Soviet expansionism, support for high levels of military spending, and repression of organized labor and civil rights. McCarthyism, therefore, combined a backward-looking nostalgia with a recognition and fear of the rapid changes World War II had induced. By interpreting all challenges to the superiority of the American way of life as a potentially subversive threat, it was both the culmination of persistent historical themes and the manifestation of the unique politics of the period. Because organized social work reflected contrarian values and worked with people whose lives underscored the failures of the market economy, the profession and its more vocal members were regarded with suspicion and even hostility (Blau, 1997).

By the mid-1940s, prior to the appearance of "Tail Gunner Joe" McCarthy on the national political stage, federal and state officials were already using the twin specters of Communism and radicalism to justify the suppression of political dissent, much as they had done immediately following World War I. Shortly after the war ended, the Department of the Army distributed a pamphlet, *How to Spot a Communist*, to officers and enlisted personnel. The publication reveals that even in the earliest days of the Cold War the government had launched a propaganda campaign to discredit not merely political organizations but also political positions. For example, the pamphlet stated that a communist was anyone who criticized the FBI, HUAC, the American Legion, the Daughters of the American Revolution (DAR), and other "patriotic" organizations.

The pamphlet went further, however, and linked the *language of politics* to disloyal political behavior. The authors warned that communists and their sympathizers used terms like "chauvinism, book-burning, colonialism, demagogy, exploitation, progressive, reactionary, and witch hunt." Disloyal individuals also discussed such issues an "anti-subversive legislation, civil rights, 'curbs' on unions, immigration laws, peace, racial or religious 'discrimination'" (quoted in Fisher, 1987, p. 40). In 1946, in words similar to those used 30 years before in attacks on Jane Addams and Lillian Wald, Admiral Inglis, Chief of the Office of Naval Intelligence (which had listed the Soviet Union as an "enemy power" throughout the World War II), defended the idea of loyalty oaths by declaring that subversives are people who masquerade as protectors of civil liberties (Fisher, 1987). (Ironically, similar allegations against radicals surfaced again in the 1980s during the Reagan administration.)

ATTACK ON *COMMON HUMAN NEEDS*

The suppression of Charlotte Towle's book, *Common Human Needs* (1945), by the same government that had paid her to write it was a prominent example of the postwar anti-Communist furor and its relationship to domestic politics. The book was originally commissioned in 1944 by Jane Hoey, Director of the Bureau of Public Assistance (who wrote the book's preface), and published the following year by the Social Security Administration. Towle's work, which focused on welfare services as a right of citizens and an obligation of a caring society, received positive reviews and was widely used to train social workers in the public sector. Two years later, however, caught up in the frenzy of anti-Communist witch hunts, the U.S. Government Printing Office ordered the removal of all copies of the book from circulation and, in 1951, destroyed its printing plates (Posner, 1995).

The attack on *Common Human Needs*, whose first chapter was entitled "The Place of Public Assistance in a Democracy," was a minor and somewhat absurd skirmish in the war against the expansion of the New Deal. Towle's detractors took objection to her book's "socialistic" themes, which they equated with the promotion of the welfare state. They cited one sentence of the book as evidence of its ideological persuasion: "Social security and public assistance programs are a basic essential *for attainment of the socialized state envisaged in democratic ideology*, a way of life which so far has been realized only in slight measure" (Towle, 1945, p. 57, emphasis added).

Nothing that Towle wrote or proposed went beyond the social policies already implemented by Great Britain and the Scandinavian countries. Nevertheless, for the next four years, opportunistic politicians in Washington kept up the conservative drumbeat over the book. The American Medical Association (AMA) exploited the controversy over the book for political advantage in its successful campaign to defeat President Truman's proposal to establish national health insurance (Starr, 1982).

To its credit, the American Association of Social Workers (AASW) defended Towle as did students at the University of Illinois (letters of Charles Plapp, May 16 and 17, 1951, Evelyn Butler Archive, University of Pennsylvania). In early 1952, the AASW published a revised edition of her book and put it back in circulation (National Association of Social Workers [NASW] Papers, SWHA 1952). In the revised edition, however, Towle reworded the controversial sentence, eliminating the phrase "socialized state" (Towle, 1952, p. 57).

Over the years, despite these professional setbacks, Towle maintained a "hardened approach to public criticism." She wrote many papers and a well-received book, *The Learner in Education for the Professions* (1954). Yet the criticisms she endured because of *Common Human Needs* produced both her greatest notoriety and considerable and persistent personal suffering. For example, in 1954, Towle was denied a passport because of her alleged involvement in suspect organizations and for signing a petition seeking clemency for the Rosenbergs.

GOVERNMENT AND PRIVATE SECTOR PURGES

As a tenured professor at the University of Chicago, Towle held a relatively secure position, particularly in an institution with a long history of tolerance for dissenting ideas. Most other social workers did not have the same formal or informal protections, particularly after President Truman signed Executive Order 9835 on March 22, 1947. This order not only barred Communists from federal posts, but also barred from such employment anyone guilty of "sympathetic association" with them or their organizations. According to Francis Biddle, Attorney General during the Truman administration when the order was approved, Truman's purpose in signing the order was to undercut the anti-Communist posturing of his Republican opponents. Biddle felt that although the purge of suspected public employees was politically necessary, it represented "this vast amateur and childish yet brutal and stupid mechanism for our protection" (Fisher, 1987, p. 19).

Backed by both major political parties and supported by a large majority of the public—whose postwar economic insecurities were exacerbated by the anxieties of the Cold War—Truman's action had important consequences. It produced a wave of suspicion and anonymous accusations against thousands of federal workers that reverberated throughout other sectors of the nation, from public schools to the motion picture industry (Navasky, 1980; Schrecker, 1998). In general, there was little organized opposition to the loyalty oath campaign. The United Public Workers of America (UPWA), the CIO union for government employees (which included social workers in its ranks), mounted the only organized opposition to the order within the federal bureaucracy. By 1950, however, the UPWA had been expelled from the Congress of Industrial Organizations (CIO) on the grounds that it was controlled by Communists (Fisher, 1987). Thus, government employees either quietly acceded to or abetted the purge of individuals with suspected left-wing ties.

Under the federal loyalty program, thousands of people who expressed (or had expressed in their past) liberal, radical, Marxist, Communist, socialist, or anarchist views were charged with possessing Communist sympathies and being potentially disloyal. Loyalty came to be synonymous with total conformity to the status quo. In the late 1940s, it required uncritical acceptance of the socioeconomic reality of the United States and unquestioning acceptance of U.S. domestic and foreign policies. People who expressed nonconformist economic, political, or social opinions, like many that had entered public service during the New Deal and World War II, were particularly suspicious (Heale, 1998; Schrecker, 1998).

Marion Hathway, herself a victim of anti-Communist vitriol, made this point at a 1951 Minnesota conference on welfare:

> These special loyalty oaths are to be sharply distinguished from an oath of allegiance to our constitutional form of government. They are based on the doctrine of guilt by association as against guilt by action. They constitute no problem to the really subversive person who will sign without a conscience. But they will intimidate and incriminate many honest and sincere people who have participated with good faith in many social movements of the past or present. (Marion Hathway Papers, Folder 124, Social Welfare History Archives, University of Minnesota)

During the 1930s and early 1940s, social workers had been prominent among those persons eager to contribute their knowledge, creativity, and experience to government efforts to promote social justice. In the postwar era, many pressing social issues, such as health care, housing, civil rights, and Social Security, remained unsolved. The loyalty oath program not only purged many patriotic and able civil servants at a time when their expertise was most needed, it also discouraged countless others from pursuing careers in government service, lowered employees' morale, led to the exercise of self-censorship, and stifled innovation in the executive branch. By the mid-1950s, studies of both specific occupational groups and a cross section of the general population found a mood of "widespread apprehension." Forty-one percent of respondents in one survey indicated they did not feel as free to express their opinions as they had in the past (Goldstein, 1978; Stouffer, 1966).

State governments soon emulated federal loyalty programs. By 1949, 22 states had introduced loyalty oaths for public sector employees, including social workers and university professors. Thirty-eight states passed general and vaguely worded antisedition laws. Twenty-one states forbade "seditious teaching" and 31 banned teachers from belonging to organizations advocating "sedition." Twelve states even authorized firing teachers for unspecified "disloyalty." Private universities, especially universities dominated by corporate trustees, and large voluntary sector social service organizations, such as the United Way, soon followed suit (Brilliant, 1990; Schrecker, 1986).

In both public and private sectors, liberals often went to extremes to prove their loyalty. Fearful of being considered communists or "fellow travelers," and of losing their precarious professional jobs or status, they participated willingly as informants against colleagues producing what two blacklisted writers, Lillian Hellman and Dalton Trumbo, termed "scoundrel time" and "the time of the toad" (Hellman, 1976; Trumbo, 1972). In an environment in which even liberal New Dealers like Senator Hubert Humphrey proposed a bill to outlaw the Communist Party and to create concentration camps for domestic radicals (Miller & Nowak, 1975), acts of individual betrayal were often couched in the language of patriotism (Fisher, 1986; Schrecker, 1998; Schreiber, 1995).

The collapse of the wartime U.S.–U.S.S.R. alliance, which dramatically altered the political climate in the United States between 1945–1947, fueled such developments. Concerns about national security increased in the wake of the "red scare" promoted by the Republican Party, largely for opportunistic political gain. To avoid the label of being "soft on Communism," President Truman took an increasingly hard line against Communists and those suspected of Communist affiliations at home and abroad (Goldstein, 1978). In 1948, a federal grand jury indicted 11 leaders of the Communist Party of the United States of America (CPUSA), charging them with conspiracy to advocate the overthrow of the U.S. government by force. Although no charges of espionage or treason were filed, the Communist leaders were convicted largely on the basis of their adherence to Marxist–Leninist principles (Heale, 1999; Klehr, 1998; Ottanelli, 1991; Schrecker, 1998).

The motion picture industry soon compiled its infamous blacklist, through the publication *Red Channels*, culminating in the well-publicized trial of the "Hollywood 10" (Navasky, 1980). Major American universities began to question faculty suspected of Communist sympathies (Schrecker, 1986). Soon, in all occupations and walks of life, Americans who professed "radical" ideas or reformist positions on domestic and international issues, and even those who simply spoke out against the suppression of civil liberties, became targets of political attack (Rovere, 1959; Schrecker, 1998). Social workers in the public and private sectors, and in higher education, did not escape this scrutiny and persecution.

PURGE OF RADICAL SOCIAL WORK UNIONS

In the 1930s and 1940s, social workers were one of the most prominent professions in the burgeoning union movement (Karger, 1988). The democratic approach to the concept of social service prompted such unions as the UPWA, the SSEU, and the United Office and Professional Workers of America (UOPWA) contrasted starkly with the hierarchical detachment from clients expressed by the AASW. The unions also differed in their radical calls for economic and social equality, their support for socialist-type solutions to social problems, and their insistence on activism as a component of social work practice (Karger, 1988).

The debate over unionization itself, which had emerged in social work in the late 1930s, was still hotly contested in social work circles after the war and was the subject of considerable study. Central questions included the right of social workers to engage in collective bargaining, the compatibility of unionization with professionalism and work with middle-class clients, the legality of open versus closed shops, and the use of strikes as a labor tactic (Conference on Union Affiliation of Employees of Voluntary Health and Welfare Agencies, June 23 and 30, 1947; King, 1946; Russell Sage Foundation, October 1945; SSEU, 1948; Wolfson, 1951). These issues often produced tensions not only within professional organizations but also between unionized social workers and management in both public and private sector agencies. Social service administrators portrayed the unions as Communist-inspired dupes, who placed their self-interest above that of their clients. The unions responded that management's failure to negotiate over legitimate workplace grievances was a deliberate provocation designed to discredit and ultimately break the union (Crosby, 1952; SSEU [flyer]; *New York Times*, November 13, 1951).

One exception to this conflict was the YWCA, whose national board endorsed the right of workers to bargain collectively and to participate in "responsible political activity." The organization pledged its cooperation "in efforts to secure and maintain a decent standard of living, reasonable hours and good working conditions" (YWCA, January 9, 1946, p. 63). In the McCarthy period, this distinguished the YWCA from many other nonprofit social service agencies, who largely accepted the right of social workers to engage in collective bargaining but continued to take the position that unionization was often incompatible with the service mission of an organization. Consequently, they often opposed such prolabor concepts as the closed shop and the use of strikes to settle employment disputes (Dawson, 1954). This view was antithetical to the ideas expressed by radical and activist social workers in the SSEU (SSEU, 1948).

Tensions over labor issues and wider domestic concerns were brewing even before the end of the war (Isserman, 1987). Organized labor was openly concerned about the domestic consequences of peacetime. Progressive unions hoped that peace would bring an expansion of civil rights and social welfare legislation, as well as greater participation by working people in the political process (Cohn, 1943). Almost immediately after the war, however, anti-Communist hysteria and antilabor legislation, particularly the Taft–Hartley Bill, put unions on the defensive. The UOPWA took a strong stance against Taft–Hartley, stating in a telegram to President Truman that "to weaken in any way the full and free right of labor to organize and bargain collectively is to undermine the structure of American democracy" (UOPWA, May 15, 1947). Signers of the telegram included such radical and progressive social workers as Herbert Aptekar, Lucy Carner, Nathan Cohen, Marion Hathway, Inabel Lindsay, Harry Lurie, Kenneth Pray, Bertha Reynolds, and Verne Weed.

In 1945, militant strikes occurred among all labor unions after several years of honoring a wartime no-strike pledge. The leading representative of public welfare workers, the State, County, and Municipal Workers of America (SCMWA), merged with the CIO's United Federal Workers to form the UPWA, creating a 60,000- to 70,000-member union that included 8,000 to10,000 public welfare workers. The union staged walkouts and strikes in several major cities on the East Coast and in Los Angeles. Among workers in the private sector, the UOPWA also grew in numbers and strength during this period through mergers (Schrecker, 1992).

In 1946–1947, however, the CIO began to expel Communists and Communist-led locals from its membership. State and national union conventions featured purges of Communists from union leadership. Long suspected of being left-wing strongholds, the SCMWA and the UOPWA were particularly attractive targets for anti-Communist labor leaders. Raids from more conservative unions exacerbated their weaknesses (Alexander, 1977), as did the demise of *Social Work Today*, long a progressive voice for radical social workers. Union newsletters could only partially fill this gap.

In March 1947, the loyalty oath program signed by President Truman further decimated the unions, who were already under attack for refusing to comply with the 1939 Hatch Act. Attacks on the UPWA grew stronger by the end of 1947, especially in New York, where radical public welfare workers were blamed for increases in relief rolls, a charge refuted by both the unions and the AASW (AASW, March 1950; *Compass*, January 16, 1950; Crosby, 1952; Stern, 1950). At the 1948 and 1949 CIO conventions delegates approved first the investigation and then the ouster of the left-wing unions. By February 1950, the UOPWA and the UPWA were expelled from the CIO for following the Communist Party line (Kampelman, 1957; O'Brien, 1968). Specific allegations of being communists were levied against UPWA leaders Abram Flaxer and Eleanor Nelson.

Although they mounted a vigorous defense, attacking their enemies as "the most anti-labor, anti-democratic, and pro-war elements in our country today," the expulsions soon led to a dramatic decline in union membership. The UOPWA membership dropped from 45,000 in 1946 to 12,000 in 1950 while the collapse of the UPWA was even more precipitous: from nearly 80,000 members in 1947 to fewer than 2,500 in 1952 (Livingston, 1951; UOPWA flyer, 1949). Weakened by their expulsion from the CIO, the unions' members were vulnerable to mass dismissals in 1949–1950 in major cities like New York, Chicago, Detroit, and Los Angeles.

New York City welfare commissioner Raymond Hilliard vowed to get rid of all Communists in the welfare department and tried repeatedly to break the social workers' union (Crosby, March 20, 1952; Gailmor, 1951a; *Compass*, November 14, 1950). He claimed that Communists in the union "could grant or withhold relief for any political purpose that suited them, such as the election of a pro-Communist Congressman or a Communist member of the City Council. They could put the squeeze on our welfare clients by granting them extra favors as a reward for going along with the Communist program. In essence, they could undermine the confidence of these unfortunate people in their government, moving toward their ultimate goal, which is the destruction of the country" (quoted in Crosby, March 20, 1952). This charge was particularly ironic in view of recent rulings in Pennsylvania and other states that had declared Communists ineligible for relief (Lush, 1950).

Hilliard was especially concerned about a pamphlet entitled "Welfare in Crisis" that had been distributed by the Joint Committee of Trade Unions in Social Work at the National Conference of Social Work (NCSW) conference in Atlantic City. The pamphlet placed the blame for the city's welfare problems squarely at the feet of the commissioner. Subsequent newspaper investigations revealed how he had attempted to discredit the union and red-bait activists to deflect attention from his own failings (Crosby, 1952; *Compass*, November 14, 1950; Gailmor, 1951a).

Nevertheless, Hilliard's tactics had their intended effects. Union activists, including Christian Lewis, Murray Stein, and Edith Goldner, were dismissed on charges of inefficiency and insubordination. Workers who participated in demonstrations were investigated (Levenstein, 1981). About 200 union members were fired in New York alone. By 1953, the UPWA disbanded. Similar attacks occurred among leaders of the UOPWA and, in the same year as the UPWA disbanded, it purged itself of its leaders with Communist backgrounds, despite earlier efforts to survive by merging with other left-leaning unions (Schrecker, 1992).

These sustained attacks led mainstream professional organizations to sever their connections with the unions. In the October 1948 issue of AASW's *Social Work Journal* focusing on civil rights, an editorial declared, "There is undeniable evidence that such [Communist] infiltration has occurred . . . [and] that communist political philosophy and practice are irreconcilable with democratic, constitutional government" (p. 139). The AASW also made little comment about social service cuts in the late 1940s and early 1950s and said nothing about the firing of Jane Hoey from the Bureau of Public Assistance for protesting these cuts and defending staff accused of disloyalty (AASW, 1948).

In the early 1950s, AFSCME local 1706 supplanted the UOPWA, the so-called red union, among many social service workers in New York (Chaiklin, personal communication, 1997). By 1954, in Orwellian fashion, the official organs of the social work profession such as the *Yearbook* had nearly expunged the contributions of the labor unions from the history of the profession. Union leader Abram Flaxer was cited for contempt of Congress for refusing to testify before the Senate Subcommittee on Internal Security, a conviction later overturned by the Supreme Court. Flaxer remarked, "I was an absolute anathema to the leaders in social work. They would have never dreamed of saying anything in my defense. I didn't expect them to and they sure never did" (quoted in Hunter, 1999, p. 47).

After 1955, the AASW's successor, the National Association of Social Workers (NASW) assisted the FBI in the investigation of suspected radicals such as Meyer Schreiber and Margaret Wheeler. In addition, when Schreiber's loyalty was called into question because of his prior involvement in several "subversive" organizations, the Council on Social Work Education (CSWE) and his alma mater, Columbia University School of Social Work, also cooperated with government investigators (Schreiber, 1995). Wheeler later recalled, "The professional association shunned me when I was going through the HUAC persecution. They refused to come to my side or even offer advice. . . . Most of them were cowards, nearly all of them" (quoted in Hunter, 1999, pp. 46–47).

The equivocal attitude of mainstream social work organizations to radical unions and radical activists, alternately defending their rights and cooperating in their persecution, reflected the complex political realities of the period. The high proportion of Communists in unions like the UOPWA led mainstream social workers to shun alliances with them over the social reform goals they shared. Legitimate fears that supporters of such unions would be tarred with the same brush by anti-Communist investigators also played a role, as did the desire to preserve social work's tenuous professional status (Glazer, 1961; Haynes, 1975). In the long run, however, the failure of mainstream social work organizations to defend their radical colleagues inflicted severe damage on the profession and the social welfare causes it espoused.

SOCIAL WORK AND MCCARTHYISM

The antipathy of anti-Communists to social work and the welfare state can be traced to two political developments of the 1930s in which social workers were directly and indirectly involved, often in leadership positions. One was the enormous growth of the federal role in economic and social planning—a role promoted by a loose coalition of New Deal liberals, socialists, and communists, including many social workers, particularly women (Ware, 1981). Wartime mobilization further expanded the government's role and provoked fears of "socialism" among long-time opponents of social welfare.

The Cold War hysteria of the late 1940s provided conservatives with a unique political opportunity to undo the social reforms of the New Deal and to undermine the modest efforts of the Truman administration's "Fair Deal" to expand benefits in the areas of Social Security, health care, and housing:

> By claiming that the Democrats had condoned Soviet subversion, the conservatives in the GOP could mount an assault on the New Deal, which they could not do on social or economic grounds. . . . Legislative investigations gave the conservatives a perfect arena for their campaign against the New Deal and its supposed sympathy for communist subversion. (Schrecker, 1998, p. 7)

Whether their opposition to the New Deal was based on principle or politics, anti-Communists in both major parties displayed little concern for democratic ideals or First Amendment rights. Epithets like "subversive" were applied freely, not only to suspected communists but to liberals and civil libertarians as well (Schrecker, 1998). In public speeches and newspaper columns anti-Communists "were not always scrupulously careful to distinguish between liberals and communists . . . and seemed to say that subversives and social reformers were the same thing" (Latham, 1965, p. v). These attacks scuttled modest reforms in the areas of health care, housing, and employment policies, even as other industrialized nations expanded social welfare provision.

Social workers who had been prominent members of the New Deal coalition or members of the Rank and File Movement of the 1930s were particularly vulnerable to this type of attack (Fisher, 1980). As strong advocates for civil liberties, they were easy targets for political demagogues and their allies who equated the defense of the First Amendment and the promotion of civil rights with questionable allegiance to the state. As proponents of government intervention on behalf of the unemployed and the poor, they were open to charges of "red" or "pink" sympathies nearly a decade before the McCarthy era, much as their professional ancestors had been in the 1920s.

Based in part on their overseas experiences during and after the war, social workers were also strong supporters of internationalism, universal human rights (United Nations, 1948), and worldwide efforts to prevent future wars. The prospects for peace inspired by the foundation of the United Nations in 1945 fostered a belief in "one world" among many progressive social workers (International Institute, 1946, Evelyn Butler Archive, University of Pennsylvania). Haunted by the effects of wartime carnage and the holocaust, others wanted to take international action to prevent the reoccurrence of fascism in the future. These positions became suspect in an era when patriotism was defined in terms of unquestioning loyalty to the status quo (Commager, 1947) and challenges to U.S. foreign policy initiatives provoked accusations of communist sympathies (Williams, 1968). Many social workers who supported Henry Wallace's Presidential candidacy in 1948 and professed pacifist ideas were subsequently subject to investigations and blacklisting.

Liberal anti-Communists, including most of the mainstream leadership of the social work profession, were particularly strident in their attacks on the left.

They equated Communism with totalitarianism, the police state, and the slave labor camp, and capitalism with democracy. They argued that Communists and reactionaries had essentially the same ideas about human beings and their problems.

Of particular importance to the field of social welfare, liberals attacked Communists and their supporters for identifying "economic security with the suppression of freedom" (Lehman, 1950, p. 10). Social welfare, in the liberals' view, was a means "to promote the *well-being of individuals* in such a way as to strengthen our democracy and *our system of free enterprise*" (Altmeyer, 1951, p. 2; emphasis added). Although socialists like Norman Thomas continued to equate socialism with social welfare, liberals argued that the welfare state was a means of bolstering capitalism and protecting human independence (Denny, 1950; Smith, 1947, Evelyn Butler Archive, University of Pennsylvania). Inadvertently, this played into the hands of inveterate critics of the New Deal and the welfare state, particularly in the corporate sector, who regarded welfare provision as fiscally dangerous and stifling of entrepreneurial incentive and worker enterprise (Hirschfeld, 1943).

Congressional hearings gave conservatives a public forum to campaign against the New Deal and its alleged sympathy for Communist subversion. Among the many organizations accused during HUAC hearings of being Communist fronts were groups in which social workers played important roles, such as the American Civil Liberties Union (ACLU), the American Student Union, the National Consumers League, and the American Labor Party. This facilitated the destruction of the New Deal coalition and the defeat of the New Deal's unfinished agenda, such as national health insurance.

Radicals, however, chastised liberal critics for their acquiescence to Cold War propaganda, for accepting the "false choice between war and Communism," rather than confronting their "fear of a faulty capitalist economy full swing on a course that is bound for catastrophe" (Marcus, 1948, p. 4). For radical social workers and their allies, democracy had a deeper meaning than political participation. It involved "the extension of the fundamental opportunities, rights and responsibilities to all members of our society, regardless of differences in their economic condition, their color, religion or national origin" (Pray, 1945, p. 6). Radical social workers maintained that democracy also included the need for people to make fundamental decisions about their lives (Pray, 1945).

One issue around which liberal and radical social workers united was support for permanent Fair Employment Practices Commission (FEPC) legislation. Liberal and radical groups cosponsored publications that refuted the racist arguments against the permanent FEPC and the claims that it would subvert the free enterprise system (National Council for a Permanent FEPC, 1947). Another issue that united the profession was defense of public assistance against attacks by local and state officials and the media under the guise of preventing dependency or protecting states' rights against federal interference (Gailmor, 1951b, 1952b; O'Brien, 1951; Rosen, 1950). The promotion of civil rights and open housing was a third unifying issue (AASW, 1948, Evelyn Butler Archive, University of Pennsylvania).

SOCIAL WORK AND THE PROGRESSIVE PARTY: PERSECUTION OF MARION HATHWAY

Social work in Pittsburgh is dominated by the University of Pittsburgh School of Social Work, which in turn is dominated by Dr. Marion Hathaway [*sic*]. [She] has belonged to various Communist fronts for years but she has never been molested, even when Pitt was cleaning out its legitimate liberals. . . . [She] is careful about pushing stuff in her lectures but her students are subjected to a regular barrage of petitions, leaflets, newspaper clippings, discussions, etc. The Community Fund-Social Work bureaucracy is helpless or complacent in the face of this performance. (Rice, 1948)

This attack on Marion Hathway in one of Pittsburgh's leading newspapers was prompted by her active support of Henry Wallace's presidential candidacy on the Progressive Party ticket. As she recalled, "It was the international program and the peace issue that carried me into the party. The leadership of Henry Wallace symbolized that issue"(Marion Hathway Papers). Hathway had long supported organized labor, civil rights, and the expansion of economic security for all Americans. She was also a strong advocate for internationalism and peace (Andrews & Brenden, 1993) as demonstrated by her participation in the Pittsburgh Council on American-Soviet Friendship, the Russian War Relief Committee, and the American Committee for the Protection of the Foreign Born (Marion Hathway Papers). Throughout her career, she distinguished between support for democratic principles and blind allegiance to the American way of life. In 1942, Hathway wrote "In the present world conflict, we are struggling to defend the democratic ideology, not to defend an existing system" (Hathway, 1942, p. 18).

By the late 1940s, Hathway had already had a long and distinguished career in social work and social work education and established a national reputation as a progressive. (See Chapter 4.) She worked for the YWCA in 1920–1922 and joined the Pittsburgh faculty in 1932. After serving as executive secretary of AASW from 1938 to 1941, she was elected its president in 1942. She would shortly be elected secretary of the NCSW in 1950. The story of her persecution in Pittsburgh is a remarkable case study of the repression of social work radicals during the McCarthy era.

At the January 1948 AASW conference in Minneapolis, Hathway gave a paper entitled "Our Responsibility—1948: Preparation for Social Responsibility." In her presentation, Hathway spoke of the "fusion of the concept of individual freedom and collective security . . . as found in the document known as the Economic Bill of Rights." The principles underlying this document included useful and remunerative employment, the end of monopoly control of the economy, decent housing, medical care and good health, and freedom from fears of old age, sickness, accident, and unemployment" (Hathway, 1948).

Hathway argued that if social workers accepted the goals of freedom and security for all, the old social philosophies upon which the profession had been founded needed to be revised. She went on to defend social action as "a part of all professional practice," which rests upon historical understanding and the conviction about future trends in social welfare services. Public responsibility in the field of social work, she asserted, establishes firmly the place of professional practice in public service in both the government and private nonprofit sectors. Social service agencies supported by voluntary contributions from the community, therefore, are responsible to the community in the same way as government agencies are responsible to their constituents and should be governed by the same principles of civil liberties (Hathaway, 1948).

Hathway's views did not go unnoticed in her hometown. In August 1948, Msgr. Charles Owens Rice, a labor priest and anti-Communist, attacked her in his weekly column in the *Pittsburgh Catholic*, the official organ of the archdiocese. Msgr. Rice accused Hathway of dominating the School of Social Work and social work activities in the city of Pittsburgh and engaging in Communist-inspired propaganda. He linked his attack on Hathway to her political activities in support of the Wallace campaign and her connections to the UOPWA whose leaders had already been accused of Communist sympathies (Rice, 1948). (Hathway had written part of a pamphlet entitled "Henry Wallace speaks to Social Workers" published in Catholic newspapers in Pittsburgh.)

On August 30, the Executive Committee of the Pittsburgh chapter of AASW wrote a letter stating that although Father Rice's column in the *Pittsburgh Catholic* focused on Hathway, it was, "in essence, [an attack on] professional social work and academic freedom" (AASW, 1948). The letter refuted Rice's charges and defended Hathway's freedom to engage in legitimate political activities.

The following spring, however, the attacks on Hathway resumed in earnest. On May 1, 1949, Judge Blair Gunther was quoted in two leading Pittsburgh newspapers, the *Press* and the *Gazette*, as saying to high school seniors "Marion Hathway, a Pittsburgh professor, has been active in every communist movement in Pittsburgh and should be dismissed but we have not yet had the courage in Pittsburgh to do that" (Gunther, 1949). As evidence, Gunther cited Hathway's interests in areas such as unemployment relief, public assistance, and work relief, and her support for Roosevelt and the Wallace campaign. Members of the university's board of trustees soon picked up the clamor for Hathway's resignation.

Four days later, Hathway wrote to Pittsburgh's Chancellor Rufus Fitzgerald in response to Gunther's remarks. She admitted helping to organize the Pittsburgh Council of American-Soviet Friendship during World War II but reminded the chancellor that Gunther had also served as a member of the Council's Board and that the organization had dissolved in 1945–1946. She admitted that she was still involved in the American Committee for Protection of the Foreign

Born, which, like the council, was on Attorney General Clark's list of subversive organizations. Hathway also acknowledged she was on the national "Wallace for President" committee and had appeared at numerous Wallace rallies and on broadcasts of the American Slav Congress of Western Pennsylvania. (This organization was listed by the U.S. Attorney General as a Communist front.) She denied, however, that she had ever been a Communist Party member (letter of Hathway, May 5, 1949, Marion Hathway papers, University of Pittsburgh).

Despite Hathway's response, the university took the charges against her seriously particularly after Chancellor Fitzgerald received a May 11, 1949, letter from Harbaugh Miller, an attorney and university trustee, inquiring about the need for the university to take action about Hathway and to appraise the atmosphere at the School of Social Work. Alluding to the interest of donors and legislators, Miller wrote, "In my own experience, I have frequently been appalled at the type of thinking that all too often characterizes the attitude of the average social worker. . . . I cannot help but wonder at times just what is being taught in our School of Social Work. I know that I am not alone [in the region]" (letter of Miller, May 11, 1949, Marion Hathway Papers, University of Pittsburgh). On May 23, Fitzgerald briefly acknowledged the issue Miller raised as "one of the delicate problems facing American universities today" (Fitzgerald, 1949).

Diplomatic letters from the Pittsburgh administration could not make the Hathway problem go away. The chancellor soon received another letter from a prominent businessman in the community, Roy McKenna, who stated he had learned from a female attorney who "is in a position to have knowledge of all subversive activities" that Hathway is "an avowed communist." McKenna concluded "It was the judgement of the group [of businessmen] that the continuing of Dr. Hathway as a teacher in the university would seriously handicap the Committee in the solicitation of funds" (McKenna, 1949).

Action was also stirring in Hathway's defense. On May 10, about 110 students (including future social work educators Bernard Ross, Richard Lodge, James Hackshaw, and Kermit Wiltse) wrote the Chancellor in support of Hathway. On May 19th, students requested a meeting with the chancellor but received no reply (Lamborn, 1949). Two days later, Celia Moss, President of the School's Alumni Association, reaffirmed the support for Hathway the group had previously expressed in its letter of August 21, 1948, after the Rice column appeared (Moss, 1949).

> Within the profession of social work [she wrote] there are differences in political opinion as there are among members of any profession. We have conviction that each individual has the right to exercise his citizenship responsibility as he sees fit within the framework of a stable democratic society. (Marion Hathway Papers, folder 52, Social Welfare History Archives, University of Minnesota)

On May 25th, another student group unanimously defended Hathway. The same day, the chancellor stalled for time in a letter he dictated to the secretary of

Wilbur Newstetter, dean of the School of Social Work, giving a broadly worded defense of academic freedom (Marion Hathway Papers, University of Pittsburgh).

Two weeks later, the dean and 15 faculty wrote Fitzgerald expressing "appreciation of your support of the principles of academic freedom involved in the recent attacks in the press upon the University of Pittsburgh." This freedom, they asserted, "includes the right and the responsibility, as a citizen, to take a stand on public issues, support candidates, and take part in political activities." Signers of the letter included Hathway, Grace Marcus, Meyer Schreiber, Gladys Ryland, Gertrude Wilson, and Ruth Smalley (Letter of June 8, 1949, Marion Hathway Papers, University of Pittsburgh).

Handwritten materials from the chancellor's office reveal the extent of the struggle involved in defining the university's position regarding the charges made against Hathway and allegations that there were other Communists on the Pittsburgh faculty. Although Fitzgerald repeatedly stressed the importance of due process, he wrote the following questions and answers in response to hypothetical written inquiries:

1. Does the University have communists on its staff? *We do not believe that we have. However, we cannot be absolutely sure these days that they have not infiltrated into any organization, including the government itself.*
2. What would we do if we did have? *We would recommend their dismissal since in my opinion they are not free to meet the objective attitude requirement of the American university classroom.*
3. If conclusive evidence should be found . . . *we would recommend his dismissal in accordance with procedures under existing tenure policies. . . .* And then, finally,
4. What shall we proceed with the Hathway case? [*no response was written*]

Chancellor Fitzgerald cited the Cold War as the reason why "it is natural for individuals to be concerned about the presence of communists in our midst for there is proof that they are in my opinion not free to meet the objective requirement of the American university classroom." Then, using the language of academic freedom, he justified the dismissal of suspected Communists from university posts:

We cannot and do not wish to discharge a faculty member because he or she has political, religious or economic views which most of us do not share. To do so would be to violate the spirit if not the letter of the Constitution. On the other hand, no university should permit incompetent persons to serve on its faculty. [*We believe that a person is incompetent if he uses the classroom as a means of presenting biased views on controversial matters instead of preserving the objective point of view necessary to scientific inquiry.] We [also] believe that a Communist is incompetent to teach in a University because he is not free to engage in unbiased research and teaching but rather obliged to follow the party line.* If any person on our faculty is shown to be incompetent [either because of improper classroom activity or] by reason of membership in the Communist Party his connection with the University should be terminated." (Fitzgerald, 1949)

The chancellor went on, however, to defend Hathway and denied the charges alleged about her: "No substantial evidence that Dr. X is a Communist has been presented to the administration." He stressed the need for a fair hearing and due process, the "need to act fairly and in accordance with approved procedures," and the potential danger to faculty members and the university (Nutting, 1949).

For eight months, there were few further developments and the turmoil over Hathway seemed to have subsided. Then on February 21, 1950, the *Pittsburgh Press* published an article about the testimony of a local FBI informer, Matt Cvetic, before a government investigating committee. Cvetic swore under oath that he had seen Hathway at many Wallace events, "but [had] no information that she is a member of the [Communist] party." He did, however, name Steve Rosner and Jack Sartosky, two area labor leaders with personal ties to students at the School of Social Work, as Communists (*Pittsburgh Press*, February 21, 1950).

A week later, however, an article in the *Pittsburgh News* named Hathway and Evelyn Abelson, a social work student, as Communists. Abelson had been a cosigner of a letter to the *Post Gazette* on May 16, 1948, attacking the Mundt–Nixon bill that proposed restrictions on the rights of political leftists. Thirty other Pittsburgh master's of social work (MSW) students signed the letter, including Rose Dobrof, Hal Lewis, and Sonny Sartosky—whose husband, Jack, had just been named a Communist at a HUAC hearing (*Pittsburgh News*, February 28, 1950; *Pittsburgh Post Gazette*, February 28, 1950). An editorial in the *Pittsburgh News* asked, "How far can 'freedom of thought and expression' go in a situation involving leftish tendencies contrary to our basic American doctrine?" (*Pittsburgh News*, February 21, 1950).

Sparked by these newspaper articles, the Hathway controversy again heated up. Pittsburgh Professor Halbrook Botset defended Judge Gunther and reported on a conversation with the judge in which Gunther claimed he was misquoted. Gunther, who may have been trying to back away from an untenable position, stated that because Hathway taught in a graduate school, "her reputed left-wing attitude was not as dangerous as if she had an opportunity to influence large numbers of the younger undergraduates" (Botset, 1950). Records of a conversation between Chancellor Fitzgerald and Professor Botset indicate that Gunther believed Hathway was still at the university because of intervention by the American Association of University Professors and the influence of the Buhl Foundation (Botset, 1950).

Other faculty, like Dr. Charles Lewis, also spoke to Chancellor Fitzgerald in defense of Judge Gunther, and the chancellor's qualified defense of academic freedom began to waver. In a meeting on March 10, Fitzgerald "made it clear to him [Lewis] that if we knew we had a communist in our group I would recommend going through the recognized process to get rid of that person." Citing a recent case at the University of Washington, the chancellor remarked that such action "was not desirable from my standpoint unless we knew whether we had somebody who was definitely a communist" because of the length of time such proceedings take. He remarked that although there was noted "some loose talk about the School of Social Work . . . Mr. Cvetik (*sic*) had said that after nine years he did not have evidence that Hathway was a communist" (Lewis, 1950).

On March 15, despite his recent retreat, Gunther again attacked Hathway by name in the context of broader remarks he made at the Hungary Club calling for unity in dismissing professors who are Communists or under Communist domination. The judge accused Hathway of "teaching the young folks that there is something wrong with this country." He cited her trip to the Polish consulate (for a social event, which Hathway stated many others attended) and asserted "she is teaching that the cost of living is too high and that there is poverty in this country. She never tells her students how much worse these things are in the Soviet Union." He suggested to the audience that they go after "pinks" to stop the legislature's annual appropriation to the university (Tyson,1950; *Pittsburgh News*, March 17, 1950). By now, Gunther's campaign against Hathway had been going on for more than a year (*Pittsburgh News*, March 21, 1950).

On March 18, 1950, Hathway wrote to the chancellor regarding the letter he had received about her from Chairman John Wood of HUAC and the publication of agent Cvetic's testimony in the *Pittsburgh Press* without any factual substantiation. Cvetic had, however, mentioned Hathway in his testimony of February 20, 1950, after being questioned by a member of the committee (Wood, March 13, 1950; Hathway, February 23, 1950). An article about the HUAC hearing listing those who had been denounced as Communists soon appeared in the *Post Gazette*. It cited Representative Woods's letter to Representative Eberharter and confirmed Hathway's claim: "There was no question asked Mr. Cvetic in an open hearing relating to Marion Hathway and no voluntary statement made by Mr. Cvetic concerning her" (*Post Gazette*, March 22, 1950).

Word of Hathway's troubles spread throughout the national social work community, prompting Bertha Reynolds to write her a supportive letter in the summer of 1949 (Reynolds, 1949). Nevertheless, the pressure on Hathway intensified, in part because of the equivocal attitude of the school's dean, Wilbur Newstetter. After several years of increasing turmoil at the school, during which prominent faculty like Grace Marcus, Gertrude Wilson, Ruth Smalley, and Alice Clendenning resigned and Gladys Ryland's contract was terminated, Hathway resigned in the spring of 1951. She accepted a position as Professor of Social Economy and Director of the Graduate Department of Social Economy and Social Research (later the School of Social Work and Social Research) at Bryn

Mawr College, where she worked until her death at the age of 60 in 1955 (Hathway et al, June 22, 1949; Alumni Association, September 26, 1950; Boysen, May 6, 1950; Abell, December 12, 1949; Billston, June 8, 1950; Wilson, June 10, 1950; Clendenning, January 17, 1950).

Articles about her resignation in the Pittsburgh papers underscored the lingering effects of the controversy surrounding her political views. One pointed out that she had sponsored the 1949 Cultural and Scientific Conference for World Peace in New York. This was an event, the *Post Gazette* declared, that was a "rah-for-Russia" gathering, where "Russian Communists and their sympathizers were invited to denounce the United States." Although the article also identified her as the leader of the Progressive Party in the city, it maintained that her departure from the university was "absolutely voluntary" (*Post Gazette*, July 25, 1951).

A related article in another paper stated that Hathway was "a controversial figure . . . because of her extreme socialist philosophies." For example, at a meeting of the "left-wing American Slav Congress in 1947, she called Henry Wallace 'the greatest living American'" (*Sun Telegraph*, April 25, 1951). Ironically, her obituary in the *New York Times* four and a half years later made no mention of the controversy in which she had been embroiled at Pittsburgh for more than three years (*New York Times*, November 20, 1955).

Social workers like Marion Hathway supported the Progressive Party in 1948 because they believed Henry Wallace represented their best hope for peace, civil rights, and the expansion of social welfare. Hathway and Inabel Lindsay took leadership roles in both the national and local aspects of the Wallace campaign. During Wallace's several visits to Pittsburgh (then a stronghold of left-wing labor unions, like the United Electrical Workers), the local Wallace for President Committee met at Hathway's house.

Gertrude Wilson, a colleague of Hathway at the School of Social Work, was also a member of the local Wallace committee. She recalled how the campaign was linked to broader efforts, both inside and outside of universities, to educate people about pressing political and social issues and to raise their level of awareness:

> Those conversations around the fireplace were parts of a valuable education in practical political science which has been very helpful to me in my professional and personal life and as a citizen. I don't think we ever thought we could win; it was a way of calling attention to public social issues such as civil liberties and the right to dissent which were ignored or given but inadequate attention by the major parties and such groups as the A.D.A. [Americans for Democratic Action, a liberal, anti-Communist organization] as well. McCarthyism was well on its way—many were reacting by silence—youth was afraid to speak out. Life on most campuses was very dull and young people needed support and encouragement to examine social issues and take a stand. Youth in the labor movement got more support than middle class ones. . . . We worked hard with our students to help people of all ages and conditions participate in activities leading to social change. (Wilson, 1978, p. 178)

Many activist social workers and future social work leaders, like Harold Lewis and Robert Glass, were students of Hathway's during this period. The group work students were particularly well organized and politically radical. One of this cohort was Miriam Rosenbloom Cohn, who entered Pitt as a "far-left Zionist" undergraduate in the 1940s and stayed on to earn her master's degree in social work. Cohn remembers that it was considered "an honor to be invited" to one of Hathway's Sunday evening "soirees," where the discussions were very political and stimulating (Cohn, personal communication, 1995).

Those social workers that supported Wallace were criticized both inside and outside the profession. Inabel Lindsay recalls a 1948 meeting of the NCSW in Atlantic City where a reception for Wallace had been organized by social workers affiliated with the labor movement. Those who came out openly for Wallace and allied themselves with organized labor embraced an "unpopular" position. Lindsay remarked that "Marion Hathway . . . and I were the only professional social workers in leadership roles in our schools who dared to stand in the receiving line with [Wallace] and give him our approval. Not another social work [leader] would join us . . . to show our support for . . . Wallace" (Lindsay, 1980).

Most social workers, even those who supported progressive causes, were unwilling to support the Progressive Party. Some felt uncomfortable associating with a single ideology and a political organization that appeared to demand a high level of conformity. Arthur Schwartz, a graduate student at the time, remembers attending several Wallace rallies and feeling that "nobody ever really discussed anything. They were parroting a lot of what I considered at the time to be propaganda. . . . It is hard to portray . . . the pressure put on the non-communist left in 1948. Either one conformed to the 'party line' or one was shut out, called names, etc." (Schwartz, personal communication, 1996).

AFRICAN AMERICAN SOCIAL WORKERS AND MCCARTHYISM

African American social workers, particularly the relative few in leadership positions, experienced unusually strong pressure to show support for left-wing organizations like the Progressive Party. Many liberal African American activists, however, felt that being considered a communist only added an additional stigma. As described by Gunnar Myrdal (1944), the so-called Negro Problem got caught up in the furor of anti-Communism and provoked political difficulties for social workers who advocated for civil rights. In the South, accusations of Communism confronted every civil rights worker, Black or white, for decades (Adler, 1998; Jackson, 1957; Kurzman, 1971; Stuart, 1992; Sytz, 1957).

Lester Granger, Executive Secretary of the National Urban League during the 1940s, was a prominent example of this phenomenon. Like many African Americans, he was not especially attracted to the Communist or Socialist Parties, despite their work on such issues as antilynching laws, labor organizing, and civil rights (Record, 1951). Granger, however, was an "outspoken advocate for interracial cooperation and equal opportunity for blacks" who was committed to the "liberal, progressive tradition of social reform" (Brown, 1991, pp. 267–268). During World War II, he served as a special advisor to Secretary of the Navy James Forrestal. As a result of his work, he received the Navy's Distinguished Civilian Service Medal in 1946 and the President's Medal for Merit in 1947. Some African Americans, however, criticized Granger for joining the Republican Party in the 1940s.

Granger was the first African American to be elected President of the NCSW. He also served as chair of the United States Committee of the International Conference of Social Work. By 1961, he was president of that organization. He is best known for his work with the National Urban League, where, from 1941 to 1961, he served as its executive director. Although African American social workers like Granger possessed obvious sympathy for social justice causes, the devastating effects of racism and their marginal status in U.S. economic and political life made it too risky to add the label "radical."

Nevertheless, Granger and others could not fail to note the ominous implications of the rise of fascism for African Americans. In 1944, when any speaker critical of domestic social conditions ran the risk of being labeled unpatriotic, Granger declared to a Smith College audience,

> We recognize Fascism as built by Mussolini, perfected by Hitler, and adopted by the Japanese war lords as being the same sinister creature, the same vicious enemy of mankind, no matter what its national garb or location. We have committed ourselves to a fight to the death to extirpate this monster who is the enemy of mankind. . . . How, then, can we continue to blind our eyes and hope to blind the eyes of our world neighbors to the continued existence, the tolerated existence of Fascism here at home? Whether or not we are honest enough to admit it to ourselves, the anti-Negroism of Mississippi, Alabama and Georgia, and a half-dozen other states of the Union is first cousin to— no, the direct progenitor of—Fascism at its worst in Hitler's Germany. (Granger, 1944, pp. 31–32)

Yet Granger soon tempered these statements, which were considered radical at the time, with others that focused on more traditional ideas of responsibility, service, and freedom of thought. To separate activism on behalf of civil rights from its supporters in the Communist Party, Granger told African Americans at Howard University,

> We have thought too largely as Negroes, as "liberals," as "conservatives," or in some other stereotyped fashion. We have compartmentalized our mental activity into the narrow confines of our emotional reactions. . . . There has been too much talk among numbers of our race regarding the hopelessness of ever solving racial problems in this country. . . . There have been too frequent tendencies to impeach the democratic ideal simply because democracy has not been generally practice in the social habits of this country. But either we believe in democracy or we do not. (Granger, 1944, p. 46)

During the United Front era of the late 1930s, the Communist Party had courted Granger as well as other African American reformers and activists like Walter White and A. Philip Randolph. When the United Front effort collapsed, however, Granger and others were attacked "with a fury unparalleled in the two decades of Communist activity around the Negro question" (Record, 1951, p. 186). The party denounced Granger as a paid agent of President Roosevelt, who, they alleged, was only courting African Americans to cultivate support for the war. Ironically, these attacks against leaders who were fighting for expanded job opportunities and social equality further distanced many African Americans from the Communist Party. When summoned before the HUAC, Granger explained the dilemma he faced:

> Authentic Negro leadership in this country finds itself confronted by two enemies on opposite sides. One enemy is the Communist who seeks to destroy the democratic ideal and practice which constitute the Negro's sole hope of eventual victory in his fight for equal citizenship. The other enemy is that American racist who perverts and corrupts the democratic concept into a debased philosophy of life. (Granger, 1949, p. 315)

END OF THE DECADE: PURGES GATHER MOMENTUM

As the 1940s drew to a close, the web of fear and suspicion aroused by anti-Communist purges ensnared the entire nation. Even elite sanctuaries were not immune. The *Chicago Daily Tribune*, for example, announced that three major universities—Chicago, Harvard, and Columbia—were "hives of communism" (Griffin, 1949). The article named Edith Abbott, a founder of the Children's Bureau and a long-time member of the faculty of the School of Social Service Administration at the University of Chicago, as one of the "most frequent sponsors of Communist fronts." Joseph Matthews, the former Director of Research for HUAC, justified such attacks by arguing that although faculty members like Abbott were not necessarily Communists or even Communist sympathizers, "they do the work of communism . . . [out of a] sense of frustration, of unimportance" (quoted in Griffin, 1949, p. 6).

In 1949, the University of California Regents required all professors to sign loyalty oaths pledging nonmembership and nonbelief in any organization advocating the overthrow of the U.S. government. Among the 36 Berkeley faculty who refused to sign the oath and were dismissed was Erik Erikson, a lecturer in the School of Social Welfare since 1946. Dean Milton Chernin and others at the school protested these dismissals and, as treasurer of the Faculty Committee of Assistance to Nonsigners, Chernin raised funds for their legal defense. The MSW student organization also raised donations and circulated petitions. Finally, in 1953, the California Supreme Court ruled the oath unconstitutional and the 36 faculty were offered reinstatement (Terrell, 1994, p. 27).

In the late 1940s, Eduard Lindeman, a well-known scholar and professor at the Columbia University School of Social Work, was accused of disloyalty for his civil rights activities and his attacks on McCarthyites for eroding the nation's civil liberties. He was also a target because during World War II, Lindeman had headed a committee on Democracy in Trade Unions for the American Civil Liberties Union (ACLU, 1943, p. 52). He was outspoken on the role of an informed citizenry in the preservation of democracy and the assurance of human needs through the welfare state (Lindeman, 1948). Among his faculty colleagues, however, only Alfred Kahn defended him when he was attacked. In the words of one observer, "the rest of Columbia crapped out" (Chaiklin, personal communication, 1997).

Although many social work faculty and students equivocated in the face of administrative or governmental repression, others took risks and continued to speak out on controversial issues. Harris Chaiklin, a student in the early 1950s and now a retired University of Maryland professor, recalls that "at least in my experience, there was considerable campus activism among social workers. I was in the School of Social Work at the University of Wisconsin from 1951–1953—many of us were actively involved in everything from working against McCarthy to protesting the Rosenbergs' [trial and execution]" (Chaiklin, personal communication, 1997).

During the McCarthy era, more than 150 college and university teachers appeared before investigating committees. Approximately 100 refused to cooperate and about 65 lost their jobs. Many others resigned under pressure. What is particularly striking "is the extent to which . . . colleagues concurred in their dismissals and, in so doing, essentially helped the investigating committees weed out political undesirables from the academic profession" (Schrecker, 1982, p. 2). This occurred at elite institutions, including those with schools of social work such as the University of California–Berkeley, Columbia, Michigan, New York University, Rutgers, and the University of Washington. Yet there is virtually no mention of these incidents or their consequences in standard histories of the social work profession.

In part, this might reflect retroactive embarrassment over faculty and administrative conduct during these years. Faculty committees ostensibly supported the principle of academic freedom yet, as in Pittsburgh, repeatedly found justifications to violate it. None of those investigated was ever charged with academic misconduct; it was their failure to cooperate that prompted their dismissals (Schrecker, 1986).

> Universities did not have to prove that the professors in question were communists; the professors had to prove that they were not. Not only that, if they had once been, they also had to prove that their "repudiation of party principles" was sincere. . . . It was the faculty hearings themselves . . . that indicated the extent to which the academic community was willing to collaborate with the investigating committees by imposing a political test on its members, a test . . . created by HUAC. (Schrecker, 1982, pp. 14, 16–17).

THE RECONCEPTUALIZATION
OF SOCIAL WORK PRACTICE

The impact of the war and the post-war anti-Communist purges also led social workers to reconceptualize practice in the context of a rapidly changing world. Proponents of the Functional School, like Kenneth Pray, now linked social process—a basic ingredient of practice—with the democratic process. Social work practice, in this view, "validated democracy not on theoretical or humanitarian grounds alone, but in the demonstrable outcomes of its own responsible service of real people in real situations" (Pray, 1946, p. 18). This required social workers to abandon unnecessary allegiance to the status quo and embrace the inevitability, even the desirability, of change (Pray, 1947b). This view could be used by both radicals and their liberal critics to justify their ideological position.

By the mid- and late 1940s, mainstream social work organizations recognized, at least in their public pronouncements, the importance of working *with*, not merely *for*, clients and constituents (AASW, 1944, p. 8). Distinctions persisted, however, between liberal and radical social workers over such fundamental issues as the concept of need. Most mainstream practitioners continued to regard need as residing in the individual, and as requiring professional intervention to facilitate individual adjustment whether through the application of technical skills or the construction of social relationships (Hoffman, n.d.; Pray, 1947).

Even the literature of group work and community organization, whose practitioners strove to obtain professional recognition during this period, employed the language of adjustment and focused on the importance of relationship building, albeit at a larger systems level (Cleveland Federation of Settlements, June 17, 1946; Dunham, 1948; Pray, 1947; Ross, 1954). Radicals, like Bertha Reynolds, Grace Marcus, and Marion Hathway, however, viewed individual, group, community, and societal needs as inextricably connected. The well-being of people, in their view, could not be separated from the overall well-being of the society (Reynolds, 1951; Hathway, March 1948; Marcus, n.d.).

Although settlement houses had long moved away from their earlier radicalism, they still incurred the wrath of anti-Communists. Their support for grassroots neighborhood movements, social action on behalf of public assistance and child welfare legislation, and their promotion of inter-racial, inter-religious, and international cooperation made them suspect. The antidiscrimination provisions adopted after the war by the National Federation of Settlements, which included "political or union affiliation" along with race, creed, marital status, and gender, also set the settlements apart from the conservative climate of the day (Carner, 1945; Cleveland Federation of Settlements, June 17, 1946; The Hull-House Association, 1948; International Institute of Philadelphia, 1947; Letter of Lee Marshall, January 29, 1948; Murray, 1944; National Federation of Settlements, September 14, 1947, p. 1). Similarly, efforts by social workers in the settlements and affiliated organizations on behalf of peace and refugee assistance, particularly in conjunction with the United Nations, aroused the suspicions of anti-Communists (American Friends Service Committee [AFSC], 1950; Williams, 1946).

CONCLUSION

At one moment in the McCarthy era, there were 212 separate pieces of repressive legislation being considered in Congress. Although some were aimed explicitly at Communists, the majority sought to abrogate labor rights. Investigations of Communists and "Communist influences" abounded in state and local legislatures, churches, unions, nonprofit organizations, schools, and universities. Several states enacted unenforceable laws banning Communists from their territories. The governor of Texas proposed the death sentence for Communists. This environment drove the Communist Party underground, isolated the organized left, purged unions and faculties of their most outspoken (and often their most talented) individuals, reduced leftist influence in the civil rights movement, and shattered the left-liberal coalitions that had supported the establishment and expansion of social welfare (Heale, 1998; Schrecker, 1998).

In the decade following World War II, this sharp rightward swing in the U.S. political pendulum had a significant impact on the social work profession. The climate of suspicion, investigation, and ostracism affected all social workers, but particularly those who spoke out on behalf of human rights, peace, and social reform. In the face of such attacks, the organized social work profession largely retreated from its previous advocacy for social justice and focused most of its energies on the process of profession building and the refinement of professional technique. The effort to unite various social work organizations into what became the NASW began at the height of the McCarthy era. This effort was accompanied by a flood of articles that attempted to define professionalism in social work and reflected increasing concern with the profession's public image (Andrews, 1987; Specht & Courtney, 1994; Wenocur & Reisch, 1989). The effects of this reorientation were long-lasting:

> By the time McCarthyism had outlived its usefulness to the Government, American liberalism and radicalism had been permanently weakened, never fully to regain the organized strength they displayed between 1935 and 1945. The once influential [New Deal] coalition had been destroyed, never fully to recover. The activists of the 1960s had to start over from point zero, a new breed with little support from the old. (Dennis, 1981, p. 21)

The insecurity many social workers felt about their jobs combined with the profession's chronic insecurity about losing its tenuous occupational status. Unlike the 1930s or the Progressive Era, when social workers were among the leading spokespersons for dramatic social reforms, social workers in the postwar era became increasingly passive on social issues like civil rights, welfare, and housing:

> Social workers at every level had abandoned the reform impulse and active political engagement that had once been an important component of their profession. As a result, when the issue of welfare returned to the nation's agenda, social workers did not enter the debate on behalf of their clients and counter the hostile stereotyping of welfare recipients. The McCarthy era purges had silenced those voices that might have raised the issues of poverty and unemployment without blaming the victim. (Schrecker, 1998, p. 386)

As the stories in this chapter reveal, the personal consequences of McCarthyism for many social workers were both painful and long lasting. The persecution of social workers during these years was not even limited to active radicals. Mary van Kleeck, a leader in the Rank and File Movement of the 1930s, retired from the Russell Sage Foundation in 1948 after a long and distinguished career yet remained politically active. She backed Henry Wallace's bid for President while herself running unsuccessfully for the New York State Senate on the American Labor Party ticket. Although she was in her seventies, the McCarthy committee subpoenaed van Kleeck in 1953 because of her support for Wallace, her long history of activism, and her leadership during the late 1930s of the Social Workers Committee to Aid Spanish Democracy (Hagen, 1986, p. 727). In hindsight, the dismantling of such so-called front organizations and the left-wing unions in which social workers were actively involved was, perhaps, the most serious tangible consequence of the McCarthy era (Schrecker, 1998).

What are more difficult to assess than the immediate personal consequences of McCarthyism are their long-term effects on the policies of the nation and on public attitudes toward individual and community needs. Without McCarthyism, would a Democratic President have signed a bill ending "welfare as we know it"? Would NASW have virtually acquiesced to such a decision in 1996? Would efforts in the 1990s to reform health care have failed? In fact, would they even have been necessary? Would the idea of privatizing Social Security and utilizing private school vouchers ever have made it onto the political agenda?

The main impact of McCarthyism on social work, therefore, may well have been on what did *not* happen during the postwar era and what, ultimately, cannot be measured: the social reforms that were never implemented, the workers who were never organized into unions, books and articles that were never written or published, the people who were never hired or even considered becoming social workers. Would the profession be better able today to transform its noble rhetoric about social justice into practice, research, and education without the residual fear of political purges?

But not all social workers in the McCarthy era were silent. In the face of very real threats of reprisals and severe professional ostracism, a small but vocal group continued to speak out at professional meetings and in professional journals against injustice and the abrogation of civil liberties. Some who had belonged to organizations now labeled "Communist" maintained their defiance. Others went underground. Still others attempted to separate themselves from Communist affiliations but continued to argue on behalf of their First Amendment right to express their opinions and, in Roosevelt's words, to support "freedom from fear." Their stories, to which we now turn, provide important lessons for the future.

6

Social Work Response
to McCarthyism

*We are faced with a choice between contradictory forces in
our society: those which are moving toward the welfare of
the people, as the people's own concern and responsibility,
and those which destroy human life in preventable misery
and war, and relieve poverty only grudgingly to keep the
privileged position they hold.*
—Bertha Reynolds, *Social Work and Social Living*

*If we as social workers owe anything to our society out of
our professional knowledge and our professional experience,
we owe it our refusal to go along one single inch with this
crusade against Communism abroad and at home; we owe it
our most strenuous, active efforts to prevent the confusion of
the minds of the American people by a propaganda of fear.*
—Grace Marcus, *A Social Work Platform in 1948.*

THE BLACKLISTING OF BERTHA CAPEN REYNOLDS

*I*n 1953, unable to speak at the National Conference of Social Work (NCSW)
in Cleveland because of her political views, Bertha Reynolds gave a paper
entitled "Fear in our Culture," at a meeting of the Cleveland Council of
Arts, Sciences, and Professions that was held during the same week. By now,
Reynolds, once a major figure in social work and social work education, had
been marginalized within the profession. Since her forced resignation from Smith
College in 1938, she had effectively been blacklisted because of her open association with the Communist Party and had scraped out a living as an itinerant
lecturer and teacher.

Although she was aware as early as 1942 that there was a blacklist against
her and was under frequent investigation by federal and state authorities,

Reynolds struggled throughout the 1940s and 1950s to influence social work theory and practice while avoiding damage to sympathetic colleagues.

Despite her tenuous status and precarious financial situation, Reynolds continued to speak out on controversial issues. She described the current scene as "a nightmare of fear, [where] the only remedy . . . is to wake up" (Reynolds, 1953, p. 69). Displaying little patience for those who submitted to fear and who withdrew from political participation in the face of oppressive power, Reynolds chastised those social workers who were unwilling to bring their full intelligence to bear on the issues of the day:

> When every movement for peace is characterized as "communistic," one does not know how to classify the deep longing for peace in practically everyone we meet. Are they all communists, and agents of a foreign power? What is this phantom which is worse than death, so we are told, and yet its followers cannot be convicted of anything more dangerous than believing something and teaching it? Is this against America? Is it wrong even to ask? If we are being robbed of the use of our intelligence . . . we are also victimized by being driven into individual isolation. (p. 71)

Reynolds asserted that the witch hunts and their underlying motives could be defeated if people would just "insist upon a culture we believe in . . . demand our democratic heritage of government of the people, by the people, and *for* the people" (Reynolds, 1953, p. 73). She ended her speech with a call to everyone to make a choice:

> What kind of country will we have? What kind of people will we be, as we live in this most critical time of all history? Once we get into motion with other courageous men and women, fear will dissolve in the outpouring of living energies. The point is to get to work with others, where we are, and now. (p. 74)

One year later, Reynolds met with other like-minded social workers at the annual meeting of the NCSW and helped distribute a pamphlet entitled *McCarthyism vs. Social Work*, which ultimately sold about 1,500 copies (Reynolds, 1963, p. 342). Reynolds's call to action, however, fell largely on deaf ears within the profession. Her writings, once so influential in the development of practice and educational theories, were largely ignored well into the 1960s. Texts on social work practice and social work history made scant reference to her enormous contributions to the field. In increasing obscurity, she continued to write and lecture, although the audience for her progressive vision of social work and social welfare had considerably diminished (Lindsay, 1980; Reisch, 1993b).

Nearly a generation after her speech in Cleveland, radical social workers "rediscovered" her work and convinced NASW to republish many of her books as a means of providing her with financial support in her poverty-stricken old age. A Bertha Reynolds Club was established in New York by progressive social workers, some of them associated with the Communist Party, which ultimately led to the creation of the Bertha Capen Reynolds Society in the mid-1980s. Today, that society, recently renamed the Social Welfare Action Alliance, forms one of the few organizational centers of radical social work in the United States.

THE SURVEY

Although most social workers shunned Bertha Reynolds and others who professed similar ideas during the McCarthy era and wrapped themselves in a veil of profession building, a vocal minority continuously spoke out against McCarthyism and its consequences. By the late 1940s, a few social work journals began to publish articles that criticized the political mood of the times. Most of these pieces were tentative, however, and were often couched in conciliatory language.

Even a relatively progressive publication like Paul Kellogg's *The Survey*, long a voice for social reform in the social welfare field, was influenced by the conservative climate of the postwar era. For example, a December 1949 article by John Fitch, "The CIO and its Communists," reflected the anti-Communist environment of the day in its account of the expulsion of the United Electrical Workers and other left-leaning unions from the CIO because of their "Communist" dominated leadership. Fitch uncritically used such terms as "fellow travelers" and accepted the CIO's underlying rationale for the expulsions: that these unions followed the dictates of the Soviet Union rather than their members. He also failed to place the attack on the unions in the larger context of the Cold War and severely misjudged the long-term impact of the CIO's actions on the U.S. labor movement (Fitch, 1949). One of the purged unions was the United Office and Professional Workers of America (UOPWA), the largest union of social workers in the country.

Yet other pieces in *The Survey* and *The Survey Graphic* were strongly critical of McCarthyism. An article by the historian Louise Brown in the latter asked, "Can this country afford the cost of heresy-hunting?" and concluded that the price included the creation of an intellectual vacuum that could only be filled with fear and hatred (Brown, 1948). Three years later, *The Survey* printed a speech by Paul Hoffman, "The Tyranny of Fear," given at the tenth anniversary celebration of Freedom House. The address appeared to reflect the publication's efforts to carve out a niche in the so-called anti-Communist left:

> The thought control of dictatorships is imposed by force, but discussion, criticism, and debate can be stifled by fear as well as by force. Persecution by public opinion can be as powerful as purges and pogroms. . . . Of late, some of our people . . . have been blindly spreading just this kind of fear. In their zeal to combat communism they have been betrayed into using methods and measures which impair the sources of our strength. . . . They are forcing conformity through fear. . . . They are ready to pillory anyone who holds an unpopular view or supports an unpopular cause. As a result, too many of our

fellow citizens have been afraid to speak out. In far too many cases, decisions, often decisions in high places, have been influenced by fear. In short, the danger of Communist penetration and disruption has been compounded by the spread of panic. All of this in a nation which has grown to greatness and glory because it has recognized the rights of non-conformists and dissenters! (Hoffman, 1951, p. 480).

NATIONAL CONFERENCE ON SOCIAL WELFARE (NCSW)

As the repression of the McCarthy era intensified and deepened, speakers at the NCSW, the leading organizational voice of the social welfare field, began to criticize, if somewhat obliquely, the assault on civil liberties and on advocates of social reform. Its published proceedings, *The Social Welfare Forum*, reflected both the strength of members' convictions and the desire to distinguish the NCSW's views from Communism or "Communist-leaning" ideals. So, although the NCSW became a cautious critic of McCarthyism, like many other liberal organizations of the period, it accepted the basic premise of the McCarthyites that American society and democracy were threatened by external attack and internal subversion.

Nevertheless, some speakers at the NCSW annual meetings forthrightly addressed the implications of McCarthyism for social reform. For example, a 1948 paper by Dr. Julius Schreiber, a physician, linked the current political climate to mental health concerns. He described how persistent political persecution could undermine the mental health of the targets of McCarthyism:

> There are men and women who experience anxiety, intense resentment, and frustration . . . because of the open or concealed threat to their security, should they dare to express what they think; they find that many chest-thumping individuals, waving the flag and braying loudly about their own special brand of "patriotism," hurl at them the angry labels "radicals!" "New Dealers!" "communists!" "fascists!" (Schreiber, 1948, p. 194)

The following year, in a speech on "Civil Rights versus Civil Strife," Benjamin Youngdahl, dean of the School of Social Work at Washington University in St. Louis, remarked that "America would not be great today were it not for the freedom of thought, of expression, of movement, and of association, that has been our heritage" (Youngdahl, 1949, p. 24). He was particularly critical of loyalty oath purges that led many persons to be deemed neither innocent nor guilty of any crime, yet condemned them to "a life of impotence" (p. 28). Many of the 5,000 conference attendees testified in other sessions that freedom of thought was being threatened not only from the outside, but also from within the profession of social work itself (Close, 1949).

That same year, sociologist Louis Wirth urged social workers to take a leadership role in social action despite its "lack of prestige and power:"

One thing we can do . . . [is to] . . . refuse to join in the general hysteria which labels every progressive cause as subversive and thereby stifles every movement, however decent, patriotic, and practical, that touches a vested interest. . . . [L]et those who are responsible for retarding the march of social progress by opposing a comprehensive program of social security and civil right earn their ignoble victory if they must; but let us not hand it to them on a silver platter. . . . [T]his puts a grave responsibility upon professional social workers and others who represent the policymakers in their respective communities and organizations. . . . [S]ocial workers and those who have as their mission in life the improvement of the welfare of all our people might as well recognize that they are in a dangerous occupation. (Wirth, 1949, pp. 18–19)

These presentations, although admirable in their defense of civil liberties and social reform, also illustrate how liberals in the social welfare field strove to distance themselves from radicals inside and outside the profession. At the 1952 NCSW meeting, Youngdahl's address, "What We Believe," made a clear effort to separate Communist philosophy from social work philosophy. He asserted that social work philosophy "is completely incongruent with, in fact the antithesis of, the principles espoused and the methods and procedures used by the Communists in this country and in Russia" (Youngdahl, 1952, p. 32).

Although he acknowledged that social workers and communists often support the same causes, he insisted that "we do not run away from these problems and from our advocacy of proposals to take care of them merely because Communists support them. We must not let the advent of McCarthyism in this country compel us to reject things we really stand for or deny the espousal of programs that we really favor, on which democracy depends" (Youngdahl, 1953, p. 33). Youngdahl warned that social work was in the difficult position of opposing the tenets of Communism on the one hand, while abhorring the anti-Communists who were working so diligently to dismantle the nation's welfare system. Like many other reformers of the era, he recognized "It is not easy to be a non-Communist liberal today" (p. 33; Caute, 1978; Schlesinger, 1949).

Although most social workers supported this political and ideological balancing act, some asserted that its consequences would be far more severe than liberals were willing to admit. At the NCSW's 1953 meeting, Patrick Murphy Malin, Executive Director of the American Civil Liberties Union (ACLU), spoke powerfully of McCarthyism's impact on hiring practices in social work agencies and its suppression of the progressive wing of the social work profession:

Such intolerance and fear are producing the demand that our schools and our social work agencies should be staffed by people who are non-controversial. The result was . . . inconspicuousness having become a qualification for employment in the very professions which ought to have people of light and leadership and imagination and experiment. . . . [I]f you want to preserve your free speech, you speak freely. It is as simple, and as difficult, as that. (Malin, 1953, pp. 35–38)

ATTACK ON SOCIAL GROUP WORK

Social group workers were among the most frequent targets of the attacks Malin described to the NCSW. With roots in the fields of recreation, informal and progressive education, and social work, group work emerged as a distinct arena of social work practice in the 1930s. In 1936, group workers organized the National Association for the Study of Group Work, which, in 1939, became the American Association for the Study of Group Work, and, in 1946, the American Association of Group Workers (AAGW). Like its parent organization, the field of social group work cut across all agency, religious, racial, and even occupational lines. The AAGW focused particularly on advancing the principles and practice of democracy.

During the 1930s and 1940s, these ideals resonated favorably within the profession and the wider society. They complemented the nation's developments in the field of social welfare and appeared in sharp contrast to the spread of fascism abroad. Jewish refugees from Nazi persecution, such as Gisela Konopka and Hans Falck, strengthened the philosophical underpinnings of the field through their emphasis on humanistic values and their passion for democratic participation.

After 1945, building on the work of Grace Coyle, Gertrude Wilson, and others, and borrowing from the earlier essays of Bertha Reynolds, group workers also stressed the importance of mutual aid activities within communities and social service organizations (Simon, 1994). In 1947, Coyle clearly articulated a conception of group work as an instrument of social transformation. Its primary goal, she stated, is to "help in the replacing of the social skills necessary in the present distracted state of the world." These skills included compromise, debate, self-government, democratic leadership, and *resistance to illegitimate authority* (Coyle, 1947, pp. 17–18, emphasis added). These skills were compatible with the long-held conception of group work as "education for democracy through democracy in slow and gradual stages" (Slavson, 1955, p. 33; Lindeman, 1955). This was hardly a radical or revolutionary doctrine, except in the eyes of McCarthyites and their supporters.

Yet, although such views were regarded favorably during the New Deal and World War II, during the McCarthy era they came to be regarded with suspicion. Both inside and outside the social work profession, group workers were considered to be more political and less professional in their orientation (E. Beatt, personal communication, 1995; O. Schmidt, personal communication, 1995). Gertrude Wilson, a faculty member at the University of Pittsburgh in the 1940s and early 1950s, recalls how as a student at the University of Chicago in the 1930s, Sophonisba Breckinridge had urged her to drop her interest in group work as a waste of time for these reasons (Wilson, 1978, p. 34).

Such attitudes flourished in the postwar period. Many social workers perceived group workers as playing a leading role in promoting the acceptance of the "democratic premise within social work." Yet they regarded the field as weak in its development of a clear, unified methodology or theory of practice.

Group workers were considered those social workers who most often worked with the least advantaged segment of the population and who ensured "that the unpopular view gets heard. [They] believe in speaking up, taking issue, and in compromise to the end of agreement and action" (Bruno, 1957, pp. 421–423). It was not surprising, therefore, that a high percentage of social work leaders in the postwar period came from the group work field, despite its minority status within the profession. Nor is it surprising that group workers were the social work profession's first casualty of the Cold War period.

Harold Lewis, a group work student at the University of Pittsburgh in the late 1940s and later dean of Hunter College School of Social Work, reflected on the significance of the attack on group workers. "This was a serious loss," he asserted, "since this method of social work was the most democratic in the profession. The core concept of group work and the goal of its major proponents was participatory democracy. . . . What survived [after the McCarthy period] was the method's narrower function, therapeutic aid" (Lewis, 1992, pp. 41–42).

The attacks on group workers occurred across the country, but particularly in the East and Midwest, where group work had been most influential in the development of community organizations and neighborhood-based services and had been introduced into the curricula of schools of social work. Sometimes the persecution was direct. The FBI openly investigated Lewis and his colleague, Robert Glass, when they were assistant professors of social work at the University of Connecticut for their alleged Communist sympathies. The school's dean and former AAGW President, Harleigh Trecker, staunchly supported them and refused to cooperate with FBI agents. As a result of persistent pressure from the university and repeated personal harassment, however, both Glass and Lewis soon resigned. They, their families, and their colleagues continued to be hounded by the FBI until well into the 1960s (H. Lewis, personal communication, 1995).

Verne Weed, a long-time group worker and, later, a professor of group work at Hunter College, was also forced to defend herself against the accusations of McCarthy's Senate Committee in the early 1950s, the House Un-American Activities Committee (HUAC) in 1956, and even within the social work profession. Weed had become involved in radical social work through the Rank and File Movement while working as a caseworker with the Brooklyn Bureau of Community Services in the 1930s. In 1940, she moved to Connecticut, where she became active in Connecticut Volunteers for Civil Rights while serving as assistant executive director of Children's Services of Connecticut. After being accused as a Communist before HUAC and as an organizer of Communist front organizations raising funds for Smith Act defendants, Weed was attacked by local newspapers as part of the "red menace . . . infiltrating social services [in Connecticut] and preying on vulnerable children" (quoted in Hunter, 1999b, p. 7).

Weed never denied she was a Communist and joked that she "was a Communist and a social worker. . . . I'm not sure which was worse!" She believed that in fighting for peace and justice, she was following in the tradition of social workers like Jane Addams. She recalled, "It was years before I began to recover professionally. . . . Being called a Communist and hauled before the Committee in the middle of my studies did not exactly endear me to the professors or other students . . . most were just plain scared. The profession [was] scared shitless—what were a few red social workers to them" (Hunter, 1999b, p. 7).

As a result of these accusations, Weed lost her job and required the assistance of the state chapter of NASW to receive a year's severance pay (Rosengard, 1986, p. 4). Nevertheless, she remained an outspoken activist throughout her career. Weed was eventually hired by another target of McCarthyism, Harold Lewis, at Hunter College School of Social Work. Until her death in 1986, she served as a key link between radical generations, particularly through her leadership role in the Radical Alliance of Social Service Workers (RASSW) in the 1970s. (See Chapter 9.) She never regretted her powerful resistance to the anti-Communist hysteria of the times:

> When McCarthy attacked me for signing the Stockholm Peace Appeal, I refused to go on the defensive and reaffirmed my opposition to the A-bomb. When I was attacked as a Communist in connection with the Connecticut Smith Act trial I didn't capitulate to tremendous pressure from some NASW chapter members. (Weed, 1985, p. 84)

Nor were group workers like Weed immune from the political fixation of the era to compel individuals with suspect political backgrounds to "name names." Ira Krasner, an activist and group worker since the 1930s, joined the social work faculty at Wayne State University in Detroit in 1951. While there, he worked with several progressive organizations to oppose the efforts of Michigan Representative, Kit Clardy, to investigate Communism on campus.

Later in the decade, Krasner went to Amsterdam on a Fulbright fellowship to assist a Dutch school of social work in the development of its social group work curriculum. After one year, he was recommended for a United Nations fellowship. At that time, he received a 42-page dossier listing all the meetings he had attended throughout his career that had been sponsored by progressive organizations. He was then asked to describe his knowledge and involvement with 20 people who were listed in the dossier. Krasner refused, withdrew his application for the fellowship, and returned to the United States. When he got back to Wayne State, Charles Brink, the school's dean informed Krasner that an FBI agent had interviewed him about Krasner's membership in the ACLU, an organization, the agent commented, "known to be infiltrated with communists" (I. Krasner, personal communication, 1995).

Sometimes, the attacks on group workers took on elements of the absurd. Saul Bernstein, President of the AAGW from 1948 to 1950, recalled an experience while he was teaching at the New York School of Social Work (now Columbia University). An article he had submitted was accepted for publication in an anthology about group work. He subsequently learned that the editor was contemplating withdrawing his essay because a faculty member at City College, who also happened to be named Saul Bernstein, was suspected of being a Communist. Bernstein immediately "wrote an angry letter to the editor insisting that she be more careful about such things . . . why should my assumed membership in the Communist Party be allowed to reject the paper?" (S. Bernstein, personal communication, 1995).

Sometimes, however, the effects of McCarthyism were far more serious. Sherman Labovitz, a group worker and Communist Party organizer, was arrested in the middle of the night on June 29, 1953, and spent a month in solitary confinement in Holmesburg Prison, one of nine Philadelphians charged under the Smith Act for advocating the violent overthrow of the government. High bail was posted for Labovitz and he initially had no legal counsel.

Finally, the vice chancellor of the Philadelphia Bar Association, Thomas McBride, one of the city's most renowned criminal defense attorneys, took the case and defended Labovitz and others on First Amendment grounds. None of the defendants was actually charged with "personally advocating the overthrow of the government, much less engaging in or even discussing acts of violence. Their crime . . . was their membership in a legal political party which (so its accusers claimed) favored the overthrow of the government if it became oppressive (kind of like the Declaration of Independence)" (Guinther, 1999, p. 5).

Nevertheless, Labovitz and his codefendants were convicted after a 10-week trial and, in July 1955, he was sentenced to two years in prison. He never went to prison, however, and in November 1957, after a Supreme Court ruling in the defendants' favor, an appeals court ordered him acquitted. Since 1969, Labovitz has taught social welfare and social work at Richard Stockton College in New Jersey where he is now professor emeritus. He is still "a staunch advocate of socialism," although he severed his connection with the Communist Party in 1957 (Labovitz, 1997; Slobodzian, 1997, pp. E1, E4).

By the late 1940s, leading group workers warned their social work colleagues that the attacks on one branch of the profession threatened to undermine the broader purposes that were shared by diverse practitioners in many fields. At the 1947 AAGW conference, Nathan Cohen strongly defended the preservation of an activist orientation among group workers. Speaking in opposition to recent restrictions on social action imposed on local agencies by Community Chests, he argued, "We [must] make clear that it is not possible to have social work as we understand it without a democratic climate." Cohen urged group workers to be active at all levels of society. The challenge, he stated, is clear: social action or reaction (Cohen, 1947, pp. 8–11).

In a similar vein, that year, the AAGW changed the name of its Legislative Committee to the Social Action Committee, with the specific intention of encouraging programs of education around social issues as well as action. Such actions would include "corporate action, as well as individual effort . . . to secure social legislation to meet [the] problems of adverse social and economic conditions." Potential targets included such diverse fields as housing, health care, child welfare, youth work, and minority rights (AAGW, 1947, pp. 3–6). Two years later, at the NCSW annual conference, Grace Coyle reflected on the serious nature of the times: "We have been born into a generation confronted with social issues so momentous that they stagger our imaginations, and will render us helpless unless we can achieve some sense of social perspective" (Close, 1949, p. 380).

Gertrude Vaile stated a similar sentiment clearly at the same 1949 NCSW conference:

> The goal of all those who desire to achieve a society where each individual has equal rights . . . and an opportunity to participate in decision making . . . is an inter-professional undertaking involving teachers, clergy, doctors, lawyers, business and industrial leaders, labor leaders, recreational leaders, social workers, and all citizens. Neither social workers nor social group workers carry this responsibility alone. . . . We have faith in the capacity of human beings to develop a basis of world wide cooperative living only because we have experienced human relationships in effective groups. No human being develops faith in isolation from others. Faith is the result of a reciprocal process. (Ross, 1949, p. 382)

By the early 1950s, the situation Coyle and Vaile described had grown more serious. Settlement houses, long home to many group workers, were under constant attack by political investigators and the media. Summarizing the situation in its 1952 annual report, the National Federation of Settlements acknowledged the climate of fear:

> Intercultural tensions were heightened in 1952 by the climate of distrust and fear that was created by Senator McCarthy and by his counterparts in local communities. . . . Many settlement neighbors participated in groups which seemed progressive and constructive during depression days, but which have now been listed . . . as "subversive." . . . Newspaper reports of people losing their jobs because of such associations and questions that they themselves have faced, create a kind of timidity and fear that is quite out of keeping with the traditional American freedom we all cherish. . . . Settlement neighbors perhaps feel this more keenly than some others. Some of them know that kind of fear before they came here and in many instances it was the reason for their coming . . . this climate of fear is probably the most "un-American" thing with which settlement workers have had to deal. (National Federation of Settlements, 1952, pp. 3–4)

By the mid-1950s one consequence of these persistent attacks was the shift in the primary emphasis of group work away from broader social and political objectives toward the "enabling" of clients and the therapeutic function of groups. Yet, a minority of group workers, like Coyle and Wilson, continued to stress the importance of social issues. Others wrote of the need to preserve group work's sense of moral values and concern for the democratic climate, even as group workers strove to create a more scientific basis for their practice (Bruno, 1957, pp. 425–427). The demise of the journal *Survey* in 1952 exacerbated this trend because no other publication emerged to fill this void. As a result, "the attachment of the profession as a whole to broad social action was irrevocably weakened" in a climate that was hostile to both social criticism and social reform (Chambers, quoted in Trattner, 1995, pp. 308–309).

In this politically and professionally hostile environment, group work leaders like Harleigh Trecker (1955) argued that the key to its survival lay in the creation of closer theoretical and practical linkages to social work as a whole, in clarifying the role of the group worker in various practice settings, in recruiting more students into group work, and in helping shape the public's perception of group work services (pp. 383–385). This would require the development of "a more realistic approach to the use of group work" in social change activities, such as legislative action, and a reexamination of the connections of group work to the settlement house movement and the public social services (pp. 408–409).

At the end of the decade, William Schwartz (1959), one of the leading theoreticians in the group work field, traced the crisis in group work to the political and cultural climate of the day in which "the group experience stands accused of creating both conformity [e.g., groupthink, the organization man] and rebellion [e.g., juvenile delinquency, radical political activity]" (p. 127). Groups, he argued, were feared as somehow dangerous and subversive and "the theory and practice of social group work have been trapped, to an extent, by the pessimism of the time" (p. 127).

Schwartz argued that group work was in the midst of a transition to a new identity. Like Trecker, he maintained that this would be accomplished through the development of a new interpretation of the group work function and a merger of group work into the larger social work profession and generic social work methods. Although Schwartz acknowledged "the group will always be the most potent instrument of social change" (Schwartz, 1959, p. 137), the type of change he envisioned foresaw a role for group workers as socializing or civilizing agents acting within professional organizations, rather than instruments of community power and social action. Since the 1950s, however, group workers have discovered that, in most ways, this "merger" worked against them. Group work articles were not published in the new journal, *Social Work*. And, until its recent resurgence, the group work method virtually disappeared in schools of social work.

Thus, McCarthyism affected the character of group work—and through its impact on group work, the entire social work field—long after the anti-Communist fervor of the McCarthy period began to subside. From the mid-1950s to the 1980s, social group work was "increasingly identified with the therapeutic emphasis in social casework, rather than with the developmental task-oriented and advocacy orientation [of an earlier era]" (Austin, 1986, p. 32). In schools of social work, group work came to be regarded as "part of an inclusive direct services, treatment or clinical social work practice methods" approach, instead of being considered a distinct and separate method of intervention as it had been in the 1930s and 1940s (Austin, 1986).

These vignettes highlight the ways in which group work, the most embattled element of the social work profession, began to respond to McCarthyism.

Group work's focus on democracy, mutuality, community participation, tolerance, and cooperation, and the left-leaning politics of many of its practitioners, made group workers particularly vulnerable to attack (Northen, 1994). There is also the possibility that anti-Semitism played a role, given the high proportion of Jews among social group workers. Progressive group workers recognized that, if left unchecked, the climate of fear, persecution, suspicion, and conservatism could destroy all that social workers professed.

While some radicals, like Reynolds, Weed, Glass, Krasner, Fisher, Hathway, and Lewis, maintained their beliefs despite the consequences to their careers, most social workers and social work educators criticized the effects of McCarthyism but were careful to shield themselves from any suggestions that they could have Communist leanings. They argued forcefully that civil liberties should be preserved and that the issues important to social work should not be abandoned merely because Communists also supported these causes. Yet, by accepting the basic premises of McCarthyism, the liberal reformist wing of the profession was complicit in the repression produced by the anti-Communist fervor of the period and bears some of the responsibility for its consequences.

VOLUNTARY SECTOR

Because group workers had played a major role in voluntary sector social service and community-based agencies since the 1930s, the persecution of suspected radical group workers had a particularly dramatic effect on these organizations. Here, the attack on social action and community participation implicit in McCarthyism had several long-lasting consequences. It affected the relationship between professionals and volunteers in voluntary sector agencies, the agencies' definition of their clients, and the focus of services within the agencies themselves (Wagner, 1999).

Well-established nonprofit agencies frequently abetted or failed to resist the anti-Communist climate of the period. Staff with suspected leftist politics were dismissed, agency executives volunteered information to investigators from the FBI and HUAC, and funding for social action programs was slashed (Brilliant, 1990; Surveys, personal communication, 1997; Trolander, 1987). The prestigious Jewish Board of Guardians (JBG) and the Bureau of Child Welfare in New York, who were providing services to the sons of Ethel and Julius Rosenberg and co-defendant Morton Sobell, cooperated with the government and even tried to have the Rosenberg children removed from the custody of their family and foster parents (Meeropol & Meeropol, 1975). To his credit, however, Herschel Alt, the Director of JBG and coguardian of the Rosenberg children, refused to release their case files to the FBI when requested to do so for investigative purposes (Reynolds, 1963, p. 342, n. 24; A. Schwartz, personal communication, 1997).

Voluntary sector agencies already had begun to modify staffing patterns between professionals and volunteers in the aftermath of World War II. The inward-looking drive for professionalization within social work inspired by the conservatism of the McCarthy era compelled these agencies to clarify such issues as the role of volunteers and the nature of board–staff relationships. Professionals, many of whom were trained as group workers, especially in settlement houses and the Jewish federation field, were given control over direct service functions, administration, supervision, and training. Community-based volunteers were relegated to nonprofessional duties and, with the exception of board membership, were denied a role in agency policy making or resource allocation decisions. In addition, boards of directors increasingly came to be dominated by upper-class individuals who no longer lived in the community in which the agency was located. Although this might have made sense for political or fund-raising purposes, it contradicted the long-standing spirit of group work to use agencies and their programs as training grounds for democratic participation (Brilliant, 1990; Reisch & Wenocur, 1983). At the same time, voluntary social service agencies shifted their client base from low-income to middle- and upper-income groups, whose needs were more likely to be defined as "problems of adjustment" rather than problems of socioeconomic disadvantage. Although demographic changes, such as the growth of suburbs and the expansion of public welfare contributed substantially to this new emphasis, the desire of agencies to acquire and maintain a higher status among elite sponsors by serving a more politically acceptable clientele also played a major role (Axinn & Stern, 2000; Ehrenreich, 1985).

This "disengagement from the poor" (Cloward & Ohlin, 1960) complemented the political–economic goals of the social work profession as it struggled to define its place in the changing occupational hierarchy of the United States (Wenocur & Reisch, 1989). It also reflected the growth of a consumer-oriented, service-dominated economy, in which the problems of affluence, rather than poverty, became a focus of concern (Galbraith, 1958; Lasch, 1977). In a future characterized by the "end of ideology" (Bell, 1960), technical discussions and market-influenced mechanisms would supplant philosophical debates about the direction of U.S. society. Consequently, social workers in voluntary agencies became more concerned with fund-raising techniques and board development than with methods of promoting community participation and development. As a result, the leaders of these agencies were largely unprepared for the wave of community and social activism that swept urban America in the 1960s (Reisch & Wenocur, 1983).

DRIVE FOR PROFESSIONALIZATION

The impact of the McCarthy era on social work was more severe, if not more visible, than on some other occupational groups. There were several reasons for this. Social workers primarily served poor and oppressed populations, whose very existence belied the bombastic patriotism of McCarthyites and gave credibility to the political forces anti-Communists were trying to repress. As the experience of Charlotte Towle demonstrated, social workers espoused democratic values, societal obligations, and human rights that in the political climate of the period were frequently construed as "socialistic" and foreign. The emphasis on self-determination at the heart of social work practice and on democratic participation in social group work and community organization appeared threatening in an era that promoted conformity, unquestioning patriotism, and allegiance to the status quo.

In response to persistent attacks, some social work leaders developed an effective strategy of reframing the issues raised by their opponents: from the *threat of Communism* to the *threat to democracy*. They emphasized the defense of the newly established public welfare system and its clients, under constant assault by conservatives. Correspondence on these themes frequently appeared in the late 1940s and 1950s in *The Social Welfare Forum, The Survey*, and *The Survey Graphic* (Andrews & Reisch, 1997).

The oppressive environment of the 1950s also pushed the social work profession to look inward and to define its basic concepts more clearly. In part, this was a response to what Joseph Anderson, future executive director of NASW, euphemistically termed the "present challenge"—the attack on the philosophy and principles that lay at the foundation of the entire U.S. social welfare system (Anderson, 1951). Acknowledging that many of the attacks stemmed from fear, Anderson tried to respond to criticisms of social welfare as socialistic by staking out a middle ground:

> Too many people have reached the conclusion that there are only two choices before us: One is that we must have a society which offers security with no freedom, such as the totalitarian states offer. The other choice is to have freedom but little security, and that is what people say democracy offers. Social workers say that there is another choice, which is that we have a democratic society where government can preserve freedom and personal initiative and a democratic way of life and still have the government discharge responsibility in helping to meet the health and welfare needs of all the people. (p. 56)

Anderson's advocacy of government responsibility for social welfare, minimum standards of health, welfare and educational services, universal services, and expanded opportunity for the poor (rather than moral reform) was, in essence, a defense of the New Deal (Anderson, 1951, p. 57). Yet he failed to acknowledge that it was precisely their association with New Deal principles and policies that led to attacks on social workers by the McCarthy forces. The support of such concepts as public welfare, civil rights, and democracy were regarded as signs of communist leanings. There was little to distinguish the basic concepts Anderson articulated from those Charlotte Towle had been vilified for six years earlier.

Like Anderson, some social workers agreed with the McCarthyites that there existed a strong and well-organized Communist Party. They insisted, however, that people must still be allowed to speak out against social evils and engage in social action. They argued that social responsibility, professionalism, and patriotism were not incompatible, despite the attempts of many politicians to equate social reform and socialism.

During the mid- and late 1950s mainstream leaders of the profession and major social work organizations attempted to define a role for social action while avoiding the twin risks of political attack and public approbation. They did this in several ways. Under Anderson's leadership, the AASW published a pamphlet entitled "How to Influence Public Policy: A Short Manual on Social Action" (Wickenden, 1954). It defended social action as an essential feature of democratic government while emphasizing the importance of the rule of law, the virtues of compromise, and the distinctions between democratic and totalitarian political philosophies. The role of social workers in social action, however, was to serve "as the link between a vast array of social institutions and the individuals they serve" rather than as the advocate for disadvantaged groups. In other words, it was the technical skill of the social worker in "pointing up [the] inadequacies of our social machinery" and not the worker's ideological commitment that was of critical importance. This was consistent with the emerging view in politics and the social sciences that the problems of contemporary society were technical rather than ideological (Bell, 1960; Galbraith, 1958).

Second, social action was to occur primarily through the vehicle of the professional organization itself. This involved not only attempting to influence the public and political decisionmakers but also "eternal vigilance by the profession in policing itself" (NASW, 1958, p. 1). The protective cover of professional organizations, it was believed, could help social workers overcome their "disinclination to take stands on controversial matters which may evoke adverse reactions . . . a remnant of the era of restriction and fear which is still fresh in our memories and whose consequences linger as inhibitors of social action" (Solender, 1957, p. 15).

Third, successful social action required social workers to overcome both "the low status which society assigns to politics and political activity" and "a sense of professional insecurity" emerging out of a fear of being labeled "impractical idealists" and of repeating "previous unsatisfactory experiences" (Solender, 1957, pp. 15–18). These problems could be solved through enhanced interagency cooperation, the promotion of leadership development by professional organizations like NASW, and "greater attention to the intellectual side of [social work] and the substantive knowledge upon which it draws" (de Schweinitz, 1956, p. 3; Solender, 1957). Schools of social work, Grace Coyle wrote, have the dual function of providing students with the requisite knowledge and skills to engage "in the new area of policymaking in its social, political and economic aspects," and of teaching "a social philosophy and a system of values related to the kind of society we desire" (Coyle, 1958, pp. 21–22).

In another era, the rationality and strength of conviction behind these arguments might have influenced public opinion. The McCarthy period, however, was characterized by a retreat from reason. Ironically, by attempting to distance the social work profession from contemporary radicalism inside and outside the profession, social work leaders like Anderson inadvertently separated social workers from their radical past and from the broad-based coalitions that supported precisely the reforms they desired. This made the field more, rather than less, vulnerable to partisan attack.

It is understandable that social workers would attempt to reconceptualize the profession as a defense against an increasingly repressive environment. Yet, for most social workers, McCarthyism did not inspire a renewed, if redefined, commitment to social reform. A more common response was to retreat from social reform and adopt a growing interest in professionalization. A major focus of such efforts was the formation of the NASW in 1955.

Much of the literature on professions and professionalism, inside and outside social work, emerged during the 1950s, largely written from a structural–functionalist perspective. Authors rationalized the growth of professionalization within social work and, much like Abraham Flexner had 40 years before (Flexner, 1915), defined the primary components of a profession as the acquisition of scientific–technical expertise and skills and an inwardly directed ethical code (Greenwood, 1957; Lubove, 1965). "This image [of professions] justifie[d] the proposition that professionals represent an intellectual status group or class which can guide the public interest because they somehow operate beyond the bounds of [class interests]" (Wenocur & Reisch, 1983, p. 692). Professionalism thus simultaneously denied the existence of class divisions within society while rewarding a particular occupation for its specific expertise.

Ironically, the drive for professionalization within social work diminished, rather than expanded, the profession's attention to the public interest through social reform activities. The growing emphasis on services to individuals, instead of groups, contributed to the reduction in clients' "ability to collectively define problems, needs, and roles, and . . . potentially to [influence] the demand for certain kinds of benefits or services" (Wenocur & Reisch, 1983, pp. 714–715). By reducing clients' control over services, professionalization directly contradicted the democratic ideal that had guided the social work field for decades. As illustrated by the Council on Social Work Education's *Curriculum Study* (1959), professionalization encouraged conformity, instead of diversity, in practice models, theoretical perspectives, and program designs.

Another aspect of the professionalizing impulse was the growing emphasis on the acquisition of technical expertise as the primary goal of social work education and practice. This was accompanied by the omission of any discussions of the ideological or political bases of practice. Evidence for this shift can be found in textbooks written during and after the McCarthy period, books that shaped a whole generation of practitioners and teachers.

These texts provided "a definition of practice skills based on conceptions of the political and social order without necessarily [explicating] the [author's] ideological foundation" (Ephross & Reisch, 1982, p. 277). By ignoring the impact of McCarthyism and its underlying political and ideological subtexts, social work educators contributed to the growing dissonance between the stated social justice goals of social work practice and the conditions practitioners experienced in their daily work. Some social work leaders expressed concern about this trend in the late 1950s.

Alvin Schorr, who would later become the dean of New York University's School of Social Work and director of the Community Services Society in New York City, decried the spread of "the cult of the technician" (Schorr, 1959, p. 29). Ginsberg and Miller commented that "the concern with and necessity for developing method and process disposes people to neutralism" (1957, p. 1). This apolitical legacy persisted well into the 1970s despite the ideological turmoil of the intervening decade.

The emphasis on professionalization also obscured the personal and social effects of the political climate. As a result, many social workers displayed no more than intellectual curiosity about McCarthyism (E. Beatt, personal communication, 1995). This aroused considerable concern among some social work leaders, like Lester Granger. In his Presidential address to the 1952 NCSW conference, Granger acknowledged the importance of the professionalization of social work and its commitment to the codification of professional standards and practices. Yet he was concerned that by ignoring the political environment social workers would not be prepared to deal with its effects. Granger lamented,

> We in social work have been so occupied with learning our own way . . . that we have seldom been able to offer guidance and reassurance to our even more bewildered public. We have developed standards of professional practice . . . but frequently these standards have had slight relationship to professional resources and have been considered . . . as having little validity. And, often, as we have defined our standards of practice, we have seen our practitioners' resources swept away by careless, brutish action of half-informed legislators and incompetent administrators. (Granger, 1952, p. 11)

For African American social workers like Granger the retreat from social action presented a particularly vexing problem. Even after the Supreme Court's 1954 decision in the Brown case and the desegregation of such varied institutions as the armed forces and organized baseball in the postwar era, segregation among the staff and clients of social service agencies persisted. The failure of social workers to follow suit, one critic charged, "place[d] the democratic goal in double jeopardy. [It denied] service to certain people and by so doing, set a low tone for community activity toward integration" (Berry, 1955, p. 3).

LEGACY OF MCCARTHYISM

The climate of fear and political persecution during the McCarthy period diminished the gains the social work profession had made in the 1930s and 1940s through its participation in progressive coalitions. Nevertheless, some social workers persisted in their defense of social welfare programs (Dunn, 1952; Granger, 1952; Youngdahl, 1952). After McCarthy's censure by the Senate in 1954, it became somewhat safer to speak out in favor of public welfare and other social reforms. It is important to point out, however, that political persecution and the repression of unpopular views continued inside and outside the profession well into the 1960s. (See Chapter 7.)

The attacks against radicals left the profession ill prepared to respond to the resurgence of social activism of the 1960s and 1970s. Many of the domestic political issues that dominated the post–World War II decade—such as civil liberties and academic freedom, advocacy for the poor and the oppressed, and support for politically unpopular positions—continue to challenge social workers today. In a very real sense, today's struggles against political ideologies and cultural mindsets that are fundamentally anti–social work in their orientation are reminiscent of those of the McCarthy era. For this reason, it is important to recall the history of that period as a reminder that such persecutions could happen again. The vignettes in this chapter represent stories of fear and defeat, but also of strength, courage, and persistence. They illustrate that the fate of social work is intimately bound to the political, economic, and social philosophy of our society.

Reflecting on this experience 40 years later, Ira Krasner stated that while his political philosophy is "deeply rooted in the class struggle and the importance of socialism. . . . Social work, in the main, has moved away from social change and is more vested in treatment modalities." He saw distinct parallels between the McCarthy era and the climate of the 1990s:

> We should have learned from McCarthyism that there would be a time when it would return. . . . I think we are witnessing that today in terms of the religious right and the conservative movement and the control of Congress by the Republicans. . . . We fought McCarthyism in the '40s and '50s and into the '60s, but today, by and large, our students are not prepared from schools of social work to understand the coming power that is being developed by the conservatives and the religious right. And social workers in general are not adequately prepared to deal with the coming onslaught. (I. Krasner, personal communication, 1995)

Not all social workers shared the perspective of Krasner and his progressive contemporaries about the negative effects of McCarthyism on the practice of social work. Many truly feared Communism. Maybel Berg, a public welfare worker in Minnesota, felt that the "hunt for communists was good, but it eventually went too far" (M. Berg, personal communication, 1995). Her colleague, Jane Foster, believed that there were subversive activities that needed to be stopped, but that "innocent people were hurt" (J. Foster, personal communication, 1995). Both asserted that the height of the McCarthy era, the 1950s, was a good time for the social work profession.

University of Maryland professor Paul Ephross places McCarthyism in another aspect of the broader historical context. He points out that the McCarthy era was "also a period during which we progressive people learned a lot about the horrors of Stalin. When the former [McCarthy] had been shot down, the latter knowledge remained, only to be reinforced by other revelations" (P.

Ephross, personal communication, 1995). Although Ephross maintains that there was a legitimate concern about Communism in the postwar period, he acknowledges that one of the legacies of McCarthyism "is a fear of being found ideologically incorrect, even in the future. . . . [This] I believe is still at work today. . . . [I]t began the habit of viewing speakers as disloyal, or un-American, or something terrible, because the rest of us don't like their words or their opinions" (P. Ephronss, personal communication, 1995).

By dividing the progressive and liberal communities, McCarthyism fractured the New Deal coalition that had served as the political foundation for the creation and expansion of the U.S. welfare state in the 1930s and 1940s. It helped delay the expansion of Social Security and public welfare benefits and blocked the passage of a national health program, as proposed by President Truman. It severely weakened the power of the labor movement in U.S. politics and the influence of unionism within the social work field. It fostered a climate of opinion that shaped American intellectual and cultural life until the mid-1960s and even beyond. It made possible the rise of conservative ideologies and the discrediting of government as a potential vehicle to solve persistent economic and social problems. Its consequences continue to be felt today.

McCarthyism also imposed a climate of official or self-censorship that influenced the nation's intellectual and cultural life for nearly two decades and that some activists believe persists to this day. (See Chapter 10.) It led many liberal social workers to turn against radical colleagues to distance themselves from the wrath of anti-Communists. Just as individual social workers feared losing their jobs, the social work profession experienced a form of collective anxiety over its tenuous occupational and political status. Consequently, most social workers became increasingly passive on social issues because "to propose a measure to relieve poverty or to combat racism was to risk being called 'communist'" (Ehrenreich, 1985, p. 142).

Although in many ways unique, the McCarthy period reflected political and ideological tendencies similar to those of previous eras. Throughout its history, the United States has periodically experienced times of antiradicalism, xenophobia, fear, and political hysteria. Political leaders often have used repressive tactics to intimidate opponents and to solve alleged crises of social disintegration. Yet "the idea that systems of 'order maintenance' rarely get dismantled after the crisis that provoked them has eased, has not penetrated the public historical imagination" (Belfrage, 1989, p. xvi).

Although a minority of social workers in the McCarthy era took great risks to fight for social justice, many of their colleagues stood by in silence and publicly retreated from progressive stands in the face of political or professional threats. The current chair of the Social Welfare Action Alliance, formerly the Bertha Capen Reynolds Society, Fred Newdom, concludes that "social work's progressive roots only seem to flourish in the sunlight. When darkness overtakes the land, we hunker down and neither curse that darkness nor light a candle" (Newdom, 1993, p. 77).

As Newdon implies, witch hunts and the persecution of radical social workers did not end with Joseph McCarthy's demise. During the 1960s and early 1970s, long regarded as an era of social upheaval, social workers were largely unprepared to capitalize on the changing political climate. With a few notable exceptions, they did not establish coalitions with low-income groups, communities of color, and labor unions that could have moved the field of social welfare and the profession as a whole in a more progressive direction. To a considerable extent, the failure to take this alternate path was a consequence of the purges and persecution of the McCarthy period. It is to that lost opportunity that we now turn.

7

Revival of Radicalism in Social Work

The whole world is watching, the whole world is watching
—Antiwar protesters outside the 1968 Democratic
Party Convention in Chicago

NATIONAL WELFARE RIGHTS ORGANIZATION (NWRO) VERSUS THE NATIONAL CONFERENCE ON SOCIAL WELFARE (NCSW)

In late May 1969, the National Conference on Social Welfare (NCSW) held its 96th annual meeting at the Hilton Hotel in New York. Long the liberal voice of social work and social welfare in the United States, the NCSW found itself floundering in the late 1960s—both financially and philosophically—as it struggled to find a niche for the profession in a rapidly changing political environment. Under considerable pressure from activists in the field, it created a Social Action Task Force in November 1968 to draft a social action platform for the organization. Conference planners even scheduled a social action forum for the evening of May 27 at which resolutions offered by the National Federation of Settlements and Neighborhood Centers, the recently formed National Association of Black Social Workers (NABSW), the National Federation of Student Social Workers (NFSSW), and the NWRO would be considered. The opening plenary session, however, demonstrated how large a gap had emerged by the late 1960s between liberal and radical forces within the profession.

The scheduled keynote speaker was Livingston Wingate, whose address was titled "Community Control: Principles and Implications for Practice." In the *Daily Bulletin* announcing the keynote was a "Greetings to the Conference" column from President Richard Nixon, whose message stated, "Only the combined energies and creative talents of millions of committed Americans . . . can successfully build the bridge we seek from dependency to dignity. Only an

135

all-out effort such as this can close the unfortunate gap between black and white, affluent and needy, dissenter and traditionalist" (NCSW, May 27, 1969).

Before Wingate's speech, George Wiley, a former professor of chemistry and the founder and head of the NWRO, was scheduled to give a brief presentation asking the sympathetic audience for financial support. Before Wiley could speak, however, the agenda called for numerous other speakers to discuss a broad range of issues. The women who dominated the NWRO board grew impatient, in part because of their frustration over the failure of NCSW to meet their demand to waive the conference registration fee. They decided to practice the confrontational tactics that had catapulted their organization to national prominence.

One of their leaders, Beulah Sanders, shouted "Block the doors!" The audience was stunned. Johnnie Tillmon, national chair of NWRO, announced, "We demand $35,000 or you're not going to leave this room." With the help of supporters from NABSW, the student-based Social Welfare Workers Movement (SWWM), and the newly formed Women of the American Revolution, NWRO members blocked the exits and demanded that each delegate contribute a $1 "poor people's surcharge" (NWRO flyer, May 1969). Several fights broke out. Only police intervention enabled the delegates to escape (Clendenin, 1969; Kotz & Kotz, 1977, p. 281).

The next evening about 300 NWRO members, aided by supporters from NABSW and SWWM, again attempted to take over the conference. Wiley exhorted the audience to stop talking about outdated proposals and to "get behind the recipients [of welfare]." Meanwhile, women from NWRO circulated throughout the hall and collected nearly $2,000 in donations (Taubman & Polster, 1969).

The NWRO's pressure tactics succeeded in part: The NCSW gave $35,000 to support summer interns from schools of social work to address poverty-related issues. The NWRO later claimed that the conference had voted to raise an equivalent sum to bring 250 welfare recipients to the 1970 conference in Chicago (NWRO, May 1969). NCSW officials disputed this claim and eventually provided only $4,000 to the NWRO for this purpose (Boehm, 1970). Whether NCSW had abrogated its agreement with NWRO became a subject of contention at the Chicago event the following year (Boehm, 1970; Prunty, 1970; Horchow, 1970).

The takeover of the 1969 conference, however, provided the NWRO with media coverage that boosted its flagging fortunes. On the final day of the conference, social workers joined about 500 NWRO members in a march from Times Square to the city's garment district to hold a demonstration against Sears Roebuck, which had refused to provide $150 in credit to NWRO members: "Social workers burned their Sears credit cards in a display of unity with the NWRO campaign-boycott," the NWRO's newspaper declared (NWRO, May 1969). Yet, as Willard Richan later pointed out, activists quickly discovered that "to take over the Conference was to take over very little of real consequence for social welfare" (1973, p. 150).

This incident revealed a deep and irreconcilable split between radical activists inside and outside the social work profession and their erstwhile liberal allies, recalling the divisions in the social welfare field that emerged during the 1930s. Although individual social workers were directly and indirectly involved with activist groups like NWRO, the split reflected serious divisions over strategy, tactics, and philosophy, wrapped in the language and symbols of the racial, class, and gender politics of the period. It demonstrated the difficulty, if not the impossibility, of social work becoming a truly radical profession (Rein, 1970).

The NWRO takeover of the 1969 NCSW conference marked the high water of social welfare radicalism in the 1960s. Yet it occurred while the legacy of McCarthyism continued to haunt the social work profession. Consequently, throughout the 1960s the profession was besieged by political attacks from both ends of the ideological spectrum. Conservatives continued to persecute progressive social workers through media attacks, legislative inquiries, and the lingering professional blacklist, while radical activists denounced the profession as a tool of social control of the poor and oppressed. To understand how so much could change so rapidly, it is necessary to examine the historical context that shaped radical social work during this tumultuous decade.

BACKGROUND TO THE WAR ON POVERTY

Between 1940–1960, economic growth, a progressive income tax, and modestly redistributive social policies provided many Americans with a better life and hope for a brighter future. The Gross National Product increased over 150% and unemployment ranged between 3–5%. Dramatic demographic shifts accompanied this rapid economic expansion, especially the northern migration of more than four million African Americans. New Deal programs, particularly Social Security, helped maintain a floor on workers' spending power, contributed substantially to the physical transformation of U.S. cities, and laid the foundation for the postwar growth of suburbs (Patterson, 1994). The long-term implications of these phenomena, however, were little understood by policymakers at the time (Lemann, 1991).

By the end of the 1950s, the boom that fueled the postwar recovery began to subside. Industrial unemployment increased among semiskilled blue-collar workers, particularly in the urban North and Midwest where most Americans still lived. Yet the growth of suburbs and the appearance of universal material well-being fostered by the media, particularly television, and heralded by liberal intellectuals (Galbraith, 1958) contributed to the increasing "invisibility of the poor" despite their growing presence in urban ghettos and isolated rural areas (Caudill, 1963; Harrington, 1962). At the same time, hostility and fear toward the poor and socially "deviant" flourished among the middle class, leading to punitive efforts to cut welfare (Axinn & Stern, 2000; Jones, 1992).

The repressive political climate of the Cold War and McCarthyism abetted such attempts to roll back the policies of the New Deal and discouraged the emergence of social activism in their defense (Andrews & Reisch, 1997). As a result, the myth that the preponderance of tax dollars was being spent on increasing numbers of "undeserving" non-White urban welfare recipients went largely unchallenged. One exception occurred in 1961 when the city manager of Newburgh, New York, Joseph Mitchell, blasted both welfare recipients and social workers in his effort to reduce the city's welfare costs. Two progressive leaders of the profession, Norman Lourie, president of NASW, and Ruth Smalley, president of CSWE, denounced Mitchell and those who shared his views:

> The get-tough advocates, the people who call for thought control and dictatorial methods have always pretended to be the realist. A reading of history proves them time and again poor bargains. They have cried "socialism" at every step of human progress. We believe the American people will see through the thin tissue of the Newburgh plan and agree that irresponsible efforts to reduce assistance rolls is not the answer there or in any other community. The nation can be strong only as it faces up to social problems and seeks to remove the causes of poverty and family breakdown which compel people to seek public assistance in the first place. (Lourie & Smalley, 1961, p. 4)

As the Newburgh incident revealed, however, this resentment of the urban poor was deep and widespread. It resulted in large part from a shift in the racial composition of the welfare rolls (Danziger & Weinberg, 1994; Edsall, 1991; Quadagno, 1994). Both the changing demographics of the welfare population and the racist attitudes that accompanied them would later undermine federal antipoverty efforts in the 1960s. The "rediscovery of poverty" around 1960 that inspired the antipoverty programs and social unrest of the decade must be understood in this context.

In the late 1950s, radical new perspectives on social problems emerged within American universities that ultimately shaped social policy responses to poverty in the 1960s. In such areas as juvenile delinquency and urban poverty (Cloward & Ohlin, 1960; Mills, 1956, 1959), academics propagated a new "structuralist" perspective that focused on issues of opportunity rather than pathology. This view initially caused a schism between its proponents (largely sociologists) and mainstream social workers who still tended to regard family dysfunction as the source of deviant behavior. Despite these differences, the work of sociologists like Lloyd Ohlin and Richard Cloward inspired the development of a new kind of social service organization in cities like New York and Chicago that stressed personal freedom and client self-determination (Lemann, 1988–1989; Ohlin, 1957). In the 1960s, initiatives implemented by the Kennedy and Johnson administrations emulated this model and reinvigorated the community organization component within the social work profession (Reisch & Wenocur, 1986).

A major influence on the Kennedy administration was the Ford Foundation's "Gray Areas Project," which funded urban community action agencies and initiatives that addressed the physical and social needs of low-income city residents (Libros, 1962). Another was Mobilization for Youth (MFY), a New York City project originally designed and implemented in the late 1950s by the Henry Street Settlement under the direction of long-time settlement leader, Helen Hall (Andrews, 1993). By 1960, MFY was an independent agency and, in 1962, the Kennedy administration created a package of $12.6 million for the program (Gillette, 1996). MFY "epitomized the shift from relatively paternalistic if innovative notions of uplift for the disadvantaged to an alignment of the service staff with the clientele against welfare and other service systems" (Richan, 1973, p. 155). Its confrontational stance tapped into a deep reservoir of mistrust of existing social welfare institutions at the community level and contributed to the radicalization of young social workers and social work students.

WAR ON POVERTY

In January 1964, two months after the assassination of President Kennedy, President Lyndon Johnson proclaimed an "unconditional" War on Poverty in his first State of the Union Address. The administration's legislative package included economic stimuli, full employment and health care programs, urban and rural rehabilitation, expanded educational and labor opportunities for youth and adults, and increased assistance for the elderly and the disabled (Danziger, 1991; Gillette, 1996). Johnson's agenda expanded on the Kennedy administration's service-centered initiatives, such as the 1962 Social Security Amendments, which had been supported by both reformist and radical social workers (Lourie & Vasey, 1962; Mencher, 1962). In essence, Johnson put a liberal spin on many formerly radical ideas.

The primary instrument of the War on Poverty was the Economic Opportunity Act (EOA), which created such programs as the Job Corps, VISTA, Upward Bound, the Neighborhood Youth Corps, Community Action, Head Start, Legal Services, Foster Grandparents, and the Office of Economic Opportunity (OEO). Mainstream social work organizations quickly endorsed these initiatives as the instrument of achieving "victory over poverty," particularly among women and children on a case-by-case (rather than structural) basis (Bouterse, 1964; Sylvester, 1964; Women's Bureau, July 1964). Two years later, the Model Cities Act moved beyond an individually oriented approach and targeted certain urban areas with comprehensive services. Emphasizing the concept of community control, funds for Model Cities would pass through municipal governments yet be controlled by boards comprised equally of elected officials, low-income people, and representatives of community organizations. Although reformers were optimistic about this approach, it soon proved to be an explosive formula and tensions between largely White politicians and African American and Latino activists led to angry confrontations (Lazarus, 1965; Lemann, 1988–1989; Rose, 1972).

THE "GREAT SOCIETY"

Following his landslide election in November 1964, President Johnson proposed the creation of a "Great Society." This sweeping vision was closely linked with a civil rights agenda, the movement toward community control, and efforts to ameliorate the plight of poor children. Progressive social work organizations, like the Young Women's Christian Association (YWCA), quickly embraced the program, particularly its antidiscrimination measures (YWCA, 1965). Long before most social work organizations, the YWCA had promoted racial equality. It held an interracial conference a half century before in Louisville, Kentucky, and had approved an interracial charter nearly a generation before the civil rights legislation of the 1960s. Unlike many liberal groups, who retreated from their support of civil rights and antipoverty legislation in the late 1960s as African Americans became more radical in their demands and tactics, the YWCA continued to "struggle for peace, justice, freedom and dignity" (YWCA, 1969–1970, pp. 2–3).

The centerpiece of Johnson's Great Society was the creation of semiautonomous Community Action Programs (CAPs) in virtually every city in the United States. Together with VISTA and local legal assistance services previously established under the EOA, the CAPs essentially developed alternative centers of political power in low-income urban neighborhoods, becoming actively involved in local electoral politics (Philadelphia Anti-Poverty Action Committee, 1967; Rose, 1972). Big city mayors soon openly opposed CAPs as potential threats to the local political balance of power (Katz, 1989; Matusow, 1984). Both rural and urban conservative critics of OEO and the Great Society alleged that such programs promoted a socialist agenda. As early as 1966, they called for major reductions in federal spending for such egalitarian purposes (Quadagno, 1994).

Despite these allegations of radical goals and the participation of radical activists and radical social workers in the antipoverty programs of the period, the policies of the Johnson administration were in line with long-standing liberal/reformist traditions in the United States. They emphasized employment over welfare and reinforced long-held American values such as political decentralization, individualism, and self-reliance. Economic growth, rather than resource distribution, was regarded as the key to solving urban problems (Gillette, 1996).

In the mid-1960s, however, increasingly violent disturbances in cities like Detroit and Newark and the rapid expansion of the welfare rolls undermined even this reformist agenda. Citing the government's promise of "maximum feasible participation" in the design and implementation of the community action programs, organized groups began asserting their power at the local level (Moynihan, 1969). This soon alarmed conservative urban politicians, who pressured the federal government to dismantle or cut many antipoverty initiatives, particularly Community Action (Edsall, 1991; Katz, 1989; Lemann, 1988–1989; Patterson, 1994). The continuing militancy of welfare recipients and community action leaders, the spread of civil unrest in urban ghettos, and the growing cost of public assistance further contributed to a rightward political shift. In the 1968 election, Richard Nixon eked out a narrow victory by effectively exploiting these fears and resentments and appealing to racial and class resentments in carefully coded language (Matusow, 1984). Ironically, in the same year, radical movements in the social services reached their maximum power and influence.

MILT COHEN VERSUS HUAC

In the midst of the social upheavals of the 1960s, the legacy of McCarthyism lingered in new forms—a persistent reminder of the risks of radicalism. Throughout the decade, the FBI spent lavishly to infiltrate social protest and radical movements, and targeted civil rights and antiwar activists. Even welfare rights groups were subject to investigation (Branch, 1998, 1988; Garrow, 1986; Gitlin, 1987, 1980; West, 1981). As the government attempted to subvert the so-called New Left through legal harassment, the use of agents provocateurs, and what some termed political assassination, it continued to harass members of the Old Left, including some leading social workers.

In 1965, after Lyndon Johnson had proposed the creation of the Great Society, Milt Cohen, the executive director of the Parkview Home for the Aged in Chicago, was called before the House Un-American Activities Committee (HUAC), on unspecified charges along with two other Chicagoans, Jeremiah Stamler and Yolanda Hall. Cohen was a lifelong social activist for leftist causes. In the early 1930s, as a high school student, he became interested in politics in response to the rise of anti-Semitism in Germany. He later fought in the Spanish Civil War as a member of the Abraham Lincoln Brigade. After World War II, Cohen participated in many peace activities and the civil rights movement.

Cohen responded to the committee's subpoena, but refused to answer any questions other than his name, because he believed that his basic rights had been denied and breached in a number of areas (*NASW News*, November 1970, p. 9). For example, the committee had failed to inform Cohen of the charges against him, denied his attorneys permission to cross-examine witnesses, and turned down his request to testify in closed session. In fact, while the committee did not even reveal the purpose of the hearings until the proceedings began, it disclosed Cohen's name and those of his colleagues to the press in advance, which is a violation of its established procedures. Not only did Cohen refuse to testify, he also was unwilling to take the Fifth Amendment and walked out of the hearing.

Cohen subsequently filed a lawsuit against the committee in which he challenged its constitutionality and "the law through which it was established" (NASW, 1970). In response, the committee indicted him for contempt, although the indictment was stayed pending the outcome of the civil suit. Two suits were denied by Judge Julius Hoffman, soon to gain notoriety as the judge in the trial of the "Chicago 7" (Lassner, 1997). The case lingered in the courts for more than eight years, during which time Cohen received substantial support from social workers. The haunting fear of McCarthyism clearly had subsided somewhat.

Joe Lassner of Loyola University, self-described as "one of Helen Phillips' boys" from the University of Pennsylvania, cochaired the defense committee for Milt Cohen vs. HUAC. Despite the highly visible role he played in support of Cohen's defense, Lassner experienced no problems with his employer. This demonstrated how far the profession had come from the cautious days of the late 1940s and 1950s.

With the backing of the Chicago Chapter of NASW, Lassner appealed for support to the NASW's national board. The board approved an open statement of support that was printed on a full page of the *NASW News* in November 1970. Whitney Young, Jr., then president of NASW, and a target of McCarthyism in the 1950s, wrote

> The NASW Board of Directors unanimously resolves support for the challenge—within the established system of courts and law—of social worker Milton M. Cohen, ACSW, and two fellow Chicagoans against the . . . House Un-American Activities Committee. In taking this stand, the board stresses the significance of the . . . case on the proper conduct of social work and the legal rights of social workers. . . . Because of their courageous efforts during the past five years, the U.S. Supreme Court has permitted Mr. Cohen and his colleagues to challenge . . . the existence of HUAC and other internal security committees that so often threaten and deny the rights of Americans to the due process of law (Young, 1970).

In late 1973, nearly two decades after Joseph McCarthy had been censured by his Senate colleagues, the charges against Cohen were finally dismissed. In a personal letter, Cohen thanked his supporters and commented that the dismissal was

> a reaffirmation of the First Amendment rights of all U.S. citizens. . . . In the course of 8 ½ years of tortuous and expensive legal proceedings . . . we have not yielded the Constitutional principles which my position before the Committee, and our lawsuit, was designed to protect. I have refused to permit the Committee to inquire into my political beliefs and associations, to pillory me with star chamber procedures, and to chill the exercise of my freedom of speech. I especially want to thank my professional colleagues and . . . the National Association of Social Workers . . . for their outstanding support and help. I am proud of its fight for the First Amendment rights of one of its members. The NASW's concern for human rights includes the concern for the democratic rights of every American. (Cohen, 1973)

Cohen's bold resistance to HUAC had far-reaching consequences. It marked the first time in U.S. history that a contempt of Congress indictment for refusing to testify before HUAC was dismissed without being brought to trial. It was also the first time a citizen sued HUAC before a committee hearing involving the citizen was ever held. The success of Cohen's suit "still[ed] HUAC, chang[ed] its charter and its name [to the House Internal Security Committee], and limit[ed] its inquisitional techniques" (Lassner, February 25, 1974). According to Cohen's attorney, Richard Orlikoff (January 22, 1974), activist social workers like Lassner made the difference in the case.

Cohen's problems with HUAC were remarkably similar to those encountered by social workers in the 1940s and 1950s. Like those social workers who lost their jobs during the McCarthy era, Cohen's passion for human rights and social justice and his concerns about fascism were attacked under the guise of anti-Communist patriotism. Whereas others had failed, however, Cohen succeeded in resisting HUAC. This was due, in part, to Cohen's personal courage and persistence. It was also due to the major shifts that had occurred in the political and social environment. The anti-Communist hysteria of the post–World War II era largely had subsided. The Supreme Court had a much more liberal composition. This emboldened professional organizations like NASW to abandon their political timidity and defend their members openly and actively. Yet, although the liberal core of the profession could now defend civil liberties and reform causes with greater comfort, its concerns over professionalism precluded its acceptance of more radical approaches to social work practice or social change.

NATIONAL WELFARE RIGHTS ORGANIZATION (NWRO)

While Cohen's lawsuit dragged on in the courts, a social movement of welfare recipients and their supporters emerged that challenged the principles and status of the social work profession. Between 1966 and 1973, as the civil rights movement shifted its focus to Northern cities, the NWRO transformed the nation's view of welfare and economic justice. Led by Dr. George Wiley, a chemist and former organizer with the Congress of Racial Equality (CORE), and inspired by the antipoverty strategy developed by Richard Cloward and Francis Fox Piven at MFY in New York, the NWRO sought to organize welfare recipients to fight on their own behalf (Kotz & Kotz, 1977; Piven & Cloward, 1977; West, 1981). In a few years, the NWRO reframed the national debate over poverty. Unlike the liberal creators of the Great Society programs whose benign paternalism they frequently targeted, the NWRO asserted that poor people were entitled to public aid as a matter of legal and human rights.

The roots of the NWRO emerged from two vastly different places: the Southern-based civil rights movement and community activists in large cities like New York. By the mid-1960s, the civil rights movement had achieved notable legislative and judicial victories, culminating in the passage of the landmark Civil Rights Bill of 1964 and the Voting Rights Act of 1965. As younger activists played a more visible role and the locus of organizing switched to the North, the movement shifted its focus from an attack on segregation and discrimination (political inequality) to an attack on social and economic inequality.

It also began to challenge the strategy of integration and accommodation and replace it with one of confrontation and the development of Black Power (Branch, 1988; Morris, 1984).

The impetus for the welfare rights movement in New York emerged out of Mobilization for Youth (MFY), a controversial program developed by community organizers from the Henry Street Settlement on the Lower East Side. Instead of focusing on delinquency and other forms of social "pathology," MFY organizers identified the lack of income and welfare benefits as the most serious issues affecting the poor. Many future leaders of social work, including Richard Cloward, Francis Fox Piven, Francis (Pat) Purcell, George Brager, Harold Weissman, Bertram Beck, and Harry Specht, achieved initial prominence through their work with MFY (Brager & Purcell, 1967).

By the mid-1960s, however, complementary programs like Harlem Youth in Action (HARYOU-ACT), had moved beyond the development of alternative forms of social service to engage in dramatic social protests on behalf of low-income minority clients and their community organizations. Their tactics included rent strikes, picketing, and attacks on public officials, including public welfare leaders, the police, and the local Board of Elections (Cloward & Piven, 1964). As a result, MFY and HARYOU-ACT became the focus of political controversy and were frequently tied up by investigations of alleged fiscal improprieties (Press release of October 20, 1965, Evelyn Butler Archive, University of Pennsylvania). Liberal social work groups like NASW were lukewarm in their support for MFY's radical activism. Although a 1964 Delegate Assembly resolution recognized the value of its programs, the following year a report of the New York City chapter of NASW implicitly criticized the organization for its political activities and alleged fiscal improprieties (National NASW, October 1964; New York City NASW, June 1965). Mainstream social work leaders thus tried to walk a fine line by embracing the abstract mission of MFY and the concept of community action while not alienating conservative supporters in government and the media.

Despite these political controversies, the ideas that inspired MFY flourished and soon made their influence felt on a much bigger stage than the gritty streets of New York. As early as 1964, MFY leaders Richard Cloward, a sociologist and expert on juvenile delinquency, and Frances Fox Piven, a political scientist, had pointed out the limitations of the organization's strategy of social change. They argued that MFY's principle approach had been "to exert organizational pressure . . . upon low-income people to select strategies and tactics of social action that are consonant with those employed in elitist social action or, at least, to permit the organization to direct the overall enterprise thereby subordinating protest strategy to its particular elitist strategy" (Cloward & Piven, 1964, p. 14). This approach, they asserted, was based on questionable assumptions about social change and the social order, including the conventional wisdom that lower-class people could not be organized into an effective political force (Banfield, 1970). Instead, they proposed to mobilize low-income people and use disruptive tactics as a last resort, short of violence. This, they hoped, would "cause strain for powerful segments of the community [e.g., the welfare system] but [would] not call forth the full coercive and repressive forces of the society" (Cloward & Piven, 1964, p. 37).

The following year, Cloward expanded on this theme in "Advocacy in the Ghetto," coauthored by Richard Elman (1965). Cloward and Elman consciously linked the contemporary work of welfare rights organizations to the efforts of relief recipients and social workers through the Workers Alliance during the New Deal. In 1966, as the NWRO was being formed, Cloward and Piven drafted "A Strategy to End Poverty" and distributed it widely among clients, social workers, and community organizers. In May, it was published in *The Nation* and received widespread publicity, drawing the attention of George Wiley, the leader of the NWRO.

Cloward and Piven proposed to create a crisis in the current welfare system—by exploiting the gap between welfare law and practice—that would ultimately bring about its collapse and replace it with a system of guaranteed annual income. They hoped to accomplish this end by informing the poor of their rights to welfare assistance, encouraging them to apply for benefits and, in effect, overloading an already overburdened bureaucracy (Gelb & Sardell, 1974; Kotz & Kotz, 1977; Piven & Cloward, 1977; West, 1981). Through this "insurrectionary theory" of social change Piven and Cloward also hoped to capitalize on the social unrest of the period to mobilize welfare recipients to take action on their own behalf (Piven & Cloward, 1977).

Although Piven and Cloward opposed the formation of organizations of low-income people as an unnecessary, even counterproductive distraction, their strategy was put to the test through the NWRO, initially through its local welfare rights groups in cities like Oakland, Los Angeles, Philadelphia, and New York. In Oakland, social workers had begun to protest the intrusive policies of the Alameda County Welfare Department as early as January 1963, particularly its notorious "Operation Bedcheck." Bennie Parrish, a caseworker in the department, was fired for insubordination when he refused to participate in the raids, which the California Supreme Court later ruled were illegal. With the assistance of labor unions, however, Parrish and some of his colleagues began to work with recipients through the Oakland Welfare Rights Organization (Blawle, 1970).

By 1966, with the assistance of the Catholic archdiocese and federally funded antipoverty workers, welfare rights groups appeared throughout New York City. Even before the formation of the NWRO, a Citywide Coordinating Committee of Welfare Groups was created to implement the Cloward and Piven strategy of overloading the welfare system and to press for minimum standards of assistance. Social workers were recruited to the welfare rights movement in New York through Social Work Action for Welfare Rights (SWAWR) and, nationally, through the Poverty Rights Action Center (SWAWR flyer, 1966). Throughout the late 1960s SWAWR criticized mainstream organizations for their half-hearted measures on behalf of welfare recipients and protested against state welfare cuts.

The beginnings of mass welfare rights demonstrations in the summer of 1966 led to the formation in Chicago of the National Coordinating Committee of Welfare Rights Groups. Although tensions persisted between "top-down" and "bottom-up" approaches to organizing, by 1968 the Cloward and Piven strategy began to achieve its intended results (Gelb & Sardell, 1974). By the following year, with the assistance of local activists, including liberal clergy, the NWRO had organized more than 22,000 dues-paying members and 523 local groups (Trattner, 1995, p. 344).

Despite these successes, it is unlikely that the NWRO would have achieved national prominence so rapidly without the emergence of George Wiley as its charismatic leader. A handsome, articulate African American professor of chemistry at Syracuse University, the 35-year-old Wiley had been associate director of the Congress for Racial Equality, and director of the Washington office of the Poverty Rights Action Center, where he became attracted to Cloward and Piven's ideas about poverty and community organization. Wiley saw welfare rights organizing as a step toward the revitalization of the Civil Rights Movement. Eventually, he hoped to create a poor people's movement that would address issues of housing, education, and employment (Kotz & Kotz, 1977). In addition to adopting the aims of local welfare rights groups, such as ending the illegal practices of welfare departments, the NWRO adopted broader long-term goals that focused on adequate income, individual dignity, justice, and democracy (NWRO, August 21, 1968).

An alliance between the NWRO and the OEO-sponsored Community Legal Services Corporation soon produced a legal strategy to create a constitutional right to subsistence that complemented the NWRO's confrontational political tactics. Spearheaded by the Center for Social Welfare Policy and Law, this approach initially met with considerable success. In 1966, the Warren Court established the principle that wealth-based discrimination was equivalent to "invidious" racial discrimination. This expanded the concept of fundamental rights to include those rights not explicitly listed in the Constitution.

Inspired by these rulings, welfare rights advocates forged a strategy to convince the court to find a "right to live" within the Equal Protection Clause of the Fourteenth Amendment. Relying on natural law tradition and universalist arguments, they sought to eradicate the distinction between positive and negative rights. By 1968, prospects looked hopeful that this bold strategy would prevail (Bussiere, 1997).

Although their long-term goals were compatible, Wiley, Piven, and Cloward disagreed on organizing strategy and tactics from the outset. Wiley wanted to develop a grassroots organization of poor people controlled by poor people. Piven and Cloward, on the other hand, argued that organizing used scarce resources and had little hope of gaining any significant power. They emphasized protest, rather than organization building, as the best way to mobilize resources for the poor (Piven & Cloward, 1977). Nevertheless, spurred on by the women with whom he worked, Wiley and his staff (which included Tim Sampson, a community organizing graduate of the University of Southern California and later a professor of social work at San Francisco State University) quickly established a national organization with semiautonomous local chapters in both urban and rural areas (West, 1981). In 1967, Johnnie Tillmon, a welfare recipient and mother, was elected chair.

Despite their disagreements over strategy and tactics, the presence of supporters like Piven and Cloward provided credibility for the welfare rights movement among left-wing intellectuals and a bridge to the radical and liberal elements within the social work profession. The appearance of Whitney Young, NASW President and Director of the National Urban League, as the keynote speaker at the 1969 NWRO convention gave the movement added legitimacy among mainstream professionals. Many social workers, particularly those in settlement houses and community action agencies, became active as "friends of the NWRO."

These linkages soon produced concrete benefits. Community Action Councils used OEO-funded resources and staff to help organize welfare recipients. Local United Fund campaigns, such as in the San Francisco Bay Area, provided emergency assistance to welfare rights organizations. Schools of social work like Columbia worked in cooperation with law schools, civil rights groups, and foundations to train both professionals and paraprofessionals to work with low-income people. Many social workers provided technical assistance to the NWRO on welfare regulations, organizing skills, and political strategy (Gelb & Sardell, 1974; Blawle, 1970). With the cooperation of some schools of social work, NWRO launched a "summer student project" that provided MSW students with field placement supervision and credit (NWRO brochure, "Students NOW," 1968).

Even with the active support and involvement of many progressive social workers, NWRO continued to criticize social workers for their role as control agents of a repressive welfare system. Social workers who supported the NWRO agreed with these criticisms. SWAWR, a New York advocacy group, declared: "For too long, social workers have permitted themselves to be used as the instruments of oppressive welfare programs, instead of directing their energies and professional skills to fighting for programs beneficial to their clients" (SWAWR, 1969, p. 1). In many ways, the NWRO brought to the fore the tensions between the liberal (reformist) and radical factions within the social work field.

John Ramey, who helped support the NWRO through his work at the Greater Cincinnati Federation of Settlements, argues that many social workers continue to deny the profession's contribution to the movement. Ramey asserts this was because social workers often felt pressured by the NWRO's tactics, which included frequent denunciations of their social control function: "When people take extreme positions, there's no room for negotiation" (J. Ramey, personal communication, 1998).

Although Wiley's original vision was to create an umbrella social movement organization, the NWRO soon became a movement dominated by African American women AFDC recipients, particularly at the national level. It was one of the only nationally organized movements of poor people in the nation's history and the only movement of its kind composed predominantly of women, the vast majority of whom were women of color. In the Midwest, however, membership in most states was largely White. In Minnesota, for example, the overwhelming majority of members were White women from small, rural, poverty-ridden counties (Hertz, 1981).

Ironically, the NWRO's unique composition was both the source of the movement's strength and, ultimately, its collapse. When AFDC rolls exploded in the late 1960s, membership in the NWRO did as well, particularly in New York and Boston (Levine, 1968). Bolstered by significant court decisions in its favor and a receptive political climate, the NWRO appeared close to winning a legal right to welfare (Bussiere, 1997). This was the most revolutionary aspect of the movement: that the poor should receive benefits from the government on the basis of their rights as citizens, mothers, consumers, and most importantly, human beings. This claim challenged the fundamental capitalist notion of paid labor conferring the right to individuals to participate in the consumer culture. The NWRO promoted a "right to live" philosophy that was not tied to the concept of work. In this way, the organization

> pushed the postwar welfare state to new limits. They also articulated a historically remarkable theory of citizenship. When they insisted that welfare departments fulfill their "rightly needs" and pressed private companies to help them acquire "the better things in life," the NWRO activists reconfigured familiar Anglo-American ideas about rights and obligations. (Kornbluh, 1997, p. 103)

Hopeful of ultimate victory in the courts, in late 1968 and early 1969, prior to its attempted takeover of the 1969 NCSW, the NWRO prepared for a Poor People's March that summer in Washington and launched a national campaign for a "right to welfare" and a guaranteed annual income (Buchen, 1968; NWRO, December 1968, January 1969). The campaign was intended to counteract an increasingly hostile press, FBI investigations of welfare protests, proposed state cuts in welfare grants, and what Cloward and Piven termed the "finessing of the poor" by politicians and local welfare officials (Cloward & Piven, 1968; Perlmutter, 1969; *Time Magazine*, December 13, 1968; *Toledo Times*, November 20, 1968). It also sought to take advantage of shifting attitudes about the poor among the general public, particularly growing sympathy for low-income children (Newman, 1969).

To promote the campaign, the NWRO sought allies among former foes, including Jack Goldberg, the Commissioner of Welfare in New York, as well as in the Nation of Islam and labor groups like the United Farm Workers and the Social Service Employees Union (SSEU; Himmelstein, 1969; Levine, 1968; NOW!, December 1968; Walker, 1968). The latter had grown in political influence for several years as a consequence "of general social unrest, the desire for involvement, . . . the protest movements . . . in . . . large cities, . . . [and] a campaign to organize public employees at the State and local level" (Department of

Health, Education and Welfare, May 17, 1967). Although the NWRO continued to grow in numbers and influence through these efforts—by June 1969 it
had 250 affiliates in 46 states and more than 100 cities (NWRO, June 11, 1969)—
it also contributed to the growing divisions among liberal and radical civil rights
groups (Herbers, 1969). Nevertheless, the NWRO promoted its proposals for a
"guaranteed adequate income," based in part on the idea of a Family Investment Program developed by local welfare rights groups such as in Philadelphia
(Philadelphia Welfare Rights Organization, n.d.; NWRO, June 11, 1969; NOW!,
July 1969; Massachusetts Welfare Rights Organization, 1969).

In response, the Nixon administration developed its own version of a guaranteed annual income through a Family Assistance Plan (FAP). This proposal
was soon attacked by the NWRO, which successfully lobbied NASW to testify
against its provisions and enlisted other liberal groups to oppose it as well (NASW,
October 1969; *NASW News*, September, 1970, pp. 3–4; Young & Lourie, November 3, 1969). Ultimately, the FAP was defeated by an unusual coalition of
conservatives and progressives (Moynihan, 1973). The former continued to express contempt for welfare, while the latter maintained that the FAP would
provide inadequate benefits (Edstrom, 1970; Scherr, 1970). Ironically, shortly
after the battle over FAP thrust the NWRO into the center of national policymaking debates, the movement began to decline (West, 1981).

Local NWRO chapters were frequently put on the defensive by the public's
increasing hostility toward antipoverty programs and political efforts to freeze
or roll back welfare grants (Bailis, 1974; *Boston Globe*, July 1969; Gelb & Sardell,
1974; Pope, 1990). The NWRO responded, in part, by forging new alliances
with labor groups and other radical organizations around issues such as housing
(Philadelphia NWRO, January 1973). In February 1972, Wiley and Tillmon
shifted the national organization's tactics, calling for an end to the war in Indo-
China and a focus on the survival needs of children (Letter of February 7, 1972).
Wiley announced a "Children's March for Survival," to be held in Washington
on March 25 (Wiley, February 8, 1972). Like the Poor People's Campaign of
1969, however, the march was a failure. It would be years before the plight of
low-income children would again capture the full attention of advocates and
the nation.

Wiley's resignation from the NWRO in 1973, coupled with several important defeats in the Supreme Court (Bussiere, 1997), soon led to the movement's
virtual disappearance on the national stage. Only a few local chapters remained
active (Pope, 1990). With the same intensity that had built the NWRO, Wiley
threw himself into the development of a broader movement for economic justice. Tragically, his life was cut short at age 42 by a boating accident shortly after
he left the NWRO. Although they continued to write about welfare issues, Piven
and Cloward refocused their community work on the issue of voting and soon
formed the Human Serve Voter Registration Project (Piven & Cloward, 1988).

The NWRO strategy was ultimately unsuccessful, in part, because of its
reliance on a judicially oriented approach and, in part, because of internal con-

flicts between male founders like Wiley and female leaders like Johnnie Tillmon. At the organizational level, its strategy failed because grassroots NWRO leaders increasingly resisted the use of a "maternalist" argument in support of welfare rights (West, 1981). Conflicts also emerged between local welfare rights groups and the parent organization over issues of autonomy and tactical flexibility. Persistent class and racial divisions and the difficulty of sustaining a posture of perpetual mobilization also undermined the movement (Pope, 1990).

The principle explanation for the failure of the NWRO, however, lies in the advocates' legal strategy, not ideology. Court victories led to natural rights being defined as mere statutory entitlements rather than constitutional guarantees. Thus, in the late 1960s, just as antipoverty programs were beginning to lose their broad base of public support in the aftermath of civil disturbances, judicial decisions neutralized the universal appeal of advocates' arguments and limited their redistributive potential (Bussiere, 1997; West, 1981). Although this approach initially increased both total welfare spending and average benefit levels, in the long run it inadvertently "tended to set different groups of poor people against each other in the pluralist political arena . . . in a fierce competition for diminishing public resources" (Bussiere, 1997, p. 119). It also fostered a climate in which advocates for disadvantaged groups were ill prepared a decade later to defend against the anti-welfare policies of the Reagan–Bush era.

Ironically, the NWRO mirrored in its composition and leadership the social work profession against which its members frequently railed. Although most of the members were women, the organization's real leaders were men. Gender issues, however, rarely were used as a political strategy. In fact, Elizabeth Bussiere argues that the split over the emphasis on gender and the divisions between maternalist and universalist strategies contributed to the movement's downfall (Bussiere, 1997).

The political and intellectual leaders of the Black movement, and their allies among the New Left, were unwilling to acknowledge gender differences in the NWRO because they believed that to do so would be "potentially divisive." Consequently, race, poverty, and gender "interfaced to develop a double and occasionally triple handicap on the political activities of poor women" (Hertz, 1981, p. 182). Wiley's response to the NWRO confrontation at the 1969 NCSW conference illustrated this problem all too vividly. Visibly upset over the departure of many of the social workers from the ballroom, Wiley pleaded on behalf of the poor women before the shrinking audience. Yet his words made no reference to the women for whom he spoke: "Black men," he said, "are getting tired of the brutality, intimidation, and indignities organized against them by white society" (Clendenin, 1969, p. 5).

By the time Black feminists began to champion the cause of their sisters on AFDC in the mid-1970s, it was "too late . . . to help save the NWRO" (West, 1981, p. 240). Yet their support "provide[d] new impetus and legitimacy to the cause of welfare as a women's issue by incorporating this problem into their agendas and some NWRO leaders and poor women into their organizations"

(p. 240). By the end of the 1970s, African American feminists such as Florence Kennedy, Margaret Sloan, Shirley Chisholm, and Maya Angelou openly supported the need not only to end racism, but sexism as well.

In contrast, White feminists, including many social workers, gave little assistance to the NWRO. This occurred for two reasons. First, the concept of the "feminization of poverty" had not yet been recognized and articulated in feminist thought. White feminists focused largely on issues of concern to middle- and upper-middle-class women such as abortion rights and employment discrimination (Deckard, 1979; Freeman, 1975). By the 1980s, when White feminists began to emphasize issues of poverty and economic inequality, the gap between them and women of color had become virtually unbridgeable (Goldberg & Kremen, 1990). Second, through the 1970s many nonpoor women, particularly from the professional classes, continued to view poverty among women as rooted in, or at least linked to, personal deficiencies and poor decision making. This split along class and racial lines within the feminist movement proved to be a portent of schisms to come in the 1980s and 1990s, divisions that are still affecting the progressive community and the social work profession (Deckard, 1979; Rosenberg, 1992).

Although the welfare rights movement was short lived, it did achieve some limited success. One major accomplishment of the NWRO was "to ignite and fuel the explosion of the welfare rolls, with six million more people getting benefits and benefits rising by four billion dollars in the seven years following its birth" (Kotz & Kotz, 1977, p. 305). Through the publication of welfare rights handbooks by local chapters, welfare recipients and their advocates became better informed about legal requirements and application procedures (Massachusetts Welfare Rights, June 1969; Philadelphia Welfare Rights, February 1970). Rallies, demonstrations, and hearings, involving national leaders like Wiley and sympathetic supporters like Dr. Benjamin Spock, local organizers like Mel King (executive director of the New Urban League in Boston) and Hubert Jones (chairman of the Welfare Coalition in Boston and later dean of the Boston University School of Social Work), grassroots welfare rights leaders, union representatives, social workers, and social work students, increased public awareness of poverty and welfare issues (Massachusetts Welfare Rights Flyer, June 1969; Pope, July 1969; SWAWR, 1969).

Welfare rights groups also formed alliances with concerned trade unionists, social workers, and other professionals around health and welfare issues (SWAWR, May 1969). Some welfare laws were liberalized, employment opportunities for some NWRO participants emerged, and the movement produced a heightened sensitivity to issues involving poor women. Ultimately, this led to the formulation of the concept of the feminization of poverty. These accomplishments, however, could not be achieved without long-term costs:

> At the local level welfare groups achieved short-term success . . . through the inability or unwillingness of key decision makers to suppress demands for change. In the long run, without support and in a political environment

hostile to public welfare spending, the movement met defeat. (Gelb & Sardell, 1974, p. 524)

Some progressives acknowledged the gains secured by NWRO activists but shied away from its confrontational tactics. Others felt uncomfortable ceding their professional or intellectual leadership to low-income, minority women. For many liberal social workers, self-determination looked fine on paper, but, as in the community action programs of the 1960s, it looked different in practice (Rose, 1972; Simon, 1994).

Conservatives viewed the movement as a national disaster and, particularly at the state level, took a hard line in controlling welfare benefits. As a result, after the collapse of the NWRO in 1973, welfare benefits began to lose their value. The virtual freeze on welfare benefits during the Reagan-Bush era produced a 50% drop in their purchasing power between 1970 and 1997 (Green Book, 1998, Table 7-14, p. 431). In sum, welfare protests produced a punitive response toward recipients among conservatives and a fatalism about the system's failings among liberals, including many social workers. This combination ultimately paved the way for the 1996 Personal Responsibility and Work Opportunity Reconciliation Act—signed by a Democratic President—that destroyed the much-maligned welfare system without replacing it with anything like the guaranteed income Piven and Cloward and the NWRO had proposed thirty years before.

SOCIAL WELFARE WORKERS MOVEMENT (SWWM)

Although the radical tactics of the NWRO failed to attract liberal social workers to its cause, the confrontation at the 1969 NCSW conference spurred the creation of a short-lived radical movement *within* the profession—the SWWM. With ideological roots in New Left theories of social change, the SWWM promoted a "socialistic vision of a planned cooperative society, a participatory democracy where people truly have control over the institutions that affect their lives" (Wenocur, 1975, pp. 3–4). The primary focus of the SWWM was on radical consciousness raising through teach-ins, publications, study groups, and direct action.

The movement actually began earlier that spring in Boston, New York, Philadelphia, and other cities among a small group of radical social workers concerned about the indifference of the public welfare bureaucracy and the conservatism of the social welfare system. SWWM was conceived as a "political movement in social welfare," an alternative to NASW, and a response to the failure of mainstream social work organizations to support the demands of the Coalition for Action Now (CAN), the movement's predecessor (SWWM, 1969). SWWM's core goals were "community-worker control of social agencies, an end to meaningless professionalism, and a redistribution of [the] country's resources" (Philadelphia SWWM, 1970, p. 1; Boston SWWM, April,1969). In late April, an interim organizing committee drafted a provisional position statement that served as the basis for organizing up to and during the May NCSW conference. This statement outlined the "common conditions of work" that united all welfare workers, the movement's assumptions about the structure of U.S. society, and a five-point minimum program of action. It focused on decentralization and deprofessionalization, exposure of social inequalities, resistance to dehumanizing social welfare policies, support for sweeping political and economic changes, and coalition building with allies in the human services and other professions (SWWM, April 1969).

Most members of the group were young people who entered social work as public welfare workers during the rapid expansion of the field in the 1960s, much like the Rank and Filers of the 1930s. They included professionals, paraprofessionals, clerical workers, and students, who were employed by welfare departments, antipoverty programs, settlement houses, schools, and other private sector agencies (SWWM, 1969). Inspired by the social movements of the period, particularly the welfare rights movement, and New Left ideas, they "view[ed] their work as a way to advance social change" (Wagner, 1990, p. 2). Both practitioners and students began questioning the profession's narrow focus on casework and pushed for more emphasis on group work and community organization. Within four days of the dramatic NCSW conference, the movement had taken on a national character (SWWM flyer, June 1969).

Influenced by grassroots practitioners and low-income clients, SWWM argued that casework was more harmful than helpful, as reflected in one of its slogans: "MSW = Maintaining Social Wrongs" (Trattner, 1995, p. 345). Low ($5) membership dues encouraged recruitment of minorities and lower-income students. SWWM's emphasis on community organizing further strengthened radical tendencies among students and young social workers. In addition to participating in broader social movements outside of social work, it organized various collectives, caucuses, and movement chapters in places like Boston, New York, Chicago, Michigan, Pennsylvania, Ohio, and California (Kidneigh, 1969; Prunty, 1969; Wenocur, 1975).

The Boston group—one of the movement's most effective chapters—was composed exclusively of White workers, both men and women, roughly 24–35 years old (Wenocur, 1975). It began meeting weekly in the spring of 1969 to share members' concerns regarding the failure of the social welfare system to respond adequately to the poverty and oppression experienced by their clients. The group's early efforts to promote social change from within the system, however, were stymied by the public welfare bureaucracy and the absence of a clear social change orientation within existing professional organizations (Wenocur, 1969). The protests of the NWRO, the NABSW, and other dissident groups at the 1969 NCSW conference radicalized the Boston social workers and served as the catalyst for the creation of SWWM chapters across the country.

The movement's mission statement (SWWM, April, 1969) challenged social workers to examine their contributions to a repressive social welfare system:

> The services we are asked to tender as clinicians, public service workers, organizers, community workers, clerical and technical workers, and students have become devastating instruments for promoting acquiescence to social injustice in the most deprived portions of the American population. The social institutions in which we work tend not only to pacify those who are oppressed and defend the stability of the present socio-economic system, but also to define the lifestyles and status of the people that it oppresses. This is particularly true in the way it molds the nature of family life, defines the role of women in our society, and through its control of economic resources, perpetuates and institutionalizes race, class, and sex stratification. (p. 1)

Members of the movement assumed that the United States was unable with its "present political, economic, and social structure to make adequate, just allocation of its wealth and to set human priorities above property, profit, and military and corporate power" (SWWM, April, 1969, p. 2). Based on this radical vision, the group organized around two major goals. One was the establishment of an organization that practiced participatory democracy through a decentralized structure and an emphasis on deprofessionalization. The other was to obtain eventual control over social welfare institutions by workers and communities. The SWWM hoped to achieve this second goal through the formation of alliances with client groups like local welfare rights organizations and participation in collective protests against the social welfare establishment. This inevitably led the SWWM to attack the social work profession itself, including mainstream social work organizations like NASW and many professional colleagues (Richan & Mendlesohn, 1973; Rose & Black, 1985).

Through a monthly national newspaper, *Hotch Pot*, which the movement supported without formal affiliation and circulated to approximately 1,200 people, the SWWM promoted its analysis of social welfare issues and attempted to stimulate social action at the community level from a distinctly, if eclectically, socialist perspective. The newspaper resembled—in content, language, symbols, and format—other radical media of the period, such as the *Radicals in the Professions Newsletter*, although its politics tended to be less sectarian (Allen, 1969). It covered a wide range of topics, including national health insurance, union organizing, the mobilization of social work students, welfare rights, and what might broadly be termed "movement news." It also covered alternative fund campaigns around the country that had sprung up in protest of the perceived elitism of United Way fund-raising and charitable distribution activities (Brilliant, 1990; Wenocur, 1975; *Hotch Pot*, 1969–1971).

Contributors to *Hotch Pot* frequently asserted that mainstream professional organizations like the NCSW, NASW, and the Council on Social Work Education (CSWE) were ultimately under the control of corporate America. For example, an article in the May 1970 issue entitled "NCSW Is a Delusion" included a version of the slogan made famous by the student revolutionaries in Paris in May 1968: "I participate, you participate, she participates, we participate, they rule." It went on to assert.

> The ideas of the business community are taught in every school of social work in the country. . . . They control the voluntary agencies from which the professional participants in the NCSW leadership come. The NCSW continues to exist, financially, from the memberships of those agencies and agency federations and from the agency and school-supported conference fees, because it continues to serve purposes which the business community approves. (*Hotch Pot*, May 1970, p. 5)

In the same issue, *Hotch Pot* had a two-page centerfold advertising the upcoming NCSW annual meeting in Chicago. It included a full-page photograph of police beating demonstrators (presumably from the 1968 Democratic Convention in Chicago), a clenched fist, and the slogan "fight professionalism" (pp. 6–7). Local chapters also published their own newsletters that combined analyses of state welfare issues with sweeping, often revolutionary, broadsides against U.S. foreign and military policy and discussions of union activities in the social welfare field (Boston SWWM, January 1970; Los Angeles SWWM, December 1970).

Although *Hotch Pot* continued to be published through 1971, SWWM's influence peaked at the local level from late 1969 to mid-1970. During these months, the Philadelphia and San Francisco Bay Area chapters focused primarily on welfare rights, sometimes working with or through sympathetic local chapters of NASW or progressive churches (SWWM documents, 1969–1970). Through the summer and fall of 1969, the Boston chapter engaged in a spirited but unsuccessful campaign to defeat a punitive welfare bill passed by the Massachusetts legislature (SWWM materials, 1969). After initially boycotting the annual meeting of the Massachusetts Conference on Social Welfare in November, it persuaded the conference to pass resolutions calling for a guaranteed annual income, protest against the workfare provisions in President Nixon's welfare reform proposal, and condemn racism in U.S. society (*Boston Globe*, December 5, 1969; *Boston Herald Traveler*, December 5, 1969; *Boston Record American*, December 5, 1969; Massachusetts CSW, December 1969). Less successful was its support for open admissions to all the health science schools for Black and Spanish-speaking residents of the state (Open Admissions Committee, 1969).

Although it organized frequent teach-ins and workshops at the local level, the SWWM had a short-lived existence as a national organization. At the 1970 NCSW conference in Chicago, SWWM worked with the NWRO, NFSSW, NABSW, the newly formed La Raza, and two American Indian organizations to overcome "the startling indifference of the whites in attendance" through a variety of tactics, including direct confrontation, disruption, conference wide participation, and quiet diplomacy (Prunty, 1970, p. 158). Their efforts, however, had little impact on the NCSW membership, nor did attempts by another group, the Social Workers Radical Caucus (formerly the Social Fund for the Conspiracy), to hold a general session on the "Chicago 7" trial (Horchow, 1970).

Recruitment of new members to SWWM was a chronic problem. The movement also was hampered by the absence of a clear sense of group identity or organizational purpose (that is, was it a social movement or a support group?) perhaps because of its lack of a clear theoretical foundation (Wenocur, 1975). Although it often worked closely with welfare rights organizations around legislative issues, SWWM's failure to establish strong and lasting linkages to broad-based social justice organizations also undermined the movement's success. The turning point occurred at the 1970 NCSW conference in Chicago, barely one year after the movement's inception. SWWM members could not agree on any strategies for action at the meeting and the Boston SWWM could not long sustain itself.

Later that year, radical social workers in Boston attempted to create another organization, the Alliance for Radical Change, with the hope of strengthening SWWM by aligning it with other local radical groups such as the Boston Teachers New Caucus and the Somerville Tenants Union (SWWM flyer, 1970). As its basic philosophy, the group adopted the principles expressed in a monograph, "Towards an Alliance for Radical Change," written by Ed Schwartz (1970), a radical lawyer and Robert Kennedy Foundation fellow assigned to work with the Massachusetts Welfare Rights Organization. Schwartz had been the architect of the bold and innovative legal strategy to create a "right to welfare" that had almost succeeded in revolutionizing public welfare in the United States (Bussiere, 1997). (He continues to work for radical change today as the director of the Center for the Study of Civic Values in Philadelphia.)

With Schwartz's ideas as a guide, the Alliance for Radical Change proclaimed that its goal was to "foster a national movement of local activists; to establish an association among post-graduates with a major investment in change; to build an organization of advocates for the 'explosive regeneration' of the nation and the world" (Schwartz, 1970, p. 9). This goal, however, proved to be overly ambitious. The groups that formed the alliance lacked both the political power and the organization to sustain the coalition or to pursue such lofty ends.

Stan Wenocur, a founding member of SWWM and later a professor of social work at the University of Maryland, suggests that SWWM members could not "surmount their own social class positions." Like many other movements based in the middle or professional classes, before and since, many social workers simply found it too difficult to invest simultaneously in a career and social action and too risky to be identified as a radical (Wenocur, 1975, p. 16). Consequently, efforts to recruit social workers to full-time political activism through the distribution of pamphlets drafted by the Movement for a Democratic Society, based in Cleveland and New York, largely failed (Smukler, McEldowney, & Coblentz, 1970a; 1970b).

Other related, short-lived radical movements emerged within social work during this period. One was a Washington-area group, led by such long-time activists as Nancy Amidei, called in Defense of Dissent (DOD). DOD was affiliated with California's CAN, the SWWM, and other radical caucuses and published a newsletter entitled *Resistance* in 1970. Although DOD grew out of the same concerns as the SWWM, it came together specifically in response to a report by the Catholic University Faculty Grievance Committee charging the School of Social Service with punishing dissent and violating a faculty member's academic and civil rights (*Resistance*, April 1970).

Another short-lived radical organization of the period was a secretive group that appeared in Connecticut in the spring of 1970, calling itself "The Inner Circle." This group sought to create a new organization of social workers, clients, and supporters, separate from the SWWM. Its goals included major systems change in the United States, improvements in state welfare policies and the administration of welfare programs, and the enhancement of educational programs in universities and agencies (Confidential memo, April 6, 1970, Evelyn Butler Archive, University of Pennsylvania).

A more lasting radical group was the Human Services Movement. It focused on social change, grassroots organizing, client empowerment, and community development, and its members worked with the most oppressed clients such as prisoners and welfare recipients. It opposed mainstream social work's emphasis on professionalism and argued for more inclusive standards of membership, much as the Rank and File Movement and Bertha Reynolds had in the 1930s. The principle legacy of its actions was the acceptance of bachelor-degree-level social workers into NASW in 1969 and the decision of CSWE to accredit undergraduate education programs. These decisions were not without controversy, however, and even were opposed by some radicals in the profession, such as Harold Lewis (1982, 1972), because of their potentially deleterious effects on services to low-income clients.

RADICAL LEGACY OF THE 1960S

The resurgence of radicalism in social work during the 1960s took place in the context of rapid social change and the emergence of turbulent social movements unparalleled since the era of the Great Depression. Activists in many sectors of society "aimed to remake virtually every social arrangement America had settled into after World War II" (Gitlin, 1987, p. 5). The optimism nurtured by the early successes of the civil rights movement and the War on Poverty led many social workers and social reformers to believe that "government could solve even the most intractable of society's ailments" if sufficient resources were provided (Gillette, 1996).

Social work radicals participated as citizens in virtually all of the social movements of the period, although, unlike in previous eras, they did not occupy national leadership roles in any of them with the exception of welfare rights. In the early 1960s, despite the setbacks of the McCarthy era, unions made some progress organizing public sector workers and encouraging political activism among social workers within the Jewish center field (Brindle, 1962; Karger, 1988; Metropolitan Association of Jewish Center Workers, 1961). Some social service agencies assisted radical labor efforts, for example among California farm workers (Dutton, 1984). Although organized social workers were viewed as more militant than their colleagues, there was little evidence that the union-centered radicalism of the postwar period had survived the purges of McCarthyism (Department of Health and Human Services, May 1967, Evelyn Butler Archive, University of Pennsylvania).

At the same time, peace activists within the profession continued to advocate for economic conversion and nuclear disarmament. In 1961, they persuaded the NASW Delegate Assembly to endorse their position on universal disarmament (*NASW News*, February 1961; Chicago Social Workers, May 1961). Social Workers for Peace and Nuclear Disarmament (SWPND; later renamed Social Workers for Peace and Social Justice) was formed under the auspices of national NASW, with small local chapters in many states. Yet, unlike in previous eras, social workers were not prominent in national peace movements or national organizations opposed to the war in Vietnam (Zaroulis & Sullivan, 1984). (See Chapter 8.)

RADICAL INFLUENCE ON SOCIAL WORK PRACTICE

The most notable contributions of social work radicals to the social work profession during the 1960s occurred through the more experimental aspects of the War on Poverty, such as MFY and CAP, through movement organizations like the NWRO, and a few social work-focused collectives and organizations. Social work radicals in the late 1960s and early 1970s also influenced changes in NASW's bylaws so that social workers had an obligation to use "both social work methods . . . and social action." Major social service agencies, such as the Community Service Society in New York, temporarily discontinued casework to focus on the "pathology of the ghetto" rather than the individual problems of its inhabitants. It was the War on Poverty, however, probably more than any other external force, that shifted the focus of the profession to community organization, social policy development, deprofessionalization, and social action (Ehrenreich, 1985; Specht & Courtney, 1994).

Social activism, inside and outside the profession, heightened existing tensions within the social work profession between reformers and radicals, micro and macro practitioners, faculty and students. The civil rights movement played a particularly important role in shaking off the apathy of the previous decade. One social work observer commented that it marked "a final step in the liberation from the heritage of McCarthyism" (Thursz, 1966).

By the late 1960s, the major social work organizations had embraced the concept of social action, particularly on behalf of the poor, as "the business of social work." In April 1968, NASW sponsored a National Social Action Workshop "The Urban Crisis: A Challenge to the Profession/Strategies for Action," which was dominated by liberal agency directors but included workshops on direct action and participation by Piven, Cloward, and representatives from NWRO, MFY, and the Coalition for a Sane Nuclear Policy (SANE), the long-standing left-wing peace group. In the words of Daniel Thursz (1966), chair of NASW's Commission on Social Action and later dean of the University of Maryland School of Social Work, this reflected the acceptance of social conflict as a constructive and necessary tool to promote social change and the recognition that "social work cannot be wholly scientific."

Yet most social workers continued to reject both radical goals and radical tactics, preferring roles and strategies that operated well within mainstream guidelines and that could be controlled by professionals. These included legislative advocacy, community-based social planning, advocacy, and coalition building (Brody, 1969; Cohen, 1966; Kurzman & Solomon, 1970; Sanders, 1964). This conception of social action had changed little from the well-intentioned, professionally dominated model that prevailed before the movements of the 1960s erupted (United Community Funds and Councils of America, 1961). Even radicals like Cloward briefly considered the possibility of a mediating role for affluent professionals as ombudsmen for the poor (Cloward & Elman, 1966).

Although proponents of social action acknowledged the utility of disruption and civil disobedience, most considered the use of violence unacceptable under any circumstances (Thursz, 1971). In a famous paper, "Disruptive Tactics," presented at the 1968 NCSW conference, Harry Specht (1968) argued that the ideas of Third World revolutionaries like Che Guevara, Franz Fanon, and Regis Debray "can provide vicarious pleasures for American radicals, but not realistic action strategies" (p. 22). Echoing the views of both conservative and liberal academics, Specht asserted that real radical change in the United States could only occur by working through existing institutions (Gamson, 1968; Lipsky, 1968). If that was impossible, he declared, "then God help us all, for we must then either continue to act in a drama which has lost its purpose or join in its destruction. Disruption and violence can contribute to change, but more than that is required for reconciliation; more than that is required to transform America" (Specht, 1968, p. 24).

Many social workers who were active in the antiwar and civil rights movements agreed with Specht that nonconfrontational tactics were preferable to violent approaches. Although they still rejected working through the system, they opted for nonviolent forms of protest, using the ideas of Martin Luther King, Jr., and Gandhi as models. Another source of tension during the 1960s emerged when older, White female heads of settlement houses, like Helen Hall at Henry Street, were replaced by younger, male activists, many of them African American or Latino.

Liberal social work groups like the National Federation of Settlements and Neighborhood Centers (NFSNC) continued to wrap themselves in the mantle of Jane Addams while endorsing a noncontroversial reformist agenda (NFSNC, 1968, 1970, 1972). Among practitioners, Epstein (1970) found that "caseworkers were . . . more conservative than group workers and community organizers at almost every point in the organizational-professional hierarchy," but that professional status also diminished the radicalism of macro practitioners, particularly in public welfare agencies (p. 130). Many practitioners viewed community organization as a "lusty adolescent sub-specialty" in which rhetoric often substituted for competence (Brown, 1968). Others sought to respond to "the challenge of social change" through efforts to unify the profession under a common theoretical, research, and organizational banner that was essentially politically neutered (Johnson, 1964). In the 1970s, this led to the nearly universal acceptance of apolitical systems theory and, later, the ecological model of practice within the field (Meyer, 1970, 1983, 1998; Pincus & Minahan, 1973).

IMAGE BUILDING IN THE PROFESSION

Even the support and participation of NASW in a controversial CBS television series, *East Side/West Side*, starring George C. Scott and Cicely Tyson, in 1963–1964 caused friction within the profession. The series, produced by David Susskind, reflected a progressive interpretation of social problems and human misery that served as the conceptual foundation for the decade's activism. It marked the only time a weekly program dealing primarily with social work appeared on network television (Andrews, 1987).

East Side/West Side focused on a community-based social service agency on the Lower East Side of New York City. Unusual for the television medium of the period, the show addressed issues such as poverty, tenant/landlord conflicts, public health, unresponsive welfare bureaucracies, and race relations. Susskind's left-of-center interpretation of social problems and social work practice won applause from social work leaders and drew criticism from some frontline workers, corporate sponsors, but local CBS affiliates, particularly in the South.

Bertram Beck, associate director of NASW, served as consultant to the series. This overt support of the program by NASW was not well received by all social workers. Some were concerned that social work practice methods were distorted for the sake of dramatization; others complained that too much attention was given to larger system issues like poverty and oppression and that the interpersonal problems that most social workers addressed were largely ignored. Many social workers went so far as to criticize the physical appearance of the lead character, Neil Brock, as portrayed by the series' star, George C. Scott, particularly his casual attire. (He did not tightly secure his tie.) Reflecting on the series years later, Beck noted,

> The fact that so many social workers in the United States were more concerned with Neil Brock's necktie than with the essential message of the program, reflected the tensions within the profession that existed then and still exist today. (B. Beck, personal communication, 1981)

Because of *East Side/West Side's* controversial message about the structural roots of social problems and its sympathetic portrayal of interracial relationships, many local stations refused to air specific episodes and corporate sponsors withdrew their support of the show. Many viewers were also not ready for a weekly television show that explicitly showed the impact of poverty and racism on the lives of families (Andrews, 1984). Internal bickering among social workers, particularly in the early months of the show, also weakened the show's prospects.

Under considerable pressure from sponsors and local affiliates, particularly in the South and Midwest, CBS did not renew the series for a second year despite favorable reviews and satisfactory ratings. Although social work leaders and some progressive practitioners applauded the show's political nature and its contribution to the image-building efforts of the profession, persistent internal tensions over the goals and nature of the profession surfaced during the series (Andrews, 1984; B. Beck, personal communication, 1981). Many social workers viewed the progressive interpretation of social issues at the heart of the program as a threat to their professional aspirations. The split this reflected between leaders and membership over the issue of activism *vs.* professionalism intensified throughout the decade, culminating in open attacks on professionalism by groups like the NWRO and the SWWM. Micro/macro tension, present since the beginnings of the social work field, also tore the profession apart during the early 1960s. The debate over *East Side/West Side* merely symbolized this schism, sometimes in ridiculous ways.

IMPACT ON PRACTICE AND EDUCATION

The social change orientation of the 1960s also influenced the development of social work practice methods and social work education. Schools of social work began to alter course offerings and emphases to educate social workers for social change and community action. More students of color entered graduate social work programs. By the end of the decade, "school after school found itself in the throes of internal conflict which sometimes saw younger faculty members aligned with students against their older colleagues" (Richan, 1973, p. 156).

As Berkeley was the birthplace of the Free Speech movement on college campuses, it is not surprising that the School of Social Welfare there went through a particularly contentious decade of struggle. After a short period of cooperation between student activists and the school administration, sharp schisms appeared in the late 1960s over several core issues, particularly those focused on charges of institutional racism and the relevance of the curriculum. Although the school hired a few radical minority faculty, like Andrew Billingsley, and introduced courses on community organization in 1965 (with guest lectures by Black Panther leaders), students repeatedly decried its failure to "work actively to close the gap between social work theory and social work practice to third world and poverty-stricken communities" (Terrell, 1994, p. 37). Adjunct faculty, many of whom had experience in community agencies, largely sided with the students. The dean, Milton Chernin, and most tenured faculty, however, "could not . . . sympathize with those radicals who dismissed academic standards as another form of institutional racism or who demanded that the School put aside its universalistic values and establish a separate curriculum for disadvantaged minorities, with faculty, students, and curriculum decided by reference to their ideas of social justice" (Leiby, 1994, pp. 23–24).

As the struggle for power within the school and the university intensified, relations among faculty, students, and administrators became increasingly hostile, culminating in a strike by Third World students in February 1969 (Miller, 1994). This drew the critical attention of professional organizations such as NASW and CSWE and led to a decline in external funding. As in other schools, the long-term impact of this conflict was less dramatic. The school eventually retained its accreditation, some diversification of the student body and faculty occurred, and modest changes were introduced to the MSW curriculum—hardly radical accomplishments (Specht, 1994).

Meanwhile, across the Bay at San Francisco State College (now University), social work faculty and students, who had created a social work program with a distinctly radical mission, played key roles in the campus strike called in support of the demands of Third World students. One faculty member, Stanley Ofsevit, formerly a social worker in New York, was fired for his political activism during the strike. After years of litigation, his faculty status was restored and he received back pay from the state (S. Ofsevit, personal communication, 1997).

These struggles made a lasting impact on some students. Schools of social work opened themselves up to new ideas—about women, African Americans, and Latinos—and introduced concepts that ultimately evolved into empowerment theory and the "strengths perspective" on practice (Saleeby, 1997; Simon, 1994; Young, 1970). Many radicals of the 1970s and 1980s cite the crucial role of faculty in shaping the development of their political perspectives (Wagner, 1989b).

Radical social work students also began to organize nationally on their own behalf in the aftermath of the NWRO takeover of the 1969 NCSW conference and the formation of the SWWM. The first issue of the bimonthly newsletter of the National Federation of Student Social Workers (NFSSW), *The Advocate*, appeared in May 1969. Organized along regional lines, the NFSSW focused on issues like curriculum change and state licensing requirements. Although it maintained close ties to the SWWM, it deliberately chose not to be the "student arm of SWWM" but to focus on client advocacy and political activism within the context of students' educational experience (*Hotch Pot*, April 1970, pp. 3–6; NFSSW, 1969, 1970).

Through such efforts, and spurred by criticism from organizers outside of the profession, like Saul Alinsky (1969), client groups, and radicals within the profession itself (Franklin, 1990), the field of community organizing, recognized as a social work method since the 1930s, began to acquire a renewed focus on social action. The short-lived possibilities of the War on Poverty inspired a new generation of social work activists (Van Wormer, 1997). Even NASW embraced a strategy of forming alliances with clients and community-based activists. As a result, radical social workers participated and helped shape some of the more militant organizing efforts of the period (Wagner, 1990).

Yet, as a whole, the social work profession was neither able nor willing to capitalize on the abundant opportunities to forge lasting alignments with organizations created by their clients and constituents among the poor and oppressed populations of U.S. society. There were several reasons for this failure. One was the persistent fear of government repression—the shadow of McCarthyism—that continued to inhibit the social activism of individual social workers and the larger social work community. (See Chapter 10.)

Throughout the 1960s, the government compiled dossiers on radicals in the civil rights, student, and peace movements, and periodically circulated a new version of a blacklist. The FBI had a list of 26,000 alleged radicals, including Martin Luther King, Jr., to be incarcerated in case of a "national emergency" (Branch, 1988, 1998; Davis, 1970; Garrow, 1986; Gitlin, 1980, 1987). In 1975, a Senate Committee chaired by Frank Church (D-Idaho) found that the FBI also maintained files on one million Americans during this period and investigated 500,000 individuals as suspected subversives, without producing a single conviction. Meanwhile, the CIA continued to open citizens' mail and the Internal Revenue Service routinely conducted tax audits as a form of political harassment (Black, 2000).

Social work radicals like Harold Lewis continued to be investigated long after the demise of McCarthy even while on the faculty of prestigious universities like the University of Pennsylvania (H. Lewis, personal communication, 1997). Activists within the War on Poverty like Sanford Kravitz, the creator of the Foster Grandparents Program, and later founding dean of the School of Social Welfare at the State University of New York at Stony Brook, discovered that the FBI had been keeping a file on him since he was a high school student in Connecticut in the late 1940s (S. Kravitz, personal communication, 1995). Lesser known radical social workers also report similar harassment during these years. (See Chapter 10.)

A second reason was the profession's all-consuming drive for professionalization that encouraged social workers to separate from, rather than form coalitions with, the very groups that produced a reorientation of the field and the fulfillment of social work's rhetorical commitment to social justice. Although mainstream organizations like NASW and CSWE formally called for the abolition of White racism (NASW, 1969) and usually endorsed the antipoverty measures of the period, "they were concerned about the bypassing of traditional social work agencies and the stress on 'indigenous,' non-professional staff" (Leighninger, 1999, p. 23). This narrow focus on professional status restricted the ability of social workers to influence the policies of agencies like the OEO because it reinforced the view that social workers could not break out of traditional, patronizing methods of working with low-income people. When a more individualistic approach to people's problems reemerged in the 1970s, the professionalizing impulse in social work shifted once more into high gear. The renewed interest in clinical practice, the professionalization of bachelor of social work (BSW) graduates, and the focus on state licensure of social workers are three prominent consequences of this development.

Some intellectual leaders of the profession, however, embraced the new stress on client participation and rights, and the use of indigenous personnel. They found precedents for this development in the values of radical social workers from the 1930s and 1940s, such as Bertha Reynolds, Grace Marcus, Ruth Smalley, and Kenneth Pray. Alan Keith-Lucas (1967) asserted that contemporary social work radicals were not antiskill, but rather opposed to "the use of skill to control, to influence, to boss another." Theirs was "a cry to be free from domination, to harness social work knowledge and skill for client's rights, for a partnership" (pp. 19–20).

A third reason was that the age and class position of the majority of older social work radicals (who had entered the field in the 1930s through the 1950s) shaped whether and how they were able and willing to remain radicalized. The professional and psychological legacy of McCarthyism continued to take its toll. (See Chapter 10.) Some of the issues raised by the new radicalism of the 1960s— issues of race, gender, and (later) sexual orientation—further divided old and young radicals within the profession even as they stimulated a growth of radical activities among practitioners.

A particularly divisive issue to some practitioners and educators was the growing tensions between African Americans and Jews as some schools moved to establish required courses on racism often in response to strikes organized by African American students (Arnold, 1970; Moore, 1970). Some Jewish faculty and students accused colleagues of hypocrisy for excusing incidents of Black anti-Semitism and allowing the equation of White racism with Jewish racism to go unchallenged (Becker, 1971). Even the radical SWWM struggled with these issues, although it eventually "deplore[d] and condemn[ed] . . . any expression or manifestation of anti-Semitism . . . [as] . . . irrelevant to the tasks and issues which demand attention and . . . as a deliberate ploy . . . to attenuate the efforts of the black community to take its rightful place in the American political, social, and economic order" (SWWM, 1970). The effects of these divisions became particularly pronounced during the 1970s as the general political climate of the nation grew more conservative again. In some schools, this tension persisted throughout the 1990s, often in unspoken ways.

RADICALISM AND PROFESSIONALISM

Throughout the 1960s, radical social workers tried to transform the social work profession as well as the larger social welfare system of the nation. Yet, in an era in which radical ideas and action acquired some broader acceptance and even cultural cache, social work as a whole did not move in a more radical direction. For most social workers, a professional career with job security and decent wages proved far more attractive than radical ideas and their implications for practice. Consequently, some radicals of the period retreated into universities, which provided a safer although less activist environment for the exploration of radical theory. (Their efforts will be discussed in Chapters 8 and 9.) Other social work radicals left the field entirely to continue to pursue a radical vision of U.S. society. To some extent, social workers in the burgeoning area of community organizing and advocacy could continue to practice a radical approach to social change while maintaining their identity as social workers.

The radical legacy of the 1960s lingers on, however, in both the myth and fact of the profession. In a study of self-identified radical social workers conducted in the late 1990s by the authors, respondents frequently commented about the effects of the 1960s on their work. Regardless of whether these were their formative years, whether they practiced social work at that time, or simply knew about the 1960s from other sources, the events of the decade had a lasting impact on their consciousness (Reisch & Andrews, 1999). Contemporary social work radicals still identify the works of such authors and activists of the period as William Ryan, Michael Harrington, Piven and Cloward, Si Kahn, Saul Alinsky, Cesar Chavez, and Stokely Carmichael as providing the intellectual roots of their radicalism. One respondent said "As a college student in the late sixties, I became more conscious of my radicalism as I . . . began to read radical literature, talk radical talk, and participate in left political activities" (Trent, personal communication, 1997).

The numerous social movements of the period also contributed to the development of the current generation of social work radicals (Eamon, Hertzberg, K. Van Wormer, A. K. Lucas, Teague, Kilty, Simmons, personal communications, 1997). Many share the sentiment expressed by one social worker that "We must find a way to ignite that dormant fire of the 60s and let it burn in the name of freedom" (Baum, personal communication, 1997). The idealism of the period—"a time of flower children, psychedelics, free love, and rock and roll, when everything was touched with beauty and love was the key word, when dreams grew into possibilities and possibilities could come true" (Day, 1997, p. 343)—thus remains alive in the hearts of those radical social workers who lived through it.

8

The Redefinition of Social Radicalism, 1970-1999, Part I

The crisis consists precisely in the fact that the old is dying and the new cannot be born; in this interregnum a great variety of morbid symptoms appears.
— Antonio Gramsci, *Selections from the Prison Notebooks of Antonio Gramsci*

AN OVERVIEW OF LATE TWENTIETH CENTURY RADICALISM IN SOCIAL WORK

Just as the radical social movements of the 1960s provoked a backlash in American society and politics, the brief surge of radicalism in the social work field during these years produced a defensive, even hostile, reaction in the social work mainstream. Many social workers felt that radical political activism was either inimical to social work professionalism or should be a separate, subjective activity distinct from scientifically based, objective social work practice (Specht, 1968, 1994). Attacks by radicals on the welfare system and the nature of the social work profession itself—exemplified by their association with the confrontational tactics of the National Welfare Rights Organization (NWRO)—led even reform-minded leaders to rise in defense of existing institutions and organizations. Consequently, as the political–economic and ideological climate shifted in the United States during the 1970s, laying the foundation for the Reagan-Bush era and the "end of welfare" under Clinton, so did the field of social work.

For the next three decades, social work radicals continued their efforts to create alternative organizations and reorient the direction of the profession. They struggled to define radical ideology and theory and to sustain the social

167

changes initiated in the tumultuous 1960s even as conservative trends reemerged and took root in both the society and the social work field. Pressures to broaden the scope of radical thought and action, to incorporate feminist ideas, and to include the perspectives of people of color, gays, and lesbians, presented unprecedented challenges to radical social workers during this period.

In the 1970s, radical social workers were also motivated by the policies of the Nixon, Ford, and Carter administrations, which reflected an antipoor and antiurban bias. (Recall the famous tabloid headline of 1976: "Ford to New York— 'Drop Dead!'") During these years, the tax structure of the United States became increasingly regressive. State and local governments froze revenues through ballot initiatives such as Proposition 13 in California and instituted a virtual freeze on public assistance payments. With the exception of the elderly, who benefited from the indexing of Social Security and the expansion of Medicare, the plight of low-income populations became increasingly grave (Danziger & Weinberg, 1994; Edsall, 1991; Jones, 1992; Katz, 1989; Patterson, 1994).

Unlike conservative critics who regarded the antipoverty programs instituted during the 1960s as wasteful, and liberals who viewed them as well intentioned but insufficient, radical social workers linked the rise and fall of social spending in the 1960s and 1970s to broader political–economic trends (Abramovitz, 1992; Danziger, 1991; Katz, 1989; Keisling, 1984; Lemann, 1988, 1989; Murray, 1984; Piven & Cloward, 1995; Quadagno, 1994). One was the desire of the government to dampen growing social unrest by controlling access to the labor market and its benefits (Piven & Cloward, 1995). Another was the use of social spending to reinforce prevailing gender roles regarding work and the family (Abramovitz, 1999). A third influence was the persistence of institutional racism, a perspective shared by some liberal analysts as well (Edsall, 1991). Finally, radicals argued that social action, not government benevolence, had produced the modest reforms of the past and that, ultimately, more sweeping, egalitarian policies would run counter to what O'Connor (1973) termed the "accumulation" function of the capitalist system. The evolution of radical social work theory and action at the end of the twentieth century must be seen in light of these analyses.

After some short-lived successes in the mid- and late 1970s, largely at the local level, the onset of Reaganism in 1981 demoralized many social work radicals and led to the collapse of several radical social work organizations. By the late 1980s, however, radical social work—often under different labels such as progressive or empowerment-based practice—had made a minor resurgence in both schools of social work and the practice arena (Reisch, 1987a). At the same time, concepts with radical implications, such as social justice, multiculturalism, and the imperative to work for social change, were adopted— at least rhetorically—by mainstream organizations such as the National Association of Social Workers (NASW) and the Council on Social Work Education (CSWE).

Ironically, the increasingly diverse nature of social work radicalism and the appearance that some of its principles had been accepted by the profession both expanded the number of its adherents and made it more difficult to articulate or implement a unified, coherent radical vision. These problems persisted throughout the 1990s and many of the issues that had initially emerged in the early 1970s remained unresolved. At the end of the century, social work radicals once again found themselves and their ideas on the defensive as attacks mounted on the remnants of the U.S. welfare state. Despite superficial appearances to the contrary, radicals remained marginalized in professional organizations and schools of social work. (See Chapter 10.)

REACTION TO RADICAL ACTIVISM IN SOCIAL WORK

One of the earliest and sharpest critics of 1960s-style social work radicalism was Harry Specht, professor and later dean at the University of California-Berkeley School of Social Welfare, who criticized the "disruptive tactics" of 1960s radicals in 1968 (see Chapter 7) and later decried the "deprofessionalization" of social work in a widely circulated *Social Work* article in March 1972. Stung by his experiences with student radicals at Berkeley, Specht attacked their activism as a demonstration of social workers' naivete, citing efforts against institutional racism as an example of "dogma without content" (Specht, 1972, p. 5). Such political activism, in his view, "downgraded professional practice" through its emphasis on anti-individualism, communalism, and environmental determinism.

Ironically, Specht had been one of the major proponents of grassroots community organizing in the early 1960s when he worked at Mobilization for Youth (MFY) in New York. He contributed several classic essays to community organizing literature. By the early 1970s, however, his views had shifted. Shrewdly citing C. Wright Mills, long an icon of the American left, Specht critcized the linkage of political activism with professional practice and education, which he regarded as an "abuse of the function of the profession" (Specht, 1972, p. 13).

His outspoken views, however, naturally put Specht at odds with social work radicals. Yet, even other acknowledged liberal leaders of the social work profession, such as Daniel Thursz, dean of the University of Maryland School of Social Work (1971), and Chauncey Alexander, executive director of NASW throughout most of the 1970s challenged his positions. They believed that professionalism and activism were not in conflict; in fact, they argued that social work's mission required social workers to be politically active as part of their professional responsibility.

At the 1977 NASW Delegate Assembly in Portland, Oregon, Alexander (1977) declared that social workers must "recognize, and be proud . . . that within the demand for professional recognition and practice is the willingness to be responsible and accountable for decent service to people. Commitment to advocacy of social . . . change is inherent in our socially based theory and practice" (p. 2). The profession's *Code of Ethics* (1976, 1996) created an ethical imperative for social workers to engage in political action on behalf of vulnerable populations. Because the focus of the *Code*, however, remained on advocacy for people, there is some question as to whether it reflected, even rhetorically, a truly radical position (Simon, 1994).

As they debated the ethics and efficacy of activism, social workers were under attack from both conservative politicians and organized client groups. At the 1970 National Conference on Social Welfare conference, Johnnie Tillmon, the leader of the NWRO, blamed social workers (rather than the socio-economic system) for the problems welfare recipients faced. At the other end of the political spectrum the Nixon administration frequently trumpeted the view that social workers promoted community programs out of self-interest. Given this climate, it was no surprise that a popular book of the time referred to social work as "The Unloved Profession" (Richan & Mendelsohn, 1973). Social workers, in Tom Wolfe's (1970) memorable phrase, had become one of the "flak catchers" of a turbulent society—bombarded with criticisms from ideological opponents of the left and the right.

Despite the presence of radical social workers in several movements of the 1960s which focused on civil rights for people of color and welfare rights for the poor, the radical movement in social work had been predominantly White. The emergence of social movements within the profession based on race, gender, and sexual orientation altered the nature of radical social work during the post-1960s period and influenced even mainstream organizations, such as NASW and CSWE, beginning in the late 1960s and early 1970s. Minority caucuses appeared between 1968 and 1971, representing African Americans, Puerto Ricans, Asian Americans, and American Indians. CSWE created Commissions on the Status of Women, on Race and Ethnicity and, later, on Gay Men and Lesbian Women. In part, these changes occurred because of the sheer growth in the size and diversity of the profession. And, in part, they emerged because the consciousness and sensitivity of the general population around these issues gradually had increased.

Articles on issues of race and racism by social workers of color and on feminist perspectives on practice began to appear in the early 1970s. Through groups like the National Association of Black Social Workers (NABSW) and local Black United Funds, African Americans focused on broad issues of economic and social inequality and specific concerns like transracial adoption, often from a perspective of Black Liberation or Black Nationalism. The antecedents of today's Afrocentric views on practice and education can be identified in some of the writings of the period (Harvey & Coleman, 1997; Harvey & Rauch, 1997; Mathis, 1977; *Survival Magazine*, February 1970; United South End Settlement papers, April–May 1970).

In many ways, social work was slow, compared with other professions, to tackle these tough issues. The "Institutes to Eliminate Racism" (1971) organized by the Young Women's Christian Association (YWCA), as well as that organization's long-standing focus on feminist issues, were a notable exception. Nevertheless, the incorporation of new perspectives simultaneously broadened the scope of radicalism within the field and divided the radical wing of the profession. Ultimately, so-called identity politics moved radical social workers into new and important arenas of social and ideological debate while limiting the possibility of lasting radical change within the profession and the political environment.

FEMINIST PRACTICE: A NOT ALWAYS RADICAL ALTERNATIVE

In the early 1970s, during the second wave of the women's movement, feminist social workers began to pay increasing attention to issues of gender in social work practice, to question the nature of knowledge, and to challenge the process of research itself. Despite the numerical dominance of women in social work, women's issues had not been given a great deal of attention by the profession since the 1920s (Chambers, 1986). Although colleagues in psychology and sociology responded to the ideas inspired by the women's movement relatively quickly, it was not until 1977 that *Social Work* devoted a special issue to women's concerns.

At first, feminist social workers were not directly involved in the formulation of radical feminist social work theory. But they soon challenged the unequal distribution of power, status, and income within the profession and pointed out sexist gaps in the presentation of social work history (Hooyman & Bricker-Jenkins, 1984; van den Bergh & Cooper, 1986; Weick & Vandiver, 1982). Much of this early feminist work, however, was not specifically radical in its orientation. It focused instead on analyzing and responding to the special problems of women and resulted in the creation of much-needed community-based services such as battered women's shelters, women's health centers, programs for displaced homemakers, and alternatives to traditional counseling. These were often services focused on White, middle-class women, rather than low-income clients or women of color (Abramovitz, 1999).

Nevertheless, the growth of the women's movement in the late 1960s and early 1970s slowly influenced social work theory and practice through traditional women's groups, professional associations, and newly established feminist policy networks. NASW and CSWE created women's caucuses, which, despite substantial initial resistance, were successful in promoting important changes in the structure of both organizations and the accreditation guidelines of social work programs.

As the concept of the "feminization of poverty" acquired increased currency and saliency in the late 1970s, issues of poverty and inequitable wages became cutting-edge women's concerns (Goldberg & Kremen, 1990). The linkage of poverty and gender inequality enabled many female social workers to address issues that affected low-income and low-power women, including women of color. This helped somewhat to bridge the gaps of class and race that plagued the feminist movement since its inception (Deckard, 1979; Rosenberg, 1992). Over the next two decades, activism among women social workers continued to

increase, particularly around issues such as poverty, civil rights, domestic violence, and nuclear disarmament (Reeser, 1988). One consequence of this activism was that formerly radical issues became incorporated into the liberal agendas of mainstream social work organizations.

An example of the transmission of feminist ideas into the social service
arena was the emergence of the rape crisis movement. Although initially based
upon radical feminist ideology, by the early 1980s the movement adopted more
of a liberal-reformist orientation. It became increasingly professionalized, institutionalized, and homogenized (Collins & Whalen, 1989). Other self-help and
mutual aid organizations founded by women went through similar transforma-
tions during this period (Withorn, 1984).

In addition to the impact of professionalization, these developments reflected a division among feminist social workers along liberal, socialist, and radical
lines that often belied the image of united "sisterhood" so carefully nurtured by
movement leaders. In the social work field, these distinctions were reflected in
the practice arena over matters of problem identification, assessment, treatment
strategies, and goals (Nes & Iadicola, 1989). Radical and socialist feminists, in
particular, operated from assumptions that challenged prevailing conceptual
frameworks. They argued that feminism without a radical perspective and goals
would lose its fundamental meaning and purpose: "Simply put, feminism is trans-
formational politics. It seeks individual liberation through collective activity,
embracing both personal and social change. The broad goal of feminism is not
limited to the elimination of dominant-subordinate relationships between sex
groups but . . . the dismantling of all permanent power hierarchies" (Morell,
1987, pp. 147–148).

By the 1980s, some radical feminist ideas, particularly the popular notion
that "the personal is political" began to penetrate mainstream social work publications and organizations (Bricker-Jenkins & Hooyman, 1986; van den Bergh
& Cooper, 1986; Weick & Vandiver, 1982). Inspired by the special issue of Social Work on women, NASW instituted "the feminist practice project" in the
early 1980s led by Nancy Hooyman and Mary Bricker-Jenkins. Women faculty
and administrators at institutions such as the University of Pennsylvania were
instrumental in promoting Affirmative Action policies in schools and field agencies, which helped diversify faculty and student bodies in institutions that were
racially homogeneous and male dominated even in the late 1960s (Staples, 1983).

In 1986, the first feminist social work journal, *Affilia*, appeared, published
by the Feminist Press. It immediately had 500 subscribers, a number that grew
considerably after the journal signed a publishing agreement with Sage Publications in 1988. *Affilia* not only published articles about women's issues, it was
and continues to be run entirely by women, operating under feminist process
principles. Although not an exclusively radical publication, it frequently published essays by radical feminists, most recently in a special issue on the impact
of welfare reform (*Affilia*, Summer 2000).

Feminist ideas also shaped the theory and practice of other oppressed
groups, particularly gays and lesbians. Influential themes introduced and popu-

larized by feminist social workers included empowerment, identifying and over-coming oppression, the importance of process, an emphasis on consciousness raising and self-help, an attack on patriarchy, and increased attention to nonrational ways of knowing and depicting the world (Morell, 1987; Withorn, 1984). The latter helped make social workers increasingly receptive to postmodern theory in the 1990s (Sands & Nuccio, 1992).

In March 1984, the Association for Women in Social Work (AWSW) was formed for the purposes of promoting

> the development of feminist values, knowledge, assumptions, research, and behaviors [and promoting] their infusion into social work practice and education; the formation of feminist networks, support groups and work groups . . . ; the development of learning and practice environments which reflect feminist values and concerns . . . ; the development of knowledge and skills—to protect women from the effects of oppression . . . ; . . . the interests of women in mainstream and alternative organizations; the development and legitimization of policies and service to meet the special needs and concerns of women; [and] . . . the infusion of feminist values, principles, priorities, and content within the standing organizations of the profession. (AWSW, May 1995, pp. 9–10).

Feminist practice and female-centered social work organizations offered an opportunity for social workers to bridge the cause/function gap that had split the profession since the 1920s. A feminist approach provided "services within the context of a change-oriented politics" while working to create "a collective movement that changes social structure" (Morell, 1987, p. 149). The feminist notion of integrating cause and function also was expressed by radical male social workers in the 1980s, notably Harold Lewis. From a theoretical perspective influenced by Marx, Rawls, and Freire, Lewis argued that the "cause" of social work was embedded *in* the "function" rather than being distinct from it as mainstream leaders had long implied (1976–1977). By the mid-1980s, therefore, it certainly seemed that "the feminist future [was] not for women only" (Hooyman & Bricker-Jenkins, 1984).

Feminist ideas had a lasting impact on the social work profession during these 30 years. After a decline in the 1960s and 1970s, more women moved into leadership positions in schools of social work and professional organizations like NASW and CSWE. Articles, books, and conference papers with feminist themes, like empowerment, and around issues concerning women, such as violence and welfare reform, flourished, occasionally even in mainstream journals (Abramovitz, 1999; Mandell, 1996, 1997; Prigoff, 1996; Van Soest, 1997; Van Soest & Bryant, 1995). Throughout the 1980s and 1990s, largely through the influence of feminist editors, the *Journal of Progressive Human Services* (*JPHS*), as well as more traditional publications like *Social Work* and the *Journal of Social Work Education*, consistently reflected feminist ideas in their articles and editorial policies. Not all of these ideas, however, were of a radical nature.

During the 1990s, the AWSW and the CSWE Commission on the Status of

Women continued to serve as focal points for the expression of feminist views on practice and education in the profession. Although they had limited impact on either national or organizational policies, the concentration of women in these groups kept feminist issues alive during conservative times and provided important personal supports for women in the field. In the mid-1990s, through the leadership of individuals like Mimi Abramovitz and Mary Bricker-Jenkins, AWSW began to strengthen its connection to radical groups within social work like the Bertha Capen Reynolds Society (BCRS) and outside the field like the Kensington Welfare Rights Union (AWSW, October 1995–June 1997).

EXPLOSION OF RADICAL SOCIAL WORK THEORY

Feminist ideas represented only part of the virtual explosion of radical social work literature that appeared in the 1970s. For the first time, concerted efforts were made to define radical social work practice. In effect, this was a radical version of the inward-looking tendencies that have characterized the social work profession during periods of political conservatism (Wenocur & Reisch, 1989). Because the scope of political activities among radical social workers decreased during the late twentieth century, the development of radical theory took on an increasingly significant dimension. It is largely through the development of that theory that radical social work continues to have some influence on the field and the society as a whole.

Some radicals, like Piven and Cloward (1971), focused on issues of social policy and community organization, based on an interpretation of their experience as activists with the NWRO and MFY during the 1960s. Other authors (Galper, 1975, 1980; Lichtenberg, 1976) attempted to formulate a model of radical practice that could be equally applied to work with individuals and communities. During this period, U.S. radicals often looked abroad—to Great Britain, Canada, France, The Netherlands, and Latin America—for new theoretical models (Bailey & Brake, 1975; Corrigan & Leonard, 1978; Freire, 1970). Much of the literature that emerged was influenced by Marxist or neo-Marxist ideas, often under new labels like "structural social work" (Moreau, 1979). Ideas that prefigured the postmodern approaches of the 1980s and 1990s also began to appear. For the first time, essays with radical themes were published in mainstream social work journals like *Social Work, Social Service Review,* and the *Journal of Education for Social Work* (Epstein, 1970; Lichtenberg, 1976; Rein, 1970). Most of these articles focused on the nature of the profession or the professional role from an openly radical perspective.

Writing at the height of the social work activism of the 1960s, Martin Rein (1970) defined radical social work in terms of four basic components. These were resistance to practice norms and standards, a commitment to the redistribution of societal resources and power, the reduction or elimination of economic and social inequalities, and the altering of social/structural conditions. These components of social work radicalism, he argued, were preconditions for individual change. Rein, therefore, distinguished between radical social action as a means to produce individual change and change produced "by the total submission of the individual in the collectivity" (p. 18), a view of radicalism comparable to Rousseau's conception of the General Will (Crocker, 1968). It was the latter view that liberals like Harry Specht found so threatening to the status of the profession.

Unlike most radical social workers of earlier generations, Rein did not equate radicalism with any particular ideology. Instead, he conceived of radicalism as a sustained commitment to a set of policy and practice principles that were critical of the emerging shape of the U.S. welfare state and that linked social work practice with political action. One of Rein's colleagues at Bryn Mawr College, Philip Lichtenberg (1976), argued that "the radical thrust or potential in casework appears to stem from the very nature of the tasks to which the field addresses itself," that is through its focus on systemic or structural change. In this conception of practice, individual change is not possible "without the world being turned upside down" (p. 259).

Lichtenberg (1990) was among the first of many radical social workers in the 1970s and 1980s to connect the issue of social struggle with the identification and overcoming of *all forms* of societal oppression. This became a central tenet of social work radicals during the next three decades, particularly among women, persons of color, and gays and lesbians. While broadening the potential scope of radical social work, however, it fragmented the previously unified conception of radicalism in the field and made the formation of radical coalitions more difficult to develop and sustain, paralleling conditions in the wider society (Gitlin, 1995).

Other social workers during this period, whom Daphne Statham (1978) called "liberal radicals," attempted to produce structural changes within the rules of society or to challenge existing institutional arrangements through legitimate means (J. Blau, personal communication, 1997). Their professional ancestors date back to the Progressive Era, with role models like Florence Kelley (Sklar, 1995). Among their tactics was a form of institutional insurgency to humanize social policies and bureaucratic procedures (Needleman & Needleman, 1974). These social work radicals of the 1970s emphasized the principle of justice as a counterweight to the ideological status quo (Lewis, 1972). They adopted social action strategies, including social conflict approaches, that operated outside conventional political channels but not usually outside the law, and directed their efforts at systemic or structural transformation (Epstein, 1970). In his book, *The Challenge of Social Equality*, David Gil (1976a) articulated this sentiment clearly. He argued that, above all, radicalism involved the peaceful replacement of the existing political–economic system and the values upon which it was founded.

Norman Goroff (n.d., e, f), a leader in the group work field, outlined similar goals for social work in more explicitly socialist language. He described the ultimate aim of radical practice as "a radical transformation . . . to replace a competitive, alienating and alienated society, which because it is capitalist, exploitive, individualistic and hierarchically structured developes (*sic*) grossly unequal life chances for its citizens, with a society based on cooperation, egalitarianism and non-exploitive relationships, where production of goods and services are for use and not intended solely for profit" (Goroff, n.d., d, p. 1). Goroff's views reflected a growing tendency among those David Wagner (1989a) termed the "militant radical" professionals of the mid-1970s to define their radicalism in anticapitalist terms.

Jeffry Galper's definition (1975, 1980) of radical social work perhaps best reflected Wagner's typology. Galper regarded it as "social work that contributes to building a movement for the transformation to socialism by its efforts in and through the social services. *Radical social work . . . is socialist social work*. Those who practice radical social work are those who struggle for socialism from their position within the social services" (1980, p. 10, emphasis added). This involved an understanding of capitalism, racism, imperialism, and the theories and values that support them (Joseph, 1975).

Other social work radicals like Robert Knickmeyer (1972) and John Longres (1977, 1986) adopted an explicitly Marxist analysis. Knickmeyer differentiated between Marxist-oriented social service and those promoted by reformist organizations such as NASW in three major ways. First, it regarded social welfare as an expression of the hegemonic forces in society. Second, it involved face-to-face contact between workers and clients without the mediation of official channels of communication and contact. Third, it considered the agency and not the legislature as a primary focus of political struggle. In Knickmeyer's view, the target of radical social work "is not the politicians who are accountable to a ruling elite, but rather fellow human service workers who are ready to reject a violent social system" (Knickmeyer, 1972, p. 63).

Longres asserted that radical social casework "encourage[s] social, political and economic change . . . consonant with a Marxist social vision. [It] promotes the ideals of socialism as an alternative and works toward the alleviation of the conditions of alienation" (1977). He deduced four practice principles from Marxist theory. These focused on the centrality of the concept of alienation, the importance of analyzing practice from a working-class perspective, the use of social work intervention to eliminate alienation, and the importance of "promot[ing] class consciousness and the pursuit of collective interests" (1986, p. 27).

Ann Withorn (1984) also regarded an anticapitalist stance as a primary element of radical social work, along with class consciousness and egalitarianism. Withorn, like Cloward and Piven (1975), and unlike Rein, Lichtenberg, Gil, and Lewis, regarded deprofessionalization as a precondition for radical practice. In the 1980s and 1990s, through her leadership in the Bertha Capen Reynolds Society (BCRS) (now the Social Welfare Action Alliance), Withorn moved the organization increasingly toward a stance against professionalization and in alliance with welfare rights groups (Newdom, 1996, 1997). (See Chapter 9.)

These views became popular among young radical social workers and social work students during the 1970s. For example, students in the Radical So-

cial Work Collective at the University of Connecticut (1975) stated that "Radical social work . . . emphasizes the importance of the socio-economic system as
a source of people's problems rather than looking solely to intra-psychic or interpersonal explanations. It emphasizes change instead of adjustment" (p. 1).
In their view, such practice seeks collective solutions within people, not for
people, thereby demystifying the professional role. It challenges the present
inegalitarian socioeconomic system and promotes a more just distribution of
power and resources.

Thus, the definition of radicalism within social work during the post-1960s
era encompassed increasingly diverse ideological perspectives. It included radicals who regarded the structure of society and, sometimes, even the nature of
the social work profession as the primary sources of individual, family, and community problems. Their view of social and economic problems, public policies
that attempted to address them, and the theoretical frameworks of social work
practice rested upon a critique of capitalism as a socioeconomic and cultural/
ideological system, without always adopting explicitly socialist or Marxist language.

DEBATE OVER PROFESSIONALISM

A significant and lasting debate began in the 1970s among radical social workers between those who advocated antiprofessional models of practice and regarded social workers as mere agents of control and those who viewed social
workers as advocates who could help clients develop their own power (Wagner,
1990). This debate was important because it enabled some radicals to establish
a rationale for working within the system rather than being solely "outside agitators" railing against it. Their goals could now include radicalizing the social
service organization to improve services to low-income and oppressed groups
(Needleman & Needleman, 1974). Ultimately, many of those who adopted this
perspective embraced an empowerment approach to practice that continues to
influence the profession to this day (Gutierrez, Parsons, & Cox, 1998). The
ongoing struggle over these different conceptions of the social work role resembled the intraprofessional conflicts of the 1930s and occurred within educational institutions as well as the practice arena.

Two contrasting analyses appeared during this period. Some American radicals, like Piven and Cloward (1975, 1977), Withorn (1984), and Galper (1975,
1980), and their British counterparts, such as Peter Leonard (1975), Mike Brake
and Roy Bailey (1975, 1980), regarded—albeit to different degrees—the *organizational and theoretical structure of professional social work itself* as an im-
pediment to the creation of a truly radical practice. Other self-described radical
social workers in the United States did not see a direct contradiction between
social work professionalism and so-called transformative practice (Knickmeyer,
1972; Lewis, 1982; Longres, 1986; Needleman & Needleman, 1974).

For the former group, radical social work practice involved several critical elements. One was a decentralized, nonhierarchical, collective practice in which clients and workers cooperated in breaking down professional status distinctions and power differentials. A second was welfare state trade union politics and linkages to other unions. A third was consistent connections between practice with individuals and families and community politics and issues. A fourth was the decentralization and democratization of work in social service agencies (Brake & Bailey, 1980).

Critics of professionalism also included academic activists like Tim Sampson, a faculty member at San Francisco State University, a founder of the National Welfare Rights Organization, past president of the Citizens Action League in California, and a long-time leader of the California Faculty Association. In a debate with Mark Battle, executive director of NASW, and Harry Specht, dean of the University of California-Berkeley School of Social Welfare, published in *Public Welfare* (Summer 1981), Sampson assessed the value of professionalism against three primary objectives: "Does it build power for change? Does it help create community? Does it help people reflect and develop their own political analysis and ideas for change?" Sampson maintained that the virtues of professionalism were "outweighed by its two fatal flaws: (1) its tendency to separate the professional from those served and (2) the related tendency to involve the professional in the pursuit of a pernicious set of self-interests: status, prestige, money." He proposed a model of human service provision that was based on dialectical theory, mutuality of workers–clients, client/community ownership and control of services, and a focus on political as well as personal goals.

In an essay in the influential book *Radical Social Work*, Peter Leonard (1975) adopted a critical perspective on professionalism that fell short of the strident antiprofessional stance of some American radicals. He argued that the situation of social work under capitalism was far more complex than portrayed by some of its critics. Radical practice, he asserted, developed within a dialectical context of people and institutions, the simultaneous and seemingly contradictory existence of both oppressive and supportive systems, and the development of individual consciousness. Its aims were education, linking people with systems, building alternative systems of services and power, and the creation of both individual and structural responses to oppression. Radical practice, in Leonard's views, emerged through the development of dialogical relationships, the promotion of critical consciousness (what Freire had called conscientization), and through focused organization and planning. Apart from differences in terminology, social work radicals in the United States have embodied many of these characteristics since the late nineteenth century (Leonard, 1975). Other British radicals like George and Wilding (1976, 1985, 1994) pushed this argument further by identifying the contradictory elements inherent in the concept of the welfare state itself.

Some of their American counterparts, however, took an uncompromising stance against professionalism. In their essay, "Notes Toward a Radical Social Work" (1975), Cloward and Piven identified four "tenets for radical action": (1) the rejection of the idea that social welfare institutions have benign motives; (2)

the rejection of the notion that social service agencies and their clients have complementary interests; (3) the identification of clients' problems in the socioeconomic system and not in their personality; and (4) the development of awareness as to *how professionalism (theories, status, roles) legitimate professional dominance over people's lives* (pp. XXII–XXVIII, emphasis added). Once they recognize that their struggle is against the institutions of capitalism, radical social workers engage in many forms of resistance, including the use of external pressures to produce institutional change. Their educational work strives to underscore the contradictions within the design and delivery of social services.

Daphne Statham (1978) disagreed with this dichotomous view of social work radicalism. She commented that "degrees of radicalism cannot be determined by crude measures of whether a person is inside or outside traditional social work, working within the liberal tradition or outside it" (p. 14). In fact, Reeser and Epstein's study of social work activism (1990) provides some evidence that greater professionalization does not lead to less activism. The goals of such activism, however, can reflect either liberal or radical orientations. The key questions are: What is the focus of this activism? Do social work activists maintain the same level of militancy? Are they active in pursuit of social justice or in the service of their own professional enhancement? As Collins and Whalen (1989) pointed out in their essay on the rape crisis movement, without radical goals, many reform efforts simply maintain the status quo. The history of social work radicalism over the past century frequently proves their assertion.

PEACE AND SOCIAL JUSTICE

As it had in the past, the issue of peace and nuclear disarmament offered the potential of uniting and mobilizing radical and liberal social workers, particularly in response to the military buildup and bellicose rhetoric of the Reagan administration during the 1980s. Ironically, NASW's committee, Social Workers for Peace and Nuclear Disarmament (SWPND), played a more effective role in this regard than did radical groups like the Radical Alliance of Social Service Workers (RASSW) or, later, the BCRS. It served as a vehicle for radicals and pacifists like David Gil, Arline Prigoff, Eleanor Belser, Fred Newdom, and Dorothy van Soest to influence the policies of NASW at the state and national levels and educate its members about the relationship between militarism and domestic policy issues (*Peace Network News*, Fall 1987).

In both 1984 and 1988, NASW's Delegate Assembly selected peace as one of four priorities for the organization's "social policy and action" agenda (NASW, 1984, 1988). In September 1985 and April 1987, at the request of SWPND, the NASW Board of Directors took a firm stand against the apartheid policies of the South African regime, well in advance of the U.S. government. The following year, SWPND persuaded the NASW Board to adopt a policy statement on "Peace and Human Rights in Central America." Although generally moderate in tone, the statement implicated the United States government "in the suffering of the Central American people" and called for the United States to cease its intervention in the region's civil wars (*Peace Network News*, Winter/Spring 1988, p. 4). Representatives for the committee also regularly participated in international social work conferences and sent delegations on human rights missions to countries like El Salvador. By the end of the 1980s, more than 35 states, New York City, and the District of Columbia had active chapters (*Peace Network News*, Summer/Fall 1988). In March 1989, the School of Social Work at the University of Illinois at Urbana-Champaign hosted an international conference on "Women and Peace."

In the early 1990s, reflecting the increasing breadth of the issues it addressed and the appearance of a diminished nuclear threat after the end of the Cold War, SWPND changed its name to Social Workers for Peace and Social Justice. With the support of Catholic peace activists, long-time social work radicals, and a few state chapters, it published a widely distributed curriculum guide, *Incorporating Peace and Justice into the Social Work Curriculum* (van Soest, 1992). Through its newsletter, the committee served primarily an educational and clearinghouse function. It reflected new vistas in the profession, such as the growing concern over global violence in its personal, political, and economic manifestations, and greater interest in international human rights issues in such regions as the Balkans and Central America.

In the mid-1990s, in addition to a continuing focus on the impact of federal budget decisions, the committee began to incorporate in its newsletter an analysis of how economic globalization was linked to issues of peace and justice (*Social Workers for Peace & Social Justice Newsletter*, Winter 1994, Spring 1995, Spring 1996, Fall 1996). In the fall of 1995, it also persuaded the NASW board to endorse the call of dozens of other organizations in the United States and abroad for a new trial for African American activist Mumia Abu-Jamal (NASW, Fall 1996). Although its efforts were diminished by NASW's fiscal crisis and the October 1996 death of Eileen McGowan Kelly, the organization's director of Peace and International Affairs since 1989, Social Workers for Peace and Social Justice (SWPSJ) continued to be an advocate for human rights into the new millennium. Paralleling developments in the profession as a whole, it now paid increased attention to issues involving people of color while expanding its focus on violence to include protests against the death penalty (Newsletter, Summer 2000).

In turn social workers of color, particularly in academic settings, stressed the importance of broadening conceptual paradigms to account for multicultural perspectives, institutional racism, and the impact of White privilege (Gutierrez, 1997; Lum, 1986, 1992, 1999; Pinderhughes, 1989). In the 1970s, CSWE created a Commission on Racial, Ethnic, and Cultural Diversity and modified its election procedures to ensure greater representation of racial minorities on its board of directors. Faculty and students at San Francisco State University established the Institute for Multicultural Research and Social Work Practice and the student-edited journal, *Social Work Perspectives*, in the late 1980s. The *Journal of Multicultural Social Work* appeared in 1991. Although they included works by some radical social workers of color, publications that focused on multiculturalism or diversity primarily emphasized emerging identify-focused issues and tended to present alternative practice models or research on persons of color, rather than broader, structural analyses. While such works underscored the persistent lack of attention to multicultural themes in mainstream journals they also reflected the liberal, ideological orientations of most authors.

Gay, lesbian, and bisexual social workers also challenged the pervasiveness of heterosexism and homophobia in society and in the professional literature. By the 1990s, CSWE established a CSWE commission to address their concerns and a distinct journal, the *Journal of Gay and Lesbian Social Services*, appeared. Although most gay and lesbian social workers were not politically radical, perhaps because of their predominantly White, middle-class backgrounds, the intellectual and cultural forces unleashed by their efforts transformed and often complicated the meaning of radicalism within the social work field. Consequently, many social workers maintained overlapping demographic and cultural identities.

Thus, even without a significant, broad-based radical movement in social work (such as the Rank and File Movement of the 1930s), radical social work theory in the 1980s exercised a steady, modest influence on practice models, education, and research. Occasionally, radical ideas were found in mainstream journals and books. The establishment of the Progressive Practice Symposium at CSWE conferences in the early 1990s kept these ideas alive and the BCRS occasionally helped solidify national unity around progressive themes, particularly through its national conferences in the late 1980s and early 1990s. The impact of the society, however, was limited by its domination by East Coast academics, the scant representation of minorities of color in its membership, and persistent confusion over its goals, which its name did not help clarify. (See Chapter 9.)

Despite these obstacles, radical social workers did not abandon their values or their commitment to social change. Wagner's (1990) study of former members of the Catalyst Collective in New York City in the late 1980s revealed that they still professed such values as more egalitarian relationships between workers and clients; a focus on combating sexism, racism, classism, ageism, and heterosexism; and preferential treatment for oppressed and excluded groups as clients or employees. Wagner also found that social work radicals continued to be unwilling to implement policies they believed to be contrary to principles of humanitarianism and democracy. They had a vision of family and work that encouraged reexamination of the work ethic and family patterns and roles. Finally, they belonged to networks of other left-leaning social workers and supported progressive organizations outside the field (Wagner, 1990, pp. 201–202).

As the nature of radicalism in the field evolved, some radical social workers expressed their views in new, occasionally unusual ways. Norm Goroff, a long-time socialist group worker, wrote several papers promoting the concept of "The Love Paradigm" (1988) as a means of overcoming the increasing violence of U.S. society and what he termed "the social construction of . . . personal inadequacy." Goroff's model contained four central components—care, responsibility, respect, and knowledge—which reflected the writings of Bertha Reynolds two generations before. Thomas Keefe's work on alienation adopted a similar line of analysis from an explicitly materialist perspective (1984).

Arline Prigoff (1987), a long-time radical who was active in the 1980s around issues of peace and U.S. intervention in Central America, focused on broadening the widely used framework of systems analysis to include class structure as a major feature. By incorporating Third World perspectives, such as those of Franz Fanon, into practice models, social workers could "intervene on behalf of empowerment and liberation at a variety of levels" (p. 9). The mode of intervention mattered less in her view than the theories and values that guided it. This was a significant departure from the radical thought of the 1960s and 1970s, which often promoted a rigid dichotomy between conservative individually oriented practice and radical community organizing or other forms of social action.

By and large, the influence of radical social workers in the 1970s and 1980s can not be found in major institutional changes, legislative breakthroughs, or the emergence of dynamic social movements. Rather, it occurred gradually, largely in the form of altered consciousness around social issues and theoretical perspectives among many practitioners and educators. In the foreword to Epstein and Reeser's study, *Professionalization and Activism in Social Work* (1990), Richard Cloward asserted, "Far more social workers today think that problems such as poverty are rooted in structural sources than thought so in the 1960s. . . . This shift in explanatory mode is a genuine legacy of the protest movements of [that period]" (p. xvi).

RADICALISM IN SOCIAL WORK EDUCATION

During the last three decades of the twentieth century, schools of social work constituted one of the most fertile arenas for the development of radical ideas, although some observers have pointed out the cyclical quality of radicalism in social work education (De Maria, 1992). Ironically, in a politically conservative era, radical perspectives on practice became more visible and explicit components of social work education than they had at times of greater activism like the 1930s and 1960s, despite the limitations of university environments, dominant paradigms, and research methods (Epstein, 1995). Students at such diverse schools as the University of Pennsylvania, the University of California-Berkeley, San Jose State University, the State University of New York at Stony Brook, the University of Michigan, Hunter College, and San Francisco State (just to name a few) organized collectives and teach-ins, formed study groups with faculty, and threw themselves into campus and community causes. They debated the relative efficacy of using analyses based on class, race, and gender and pushed faculty to define concepts like social change more clearly in the curriculum (Balter et al., 1978). Often, student radicals adopted a broad, antihierarchical perspective that either lacked or attempted to synthesize more formal socialist or feminist frameworks.

The major focus of most student radicals was on the importance of radical structural and personal change (Finnerty, 1971). Although most of this activity took place at a local level, the National Federation of Student Social Workers (NFSSW), founded in 1967, organized a conference in 1976 in Philadelphia on "Revolutionary Tactics for Human Services" under the auspices of Temple University (NFSSW, 1976). The conference included a wide range of workshops and papers on topics from "Radical Therapy and Psychosocial Liberation" to "Unionization" to "Racism in Social Work Education" (NFSSW, 1976).

In addition to their participation in groups like the RASSW and the BCRS, radical social work faculty engaged in a variety of local efforts to translate radical ideas into practice. In the early 1970s in Philadelphia, faculty at Bryn Mawr College and the University of Pennsylvania organized the People's Fund to raise money for social change organizations that fought against racism, economic exploitation, sexism, and other forms of oppression. In the first year, more than 500 contributors joined the fund to assist organizations that had been bypassed by traditional funders such as the United Way (People's Fund, 1972). Similar funds were created in Baltimore by University of Maryland faculty Stanley Wenocur and Richard Cook and in San Francisco by social work faculty members Pat Purcell, Willia Gray, and Tim Sampson, with the active participation of students, colleagues, and community practitioners.

Social work faculty also increasingly took risks around the presentation of radical ideas about policy and practice in mainstream arenas. Problems like racism that were heretofore unspoken by White radical professors began to be addressed explicitly at professional conferences and in journal articles. In January 1969, at the annual meeting of CSWE in Cleveland, Harold Lewis, soon to become dean of Hunter College School of Social Work, asserted, "Whatever our personal beliefs and public declarations, we must assume that our profession and its associated institutions perpetuate the racist practices of our society, unless in attitude and actions they prove otherwise" (1969, p. 2). Racism, he argued, was not merely a problem associated with slavery or even with the contemporary plight of African Americans. It was based on the institutional association of private property and profit that is also reflected in the increasing gap between rich and poor. Under such circumstances, social work curricula should emphasize the importance of values and ideology and not merely focus on methods (Lewis, 1969a).

Echoing other radical sentiments of the period, social work faculty challenged the ways educational institutions replicated the hierarchical relationships of the wider society (Goroff, n.d., d). Under the influence of writers like Brazilian educator Paulo Freire (1970), they began to distinguish between education and indoctrination and to promote greater egalitarianism and dialogue in the educational experience (Lewis, 1973; Cloward & Piven, 1975). They introduced the theme of distributive justice as a guiding principle for social work, even though, like their professional ancestors, they recognized that the application of this principle would incur significant opposition from political and economic elites (Lewis, 1972; Silverstein, 1975). David Gil (1976a) asserted that problems of distribution could best be solved through philosophical and institutional transformation and political action, rather than the introduction of new professional techniques. He and others argued that schools could play a critical role in the reorientation of practice along these lines (Gil, 1976b).

Other faculty advocated for the refinement and dissemination of the emerging structural approach to practice, which had been more fully developed in Canada. There, social workers had been consciously striving to integrate radical perspectives on society into practice models since at least the early 1970s (Moreau, 1979; Mullaly, 1997; Quirion, 1972). Similar to the basic principles of the Rank and File Movement of the 1930s, the main elements of structural social work included: (1) defense of and advocacy for the expansion of clients' rights and resources; (2) fostering an understanding of the living and working conditions of clients by linking them to broader oppressive structures such as capitalism, racism, patriarchy, and heterosexism; (3) a focus on personal change through empowerment; (4) the development of collective consciousness; and (5) linking political change and social justice with personal change (Carniol, 1992).

Thomas Keefe (1978a, 1978b, 1978c) argued that social work curricula should go beyond a "magical" radicalism to a more analytic historical–materialist framework that recognized the economic and ideological dimensions of current environmental changes. This curriculum, which would emphasize critical consciousness as a complement to empathy (Keefe, 1980), would enable students to identify class barriers that are fostered by social policies without denigrating the potential roles of social workers, as many radicals had done (Keefe, 1978a, p. 65). Keefe argued that social workers "must be prepared to broaden [their] role expectations . . . and find common cause with other progressive elements in [their] society just as [they] did in the 1930s and late 1960s" (Keefe, 1978a, p. 73).

In the words of Puerto Rican professor and radical activist, Carmen Rivera de Alvarado, this reorientation required social work practitioners, educators, and students to "discover the hidden, hard reality" behind persistent myths . . . [to understand] that the problems social workers address are those that disturb the upper classes and that serve to perpetuate the status quo" (de Alvarado, 1973, p. 3). It would involve the creation of a new form of profession—one that eschewed the explanations of the dominant culture for persistent social and economic problems in favor of environmental analysis and action.

In a similar vein, faculty like Jack Sternbach at the University of Pennsylvania recruited students to work with prisoners in local correctional institutions. With Jeffry Galper, Philip Lichtenberg, and Harvey Finkel from Bryn Mawr, Sternbach formed a collective dedicated to the development and dissemination of radical perspectives on practice (Finkel, Galper, Lichtenberg, & Sternbach, 1973). They attempted to synthesize a Marxist analysis with "a combination of existentialism, polemical social analysis and non-rational-mystical understandings" derived from such authors as R. D. Laing, Herbert Marcuse, and Wilhelm Reich (Sternbach, 1972a, p. 18). They applied practice principles derived from radical therapy, law, and, although not explicitly acknowledged, from past radicals such as Bertha Reynolds.

Like other radical social workers of the period, Sternbach emphasized the importance of critical consciousness raising and worker–client mutuality. He was also one of the first social work faculty to advocate for empowerment as a central principle of practice (1972a, b). Ellen Russell Dunbar, later executive director of California-NASW, proposed policy changes in the correctional system from a similar perspective (1976).

Echoing the arguments of both professional ancestors and contemporary radical practitioners, some radical social work faculty in the 1980s paid renewed attention to potential alliances with the labor movement as a vehicle for social and political change. Paul Adams (1982) argued that the collective strength of organized labor could serve as an important source of support for radical social workers, who were at risk of isolation in their agencies and universities. Collective action by social workers, particularly as part of the labor movement, could, Adams asserted, "undermine the legitimacy of the system" (p. 61).

While warning of the danger of an alliance between conservative elements of the labor movement and conservative forces in the social welfare field, William Epstein (1985) reached a similar conclusion: The welfare state could survive only in the context of supportive social attitudes including those of organized labor. The confluence of values between social workers and union leaders was a key component of such alliances. Participation in coalitions with labor groups could help social workers translate these values into concrete political objectives and overcome their reluctance to engage in social change activities (de Alvarado, 1973; Wagner, 1990). Unfortunately, few such coalitions appeared.

Despite the growing acceptance of radical ideas within social work education, the repression of social work radicals continued during the Reagan years although less openly than during the McCarthy period. Like radicals in other fields, the most vulnerable social work faculty were those who attempted to blend activism with their scholarship (Gordon, 1983). Open red-baiting no longer occurred, although in some cases it persisted in subtler forms (Interviews and Surveys, personal communications, 1997; see Chapter 10).

Certain forms of activism, however, were tolerated and even encouraged by schools. The establishment of the Human Serve voter registration project by Richard Cloward and Frances Fox Piven in the mid-1980s received considerable support from mainstream social work leaders in NASW, CSWE, and higher education. Although it never lived up to initial expectations, Human Serve appeared to offer an opportunity for social work faculty, students, and agency practitioners to be on "the cutting edge of a national human service voter registration campaign" (Cloward & Piven, 1984).

From the mid-1980s through the early 1990s, a considerable number of radical social work students and faculty openly supported the left-wing Sandinista government in Nicaragua and the Farabundo Marti National Liberation Front (FMLN) rebels in El Salvador. Some even defied the U.S. ban on travel to Cuba and participated in the first and only U.S.–Cuba Social Work Conference in 1989 (Arches, 1989). Other social work faculty and practitioners actively opposed the U.S. military buildup in the 1980s through their involvement in the Honeywell Project. These often risky activities put these social workers in direct opposition to established U.S. policies and laws and often led to their surveillance by law enforcement authorities. Their experiences in Central America and their work with refugees in the United States provide eloquent testimony of the effects of U.S. support for the Nicaraguan contras and the repressive government in El Salvador (C. Beck, J. Friedman, A. Prigoff, J. Stokan, personal communications, 1987–1991).

A major influence on radicals within social work education during the 1980s was Paulo Freire, whose book *Pedagogy of the Oppressed* (1970) had inspired the conscientization movement in Latin America. Although primarily an educator, Freire's ideas about the importance of dialogue and the cultivation of critical consciousness and his emphasis on *praxis*—the ongoing reflection on one's practice—began to appear in social work publications in the early 1980s (Burghardt, 1982; Reisch, Wenocur, & Sherman, 1981). His message that social work must be understood in the context of social structure and of the importance of linking theory and action through *praxis* shaped the mission of the BCRS and facilitated the acceptance of structural social work in the 1990s (Mullaly, 1997; Mullaly & Keating, 1991). Significantly, the *JPHS* introduced its first issue with Freire's paper, "A Critical Understanding of Social Work" (1990). Thus, a persistent dilemma for radical social workers in the 1990s involved the nature of education for contemporary practice. As Newdom (1993) put it,

> If we do not listen to the field, we are guilty of arrogance, of the contributions practice makes in the building of knowledge. If we build our curricula solely on a foundation of current agency needs, though, we are in danger of being constantly out of touch with the reality into which our students will graduate. Beyond that, we institutionalize the limitations of the practice in which the agencies engage. And that practice is circumscribed and defined by those who pay the bills—government, third party payers, and the corporations and wealthy individuals who give money to organizations which will not threaten their interests. (p. 73)

This dilemma was also reflected in the last quarter of the twentieth century in other organized efforts to translate radical or progressive ideas into action.

9

The Redefinition of Social Radicalism, 1970-1999, Part II

There are many groups who wish to change the market-oriented, money mad societies of this current era to a world with more equality, more environmental protection, mutual support in communities, and higher quality of life. To the extent that radical social workers are organizers, activists, and can work well with multi-racial, multi-ethnic coalitions, radical social workers can make major contributions to a new social movement for justice that is starting to confront transnational corporations and their servants in government who now rule society. This is the coming frontier in social struggle.

—Arline Prigoff, personal communication

CATALYST COLLECTIVE

The Catalyst Collective, through its efforts to construct radical social work theory while engaging in radical social action, represents one example of the new form that social work radicalism took in the 1970s. Based in New York, the collective consisted primarily of young White radicals, who were strongly influenced by the social movements of the 1960s and their experience in graduate schools of social work. Although they shared a general leftist political ideology, the collective included individuals who self-identified as socialists, radical or socialist feminists, anarchists, and Marxists (Wagner, 1989b). In its publication *Catalyst: A Socialist Journal of the Social Services* the collective articulated a consistently critical stance on professionalism, despite the social work careers of its members.

The collective began publishing the journal in 1978. According to one of its original members, David Wagner (1989b), it reached its peak circulation of several thousand in the late 1970s. During these years, in addition to publishing the journal, collective members spoke at professional conferences, joined radical local coalitions, spoke on progressive radio stations like WBAI in New York, and participated in mass demonstrations.

Shortly after the election of Ronald Reagan, however, the collective experienced a sharp decline in membership and focused most of its energy on survival issues (Wagner, 1989a, p. 283). The publication of *Catalyst*, always somewhat irregular, became increasingly infrequent. When the members of the collective could no longer publish the journal on a voluntary basis, it evolved into the *Journal of Progressive Human Services (JPHS)*, which first appeared in 1990. With radical social work faculty as editors and a publishing agreement with Haworth Press, the *JPHS* served for several years as an unofficial organ of the Bertha Capen Reynolds Society (BCRS; see below).

The experience of the Catalyst Collective reveals how radical social workers of the 1970s developed more comprehensive theoretical orientations and, for the most part, moved toward less confrontational but no less militant styles. In part, this redirection of radical activism was shaped by the economic crisis of the early and mid-1970s, which affected them personally and professionally through dramatic cutbacks in funding for the social services. Wagner (1990) points out,

> In the 1970s, economic conditions were primarily responsible for the movement of radical professionals taking a different turn than the social movements of students, minorities, and the poor. While the early to mid-1970s saw a general decline in militant activism among significant sectors of the population . . . the recession of 1973 and the state budget crises that followed, along with the growth of Marxist and other radical influences, led to increased militancy in the social services and among other radical professionals for a period of years. (p. 225)

RADICAL ALLIANCE OF SOCIAL SERVICE WORKERS (RASSW)

One important consequence of this increased militancy was the formation of numerous local groups of radical social work practitioners, faculty, and students in the early and mid-1970s. Perhaps the most influential and longest-lived was the RASSW in New York City, which was organized in 1974 as New Yorkers grappled with the combined effects of a deep recession and the city's traumatic fiscal crisis. The development of RASSW reflected in some ways the "coming of age" of social work radicals from the 1960s. It also demonstrated how radical ideas could be put into practice, particularly at the local level, and, in the end, which ideological and organizational barriers proved too difficult to surmount. For unlike the Rank and File Movement of the 1930s, which also began in New York, RASSW did not produce a national movement in the social work profession.

RASSW's influence peaked in 1974–1976, when as many as 300 people attended some of its meetings and its bimonthly newsletter, *The Social Service Alternate View*, reached an audience of about 1,500 (Wagner, 1989a, p. 271). During these years, like-minded and loosely linked organizations emerged among radical social workers, primarily on the East Coast and in the Midwest. These included the Philadelphia Radical Human Service Workers, the Chicago Alliance of Social Service Workers (which had a weak affiliation with RASSW), Social Workers for Welfare Rights in New York, and the Union of Radical Human Service Workers in Boston, a descendant of the short-lived Social Welfare Workers Movement of the late 1960s. Although these groups shared similar perspectives and membership and often worked cooperatively with local welfare rights organizations, they could not coalesce into a broader radical coalition. Several efforts to join forces failed because of disagreements over strategy and tactics, the last one—to create a Human Service Activists Network—in 1981 (Wagner, 1989a, p. 283, n. 27, n. 30).

From the outset, RASSW attempted to create an organization that was "radical" in both ideology and structure and to build a broad-based movement for change within the social services field. Its founders, some of whom belonged to the Catalyst Collective, hoped to unite "all those persons in the social welfare field" who accepted its guiding principles. These principles, reflected in its recruiting brochures and earliest position papers, could roughly be divided into those outlining the organization's vision and goals and those describing its fundamental political strategy:

1. Social workers must be educated on the major political and economic issues to fight effectively for clients' needs.
2. Major social welfare issues and programs must be examined from a class point of view.
3. Human services are a right, not a privilege.
4. Social welfare needs should be a government priority, not military spending or corporate profits.
5. Social action, in concert with others, is necessary to bring about basic changes.
6. Racism, sexism, and other divisive tools must be exposed and eliminated (RASSW, 1974).

These principles reflected "antagonism towards the leadership of the profession and the liberal political leadership [of the nation], encouragement of unionization and an employee identification for social workers, organizing for a massive 'fightback' against budget cuts by united groups of workers and clients, as well as developing critiques of the welfare state, specific social policies regarded as repressive . . . , opposing racism and sexism, and attempting to develop a 'radical' practice within social work"(Wagner, 1990, p. 28). They varied little from the class-based perspectives of the "old left" of the 1930s–1950s. In fact, RASSW emerged from the Bertha Reynolds Club, a small largely informal group of left-wing social workers associated with the Communist Party or its youth affiliate the Young Peoples' Liberation League. Although RASSW differed from older radical organizations in its attention to issues of race and gender, it tended initially to regard racism and sexism as obstacles to the formation of broad, class-based coalitions, rather than as issues of equal significance.

In its "Proposal on Purpose" (Kramer, Lefkowitz, Prigoff, & Russak, 1974), RASSW's founders placed a priority on the following: human needs over corporate profits; reordering the nation's priorities from military to social spending; shifting the cost of social programs to monopolies and business interests; and supporting "anti-imperialist movements *as they relate to social needs* both within the U.S. and in the countries oppressed by U.S. imperialism" (p. 1, emphasis added). RASSW's vision attempted "to examine all issues affecting social welfare both concrete and ideological from the viewpoint of a class analysis" while giving "major attention to issues of racism and sexism" as divisive instruments of the capitalist class. The association proposed to promote this vision through a broad range of activities, including education programs, publications, influencing mainstream social service organizations such as the National Association of Social Workers (NASW) "towards more effective social action," forging coalitions within the social service field and attempting to join coalitions created by labor and minority groups, and promoting trade unionism among social workers (Kramer et al., 1974).

In hindsight, RASSW's goals were too broad and laden with contradictions. For strategic reasons, it hoped to build a broad-based organization around an explicitly class analysis without placing primary emphasis on a socialist outlook or solution. It attempted to reach out to minorities of color, women, and labor groups without recognizing that, around certain key issues, such as licensure and professionalism, their interests would diverge in fundamental ways. RASSW promoted a global vision of crisis as a means of building a national movement, yet it often appeared provincial in its actions, by focusing most of its attention on the effects of the crisis in the New York area. Finally, in its organizational structure and ideology, it articulated a democratic vision while, in reality, relying on a steering committee, initially primarily composed of individuals associated with the Communist Party, to do most of the association's work.

Key members of RASSW, particularly those formerly associated with the "New Left," were aware of the dangers of such contradictions from the beginning. Within a year after its founding, a clear split emerged around what type of organization RASSW should become. Papers debating this issue reflected emerging conflicts between the so-called old guard within RASSW, who had been affiliated with the Communist Party in some way, and those whose politics had been formed in the 1960s as members of the New Left and who were part of the Catalyst Collective. Their analyses of the context did not differ in fundamental ways, but the papers had somewhat different emphases. The key issues were the targets of RASSW's organizing efforts, the nature of RASSW's program, and the organizational structure of RASSW, including the role and composition of the steering committee (RASSW, February 20, 1976).

In October 1975, four founding members (Kramer et al., October 18, 1975) drafted "Position Paper I" articulating their analysis of the "present economic crisis" and addressing the issue of how to radicalize people. They believed the crisis was the inevitable consequence of state monopoly capitalism (Baran & Sweezy, 1968; O'Connor, 1973), whose effects were felt both in the United States (e.g., in New York's fiscal crisis) and abroad (the recent CIA engineered coup in Chile). The authors adopted a classic Marxist position, regarded workers as a "vanguard force," and linked class-based exploitation with institutional racism and sexism in what they termed "a united front" strategy (although the development of class consciousness remained a priority).

The goal of RASSW in this view should be to organize and radicalize (i.e., raise class consciousness among) social service workers through education and action. RASSW should build "the broadest organization possible" and participate in coalitions engaged in similar struggles in the United States and abroad to create fundamental economic and social change. Emphasis should be on promoting "dialogue concerning alternative systems without committing the organization to given solutions" (RASSW, February 20, 1976, p. 1).

One month later, 14 RASSW members circulated two other position papers ("RASSW and the Fiscal Crisis of New York—Toward a Radical Association" [November 22, 1975l] and "Program Guidelines" [November 22, 1975b]) which presented an alternative perspective on RASSW's roles and goals. While the October (Kramer et al., October 18, 1975) paper placed RASSW's development and purpose in a global context, the November papers focused more on the fiscal crisis of New York City. Whereas the old guard proposed a fundamental restructuring of society without adopting an explicitly socialist label, the new left faction argued that RASSW "must link our demands for jobs, service and benefits with a demand for socialism." Finally, while the "old guard" proposed broad goals for the association, the "new left" warned of the inherent contradictions of radical associations, particularly against the dangers of RASSW attempting "to impose a party line" or narrow theoretical perspective, retreating from protest politics, and limiting organizational power to a core of leaders (RASSW, November 22, 1975a, pp. 1–2).

Presaging arguments that appeared later in *Catalyst*, the "new left faction" asserted that social workers both served and were part of the working class and that "traditional forms of protest and political agitation are by themselves inadequate to the current crisis" (November 22, 1975b, pp. 2–3). RASSW could play a key role, however, as "an intermediate form of political organization, a form of transition from the mass protest organization which focuses on a single issue to the revolutionary party which is all encompassing" (p. 3). The authors acknowledged, however, that the radical association as an organizational form is inherently unstable in its membership and focus, causing it to develop certain inevitable contradictions or "opposing tendencies" that undermined its ultimate purpose. Despite these tendencies, they believed that RASSW could serve a vital function as "a unifying catalyst which links the providers and . . . recipients of service in struggle against capitalist repression and exploitation" (p. 3).

RASSW's "Program Guidelines" (November 22, 1975b), also reflected the thinking of radical political economists during the "stagflation" crisis of the mid-1970s (Braverman, 1974; Navarro, 1976; O'Connor, 1973). The crisis, in this view, resulted from corporate efforts "to save capitalism by instituting economic and social policies that attack workers and consumers: [including] unemployment [now approaching double digits]; [and] the withdrawal of goods and services" (RASSW, 1975). The paper proposed that, in this context, radical social workers fight for full employment, an expanded welfare state, public ownership of utilities, and more equitable fiscal policies. This could be accomplished by forging coalitions with other workers and service consumers.

Yet, despite these differences, substantial common ground existed between the RASSW "factions." The split may have reflected conflicts of personality and generational perspectives more than ideology. By early 1976, through a series of forums and meetings, the organization's leaders approved a compromise of sorts, although the association continued to struggle with its basic purposes and strategies. RASSW created an expanded steering committee to make the organization more participatory. In its publications, the organization continued to focus on national issues, such as welfare reform and the military budget, while, in its actions, it addressed developments like service cutbacks in New York City and New York State. "Internal" professional issues, like the growing clinical trend among social workers, involvement in electoral politics, and professional licensure also became more prominent.

In fact, RASSW published its first public position paper in February 1976 on the issue of licensure. Placing the issue in the broader context of the economic crisis, the paper addressed three questions: (1) the role of NASW; (2) whether licensing of social workers was racist; and (3) the relationship of licensure to service quality and accountability. On each question, RASSW took positions that challenged the views within mainstream social work.

Reflecting a long-standing schism within the profession, which persists into the twenty-first century, RASSW argued that "a dichotomy exists within NASW between" social activists and clinical practitioners, which is exacerbated by the promotion of licensing. When all social services are threatened by the conservative political and ideological climate, a focus on licensing undermines the profession's efforts to fight for "the survival and well-being of millions" (RASSW, February 1,1976, p. 3). Citing the opposition to licensing by such groups as the National Association of Black Social Workers (NABSW), RASSW asserted that efforts by NASW to promote licensing contradict its stated intent to fight racism within the social service field and were destructive of professional unity. Promoting licensing, in lieu of uniting around this struggle "is to fiddle while Rome burns" (p. 3).

The paper also disputed the linkage between licensing and service quality. It added an interesting twist to the growing debate over professionalization by arguing that "under current political conditions licensure may actually decrease the accountability of social workers to their clients" (RASSW, February 1, 1976, p. 5). The paper concluded that licensure neither protected nor improved service quality; rather, it divided workers and undermined their job security, as the recent attack on public education in New York City had demonstrated. Instead of fighting for licensure, RASSW proposed an alternative strategy that focused on building worker–client–labor–community coalitions and combating racism in social service agencies and other institutions. No specifics were provided, however, as to how this strategy would be implemented or sustained.

A similar pattern emerged in RASSW's second major position paper, "The Economic Crisis and the Human Services: An Analysis and a Call for Action" (RASSW, Economic Crisis Committee, June 1976). This document represented a synthesis of the perspectives of the two major factions within the association. Using language similar to that employed by the Communist Party (e.g., "fightback"), the paper had several major objectives.

First, it placed New York's economic crisis in the context of monopoly capitalist development, the growing militarization of the economy, and the transfer of public dollars to benefit private sector investments. It emphasized the impact of unemployment and social service cutbacks on people of color and proposed a broad-based coalition strategy that united "all groups against those responsible for the crisis" (RASSW, June 1976, p. 4). It criticized the responses of liberal groups, such as the Community Council of New York and NASW. Although acknowledging the positive positions NASW had taken on issues such as full employment and national health insurance, it chastised national NASW for failing to make the economic crisis "an overriding priority on the profession's agenda." Meanwhile, at the local level, the lack of strong leadership in NASW had produced "a feeling of powerlessness and pessimism . . . among . . . practitioners" (p. 3).

As an alternative, RASSW proposed a sweeping agenda that attempted to fuse local and national concerns. Some of its demands were specific, but not exclusively radical. They included an end to all layoffs and cuts in social services, passage of the Humphrey–Hawkins full employment bill, and the cancellation of New York City's debt service to banks. Other demands were either very broad (and politically unfeasible) in their goals or vaguely worded, such as earmarking federal aid to cities "for essential human and social services," "reduction of the 'overkill' military budget," and shifting the nation's tax burden to large corporations and the real estate industry (RASSW, June 1976, p. 5).

RASSW's proposed action plan was equally unspecific. In broadly phrased, militant language, it called on social workers to join coalitions with community groups, labor unions, and social service agencies, "engage in actions from letter writing and lobbying to mass demonstrations and rallies," and "make our contribution as social service workers to the people's struggle *visible and uncompromising*" (RASSW, June 1976, p. 5, emphasis added). This lack of specificity can be explained in part by RASSW's recognition of the difficulty of forging a radical strategy to complement its radical analysis. Although it vacillated on the use of socialist terminology, the association articulated sentiments that were clearly socialist in origin and intent, for example in the statement "basic economic and social changes are necessary to ensure a system where people's needs come before profits" (p. 5). Yet, in a conservative political climate, RASSW recognized that its goals could only be reached through a long-term social and political process that included education, organizing, and (somewhat reluctantly) participation in mainstream professional organizations and electoral work. Over the next five years, the task of bridging the gap between radical analysis and radical action became even more difficult.

Nevertheless as the nation's economic crisis deepened during the "stagflation era" of the late 1970s, RASSW continued to provide a radical analysis within the social service field and to promote an alternative agenda. It did this through three primary means: publishing a bimonthly (and later, quarterly) newsletter, *The Social Service Alternative View*, beginning in 1975, and periodic position papers; organizing conferences and workshops for social service workers and community activists; and advocating for progressive social policies around issues of unemployment and service cutbacks, particularly in the New York region, within NASW and major social service organizations (Letter of August 4, 1976 to Gerald Beallor). The broad scope and content of RASSW's vision (particularly in its publications) contrasted sharply with the limited range of its political activities. This contradiction reflected both the organization's greatest strengths and its fundamental weaknesses.

Looking back, RASSW's major contributions to social work were its consistent critique of contemporary social policy developments and its placement of these developments in a wider political–economic and ideological context. During a period in which organized social work adopted an increasingly defensive posture and largely focused on issues of professionalism (such as licensure) or theory development, particularly around clinical practice, RASSW continued to link service cutbacks and issues like unemployment to national and international economic developments. It helped to keep alive the historic concern of social workers over peace and disarmament (*The Social Service, Alternate View*, April–May 1977 and flyer of May 25, 1978) as did Social Workers for Peace and Nuclear Disarmament, organized by NASW in the 1960s. As NASW and CSWE engaged in increasingly fractious debates over diversity and what later became known as multiculturalism, RASSW tried to synthesize a fundamentally class-based analysis with a growing focus on the eradication of racism and sexism. Ultimately, however, the practical strategic implications of this effort proved too difficult to achieve, particularly in an increasingly reactionary and divisive political environment.

RASSW failed to build a lasting radical movement among social workers for several reasons. One was the difficulty of promoting radical policy positions in a conservative era. Even the election of a moderate Democrat like Jimmy Carter in 1976 did not slow the rightward drift of policy at the local and national levels. RASSW, like other radical organizations of the period, failed to create a realistic alternative that could build a broader movement even within the social services.

Second, RASSW made several tactical mistakes. It proposed a comprehensive analysis that linked U.S. militarism and overseas intervention with social service cutbacks yet lacked both a feasible set of policy alternatives or the organization to promote them (*The Social Service Alternate View*, April–May 1977, September–October 1977, June–July 1978). Its analysis was too far reaching to generate interest at the local level, where RASSW did most of its organizing. RASSW continued to advocate for the creation of a national movement to address such issues but did little to build that movement itself.

Although RASSW promoted a broad contextual analysis of social welfare, by focusing on local issues in New York such as welfare cuts and the failure of protective services, it reinforced its image as a provincial organization out of touch with the problems experienced by colleagues and clients around the country. Attacks on New York Mayors Abraham Beame and Edward Koch, and the successful campaign to oust Blanche Bernstein, Commissioner of New York City's Human Resources Administration, had little appeal to those outside the region, particularly as RASSW's attacks took on an increasingly vitriolic personal tone. (For example, in 1978, RASSW attacked Bernstein as racist, reactionary, and inhuman, and unqualified for her position [RASSW, November 12, 1978; editorial in *The Social Service Alternate View*, June–July 1978, p. 1]. By the late 1970s, the [*The*] *Alternate View* devoted more space to the analysis of social service issues in New York than it did to national concerns (*The Social Service, Alternate View*, June–July 1978, January–February 1979).

Third, by focusing on service cutbacks, especially at the local level, RASSW placed itself increasingly in a defensive posture. More and more, its "alternate view" was one of opposition to policy developments or defense of programs, like Aid to Families with Dependent Children (AFDC), which its members had long criticized (RASSW, November 26, 1977). In October 1977, RASSW asserted, "there can be no real welfare reform unless it is tied to a national policy of full employment, of urban reconstruction, of housing, a national health service, expanded education and social services" (*The Social Service, Alternate View*, October 1977). Yet the association adopted a series of proposals that called for the defeat of Carter's welfare reform program and promoted a broad range of alternative policies that were virtually indistinguishable from those of the liberal/left wing of the Democratic Party and its labor allies. These included full employment (using public sector jobs if necessary); increases in the minimum wage and a reduction in the work week from 40 to 35 hours; a federally funded social service system; expansion of child care facilities; and an increase in welfare grants and other income maintenance programs (*The Social Service, Alternative View*, October 1977).

Finally, RASSW diverted attention from its national policy agenda by engaging in issues that had marginal connection to its long-term goals. For example, in March 1977, it became embroiled in a personnel dispute with Hunter College over the failure of the School of Social Work to renew the contract of its only Puerto Rican faculty member, Yolanda Mayo (*The Social Service, Alternate View*, April–May 1977). RASSW also sought to strengthen its position within communities of color by forcefully defending Affirmative Action, particularly around the Bakke case (Letter of January 30, 1978; RASSW, November–December 1977). Although such issues were clearly consistent with RASSW's overall mission, the association lacked the resources to pursue such a wide agenda effectively.

Perhaps sensing that the organization was at a crossroads, RASSW convened an all-day conference in October 1979 entitled "Human Services in Crisis: What Can Be Done?" At the conference, attended by more than 200 people, RASSW presented a major position paper by the same name that was subsequently revised and distributed again in April 1980. This paper captured some of the essence of radical thinking in the social service field at the time. RASSW used the paper to identify the causes for the current crisis, indicate where responsibility for the crisis could be found, and to propose solutions.

The authors refuted the "wrong explanations" for the crisis presented by many social service leaders—such as insufficient resources, antiwelfare attitudes among the public, and the low status of social work. They attacked the responses to the crisis by government officials and social service administrators, including the imposition of austerity measures and "quick fix" solutions. RASSW argued that the social service crisis "cannot be viewed in isolation from the other crises affecting the American people—the energy crisis, inflation, mass unemployment, and the drive to militarization" (RASSW, April 15, 1980, p. 5).

Essentially, RASSW's position in 1980 had not substantially changed from its original views. The roots of the crisis, it asserted, lay in the inability of the capitalist system to respond to the economy's problems at the national and international levels, the growing proportion of the federal budget allocated for military spending, and the growing partnership between government and big business. The major innovation in RASSW's paper was its recognition of the significance of the ideological dimension of the growing attack on human services.

In RASSW's analysis, the use of an antiwelfare strategy by the New Right (so-called neoconservatives) as a political weapon occurred in two ways. First, these attacks encouraged racist attitudes toward the poor, pitted races and classes against each other, and undermined the potential for united action. Second, the attacks were "part of a larger process of desensitizing the American people to human suffering [at home and abroad], . . . creat[ing] an atmosphere that neutralizes outrage at the possibility of world war" (RASSW, April 15, 1980, p. 9).

Mainstream social work organizations had failed to respond adequately to these ideological and political attacks for two reasons. By relying on government funding and professional expertise to solve the nation's social and economic ills, organized social work "precluded any attempts . . . to examine the underlying causes of social problems under capitalism. Instead, social work "increasingly adopted a limited, individualistic approach" tempered slightly by "an amiable do-goodism . . . not grounded in an understanding of basic social and economic forces." This approach, RASSW argued, "left the field intellectually and politically unprepared for the current crisis." As a result, NASW, despite its best intentions, could never venture beyond liberal reformism (RASSW, April 15, 1980, p. 4).

RASSW concluded its paper with an alternative response to the crisis that reflected a return to the popular front strategy of the 1930s. It emphasized a wide range of issues—peace, job creation, wage increases, control of energy prices, defense of income maintenance programs, support for national health insurance, tax equity, and the fight against racism. It proposed political strategies—such as forming broad coalitions and political action in the electoral arena—that were acceptable to liberals and radicals alike. The role of social workers in such strategies was as educators, advocates, and facilitators of interorganizational linkages (RASSW, April 15, 1980, pp. 15-16). RASSW concluded, "Our job is not easy, but neither is there a 'quick fix' to the problems we face. [Through informed action and mutual support] we can become important participants in the effort to shift the burden of the crisis from the backs of the people to those responsible for it" (p. 16). Within a year, the election of Ronald Reagan to the Presidency intensified this crisis and tempered even the qualified optimism of social workers in RASSW and elsewhere.

REAGANISM AND RADICAL SOCIAL WORK IN THE 1980S

A lead editorial in *The Social Service Alternate View* in September–October 1980 captured the mood of radical social workers about the upcoming election. "Once again we find ourselves faced with impossible decisions. . . . Though many of us feel despair at the consistent decline in the quality of life in the United States, our 'official' choices for the presidency have been limited to three people [Jimmy Carter, Ronald Reagan, and John Anderson] who wish to even further erode our living standards" (p. 1). After analyzing the positions of all three major candidates and finding them wanting, RASSW concluded that "there really is no *lesser* evil. In fact, with each election year the lesser evil seems to become more evil" (p. 1).

In this regard, RASSW distanced itself from NASW, which had given its "unequivocal support" to President Carter. In an October 20, 1980, letter, long-time RASSW leaders, Mary Russak and Verne Weed, attacked NASW's endorsement of Carter as a contradiction of its own stated national priorities and a repudiation of the report of the March 1980 Social Workers in Politics Conference it had organized (Letter of Russak and Weed). While neither the letter nor the newsletter editorial promoted the endorsement of candidates from more radical parties, RASSW recommended that its supporters examine these parties' positions on the issues and "vote for one of them as a real alternative" (p. 2). For its part, RASSW pledged to work with other progressive groups to create real political alternatives in the years ahead, a pledge it lacked the resources to fulfill.

After the election, NASW's executive director, Chauncey Alexander (January 1981), defended the organization's endorsement of Carter even as he conceded many of Russak's and Weed's points. Alexander maintained that "the democratic forces of this nation would have had a better opportunity under another Carter administration than they do have under the forthcoming Reagan one." In some ways, this dispute resembled the divisions within the Rank and File Movement and between Rank and Filers and liberal supporters of the New Deal in the mid-1930s.

The election confirmed the worst fears of social work radicals. Despite its earlier proclamation that all political evils were the same, RASSW was clearly stunned by the rightward drift in U.S. politics and its implications. Neverthe-less, it attempted to put the best possible face on the results by citing low voter turnout (only 26% of eligible voters supported Reagan) and placing the elec-tion in the broader political context of the previous decade (i.e., Reagan was the logical successor to Carter). Like many radicals and liberals, RASSW hoped to dispel the pessimism surrounding Reagan's election and to puncture the aura of conservative inevitability heralded by Reagan's backers (RASSW, January 1981).

RASSW proposed a preliminary six-point response to the new political reality. Its core premise was the importance of resistance rather than accommo-dation. The central issue, in RASSW's view, was peace, in particular the diffu-sion of the myth of a "Soviet threat" and the avoidance of nuclear war. Other priorities included defense of the policies and concept of the welfare state, ad-dressing the issue of institutional racism in the human services, overcoming the fragmentation of the social service field, and the development of political move-ments outside of the two party system (RASSW, January 1981, pp. 8–10).

During the first year of Reagan's presidency, RASSW focused much of its energies on attacking his administration's proposed budget, which involved a massive reordering of spending priorities from domestic programs to the mili-tary and changes in tax policies that dramatically favored upper-income earners and corporations (Omnibus Budget and Reconciliation Act, 1981). Concern over the effects of the Reagan budget also pushed RASSW to strengthen its ties with organized labor. Beginning in April 1981, the association began to educate its members about the history of trade unions within social work and to pro-mote the unionization of social workers. "Only through every social worker's full participation in unions where they exist, and in organizing them where they don't can we realistically follow through on our commitment to our clients and ourselves" (RASSW, April 1981, p. 8). Similar themes appeared in *Catalyst* at this time. RASSW members joined thousands of human service workers in the massive Solidarity Day demonstration organized in Washington on September 19, 1981 by the American Federation of Labor-Congress of Industrial Organi-zations (AFL-CIO).

Within one year of the 1980 election, the full impact of Reaganism began to be felt in the social service field (Center on Budget and Policy Priorities, 1982). Massive cutbacks in domestic spending pushed millions of people below the poverty line and eroded standards of professional service. People of color, women, children, the elderly, and the disabled were most affected by the cuts (Coalition on Women and the Budget, 1984).

The consequences of Reagan's policies, coupled with a severe recession in

1981–1982 that his administration's policies certainly exacerbated, created a real "crisis" in the social services, which dwarfed the crisis produced by the cutbacks of the mid-1970s. In response, RASSW published a special issue of its newsletter in April 1982, "Reaganism: What It Is and How To Fight It," principally authored by Bob Rosengard, a medical social worker, and Verne Weed. This distribution of this paper was, in essence, RASSW's last hurrah.

"Reaganism" they argued, "represents the economic and political program of the dominant financial interests in this country" (p. D). By dividing the American people along racial and class lines, it sought "to stifle united opposition to cuts in all the human services . . . on the basis that these services are primarily used by Blacks and Hispanics." Such divisions also distract attention from the true sources of the nation's economic crisis and the beneficiaries of recent policy shifts (p. D).

RASSW's analysis, however, went beyond the critiques of Reagan's policies that by now had become widespread among liberal think tanks, public interest organizations, advocacy groups, and pundits. Rosengard and Weed's paper challenged the long prevailing assumption—shared by liberal social workers and many radicals—"that progressive social change is initiated and implemented by government in response to a reasoned documentation of need . . . [and] supported by [other Americans] who have a stake in reform" (April 1982, p. I). This view of change led social workers to adopt a narrow view of society, one that disempowered both clients and workers and that placed both in the position of supplicants before entrenched political forces. It "also acted as a deterrent to critical examination of the socio-economic roots of problems services are supposed to correct" (p. I). This, in turn, led to a narrow conception of "prevention" itself and to the willingness of social workers to accommodate to fiscal austerity and thereby forego opportunities to forge coalitions with other social movements.

Citing the social activism of the 1930s and 1960s, Rosengard and Weed proposed an alternative conception of social change, which occurred "when the people with the greatest stake are organized into a force which struggles by a combination of methods to win wide support from potential allies and makes it impossible for those in power not to grant their demands" (RASSW, April 1982, p. J). In practical terms, this conception of change led to the following recommendations:

- Forge alliances with other social movements, particularly organized labor.
- Get involved in the electoral arena in support of independent candidates and progressive Democrats and through voter registration drives.
- Work to defeat the Reagan budget, particularly plans to dismantle federal programs, before further damage is done to domestic programs and civil liberties, and support alternative budgets such as those proposed by the Congressional Black Caucus and the Fair Action Budget Campaign.

- Support the Nuclear Freeze campaign and other efforts to transfer resources from the military to human needs.
- Organize workers through trade unions to engage in fight back efforts and "correct the elitism of our field which tends to forget that all the workers in a human service have a stake to fight against Reaganism." (pp. K–R)

RASSW's sweeping vision failed to materialize, however, and the organization quietly dissolved soon after the publication of this critique.

FROM "RADICAL" TO "PROGRESSIVE" SOCIAL WORK

By the mid-1980s, as a result of dramatic shifts in the nation's political climate and changes in the focus and composition of the social work profession, the term "radical" virtually disappeared from the social work lexicon shortly to be replaced by the more inclusive and less threatening label "progressive." By the early 1980s, RASSW was defunct and by 1987 the Catalyst Collective ceased to exist as an active organization. Its journal, *Catalyst: A Socialist Journal of the Social Services*, stopped publishing for a few years and reemerged in 1990 as the *Journal of Progressive Human Services* (JPHS) with considerable continuity in its initial editorial and consulting boards. Entries in the *Encyclopedia of Social Work* and the decline of large meetings of radicals at CSWE and NASW conferences also reflected this change.

The name of the *JPHS* exemplified how the more politically acceptable term, "progressive," came to replace the label radical. Whereas in the 1940s and 1950s the term progressive was used to connote someone associated with the Communist Party or its support organizations, by the 1980s it came to mean anyone with views to the left of center. Within this parlance, by 1992 a centrist politician like Bill Clinton could refer to himself as a progressive.

Although the focus on progressive, rather than radical, practice seemed to be a tactical retreat that diluted the thrust of radical social work analysis, there were some positive features of this new, more inclusive vocabulary. "Progressive" social workers, freed from a strictly class-based analysis, now addressed issues and articulated perspectives that radicals of the past had not often made a central concern. For example, with feminists in the forefront, progressive social workers now questioned "the nature of knowledge, the research process, and the limitations of relying solely on positivist research paradigms for social work research and theory" (Bombyk, 1995, pp. 1938).

The "progressive" emphases of feminist, empowerment, ethnic-sensitive and, later, ethnoconscious models of practice, however, were tempered by a conservative focus on clinical issues instead of broader themes of justice and equity. Opportunistic clinical social workers may have "rediscovered" the significance of unemployment for their clients in the midst of the recession of the early 1980s, but they integrated this awareness into "adjustment-oriented" therapies rather than transformative practice (Specht & Courtney, 1994). The collapse of the Soviet Union and other socialist governments in Central and Eastern Europe in 1989 and the early 1990s exacerbated these trends by producing "a reflex reaction [to radicalism because of] its association with socialism and Marxism" (Mullaly & Keating, 1991, p. 73).

Even before the height of Reaganism, however, the influence of radicalism had begun to fade within the social work field. Many local radical groups had disbanded. The Catalyst Collective nearly broke up in 1981, although it continued to publish its journal sporadically until 1988. After 1982, its focus shifted somewhat—from a socialist or Marxist perspective to a vaguer anticapitalist stance. Like RASSW's newsletter, the journal emphasized international issues such as disarmament and U.S. intervention in Central America more than it did issues surrounding the social work profession. The reactionary climate of the early 1980s compounded the sense of demoralization many radicals experienced. The need for a coalition strategy against Reaganism was one reason for the change in language and emphasis.

The disappearance of RASSW and other locally based radical social work groups and the gradual dissolution of the Catalyst Collective temporarily produced an organizational vacuum among leftist social workers. The formation of the Association of Community Organization and Social Administration (ACOSA) in the early 1980s did not fill this gap, although some of its members held radical views. For purposes of organizational development and credibility, ACOSA included practitioners and educators whose politics tended to be liberal and to focus on issues of practice effectiveness (in communities and organizations) more than structural or political concerns. Lacking a broad-based organization, many social work radicals focused their efforts in single-issue organizations that addressed welfare rights, homelessness, and other economically driven issues (Reisch, 1987a).

BERTHA CAPEN REYNOLDS SOCIETY (BCRS)

In 1985, under the leadership of Jack Kamaiko, a union activist and faculty member at Hunter College School of Social Work, an attempt was made to revive the radical movement among social workers. Two events were held, in New York City and Northampton, Massachusetts honoring the centennial of Bertha Reynolds's birth. At the Bertha Reynolds Centennial Conference in June 1985, an informal caucus produced a "call" to establish the BCRS, initially endorsed by more than 150 social workers, many of them prominent in the field. The society held a founding meeting in Chicago the following November, in which the 75 people present unanimously approved 10 evolving principles for the organization.

It is notable that neither the word "socialism" nor the word "radical" appears among the list of principles, although Marxism is mentioned as one of the organization's influential perspectives, along with feminism and antiracism (*Cata-*

lyst, 1988, pp. 93–95). Ultimately, nearly 500 social workers signed the call to join the society. By the late 1980s and 1990s, local BCRS chapters in New York, Michigan, and Northern California participated in demonstrations opposing U.S. intervention in Central America, apartheid in South Africa, the Persian Gulf War, and cutbacks in services for low-income people.

In the second issue of the society's newsletter, Ann Withorn (1986) attempted to summarize the organization's perspective on "progressive practice" and to make the radicalism of the 1930s, the heyday of the society's namesake, relevant to practice in an era of Reaganomics. From Reynolds's autobiography, she extrapolated five contemporary lessons based on the five "simple principles" of the Rank and File Movement. These included:

1. The need for more in-depth analysis of the welfare state, which had become much more complex during the past half century.
2. The need to form alliances with welfare recipients and other clients.
3. The need to avoid splitting social service and political work, and to define concepts like empowerment and non-racist, non-sexist practice more clearly.
4. The need to form alliances with other social movements in the United States and abroad around issues like nuclear disarmament and anti-apartheid work.
5. The need to establish relationships with clients based on mutuality and equality, rather than professional dominance and hierarchy, (Withorn, 1986, pp. 1–2)

PUTTING RADICAL THEORY INTO PRACTICE IN THE 1980s

Radical social work faculty formed the core of the BCRS during the 1980s and 1990s. They also demonstrated their commitment to progressive politics through growing involvement in social activism at the local level, particularly in advocacy organizations and movements focused on welfare rights and the needs of homeless persons (Fabricant & Epstein, 1986; Reisch, 1987a). Although radicals like Tim Sampson (1976) frequently criticized welfare advocacy because it perpetuated the power imbalance between social workers and clients, a new breed of radical advocates like Nancy Amidei (1982) fought to establish broad-based coalitions for maximum political impact.

A proponent of what she termed the "new activism," Amidei asserted in an invitational lecture at Smith College in the late 1980s that social work's "roots are equally important in helping individuals and in advocacy, social justice, social change. And if we ever lose sight of that, we'll have lost sight of at least half of what we are all about" (1988, p. 23). Amidei practiced what she preached as an organizer and advocate during the Reagan–Bush years in both Washington, DC, and Washington state.

So did Maryann Mahaffey, a professor at Wayne State University and long-time president of the Detroit City Council. Starting from a dialectical material-ist perspective, Mahaffey fought to mobilize mass support against the milita-rism and reactionary social policies of the Reagan administration. Mahaffey placed great faith in people's ability to develop their own organizations, estab-lish collective approaches to community problem solving, and determine "the forms the struggle will take" (1981, p. 8). Community social workers, she ar-gued, could play a critical role in these processes if they recognized the impor-tance of power as an essential ingredient of change and substituted more demo-cratic relationships for professional dominance.

Although most radical social work faculty limited their political activities to organizations like RASSW and the BCRS, a few continued to work with and through the Communist Party, particularly in New York. Alfred Kutzik, for-merly a professor at the University of Maryland, was a regular contributor to *Political Affairs*, the theoretical journal of the Communist Party of the United States (CPUSA), on social policy issues like the poverty index (Kutzik, 1986). After being forced out of the University of Maryland in 1979, he taught part time at other colleges, continued to publish, and eventually became the direc-tor of the People's School for Marxist Studies in New York. Other radical social workers ran for local office or played key roles in local and statewide political campaigns. Louise Simmons, a long-time community organizer, who is now a faculty member at the University of Connecticut, was elected to the Hartford City Council from 1991 to 1993 as a candidate of a local third party, People for Change (Simmons, 1996).

Verne Weed, who had been persecuted by the House Un-American Ac-tivities Committee (HUAC) in the 1950s, remained active in radical causes, including the Communist Party, after her retirement from the faculty of Hunter College. A frequent speaker at student meetings in the New York area, she continued to play a leadership role in RASSW until its demise and was one of the founders of the BCRS (*Daily World*, November 19, 1980). In the mid-1980s, Weed spearheaded an unrealized project by an Australian radical, Yvonne Cullen, to write a history of McCarthyism and its impact on radical social work-ers like Reynolds. Seven years after her death in 1985, Hunter College estab-lished the Verne Weed Living Archive for Progressive Social Work with the Social Welfare History Archives in Minneapolis. The collection includes mate-rials on social work practice regarding entitlement and empowerment; social work involvement in social movements, social work efforts in reform move-ments, and progressive social work theory.

RADICAL SOCIAL WORK IN THE 1990S: THE RENEWED ASSAULT ON PROFESSIONALISM

In many ways, the changes that occurred among social work radicals in the generation after the tumultuous 1960s resembled those that occurred in the late 1930s (Wagner, 1989a). Splits emerged once again between those radicals who continued to view social work as a mechanism of social control and those who asserted that practice based on principles of empowerment and the elevation of critical consciousness—whether at the individual, group, or community level—could produce progressive social change. Along similar lines, radicals were divided in their views of professionalism.

A sizable and influential group of social work radicals in the United States and abroad continued to identify professionalism as the major obstacle to progressive practice. They maintained that continued participation in existing social welfare institutions perpetuated status differentials and contributed to society's failure to respond adequately to human needs. The only solution to the contradiction between progressive politics and professionalism in this view was deprofessionalization: the restructuring of social work along more egalitarian lines with clients and community groups possessing a leading role in defining their problems and identifying potential solutions. The creation of alternative, nonhierarchical agencies—including self-help groups—and the strengthening of alliances with client-led organizations were central components of this vision (Newdom, 1996, 1997; Withorn, 1996).

Although the attack on professionalism was a central tenet of radical social work thought during the 1970s and 1980s, by the 1990s it was a subject of fierce debate in radical circles, particularly the BCRS. In her book, *Serving the People: Social Services and Social Change* (1984) and other writings, Ann Withorn, a faculty member at the University of Massachusetts and a leader of the BCRS, summarized the ways in which professionalism served as a major barrier to political struggle and social change. These views shaped the positions of the BCRS in the 1990s.

Withorn asserted that the concept of professionalism itself was based on capitalist premises about work and social status. The "ideology of professionalization" (Wenocur & Reisch, 1983) led social workers to establish a form of monopoly control of the helping process and, inevitably, to hierarchical relationships between workers and clients and the rejection of collective forms of organization such as unions. Unionization of social workers had, in fact, slowed dramatically since the early 1970s. Radical social work unions had virtually disappeared since the early 1950s despite intermittent efforts of groups like RASSW and the Radical Social Work Collective in Philadelphia to organize them (Radical Social Work Collective, April 26, 1978; RASSW, October 20, 1979; Tambor, 1981, 1973). Calls by radical social workers to form or collaborate with unions continued to fall on deaf ears into the 1990s (Epstein, 1991).

Without the countervailing influence of unions, the individualism and social status at the heart of professionalism obscured issues of social class and led "workers to identify with their agencies" rather than their clients (Withorn, 1984, p. 145). As a result, social workers were less able to engage with clients in collective struggle. The only viable solution was deprofessionalization—the sacrifice of both professional ideology and privilege—in favor of the control of social services by the people who need them (Alvarado, 1973).

An alternative perspective among social work radicals who were influenced by socialist and Marxist ideas also sought to strengthen linkages between workers and clients. It did so, however, by arguing that social workers were, above all, members of the new working class, who shared certain experiences of oppression with other workers and their clients (Fabricant & Burghardt, 1992). They stressed the importance of unionization and alliances with other labor groups and the possibility of working for change within existing organizations. This union-focused activism appears to have peaked between 1975–1980 in the aftermath of fiscal cutbacks and the severe recession of 1973–1974 (Wagner, 1989a).

RADICAL SOCIAL WORK THEORY IN THE 1990S

Thus, the concept of radicalism in social work was somewhat muddled at the beginning of the 1990s. Seemingly, radical ideas like empowerment and multiculturalism appeared to be widely accepted in the profession, yet upon closer examination much of their original meaning had been diluted. As originally developed in the 1970s, the concept of empowerment focused on practice methods that integrated the material, emotional, and psychological needs of people and communities (Solomon, 1976). It strove to create the means whereby people could meet their basic material needs while forging an awareness of their own capacity to produce change and offered a link between organizational reform and improved service delivery (Reisch, Wenocur, & Sherman, 1981).

By the early 1990s, however, most of the literature on empowerment abandoned its materialist core. The term "empowerment" seemed to be an obligatory attachment to any article or paper about practice. When the Bush administration justified cutbacks in such areas as public housing under the guise of "empowering" tenants, it proved that the concept had been co-opted if not corrupted (Reisch, 1991). Its strongest proponents like Barbara Levy Simon (1994) felt that it had become "a term that confuses even as it inspires" (Simon, 1990, p. 27). Even the term "radical" was now associated with clinical practice issues like addiction and spirituality (Morell, 1996).

In a similar fashion, multiculturalism lost much of its formerly antiracist emphasis by the 1990s and had largely become a vehicle to promote racial diversity or advocate for forms of separatist practice (Gross, 1995). Competing visions of multiculturalism threatened to obscure and hinder the attainment of worthy social and professional goals. The confluence of the terms multiculturalism with social justice and oppression further obfuscated serious discussions of these issues (CSWE conference, December 1998; Garcia & van Soest, 1997; Rosenthal, 1993; van Soest, 1996; van Soest, 1995).

While acknowledging the derivative nature of their ideas, Mullaly and Keating (1991) proposed a dialectical approach as a means of reconciling opposing views within radical social work. Radical social work, in their view, primarily had been influenced by three socialist perspectives: social democracy, revolutionary Marxism, and evolutionary Marxism. The latter "represent[ed] a compromise between the optimistic naivete of social democracy and the deterministic paralysis of revolutionary Marxism" and offered a theoretical solution to the problems of contemporary radical social work (p. 64).

Radical social work, they asserted, was now distinguished by certain basic characteristics. It rejected market-driven economies in favor of socialism, and liberal reformism in favor of "a massive reorganization or transformation of capitalism" (Mullaly & Keating, 1991, p. 51). It recognized that the welfare state as currently constructed was a bulwark of capitalism, while supporting a model of social welfare that was antithetical to capitalism in its values and goals. It believed that traditional social work perpetuated social problems by maintaining the false dichotomy between individual and social approaches to practice. Finally, in contrast to earlier social work radicalism, it incorporated into its framework an acceptance of feminist analyses, greater attention to racism and antiracist practice, and a mistrust of professionalism.

Other radical social workers in the 1990s attempted to integrate "new social movement theory" into a model of radical practice (Fisher & Kling, 1994). This would require greater understanding of "the historical dialectic between domination and resistance" and its refocusing in terms of "the interplay between class, community, and the search for new cultural orientations" (p. 16). It would also require the construction and mobilization of broad-based coalitions that move beyond single-community and single-constituency efforts. To hold power, rather than merely contest it, proponents of new social movement theory also argued that local and global efforts need to be balanced and the state be relegitimized as an arena of struggle. Finally, they proposed the development of "a more united ideological politics . . . which can draw the decentered narratives of our time toward a focal point" (p. 18).

An Australian social worker, Jan Fook (1993), pointed out that traditional social work theories—systems and ecological models, for example—have incorporated many ideas derived from radical practice, such as the central role of the social context in shaping behavior and the importance of taking a value-laden position. Radical practice, however, adds a structural dimension "to change people's situations by establishing their control over the effects of this structure on their lives" (pp. 41–42). This structural dimension could shed new light on such long-standing issues as the distinction between personal and professional values in practice, the limits of self-determination, and the boundaries of radical practice in conservative institutions.

Finally, radical social workers in the mid-1990s attempted to address the effects of postmodernism on both social welfare and socialist visions of society. Leonard (1995) argued that postmodern approaches allowed radical social workers to incorporate multicultural dimensions into earlier socialist and Marxist analyses, thereby enriching their validity in a postmodern world. Its contribution could occur in several ways: in promoting what Freire (1970) called "dialogical relationships," in challenging the assumptions of prevailing ideas and theories, in breaking down the notion of "ideal types" and promoting heterogeneous narratives, and in deconstructing the nature of professionalism itself.

CONCLUSION: RADICAL SOCIAL WORK IN ACTION IN THE 1990s

Throughout the 1990s, in addition to addressing the problem of professionalism, the leaders of the BCRS emphasized, as did other radical social workers, the impact of economic inequality and attacks on the welfare state, particularly the effects of welfare reform adopted in 1996. The BCRS also sought to promote a "national action initiative" to mobilize social workers around a progressive policy agenda and "to develop a program and strategies for a human rights agenda grounded in an understanding of the interrelationship of racism, sexism, homophobia, and classism both in [the United States] and internationally" (BCR Flyer, June 1997; *BCR Reports*, Fall 1997). The society's efforts, however, were limited by several factors.

Its membership reflected a broad range of ideological interests, yet the organization lacked a clear mission and strategy. The society adopted the rhetoric of multiculturalism, yet few of its 200-plus members were people of color. It sought to represent a range of constituencies within the field, yet the majority of its members were social work educators (Dover, 1997). Ironically, the name of the society itself proved an obstacle to attaining its goals. By the 1990s, few social work students and recent graduates knew who Bertha Reynolds was or what she represented, and the society's name appeared to symbolize an older, less inclusive view of radical social work.

To solve these problems, the BCRS took three important steps in the late 1990s. In September 1997, it revised its "statement of principles" to reflect the growing emphasis on multiple forms of oppression (BCRS, September 21, 1997). In June 1999, after considerable discussion, it changed its name to the Social Welfare Action Alliance. Of greatest significance, however, after the implementation of welfare reform in 1996, the society increasingly tied its activities and its fortunes to those of the Kensington Welfare Rights Union (KWRU), a radical group based in Philadelphia (*BCR Reports*, Fall 1998). It supported the "Partners in Crime" strategy crafted by Mary Bricker-Jenkins, a professor at Temple University, and the KWRU; joined in KWRU-led demonstrations in St. Louis, Houston, and Lansing at its 1997, 1998, and 2000 national conferences; and supported KWRU tactics such as the New Freedom Bus Tour, the Poor People's Summit in October 1998, and protests at the July 2000 Republican National Convention (*BCR Reports*, 1997–2000). Although the society was invited to a conference of social work groups convened by NASW in October 1998, it remains to be seen whether its recent initiatives will have an impact either on its long-term survival or the direction of the profession as a whole.

The transfer of editorial responsibility of the *JPHS* in 1997 to a collective based at the University of New England also symbolized the changes in radical social work at the end of the twentieth century. In their introductory editorial, the new editors envision[ed] *JPHS* as a publication which challenges dominant paradigms in social work and critically explores the political, professional, and personal issues faced by human service workers and recipients. Our theoretical interests include Feminism, Marxism, Queer Theory, and Post-Structuralism. Some of the practice paradigms which inform our work are empowerment-oriented practice, solution-oriented practice, trauma-based practice, integrated practice, community practice, social action, and consumer-directed practice. Our interests include feminist research, domestic violence, poverty and homelessness, gay and lesbian issues, and the development of alternative, non-hierarchical structures for providing social services, educating students, and editing a journal. . . . The struggles for workers and recipients will be examined, dilemmas of practice in liberal and conservative contexts will be explored, and strategies for ending classism, heterosexism, sexism, racism, ageism, ableism, and other forms of human oppression will be proposed." (*JPHS* Collective, 1997a, pp. 2–3)

In addition to broadening the scope of progressive practice, far more than their predecessors in other radical social work journals, the editors felt the need to bring "their stories" to the attention of subscribers (*JPHS*, 1997, pp. 1–5). Perhaps this reflected the emphasis on narrative popularized by postmodern theory, feminism, and movements of people of color, gays, and lesbians.

Although this inclusive approach to progressive social work appeared to promise something for everyone, by the late 1990s some discomfort with the vague label "progressive" began to surface, ironically in the *JPHS* itself. In 1998, an editorial bemoaned the decline in the number of "submissions that truly reflected radical perspectives" and the lack of a radical presence in the debate over welfare reform and its impact (Pritchard, 1998, p. 2). The author suggested "that social workers are compromising their commitments to human welfare, and that fewer and fewer are taking seriously the paradox of a people-serving profession in a people-denying society, and that social work as a profession has sacrificed being of real service by selling out to conventional arrangements" (p. 4).

A year later, in a guest editorial, David Wagner (1999, pp. 3–6), a former member of RASSW and the Catalyst Collective and a scholar of radical movements in the social services, questioned the validity of the term "progressive" (and, by implication, the wide scope of progressive social work) as a way of describing the position of leftists. The meaning of "progressive" had become tainted, he argued, because of its broad usage and current association with ideas formerly labeled liberal. Wagner preferred "more focus on radicalism," which although equally vague, "allows for a unity around an idea of *resistance*" (pp. 5–6). So, at the start of a new century, social work radicals and the field as a whole were once again at a crossroads, facing paths not fully explored at several critical historical junctures. Perhaps, this time, social workers will make a different choice.

10

Social Work
Radicalism at the End
of the Twentieth Century

> *Radical social work should advance the idea of a democrati-*
> *cally devised political economy, aimed at people's needs, not*
> *the profit of the few.*
> —Bertram Allan Weinert, personal communication, 1997

> *I hope that we can draw more students back to a concern*
> *with social justice [and an understanding] that progressive*
> *ideas are valid. We need to maintain a sense of the impor-*
> *tance of class, race, and gender, and to encourage people from*
> *a diversity of backgrounds to reach out across boundaries*
> *and to work together . . . to bring about lasting, fundamen-*
> *tal change.*
> —Keith Kilty, personal communication, 1997

WHAT'S IN A NAME?

*B*y the 1990s, the term "progressive," which emerged initially during the McCarthy period as a code word for individuals who were linked with or sympathetic to the Communist Party and other left-wing organizations, had become synonymous with anyone left of the American political center. This ambiguity contributed to the intellectual and political confusion among contemporary social workers and students of social work's past. It also helped to shift the focus of social work radicalism from class-based analysis to concerns over race, ethnicity, gender, and sexual orientation.

[T]he search for ways to alter the structural sources of inequality and discrimination have been replaced with a search to recognize and appreciate cultural and gender differences in values, beliefs, and worldviews. Disempowerment, once thought of primarily as a political and economic issue, is increasingly thought of as a personal difficulty. . . . The strengths approach . . . cautions us against problematizing the social environment. Yet, the intellectual distance of these progressive alternatives from mainstream practice seems extremely narrow. (Longres, 1996, p. 234)

As discussed in Chapters 8 and 9, some radical social workers in the 1980s and 1990s proposed to resolve the "dichotomies" between a simple theory of class oppression and a general egalitarian framework through the application of a dialectical approach to practice (Mullaly & Keating, 1991). Others suggested that clarification of the ideological differences among various perspectives and their implications would reduce the degree of confusion among students, faculty, and practitioners (Nes & Iadicola, 1989). De Maria (1992) argued that radical social work could be revived only by blending a radical analysis of society with radical action, as earlier generations of radical social workers demonstrated.

WHERE ARE THE RADICALS IN SOCIAL WORK TODAY?

Most radicals in earlier generations of U.S. social work history were not affiliated with the Communist or Socialist Parties or radical social movements, even in the tumultuous 1930s and 1960s. Yet they often espoused a radical vision of society and social work practice that is largely absent among today's self-identified "progressives." Progressive social workers tend instead to "raise questions about who controls the systems, who makes the decisions in the institutions," and to challenge the existing pattern of both public and private resource distribution (A. Prigoff, personal communication, 1997).

In the past two decades, the shifting terminology of radical social work has reflected serious splits within the left-wing elements of the social work field. Some radical social workers have espoused an explicitly Marxist approach to practice and education (Galper, 1980; Goroff, n.d.a, c; Joseph, 1975; Knickmeyer, 1972; Longres, 1977; Radical Social Work Collective, 1975; Withorn, 1984). Others have articulated radical feminist perspectives on practice and policy (Abramovitz, 1999, 1988; Bricker-Jenkins & Hooyman, 1986; Miller, 1990), although the majority of feminist social work scholars do not present specifically radical visions of policy or practice (Collins & Whalen, 1989; Nes & Iadicola, 1989; Perlmutter, 1994; van den Bergh, 1995).

Much of the literature developed by social workers of color had potentially radical implications (Iglehart & Becerra, 1995; Rivera & Erlich, 1998), only a relatively small percentage of such authors self-identified as radical. In fact, a disturbing feature of the few radical movements within the social work profession during the past several decades, such as the Social Welfare Workers Movement (SWWM), the Radical Alliance of Social Service Workers (RASSW), and Bertha Capen Reynolds Society (BCRS), was the relative absence of persons of color, at a time when the number of social workers of color had increased considerably. The emergence of separate organizations such as the National Association of Black Social Workers (NABSW) and the Association of Women in Social Work (AWSW), as well as distinct caucuses within the National Association of Social Workers (NASW) and the Council on Social Work Education (CSWE) offers only a partial explanation of this phenomenon.

The literature of multiculturalism (Gutierrez, 1997; van Soest, 1995) often incorporated the language and goals of radical social work, yet it rarely made these connections explicit. In fact, some social work radicals argue that the identity politics spawned by multiculturalism weakened the influence of social work radicals by fragmenting their energies (Longres, 1997). Others, however, applaud how a multicultural perspective broadened the horizons of radicalism in social work beyond class politics to encompass issues of race, gender, sexual orientation, and disability (Lum, 2000, van Soest, 1995). The impact of multiculturalism on radicalism within social work, therefore, deserves serious further study and analysis as it will shape the nature of social work theory and practice in the twenty-first century.

Finally, like many of the anti-World Trade Organization (WTO) protesters, some contemporary radicals in social work do not identify with a particular ideology or group at all. They emphasize instead the "transformative" aspects of practice, focus on such issues as militarism and violence in U.S. society, seek the linkage between "cause and function," formulate generalized antioppression strategies, and stress the development of dialogue, mutuality, and greater political consciousness among workers and clients (Bailey & Brake, 1975; Brake & Bailey, 1980; Burghardt & Fabricant, 1992; Gutierrez, 1990; Prigoff, 1987; van Soest, 1992). Although it has often been coopted by conservatives, empowerment theory continues to have the potential to articulate a radical view of practice and education without a specific connection to a particular ideology or political movement (Gutierrez, Parsons, & Cox, 1998).

VOICES OF RADICAL SOCIAL WORKERS IN THE 1990s

Despite this ideological confusion, there is a role for radical practice in social work today. The survey and interviews we conducted with more than 100 social workers, ranging in age from their late twenties to their eighties, gave fervent voice to this belief. To complete our analysis of social work radicalism, therefore, this chapter highlights the voices of contemporary social work radicals through the stories they shared with us.

We found these self-identified radicals, the majority of whom are social work practitioners, through several sources. These included the membership list of the BCRS (now, the Social Welfare Action Alliance); responses to ads placed in social work publications; and, less formally, from social workers who heard of our research or were suggested by other participants. In stories often filled with passion, respondents spoke of their work and their sense of mission. They talked and wrote about the roots of their radicalism, which varied widely depending on several factors. These included their family of origin, religious background, the influence of certain writings or people, the period in which they reached maturity (e.g., 1930s or 1960s), and contact with or involvement in a particular social movement such as civil rights, feminism, and peace.

Despite these differences, they expressed similar views on capitalism as a socioeconomic system, the nature of labor, the relationship of individual problems to exploitation by elites, the need for a redistribution of wealth and income, and the dominance of the social work profession by clinical or psychotherapeutic perspectives. They agreed that the profession should end what they regarded as useless debates, such as whether professionalism and activism were compatible. They also stated, with considerable regret, that in an era of identity politics social work had abandoned any discussions of social class. Like their professional ancestors over the course of the twentieth century, several respondents reported the personal difficulties they had encountered because of their political beliefs. Others reported that they always feel "out on a limb" or marginalized by colleagues because of their views. Overall, although they have remained unshaken in their beliefs, contemporary radicals feel that they have had very little impact on the profession as a whole.

Because of our method of data collection, a demographic analysis of the respondents may not accurately reflect the distribution of radical social workers in the United States. More than half (54.3%) of the respondents resided in the Northeast and Mid-Atlantic states; 18.6% in the West; 20.9% in the Midwest; and only 6.2% in the South. Nearly 59% were female. Almost half—48.7%—identified themselves as practitioners. Educators comprised 38.5% and graduate students 6.4%. The remaining 6.4% were retired or no longer working in the field of social work. The majority of the respondents did not complete the question on race/ethnicity. For those who did, there was a wide range of responses. These included Cherokee, Caucasian, White, Irish, French, Bohemian, Italian/Polish Jew, Mexican American, African American, Albanian, Scandinavian, Puerto Rican American, and Euro-American. Minorities of color were underrepresented in the sample compared with their composition in the social work profession as a whole.

MEANING OF RADICAL PRACTICE

As the following narratives illustrate, radicals identified several key areas of their work and their philosophies. They consider themselves radicals because they ask critical questions that challenge existing societal structures, particularly capitalism, which they consider an unjust economic system. They fight oppression in the world and in their agencies, although they define it in different ways. They promote grassroots, community-based practice. Not surprisingly, they are often unable to get their work published in professional journals or have their ideas accepted in social work circles, especially when they stray too far from the mainstream. Katherine Van Wormer presented the following interpretation of this phenomenon:

> The reason [many radical social workers do not write from their personal perspective] is that if they are radical or out of sync with mainstream social work they are not published. Today, the censorship is worse than ten years ago because one's manuscript is sent to a specialist in the subject of the article. The specialists tend to accept [frameworks like] DSM-IV or . . . P-I-E; alcoholism counselors . . . accept 12 step programs; social work educators on the editorial boards of mainstream journals . . . accept CSWE guidelines. (personal communication, 1997)

The radicals we surveyed agreed that in many respects, "radical social work" is a contradiction in terms because a member of a profession given status by the dominant culture is not likely to challenge the social order from which he or she benefits. Like many of the respondents, Marcie Lazzari believed, when she entered the field, that one could be *both* a radical and a social worker. After years in social work, however, she now believes that she has "been around too long and observed too much to believe that any longer." Her radicalism continues in the form of challenging status quo power relationships, creating a "somewhat radical" classroom environment in her teaching, and linking her work to feminist perspectives. She acknowledges that many social workers profess radical thinking, but "few of us put that thinking into practice" (M. Lazzari, personal communication, 1997).

Ursula Bischoff, a public policy analyst and researcher in California, echoes this sentiment. She considers radical social work as extending beyond mere "remediation, adaptation or integration" to a practice that results in "different patterns of thought and behavior that effect equitable cultural, political and economic reorganizations" (U. Bischoff, personal communication, 1997). In other words, it is not merely the expression of radical views, but it is action in pursuit of radical ideals, that distinguishes radical practice. Action, therefore, becomes the distinguishing characteristic of a radical profession (de Alvarado, 1973). As Susan Allen explained, it is not just holding opinions, but also voicing them and doing something about them that matters. In her case, she is involved in providing financial assistance to progressive movements, writing letters regarding progressive issues, working on the issues raised by the death sentence of African American journalist and activist Mumia Abu Jamal, and participating locally with citizens fighting oppressive city government policies (S. Allen, personal communication, 1997).

Some respondents, however, were troubled by the term "radical," believing it to have negative connotations. A social worker from Washington, DC, Myles Johnson, stated,

I have never described my social work activity as "radical." For me, "radical" connotes a rejection of most if not all conventional values, ideals, or methods. I am a democratic socialist in principle . . . but do not view Socialism as "radical." I am [also] a life member of the Bertha Capen Reynolds Society, but that, too, is nowhere near radical, although I suspect that many of the members see themselves as such.

Others were reluctant to use any labels to describe their affiliations or ideology. One anonymous respondent remarked, "Labels such as [radical or progressive] often carry their own baggage and do not fully or accurately convey where a person stands on a specific issue."

Some criticized radicals with whom they have worked as intolerant or ideologically rigid. Arline Prigoff, a cofounder of RASSW, does not call herself a radical for precisely this reason. Throughout her career, she found that many groups who used the term were "quite sectarian, hostile and negative in their practice, in some cases as a result of infiltration by FBI agents." She feels that "the 'vanguard concept,' which many radical groups adopted, contained aspects of elitism." Rather than affiliate with such radical groups and "marginalize [herself] . . . as a radical," she prefers to work with groups that are "consciously inclusive, progressive and democratic, both in theory and practice" (A. Prigoff, personal communication, 1997).

Joel Blau, a former member of the Catalyst Collective, defines radical social work differently than he did 25 years ago. He no longer believes that there is "as neat a divide of who's in, who's out anymore. Sometimes we're critical of liberals, sometimes we ally with them." He is troubled by the Social Welfare Action Alliance's "attack on professionalism" because he feels that "competence and the development of skill *is* professionalism and we can't get respect for what we do without maintaining that" (J. Blau, personal communication, 1997).

CHALLENGING THE STATUS QUO

There was widespread agreement among the radical social workers we surveyed that a critical feature of radicalism was a willingness to challenge the status quo—inside and outside the profession—in ways that most social workers do not. In their view this is largely because the organized profession is part of the dominant culture and, as such, does not and cannot confront the prevailing social order without undermining its occupational goals. This perspective reflects previous historical research on the profession (Andrews & Reisch, 1997; Fisher, 1994; Reisch, 1998; Specht & Courtney, 1994; Wagner, 1990; Wenocur & Reisch, 1989). Alfred Joseph commented:

In this country, it takes so little to be defined as a "radical." I think as a profession we have fallen down on the job. . . . What is really disheartening is that there are many young idealistic students looking for a movement of some consequence, and there is little or nothing out there for them.

For some radicals, challenges to the status quo emerge from a feminist perspective. A faculty member in the Northeast commented, "As my entry into the profession coincided with the beginning of my involvement in the feminist movement, one way in which I have defined my practice as 'radical' was that it was feminist—that I sought to promote the empowerment of women, as well as other marginalized groups, through my practice." She is committed to "walk [the] talk" by working in the classroom to "deconstruct and eliminate domination . . . teach them oppression and trauma are the root causes of the situations which lead clients to work with them, and help[s] them assess the social and environmental obstacles to clients' goals at least as much as the individual and personal."

For some respondents the concept of social work radicalism has evolved away from its earlier association with Marxism, socialism, and communism (Andrews & Reisch, 1997; Wagner, 1990; Wenocur & Reisch, 1989). Yet many respondents remain explicitly opposed to capitalism and believe that a capitalistic society is antithetical to the pursuit of social justice, which they regard as a central focus of their work. This contradiction is similar to the views expressed by radical social workers outside the United States (Mullaly, 1997).

Louise Simmons, however, was unapologetic in discussing her basic philosophy:

> I still define myself as a Marxist, however out of fashion that may be. I still see tremendous inequality and injustice, rampant racism, sexism and class based oppression. . . . I remain convinced that capitalism cannot correct its basic inequities and I still believe in the need for some type of Socialist society.

Shirley Crenshaw framed the issue both personally and succinctly. "I operate with one eye always looking at the gender, racial, and/or class bias endemic to capitalism, and with the understanding that it is normal, even healthy, but most of all, very human, to be a little insane while living in an insane environment." Others regarded their politics as flowing more out of social necessity than ideological conviction. They define their work as radical because, in the words of one respondent, "there is simply no justification for cultural, political, and economic arrangements that endanger basic survival, that prevent people from accessing food, shelter, and education, and that restrict their freedom to determine and cultivate social relations, then deny them the means to obtain all these things."

While oppression is a consistent theme among radical social workers, whatever their ideological roots or organizational connections, our research revealed that in both theory and practice, a gap exists between the ideas, goals, and emphases of White social workers and social workers of color. Keith Kilty commented on this issue in describing his attempts to bring a radical perspective to his early teaching: "Most Whites—including social workers—seem to want to ignore the depths of racial animosity and division in our society. . . . Whites should raise concern with the powerful forces of class, race, and gender. We cannot expect only the oppressed to do so."

COMMUNITY-BASED PRACTICE

For many respondents, radical social work practice is synonymous with grassroots community-based practice aimed at the transformation of society and its members. This is reflected in their underlying assumptions about practice, teaching, research, and writing. As David Gil points out, radical social workers assume "that individual and social ills . . . are primarily rooted in socially structured domination and exploitation of social classes and entire peoples by other classes and people." This assumption implies that "overcoming [these problems] requires helping people to organize social movements, pursuing transformation of domination and exploitation into non-oppressive and non-exploitative alternatives, and of competition and selfishness in human relations into cooperation and solidarity, rather than helping [people] to live with and adapt to oppression and injustice, as conventional social work tends to do."

Some respondents explicitly connected community practice with activities directed against "the harmful actions of corporations and government." Others linked their practice to specific issues such as hunger, homelessness, U.S. foreign policy, civil rights, or opposition to the death penalty. Many of their activities occurred outside of traditional social work organizations or were not specifically identified as social work practice. Although most respondents did not correlate radical practice with a specific mode of intervention, a few contrasted community practice with other, more conservative forms of social work intervention. Martha Spinks, a social worker in the military, stated candidly,

> I believe consciousness raising and community work are social work, while clinical practice is a flaccid permutation of psychiatry. Community work is constructive, assertive, and empowering; clinical work is a palliative that subordinates social work and social workers to a medical model which is foreign, even antagonistic, to my view of social work. . . . Sometimes I feel clinicians are unethical because they are waiting for a crisis to happen so they can fix it, rather than promoting healthy communities.

SOURCES OF POLITICAL
AND PROFESSIONAL IDEOLOGY

No single path defined how our respondents developed their radical views. For many respondents, catalytic events of the 1960s and, in a few cases, the 1930s, affected them through personal experience or study. Often, childhood events of considerably different types forged their radicalism. Many experienced poverty and oppression while growing up, or confronted racism or fascism in their youth. In other cases, parents or close relatives articulated radical ideas or lived a radical lifestyle.

Herman Curiel, a professor at the University of Oklahoma, identifies with radical social work because of his personal history. As he explained,

Given my roots as an American born of Mexican parents who divorced shortly after I was born, growing up in a poor neighborhood in Corpus Christi, Texas, and coming from a home where both parents were absent in my life, I felt a strong identification with social work consumers who shared similar life experiences. . . . I experienced a lot of anger believing that some members of the larger community had little regard or respect for members of my ethnic group.

The 1960s had an impact on many of our respondents who were involved in the antiwar and civil rights movements. Alfred Joseph noted,

I went to see Cesar Chavez once. He was building support for the strike against the growers. He ended his speech by saying that the average American lives to be 70 while the average farm worker only lives to be 50. He asked the audience, "Who are they to steal twenty years of our lives?" Those words have always stuck with me. I felt that whatever I did I should do something to stop that theft.

Some radical social workers took considerable risks in these activities.

I had the opportunity to be actively involved in two civil rights movements, and I am probably the only American to have done so. The first was in Chapel Hill in 1963; the second was in Northern Ireland, in 1969. . . . My most radical activities, however, were in the peace movement [which included] my involvement in protests at Fort Bragg . . . and due to the 500+ letters I sent to soldiers in Vietnam urging them to resist I was to be charged with treason at one time but connections with the U.S. Attorney in Alabama, and his understanding led to the case being dropped (K. van Wormer, personal communication, 1997).

I was active in the anti-war and civil rights movement in the late 60s, was arrested three times and went to Cuba with the Venceremos Brigade in 1970. My essential mistrust of government surveillance, centrist politics, the corruption of wealth in a market economy and the evils of racism and imperialism have remained similar in their core beliefs. . . . My professional commitment to anti-oppression work is deeper than it has ever been (Joshua Miller, 1997).

What is striking is how deeply rooted and consistent respondents' views are, despite the passage of time, the emergence of a different political climate in the United States, and shifting emphases in their work. One respondent, a social worker in Colorado, expressed her views this way:

Having come of age in the 1960s, I have the luxury of the idealism of those times ingrained in me. If anything, I have become more radical over time as I have lived my own life as a woman, a single mother, a divorcée, and as a proud member of the working class.

Older social workers were affected by the Spanish Civil War, the rise of Hitler, McCarthyism, the New Deal, the civil rights movement, and Henry Wallace's 1948 campaign for president. Philip Lichtenberg defines himself as a "democratic egalitarian socialist" as a result of his experiences of the New Deal, the early 1940s civil rights movement, and the Progressive Party. For Bertram Weinert, a retired activist from New York, "the Spanish Civil War was a defining factor" in his life. "It identified Fascism as the enemy and the system to be fought" and helped him to see "radicalism as a worldwide movement." Arline Prigoff learned, as a Jewish child in the United States with parents involved in support of refugees from the Holocaust, that "economic and political systems can have life and death consequences for individuals, families, and communities" (1997).

Retired social worker and folk singer Joan Goldstein was involved in early union activities, the Wallace presidential campaign, and the formation of the BCRS. Goldstein, who wrote her doctoral dissertation on Bertha Reynolds stated,

> From my student days to the present—I have been a "lefty"—always with a radical point of view in politics and in social work. I was at college in the days of the Martin Dies Committee and worked against Professor Dr. Brebanier [who] gave names . . . to the Committee resulting in the loss of [instructors'] jobs."

Professor David Gil of Brandeis University traced the sources of his radical philosophy to the "experiences of the occupation of Austria by Germany under Hitler in 1938, imprisonment of [his] father in concentration camps, traumatic separation from [his] family at age fourteen, living as a refugee in Sweden and Palestine, and encountering an alternative, non-bourgeois, egalitarian way of life in collective settlements." His story underscores the impact of personal childhood circumstances in shaping the adult experience. Gil shared his reflections:

> In trying to make sense out of my experiences, I became involved in an extended search for ways to prevent injustice, oppression, and war by reversing the vicious circles of violence and destruction. I became gradually committed to non-violent struggles against injustice and oppression, and refused to take part in armed struggles. I had come to realize that retribution against perpetrators of oppression (including my own) would merely continue rather than end the dynamics of oppression and violence.

Gil joined the War Resisters International and movements for peace among Palestinians and Jews and studied the social philosophy of Martin Buber, Peter Kropotkin, and Mohandas Ghandi. He found it difficult to find work as a conscientious objector during the war years and, in 1943, finally got a job in a home for delinquent children, the first step in his social work career. This was followed two years later with a job as a probation officer working in poor neighborhoods of Tel Aviv. As a result of these jobs, Gil "came to realize the contradictions, limitations, and futility of clinically oriented social services." Eventually in the 1960s, living in the United States, he encountered "social workers, organizations, and authors who advocated alternative approaches that stressed the political dimensions of practice and the need for combining practice with activism toward radical social change." Currently, he is cochair of the Socialist Party, USA, and is involved in local and national efforts "toward cooperation and organizational unity or alliance among democratic socialist organizations in the USA."

As in Gil's case, radical literature, ranging from Christian theology to Marxist philosophy to feminism to the writings of the Black liberation movement, introduced many contemporary radical social workers to alternative ways of viewing the world. James Trent remarked, "Jesus always seemed [to me] like a troublemaker . . . [Later] I read Michael Harrington's *Socialism* . . . and it brought together in a clear and convincing way that I was a socialist."

Radicals identified a broad range of influential authors and works. They cited Christian Greek Scriptures and Enlightenment philosophers, activists like Stokely Carmichael and Si Kahn, and intellectuals like Alexis de Tocqueville and Manning Marable. They referred to important social work ancestors like Jane Addams and Bertha Reynolds and professional contemporaries like Richard Cloward, Frances Piven, Mimi Abramovitz, Jeffry Galper, and Ann Withorn. Although many cited authors were from the United States, others from Latin America, Europe, and Israel also were mentioned. For example, Betty Reid Mandell, who began her social work career in 1948, was

> heavily influenced by the theories of Wilhelm Reich . . . [whose] theories about the links between sexual functioning and social/political functioning seemed very relevant to social work, but his theories were considered "far out" by the Columbia University School of Social Work. . . . His theories on the psychology of fascism, the authoritarian character structure, and the biological basis of repression have continued to influence my thinking.

Postmodern identity politics has, however, created a schism among some contemporary radicals. One respondent complained that

> class issues . . . are all but lost in the shift in radicalism . . . toward identity politics: gender, race and ethnicity, sexual orientation, ability status. . . . These are extremely important issues . . . but I am concerned nevertheless how in the process of promoting the broader array of causes, the cause of the working classes seems to have been put on hold. Social justice rather than economic justice seems the priority of many radicals.

For some radicals, their field placement as a student served as the catalyst for the development of radical theory and practice. Upon returning to graduate school in midlife, Californian Mary Brent Wehrli found her radicalism solidified by a field experience she had that strengthened her resolve to dedicate her work to grassroots, nonviolent activities. She explained

> I returned to UCLA to get an MSW. My concentration was macro and my first year placement was the Interfaith Hunger Coalition. That was the place where my journey toward radicalism . . . began to come together. It was there I got a political analysis that helped me understand all that I was concerned about (homelessness, the nuclear buildup, U.S. intervention in Central America) and met women who were organizing non-violent civil disobedience events on a regular basis. We became known as "women of conscience." For the next five years we protested the U.S. support of the military in Central America and went to jail countless times for our creative actions.

Wehrli was hired by UCLA as a field liaison in the early 1990s where she "brought [her] values and beliefs about a social worker's role in the community with [her] to the university and was shocked to find, [she] stood alone." She explained that "Some are supportive by tolerating me more than others. But it is clear, few share my total view of our profession."

PROFESSIONALIZATION OF SOCIAL WORK

Most respondents expressed concerns about the current emphasis on clinical or psychotherapeutic perspectives within social work, which they regard as a consequence of social work's drive for professionalization (Reisch, 1998; Wenocur & Reisch, 1989). Through this status orientation, they believe that social work lost its historic commitment to social activism and no longer takes proactive positions on social justice issues (Specht & Courtney, 1994). Many remarked how these tendencies have grown stronger since they entered the profession, eroding their optimism about the potential of the social work profession "to effectively oppose the [conservative] onslaught." Several respondents echoed the following sentiment voiced by James Trent:

> In my early years . . . I believed that social work could be a radical profession. I have lately, if reluctantly, come to the conclusion that social work's quest for professionalization has made radicalism impossible. . . . When I behave as a radical, I do not usually think of myself as a social worker. (J. Trent, personal communication, 1997)

Some respondents attributed the lack of proactive stances among social workers to the absence of progressive leadership. Others attributed it to social workers' aspirations "to being junior psychiatrists . . . [their attraction] to pathologizing models, [and submission] without a struggle to the dictates of managed care." Donna Hardina, a professor at the California State University at Fresno, perceived a connection between the social control mechanisms inherent in clinical practice "that cause some groups of people to internalize oppression or blame themselves for problems that have their origins in the social environment" and "the way the state uses social workers to suppress political dissent."

Another faculty member, Joel Blau of the State University of New York at Stony Brook, succinctly summarized the resignation and cynicism expressed by many people we interviewed:

> I once thought of social work for its liberatory potential [and that] radical practice . . . would bring about social change. I don't think that anymore. Social work needs to break out of the ghetto of being tied to poor people. We need to define our clients in a broader way . . . in universalism.

Thus, although once quite optimistic about the profession and still somewhat hopeful about its potential, many radical social workers now feel disillusioned. They have a sense that for a variety of reasons organized social work cannot advocate for a more radical agenda and that "the kind of radical change needed probably can't happen." As a result, the views of radical social workers like Keith Kilty remain unchanged, but his "philosophy has merely hardened more and more, while the profession has moved away from a concern for social justice and social change."

Several other factors contributed to this disillusionment. One respondent remarked on "the true sorry (liberal) state of U.S. social work institutions and goals." An African American organizer referred to the shocking nature of "the racism, the indifference, the insensitivity of many [social work] professors." A third reflected on how this disillusionment led her to scale back her hopes and dreams. An elderly social worker, long retired, voiced similar concerns about social work education.

> To an older generation it seems a real revolution inside the profession that new students and school curricula concentrate so much on careers as personal counselors and seek a credential which enables them to be reimbursed for inter-personal relationship counseling for courts, insurance agencies and individual fee paying clients and less on changing conditions . . . a la Addams, Reynolds or Cloward.

A few respondents, however, still harbor hope for the profession and believe that social workers "can choose to make their contributions to a better world in a variety of ways." One respondent remarked, "I am basically proud of social work because it is the only profession that . . . has such an explicit commitment to social justice. Although I am critical of much within the profession, particularly the emphasis on clinical work and private practice, I essentially value the profession's ethics and values." Another commented that although "there is a great deal of the profession that is not at all radical and indeed quite conservative (in effect if not intent), there is room for those who want to pursue social change."

INFLUENCE OF RADICAL SOCIAL WORK

Despite this potential, many respondents regretfully acknowledged that radical ideas have had little impact on social work practice and theory, or U.S. social policies. A social worker from Wisconsin, Mary Keegan Eamon, stated this view bluntly:

> I doubt if the social work profession never existed that the social policies of this country would be much different. . . . I tend to agree with the political left that the main effect of social work is one of social control. The profession does little or nothing to change the basic social and economic conditions that give rise to the problems that we "treat."

Keith Kilty framed the issue in a broader social context: "Many people seem to think that social workers are innately more sensitive and concerned about human welfare than other people in our society. [In fact] social workers are really no different than the rest of this society."

A few respondents disagreed. They argued that in the area of social policy, "radical practice helps define the center" of the political spectrum. The mainstream of the profession "relies on radical ideas for inspiration" and "takes radical thought and makes it liberal, humanistic." Those respondents who believe that radical ideology and practice have been influential regard social work's focus on community and reform as evidence that radical perspectives—"even if often a minority and subversive view"—have served as "the moral conscience and redeeming element" of the profession.

Even these respondents concede, however, that the effects of radicalism have usually been short lived and that radical ideas often are diluted and integrated into mainstream, conservative perspectives. Bertram Weinert remarked:

> The influence of [radical] social work on U.S. social policies is difficult to assess. In some ways it is like the influence of socialism. Ideas and programs proposed have often been incorporated into established political party platforms, after much time elapsed. Income tax and Social Security are two examples.

Some respondents viewed this phenomenon with dismay. Others acknowledged that radicals within the profession have kept the reform tradition alive and resisted efforts to move social work toward a more conservative agenda, particularly since the 1980s. Joel Blau described radical social workers as "one of the forces that work to block the ascendancy of conservatives."

As Gil (1998) points out, however, the extent to which radicals have influenced social work has varied over time with shifts in social and economic conditions:

> [Radicalism's impact] tended to be stronger during times of mass immigration from Europe and economic downturns and crises, when large segments of

the population including white working class people were affected by mounting social ills, and when progressive political forces were active in the public arena. It tended to be weaker during times of "prosperity," when social problems were thought to be concentrated mainly among people of color and non-European immigrants, and when conservative political forces monopolized the political discourse and public consciousness.

Many respondents asserted that "radical social work practice and ideology have been a constant, *minor theme* of the profession throughout its evolution" (emphasis added), which persists to the present largely through radical social work faculty. Most respondents were skeptical about the support for radical ideas among the rest of the profession "beyond lip service of CSWE and NASW to [radical] issues." These respondents also commented on their perception that adherence to such ideas resulted in their marginal status within the profession, even within the academy.

According to this perspective, self-interest and professional survival now take precedence over the interests of "those we say we are working to help." Priority is given to liberal rhetoric and to "promoting the profession rather than advocating for marginalized populations and social change." Yet some respondents expressed optimism about the future role of radical and progressive social workers. One respondent asserted, "[They] are some of the forces who will continue to fight the good fight despite the odds or popular sentiments that are anti-poor, racist, etc."

CONSEQUENCES OF BEING A RADICAL SOCIAL WORKER

Not surprisingly, questions about the personal and professional consequences of their radicalism evoked considerable discomfort among respondents. Earlier studies of the impact of McCarthyism on social work unearthed similar feelings (Reisch & Andrews, 1999). Several respondents asked that their replies be kept confidential. Others described their difficulties as subtle, hard to pin down and record. Many radical social workers regularly engage in self-censorship in their writings, teaching, and presentations. One remarked, "I censor myself more than anything in the classroom and in my submissions to professional journals." Another stated, "My political views are only shared in bits and pieces. . . . I have in turn been revered and reviled."

Others described themselves as being "closet radicals" because of the circumstances of their employment. They are reluctant to share their views with colleagues. As one social worker in the military, Martha Spinks, observed, "words like radical, socialism, welfare state, false consciousness, activism, and social justice make [colleagues] visibly nervous."

Much like their professional ancestors, today's radical social workers consider themselves marginalized by colleagues and believe that they are often considered troublemakers because of their political views and activities. One respondent commented, "Many of [my colleagues] see me as . . . abrasive and I know that they would prefer that I keep my mouth shut . . . so I tend to be on the fringe." Another spoke of occasionally "being socially shunned." Some radical social work educators described their difficulty in getting their syllabi approved if they included radical content.

Some respondents report being investigated by the FBI or other government agencies long after the McCarthy period ended. A considerable number have extensive files because of their political activities. Many experienced the public and private approbation of colleagues for their views, alternately being regarded as a threat and a "goof-ball" within their agencies or schools. One respondent's experience reflects this pattern clearly:

> I have spoken out a number of times over issues that I thought unjust, but mostly people see me as an oddity without much power. . . . I have had my share of being called a communist, suggested I should be shot, teased about the FBI file I have, etc.

Another respondent told of her colleagues saying privately that "my classes were too pro-Black," and publicly "that my feminist bias was a disservice to students." A practitioner reflected, "My political views have caused me problems most of my life. As a great admirer of the thinking of Karl Marx, I have been criticized, misunderstood, and shunned."

Yet respondents pointed out that it is often difficult to assess the consequences of their ideology because people in authority are careful not to ascribe political reasons for negative personnel decisions. Nonetheless, many are convinced that they are stigmatized, receive less pay, and are less likely to be recognized for their work than nonradical colleagues. A few explicitly mentioned difficulties in either the outcome or the pace of tenure and promotion processes in their agencies and universities. One commented, "The fear of retaliation may be the biggest obstacle to social change." These statements confirm the findings of previous research on the impact of McCarthyism (Andrews & Reisch, 1997).

PERSPECTIVES ON THE FUTURE OF RADICAL SOCIAL WORK

According to most respondents, radical social workers must align themselves with grassroots organizations and other social movements to promote their views and goals in the future. Some feel that there are a number of such movements in the current environment that would make natural allies. These include welfare rights organizations, labor unions, civil rights groups, and antipoverty coalitions.

They acknowledged, however, that the formation of such broad-based coalitions is a more formidable task now than ever. Today's radical social workers largely have incorporated the perspectives of 1990s "identity politics" into their thinking. They believe issues such as multiculturalism, feminism, and gay/lesbian rights should be at the center of a radical agenda. Yet more than most proponents of those issues within the profession, they feel that identity concerns need to be fused with a class perspective. One respondent stated,

> We need to . . . encourage people from a diversity of backgrounds to reach out and cross boundaries and to work together. If radicalism is to have a greater impact on the profession of social work and on American society, we need to stress a philosophy of integration and working together to bring about lasting, fundamental change.

Another expressed this synthesis:

> I think [radical social work] will have to incorporate a deeper relationship with both the new leadership and direction of the labor movement and also cultivate deeper ties with movements and issues of people of color, so that radical social workers . . . do not fall into the trap of being defined as "leftover hippies" who are a bunch of irrelevant white liberals. It must also maintain its presence and action on issues of sexism and gay and lesbian rights.

Many respondents remarked that the concept of social justice, particularly through its application to current attacks on the poor, women, and children, could serve as a unifying theme. This would also involve renewed emphasis on class-based issues. An important question for radical social workers in the years ahead, therefore, will be how to balance a more universalistic perspective with a focus on the particular needs of oppressed populations. Given the racial imbalance in our sample of self-identified radicals, this is a problem that radicals can no longer ignore.

Despite their widespread cynicism about the past and skepticism about the future, a considerable number of respondents reflected tentative optimism. One older respondent stated:

> I . . . believe that class conflict will eventually come to dominate center stage again at least at the national, policy level. My fear, however, is that . . . identity politics we will end up fostering nationalist and ethnocentric values. My own observation, based on my work in grassroots agencies, is that most ethnic and racial groups are deep down more concerned with their economic well being than with their racial identity.

CONCLUSION

This "snapshot" of social work radicals at the end of the twentieth century reflects their belief that radical social work practice in the future will require a

transformation—of theory, status, educational models, and professional goals—
in which most contemporary social workers in the United States will be unwilling or unable to engage. In part, this is a consequence of a lack of knowledge
and skills as to how to initiate and sustain such a transformation. In part, it is the
result of a reluctance to sacrifice the profession's tenuous class privileges and to
take the personal and professional risks involved. Gil (1998) points out, however, that "in unjust and oppressive societies nearly everyone is a victim, as well
as an agent and beneficiary of domination and exploitation, depending on one's
position and roles in hierarchically organized, competitive institutions. Transformative practice focused on creating a just and non-oppressive society would
require major changes in the patterns of people's actions, interactions, and social relations" (p. 39).

We believe that significant numbers of social workers would be receptive
to alternative, radical theoretical orientations and open to a critical examination
of capitalism as an economic and social system. Recent demonstrations in Seattle and Washington, DC, against the WTO may reflect the possibility of bridging
racial, gender, and ethnic barriers around a common agenda. Are we, as a profession with a historical commitment to social justice and social change, willing
to go beyond bold statements in official documents? Are we capable of developing forms of practice that respond effectively to contemporary issues while
working to create a socially just and nonoppressive environment? Our research
indicates that at least some social workers continue to struggle with these questions and attempt to translate their radical ideals into daily practice. Perhaps
their struggle and those of earlier radicals can be a model for all of us in the
future.

11

Conclusion—The Future of Radical Social Work in the United States

To be hopeful in bad times is not just foolishly romantic. It is based on the fact that human history is a history not only of cruelty, but also of compassion, sacrifice, courage, kindness. What we choose to emphasize in this complex history will determine our lives.

—Howard Zinn, *You Can't Be Neutral on a Moving Train*

RADICALISM AND THE SOCIAL CONSCIENCE

Writing recently in the *Sacramento Bee*, Scott J. Rose (2000), chief medical consultant of the California Department of Rehabilitation, mourned the changes that have occurred during the past 25 years in the social consciences of young people and their parents that have influenced their choice of careers:

And what of those who had chosen the helping professions? A generation of forty-somethings and fifty-somethings have silently observed this cruel twist of fate, sidelined by choices made earlier in their lives. Perhaps the silence comes from stunned disbelief, or perhaps it is simply an attempt to conceal envy. But what seemed, 25 years ago, to be such an obvious and easy decision for most, now feels to many like a foolish and naïve error, as they watch a younger generation leapfrog over them in terms of wealth and status. . . . [They] feel besieged within their own institutions, as private organizations cut back their ranks and status in the face of managed care, government agencies struggle through budget cuts. Devalued on the job and ignored by the larger culture, many feel the urge to throw in the towel. So what does this mean for the future . . . the one populated with flesh-and-blood human beings, the one whose inhabitants still have human needs to be met, the one whose inhabitants still crave face-to-face relationships with each other? Will there be anyone left to meet their needs when this unprecedented economic boom ends? . . . Who will be waiting to take care of us when we are sick, counsel us when we feel down, comfort us when we are dying? . . . Is service to humanity still being held out as a noble and worthy goal? Unfortunately, it appears that the answer is no. In America today, the sad reality is that the lure of material wealth and status is irresistible. . . . In contrast to previous generations, the majority of today's helping professionals are actively discouraging their children from following in their footsteps. Their mantra is this: "Too much work, too few rewards, too little recognition."

If Rose is right about the future of the helping professions, in general, what are the prospects for radicals and radicalism within social work? Does radical social work have any relevance in the global, high-tech, postmodern future? Is radical social work now an oxymoron? Has it always been?

SIGNIFICANCE OF RADICALISM FOR SOCIAL WORK

In a climate in which social work itself is criticized as increasingly anachronistic and even moribund (Abbott, 1999; Johnson, 1999; Stoesz, 1997), the past and future significance of radicalism within the field can be easily overlooked or dismissed. Most social workers would agree that radicalism has had only a marginal status in the social work field and has less influence today on the profession than it did a generation ago (Jansson, 1993; Johnson, 1999). The lack of a strong class consciousness and its organizational manifestations, such as trade unions; the myths of equal opportunity and political pluralism and the individualistic and materialist aspirations they foster; the divisiveness produced by immigration and diversity; a focus among reformers on specific needs rather than on universal rights; and the conservative influence of professionalism itself all have been presented as explanations for the failure of U.S. social work to embrace a radical perspective. In Jansson's (1999) assessment, "the absence of a powerful radical tradition . . . meant that radicals were absent when political compromises were fashioned between moderates and conservative politicians at numerous points in the nation's history" (p. 323).

This view of radical social work focuses on the search for explanations of its failures. Were radical ideas in social work largely confined to selected regions, populations, or cultures (e.g., large cities, Jewish social workers) and, therefore, marginalized from the outset? Were radical ideas, based to a considerable extent on socialism or other now-discredited ideologies, simply wrong? Were they constructed on faulty premises about the causes of social problems, human nature, and the possibility of individual or social change? Or, is it possible that radical ideas were once right but now have been consigned to the dustbin of history by sweeping economic, political, and technological changes?

As popular as such notions are, they cannot explain, without reference to radical theories, how problems very similar to those of 100 years ago still exist or how new, similar problems have emerged. Nor do they explain the persistent influence in social work—even if largely in rhetoric—of ideas and practice principles that trace their roots to radical approaches to social welfare. They do not incorporate the experiences or perspectives of social workers in other societies and the radical strategies they have developed to address social and individual needs. Finally, they ignore the possibility that new ideological frameworks and new organizational forms will appear in the twenty-first century, much as they did more than a century ago.

Our research leads us to a different, guardedly more optimistic conclusion. We agree with Wagner (1989a) that "it is doubtful that, without radical critics within the profession, major changes would have occurred, . . . though afterward new leaders and texts in the field have absorbed such changes and treated them as natural" (p. 279). Although the relative weakness of radical social workers prevented them from establishing a lasting presence in the profession, upon closer examination one can discern how at critical junctures of American history a radical vision of society and of social services played a key role in social work's development and the direction of U.S. social welfare. For example, throughout much of the twentieth century, radicals "not only influenced the profession's . . . incorporation of feminist and culturally sensitive approaches, but recommended indirect action on the political front" (Johnson, 1999, p. 329). In effect, radical social work in the United States became one of several vehicles through which abstract and often-maligned ideas, such as socialism and feminism, were translated into practical policies, programs, and means of intervention that contributed to social betterment.

It is through this influence that U.S. social welfare evolved into an awkward synthesis of capitalist and socialist views of the human condition and societal responsibility for human need (George & Wilding, 1985). Although capitalist values and institutions certainly have dominated, socialism and other forms of radicalism often have served as countervailing ideologies (Wenocur & Reisch, 1989). Although most social workers have never been radicals, fundamental concepts of social welfare—such as social justice, legal entitlement, and institutionalized compensation—and basic principles of social work practice—such as self-determination, empowerment, and respect for diversity—are clear examples of radicals' impact on U.S. society (Reamer, 1993; Titmuss, 1958; Towle, 1945). Social workers and social work educators usually have failed to acknowledge this influence, yet as previous chapters indicated, conservative politicians and professionals often have seen the imprint of radical ideologies on every proposal to expand the concept of social welfare or reconceptualize the nature of practice.

Our exploration of the sources and impact of radicalism in social work has underscored how radical social work evolved and increased in complexity within a changing historical context. Social work radicalism emphasized different issues and contained different features in response to changes in the external environment. In certain periods, its major contribution was the articulation of alternative ideologies or causative theories. At other times, its primary manifestation was behavioral—that is, in the translation of radical ideas into practical, often small-scale applications or the formation of radical organizations. The concept of radical social work, therefore, is a relativistic phenomenon; it varied depending on the period and the views of both radicals and their critics. It exhibited both expansive and adaptive qualities and incorporated new ideas, such as feminism and multiculturalism, into its critique of society and social welfare with varying degrees of success.

Conversely, the history of social work in the United States reveals how mainstream organizations adapted radical ideas and proposals to nonradical ends in such diverse areas as social insurance, health care, and workers' rights. Since radical ideas generally were interpreted by a conservative institutional structure, what was radical in one era often became reformist, mainstream, and even reactionary in future decades. This ongoing dialectic between radicalism and reformism within the field underscores the difficulty of determining the long-term impact of radical social work.

Yet the history of radical social work and its repression also reflects consistent themes during the past century. A major contribution of radical social workers has been, in good social work fashion, to ask provocative, rarely asked questions. They have challenged conventional assumptions about the "givens" that dictate our theories and policies, and the assumptions they produce about, for example, the permanence of poverty, the inevitability of racism or sexism, the nature of human need, or the virtues of economic globalization. Radicals also have called attention to how vital issues are framed. They have introduced and expanded the concept of a just society and challenged us to define the real meaning of equality and democracy. They have pondered what a society without oppression, war, or the fear of war would look like. Throughout the bloodiest century in human history, radical social workers have suggested the possibility of creating a world that operated on principles other than "might (or wealth) makes right."

Perhaps, above all, the mere act of asking "forbidden" questions has been the most significant and consistent contribution of radical social workers. For in posing such questions, they implied that new, previously unspeakable answers are possible. Today, in an increasingly diverse society, asking such questions also implies that diverse peoples and communities may have different, equally viable answers to persistent problems. The most significant aspect of the repression of radical social work, therefore, may have been the muting or outright silencing of those questions that have never been posed.

The persistence of seemingly intractable problems like inequality, even in prosperous times, underscores the importance of asking such questions by adopting what Freire (1990) called a problem-posing approach. An important lesson derived from examining social work history through a radical lens is that we must resist both cynicism about the possibility of progressive change—by recognizing the changes that have occurred because of collective efforts—and the notion that certain chronic problems are incapable of solution. As in the past, social workers could play a critical role in influencing how our society addresses (or fails to address) such problems.

The history of the past century also reveals that the expansion of human rights and the enhancement of human well-being have occurred only through long and difficult struggles. No victories that promote the general welfare are won for all time. Each generation must ask the difficult questions again, challenge prevailing assumptions, take new forms of risk, and build upon the tenuous gains of those who came before. That is why the nature of radical social work itself had to evolve during rapidly changing times.

Another important lesson from the social work radicals of the past is the necessity of choosing battles strategically and recognizing that no single solution (theory, policy, or tactic) can solve long-standing problems permanently. Divisive issues come under different banners—sometimes even radical ones. Yet division often plays into the hands of those who benefit from maintaining the status quo. Radical social workers in the future should celebrate the differences among them, but neither trivialize nor exaggerate them. Awareness of difference can be the basis of power rather than weakness, a tool for teaching, rather than stigmatizing.

Ultimately, the linkage of radical values and behavior is what distinguishes principled practice from mere posturing (de Alvarado, 1973). Such practice may not always be dramatic, as interviews with contemporary radicals reveal, but it certainly requires ongoing risk and sacrifice. In today's media-saturated age, it is not enough, therefore, to use words like "empowerment," "multiculturalism," "oppression," and "social justice." The test of social work's commitment to its underlying values lies in the willingness to struggle on an often mundane, day-to-day basis to translate these values into deeds, as our professional forebears did individually and collectively.

RADICAL SOCIAL WORK IN A WORLD
WITHOUT SOCIALISM

The socialist philosophy that inspired many radical social workers "was conceived of . . . as a movement to put the people in control of the economic conditions that determine so much about their lives" (Harrington, 1988). The values that emerged from socialism served as symbols—under different guises—of the ongoing possibilities of the socialist ideal itself. They helped forge and continue to be consistent with the concepts of empowerment, self-determination, and social justice (Simon, 1994). Yet, the significance of radical ideas like socialism is frequently obscured by our ahistorical culture, which perpetuates our ignorance of the political and ideological divisions that shaped our nation's history and the evolution of social welfare and social work. This book has attempted in a small way to chip away at that ignorance, to illuminate unseen corners of our past, and, we hope, to stimulate serious debates about our future.

Now that socialism is no longer a global counterweight to free market ideologies, can radical social work survive? Recent events provide only a partial answer. For the past generation, social workers in the United States have struggled to justify their existence in the face of a concerted political and ideological attack. Despite its rhetoric of social justice and empowerment, the mainstream profession has largely failed to present a viable alternative to the individualistically oriented philosophy that prevails throughout much of the industrialized world. In fact, many social workers have succumbed to the allure of the market mentality or appear resigned to its permanence (Specht and Courtney, 1994; Strom-Gottfried, 1997). This has limited the profession's ability to translate its rhetoric into reality around such issues as welfare reform, managed care, and the privatization of social services.

Attacks on the principles of social welfare, however, are based on untested assumptions that have acquired the character of myths. One myth is that the collapse of the former Soviet Union and the socialist governments of its Eastern European allies invalidates all the ideas upon which socialism was founded (Zinn, 1994). This myth is necessary to bolster the argument that market-driven economies and political democracies dominated by economic oligarchies are the apotheosis of world civilization (Fukuyama, 1992). Similar myths prevailed in the late nineteenth century, similarly buttressed by untested assumptions and pseudo-social science (Sumner, 1884). A major contribution of radical social workers during the past 100 years was to challenge and, in many cases, discredit these myths through research and political action. Without their efforts, many of the features of our society that provide an element of civility—public health measures, consumer protection laws, public libraries and playgrounds, social insurance, and workers' protections—would not exist.

Thus, although only a small number of American social workers have ever identified themselves as socialists, socialist ideas have clearly influenced the social work field and the quality of U.S. society. The assumption that individual and social problems cannot be solved without altering—at least to some extent—the environmental structures that created them has become a fundamental principle of social work practice. Even social workers who eschew radical ideas would find some common ground in Parenti's (1988) definition of socialism:

> Socialists do not believe that *every* human problem at *every* level of existence is caused by capitalism but that many of the most important ones are and that capitalism propagates a kind of culture and social organization that destroys human potential and guarantees the perpetuation of poverty, racism, pollution and exploitative social relations. . . . Much of the unhappiness suffered in what are considered purely "interpersonal" experiences relates to the false values and anxieties of an acquisitive, competitive capitalist society. (p. 49)

Many of social work's opponents recognize this influence more clearly than do most members of the profession. For more than a century, elites have portrayed movements toward social change, however minor, as socialistic and, therefore, subversive of the social order. Ironically, proponents of structural reforms,

including many social workers, have been maneuvered into denying these as-
sertions in order, they believed, to defend their tenuous political position and
professional status. Yet this denial has contributed to the ignorance of socialist
and radical ideas within the public and the profession and has abetted the promotion of outright falsehoods as the bases for public policy by political leaders
and their academic allies.

For example, in the mid-1990s, one of the most prominent conservative
spokespersons, Charles Murray, dismissed the ideas of universal Medicaid and
child care provision as "social democratic." In his view, the implementation of
such policies would blur the concept of a competent, independent adult and
lead to a sense of entitlement among a wider spectrum of the population. This
would be counter to society's interests, he argued, because "welfare is intrinsi-
cally at odds with the way human beings come to lead satisfying lives" (Murray,
1993). The passage of welfare reform in 1996 could not have occurred unless
this view of society and human well-being had been incorporated into the dominant culture without serious challenge.

A related and often unrecognized impact of radical ideas on social welfare
is its emphasis on peace and international cooperation—whether expressed
through the ideas of socialist internationalism, universal sisterhood, multicultural
solidarity, or the fraternity of labor. Radical social workers have consistently
linked issues of war and peace with the daily concerns that occupy people's
lives. Throughout the twentieth century, they took considerable risks to draw
connections between the eradication of militarism and war and the pursuit of
social justice. They repeatedly argued that militarism and war exacerbate existing socioeconomic inequalities. From Lillian Wald (1914) and Jane Addams
(1907) to Daniel Sanders (1991) and Dorothy van Soest (1997) they have pointed
out how the social psychology of militarism equates might with competence
and rejects the virtues of interdependence. As an alternative, they have promoted—with only limited success—the creation of a society in which people,
individually and collectively, can be free from material want *in order to realize*
their full human potential. There is similarly an unbroken line between the
arguments of Florence Kelley and Mary van Kleeck (Sklar, 1995) and modern
proponents of empowerment like Barbara Solomon (1976) and Lorraine
Gutierrez (1998; Simon, 1994).

A FINAL WORD ON PROFESSIONALISM AND RADICALISM IN SOCIAL WORK

Throughout the twentieth century, many radical social workers explicitly or
implicitly argued that radicalism and professionalism are fundamentally incompatible. This argument has been a major issue among social work radicals, particularly since the 1960s. It appears to have surfaced more frequently during
periods of relative political quiescence like today. Although there is no clear
resolution of this debate, it is important to address the enduring question as to

whether there are circumstances under which radicalism and professionalism can coexist.

Part of the difficulty in addressing this question lies in varying definitions of the concept of professionalism itself. Opponents and critics of professionalism, from Bertha Reynolds to Ann Withorn, regard its salient negative features as the perpetuation of status and salary hierarchies, elitism, patronizing views of clients, and top-down conceptions of individual and social change. Professionalism, in this view, is a by-product of capitalism as an economic and cultural system, and a means of maintaining structural and status inequalities. Professional social workers must, by this definition, be conscious or unconscious agents of social control, who adapt their own behavior and those of their clients to the demands of dominant cultural institutions (Gordon, 1998; Mullaly, 1997; Newdom, 1997; Reynolds, 1963; Withorn & Newdom, 1997).

Other radicals, however, believe that radical ideology can be reconciled with the requirements of professional practice. For them, the key components of professionalism are competence, integrity, and fairness. While mindful of the perils of capitalism, they argue that a revised form of social work practice could synthesize the best features of radicalism and professionalism. Often drawing on models outside the United States, these radicals emphasize the linkage between economic and social development and the importance of identifying common ground between workers and clients (Blau, personal communication, 1997; Lewis, 1982; Midgley, 1997; Prigoff, personal communication, 1997).

If radicalism and professionalism are fundamentally incompatible, then radical ideas and practice can only survive outside of mainstream organizations and institutions. Few radical social workers, however, have seriously examined the implications of this argument for contemporary U.S. society. What viable alternative structures—comparable to early twentieth century settlement houses or the left-wing trade unions of the 1930s and 1940s—exist or could be created in which radical ideas could be translated into practice? Where would the resources to sustain such institutions be found? Who would establish and maintain standards of practice and professional integrity? Because radical social work has traditionally regarded the state as a means to implement its vision, what alternatives to state intervention exist in an era of increasing privatization (Fisher & Karger, 1997; Johnson, 1999)?

Both sides see a partial solution to these dilemmas in a major reorientation of the nature of the social work field, its policy and program goals, and its educational institutions. This approach harks back to the models of social work proposed by radicals in earlier generations. It also borrows from more recent developments abroad, particularly from the lessons of social work activists in Latin America and South Africa (Freire, 1990; Midgley, 1997). The philosophic foundation for this change already exists in U.S. social work: the primacy of social justice; the celebration of human diversity; the synthesis of political action and social service; and the appreciation of the inevitability and desirability of individual and social change. The challenge that remains is to translate these high-minded values into practice in a society that often celebrates diametrically opposed beliefs.

One essential component of this reorientation is the development of practice frameworks that are truly multicultural. Despite a demographic transformation unprecedented in human history, the concept of multiculturalism is still largely muddled rhetoric. There is no agreement on the meaning of multiculturalism or its ultimate goals. Most of the literature of multiculturalism focuses on differences rather than common characteristics and—purposefully or not—reinforces separatist and, ultimately, self-defeating positions (Council on Social Work Education [CSWE], 1998; Gitlin, 1995; Longres, 1997). The absence of a viable multicultural framework to guide policy, practice, and education compels social workers to accept narrow, racially and class-biased formulations of complex individual and social problems. Similarly, the current celebration of individualism and market-driven competition contradicts the essentially social character of social service work (Lewis, 1983).

A second component of radical social work in the twenty-first century would involve the reintegration of politics into practice. Radical social workers have long promoted a conception of practice as more than the aggregation and application of sophisticated techniques. Radical practice involves an awareness of issues of power and partisanship in which politics and social work are inextricably linked, not incompatible. This reflects a broader view of politics itself (Fisher & Karger, 1997; Haynes & Mickelson, 2000; Reisch, 1997). In Parenti's words,

> "Politics" signifies not only the competition among groups within the present system but also the struggle to change the entire politico-economic structure, not only the desire to achieve predefined ends but the struggle to redefine ends by exposing . . . the injustices of the capitalist system and by posing alternatives to it. (1989, p. 4)

Within this definition of politics, the role of radical social workers has been to contain the antiegalitarian tendencies of the market economy, raise the level of political awareness among clients, colleagues, and constituents, and develop new methods to fight the abuses of the socioeconomic system. From the Rank and File Movement to the Social Welfare Action Alliance, this view of political social work has remained constant. It could form the basis of radical practice in the future.

A third component of a revised view of radical social work would involve efforts to translate the principle of social justice into specific policies and modes of intervention. Radical social workers need to construct a theoretical framework that simultaneously acknowledges the inherent dynamism of the social environment and the holistic nature of the human condition. The challenge, as framed by Titmuss (1958), of creating social policies that address selective needs within a universalist framework is even more viable today. The "subjective necessity" of creating new methods of practice and new means of social service delivery is still before us. Although twenty-first century society is far more complex than that of 100 years ago, our research indicates that the values that guided the radical social workers of the past have not been invalidated by the rapid economic, social, and technological changes of the past century. Despite the obvious obstacles, the road not taken still lies ahead.

Sources

PRIMARY

American Friends Service Committee (AFSC) Bulletin.

Papers of the American Civil Liberties Union, Evelyn Butler Archive, University of Pennsylvania, Philadelphia.

BCR Reports, Newsletter of the Bertha Capen Reynolds Society, New York (now the Social Welfare Action Alliance), 1986–present.

Catalyst: A Socialist Journal of the Social Services. New York: Institute for Social Service Alternatives

The Charities Review. New York: Charities Organization Society of the City of New York.

Community Service Society of New York. (1974, February), *Report and recommendations of the ad hoc committee on income redistribution*. New York: Community Service Society.

Kelley, 1920. *Congressional Record.* [Testimony].

National Federation Settlement. 1946. Evelyn Butler Archive, University of Pennsylvania, Philadelphia. [Pamphlet].

Jacob Fisher Papers, Social Welfare History Archives, University of Minnesota, Minneapolis, MN.

Marion T. Hathway Papers, University of Pittsburgh, Pittsburgh. PA.

Marion T. Hathway Papers, Social Welfare History Archives, University of Minnesota, City. *The Social Service Alternate View*, 1975–1982.

Helen Hall Papers, Social Welfare History Archives, University of Minnesota, Minneapolis, MN.

Hotchpot. Publication of the Social Welfare Workers Movement 1969–1971. Personal Collection.

Interviews, correspondence, and surveys with social workers practicing from 1940–present.

Florence Kelley Papers, Sophia Smith Collection, Smith College Library, Northampton, MA.

Harry Lurie Papers, Social Welfare History Archives, University of Minnesota, Minneapolis, MN.

Woman Patriot, January 15, 1927. Both pacifists and Reds: There is a bit of red inn every pink. [Article].

The Messenger.

National Association of Social Workers (NASW) Collection (includes the papers of the American Association of Social Work with Groups), Social Welfare History Archives, University of Minnesota, Minneapolis, MN.

National Association of Social Workers Oral History Project, Social Welfare History Archives, University of Minnesota, Minneapolis, MN.

Proceedings of the National Conference of Charities and Corrections/Social Work/Social Welfare, 1880–1980.

National Federation of Settlements Archives, New York Public Library.

Papers of the National Welfare Rights Organization, Evelyn Butler Archive, University of Pennsylvania, Philadelphia.

Personal correspondence from students and professional colleagues.

Papers of the Social Service Employees Union, Evelyn Butler Archive, University of Pennsylvania, Philadelphia.

Papers of the Radical Alliance of Social Service Workers, 1974–1982.

Papers of the Social Welfare Workers Movement.

Social Work Forum: Official Proceedings of the National Conference of Social Work and the National Conference on Social Welfare. Chicago: University of Chicago Press and New York: Columbia University Press.

Social Work Journal. New York: American Association of Social Workers.

Social Work Today. New York: National Coordinating Committee of Social Service Employee Groups.

The Survey. East Stroudsburg, PA: Survey Associates.

Survey Graphic.

U.S. Government. (1998). *Green Book*, Washington, DC: U.S. Government Printing Office.

Lillian Wald Papers, New York Public Library.

Verne Weed Collection for Progressive Social Work, Social Welfare History Archives, University of Minnesota, Minneapolis and Hunter College School of Social Work, New York.

Young Men's Christian Association (YMCA) Archives.

SECONDARY

Aaron, H., Mann, T., & Taylor, T. (1994). *Values and public policy*, Washington, DC: The Brookings Institution.

Abbott, A. (1999). Measuring social work values: A cross-cultural challenge for global practice, *International Social Work 42*(4), 455–470.

Abbott, E. (1905). *The wages of unskilled labor in the United States, 1850–1900*. Chicago: University of Chicago Press.

Abbott, E. (1909). *Women in industry: A study in American economic history*. New York: D. Appleton & Co.

Abbott, E. (1917). *Truancy and non-attendance in the Chicago schools: A study of the social aspects of the compulsory education and child labor legislation of Illinois*. Chicago: University of Chicago Press.

Abramovitz, M. (1988). *Regulating the lives of women: American social policy from colonial times to the present*. Boston: South End Press.

Abramovitz, M. (1992). The Reagan legacy: Undoing race, class, and gender accords [special issue]. *Journal of Sociology and Social Welfare 19*(1), 91–110.

Abramovitz, M. (1996). *Under attack and fighting back*. New York: Monthly Review.

Abramovitz, M. (1999). *Regulating the lives of women: U. S. social policy from colonial times to the present* (2nd ed.). Boston: South End Press.

Adams, P. (1982). Politics and social work: A radical dilemma. In Mahaffey, M., & Hanks, J. (Eds.), *Practical politics: Social workers and political responsibility* (pp. 55–65). Silver Spring, MD: NASW Press.

Adamson, M. (1984). *This mighty dream: Social protest movements in the U.S.* London: Routledge and Kegan Paul.

Addams, J. et al. (1893). *Philanthropy and social progress*. New York: Thomas Crowell & Co.

Addams, J. (1895). The settlement as a factor in the labor movement. In J. Addams (Ed.), *Hull House maps and papers* (pp. 183–204). New York: T.Y. Crowell.

Addams, J. (1902). *Democracy and social ethics*. New York: MacMillan.

Addams, J. (1907), *Newer ideals of peace*. New York MacMillan.

Addams, J. (1910). *Twenty years at Hull House*. New York: Crowell and Co.

Addams, J. (1922). *Peace and bread in time of war*. New York: MacMillan.

Addams, J. (1935). *Forty years at Hull House*. New York: MacMillan.

Adler, M. (1998). *Heretic's heart: A journey through spirit and revolution*. Boston: Beacon.

Agnew, B. L. (1880, January 1). Wisdom in administering charity. *Monthly Register,* 10.

Alchon, G. (1991). Mary van Kleeck and social-economic planning. *Journal of Policy History, 3*(1), 1–23.

Alexander, C. (1977, May). *A bold face for the social work profession*. Presented at the NASW Delegate Assembly, Portland, OR.

Alexander, L. B. (1977). *Organizing the professional social worker: The union movement in voluntary social work, 1930-1950.* Unpublished doctoral dissertation, Bryn Mawr College, Bryn Mawr, PA.

Alexander, L. B., & Speizman, M. D. (1979). The union movement in voluntary social work. *The Social Welfare Forum,* 179–187.

Alinsky, S. (1969). *Reveille for radicals.* New York: Vintage.

Alinsky, S. (1971). *Rules for radicals.* New York: Vintage.

Allen, R. (1975). *Reluctant reformers: Racism and social reform movements in the U.S.* Garden City, NY: Anchor Doubleday.

Allen, T. (1969, August). Can white radicals be radicalized? *Somethin' Else,* 2(3), 1–7.

Altmeyer, A. (1951, December 3). *Some issues facing social welfare today.* Presented at the annual meeting of the National Social Welfare Assembly, New York, Evelyn Butler Archive, Box 30, University of Pennsylvania.

American Association of Public Welfare Officials. (1931, November). *Suggestions for dealing with unemployment emergencies in smaller communities.* Chicago: Author. Evelyn Butler Archive, Box 56, University of Pennsylvania, Philadelphia, PA.

American Association for Social Security. (1933). *American doles cost more than American social insurance.* New York: Author. Evelyn Butler Archive, Box 56, University of Pennsylvania, Philadelphia, PA.

American Association of Social Workers (AASW). (1929). *Social casework: Generic and specific* [Report of the Milford Conference]. New York: Author.

American Association of Social Workers. (1937, Feburary 5). *A survey of the current relief situation in 28 selected areas of the United States.* New York: Author. Evelyn Butler Archive, Box 56, University of Pennsylvania, Philadelphia, PA.

American Association of Social Workers (AASW). (1944). *Social work as a profession.* Chicago: Author. Evelyn Butler Archive, Box 56, University of Pennsylvania, Philadelphia, PA.

American Association of Social Workers (AASW). (1948, October). Civil rights in social work, *Social Work Journal,* 29(4), 134–152.

American Association of Social Workers (AASW). (1950, March). *Newsletter.* New York: Author. Evelyn Butler Archive, Box 56, University of Pennsylvania, Philadelphia, PA.

American Civil Liberties Union (ACLU). (1936, June). *How goes the Bill of Rights? The story of the fight for civil liberty, 1935–1936.* New York: Author. Evelyn Butler Archive, Box 56, University of Pennsylvania, Philadelphia, PA.

American Civil Liberties Union (ACLU). (1939, June). *The Bill of Rights 150 years after: The story of civil liberty, 1938–1939.* New York: Author. Evelyn Butler Archive, Box 56, University of Pennsylvania, Philadelphia, PA.

American Friends of Service Committee (AFSC). (1950). *Annual report.* Philadelphia: Author.

American League Against War and Fascism. (1935, December). *Women, war, and fascism.* New York: Author. Evelyn Butler Archive, Box 56, University of Pennsylvania, Philadelphia, PA.

American Public Welfare Association (1932, November 18–20). Proceedings of conference on the maintenance of welfare standards. Chicago: Author. Evelyn Butler Archive, Box 56, University of Pennsylvania, Philadelphia, PA.

Amidei, N. (1982, Summer). How to be an advocate in bad times, *Public Welfare,* 37–42.

Amidei, N. (1988, July 22). The new activism, 1988 Helen Pinkus Memorial Lecture, Smith College School of Social Work, Northampton, MA.

Anderson, J. (1951). The response of social work to the present challenge. *The Social Welfare Forum* (pp. 47–60). New York: Columbia University Press.

Anderson, J. (1984). *Outspoken women: Speeches by American women reformers, 1635–1935.* Dubuque, IA: Kendall/Hunt.

Andrews, J. L. (1987, September). Social work public image building: "East side/west side" revisited, *Social Service Review,* 61(3), 484–497.

Andrews, J. L. (1990). Role of female social workers in the second generation, *Affilia: Journal of Women and Social Work,* 5(2), 46–59.

Andrews, J. L. (Ed.). (1993a). *From vision to action: Social workers of the second generation.* St. Paul, MN: University of St. Thomas.

Andrews, J. L. (1993b). Social reformer and

settlement leader: Helen Hall and her neighbors. In J. L. Andrews (Ed.), *From vision to action: Social workers of the second generation* (pp. 43–57). St. Paul, MN: University of St. Thomas.

Andrews, J. L., & Brenden, M. (1993). Leading from the left: Three prominent female social workers, *Arete, 18,* 20-33.

Andrews, J. L., & Reisch, M. (1997). Social work and anti-communism: A historical analysis of the McCarthy era. *Journal of Progressive Human Services, 8*(2), 29–49.

Aptheker, H. (1966, October). DuBois on Florence Kelley. *Social Work, 12*(1), 98-100.

Arches, J. L. (1989, January). *Clinical social work in the United States: Theories, trends, and troubles.* Paper presented at the 1st U.S.-Cuba Social Work Conference, Havana, Cuba.

Association for the Improvement of the Condition of the Poor (AICP). (1880). *Annual report,* New York: Author.

Austin, D. M. (1986). *A history of social work education.* Austin: University of Texas School of Social Work.

Austin, D. M. (1997). The institutional development of social work education: The first 100 years—and beyond. *Journal of Social Work Education, 33*(3), 599–612.

Austin, M, & Betten, N. (1990). *The roots of community organization, 1917–1939.* Philadelphia: Temple University Press.

Axinn, J., & Levin, H. (1997). *Social welfare: A history of the American response to need* (4th ed.). White Plains, NY: Addison Wesley Longman.

Bailey, R., & Brake, M. (Eds.). (1975). *Radical social work.* New York: Pantheon.

Bailis, L. (1974). *Bread or justice: Grassroots organizing in the welfare rights movement.* Lexington, MA: D.C. Heath.

Baldwin, R. (1924). The challenge of social work to the changing control of industry. *Proceedings of the National Conference on Social Work, 51,* Toronto, Canada.

Balter, K. et al. (1978). Process Piece, from *Radical social work: An experience in praxis.* Philadelphia: University of Pennsylvania.

Banfield, E. (1970). *The unheavenly city: The nation and the future of our urban crisis.* Boston: Little, Brown.

Baran, P., & Sweezy, P. (1968). *Monopoly capital: An essay on the economic and social order.* New York: Modern Reader Paperbacks.

Barnes, J. (1980, November 19). Social work students brave the 80s. *Daily World.*

Barrett, E. L. (1951). *The Tenney Committee: Legislative investigation of subversive activities in California.* Ithaca, NY: Cornell University Press.

Battle, M., Sampson, T., Specht, H., & Utting, B. (1981, Summer). Professionalism: Weighed and found wanting. *Public Welfare,* 1–2.

Becker, D. G. (1968, February). Social welfare leaders as spokesmen for the poor. *Social Casework* 99(1), 82–89.

Becker, D. G. (1971, Spring). [Letter to the editor]. *Journal of Education for Social Work,* 5–6.

Belfrage, C. (1989). *The American inquisition, 1945–1960.* New York: Thunder Mouth Press.

Bell, D. (1960). *The end of ideology: On the exhaustion of political policy in the fifties.* Glencoe, IL: Free Press.

Bell, J. O., & Wilkins, H. (1944). *Interracial practices in community YWCA's.* New York: National Board of the YWCA.

Bell, W. (1965). *Aid to dependent children.* New York: Columbia University Press.

Bender, T. (1982). *Community and social change in America.* Baltimore: Johns Hopkins University Press.

Black, E. (2000, July 7). Unfounded fear spurred FBI spying abuses of '60s and '70s, Mondale says. *Minneapolis Star Tribune,* p. A7.

Blawle, M. J.(1970, September). *Law and politics of welfare rights organizations.* Paper presented at the 66th Annual Meeting of the American Political Science Association, Los Angeles. Evelyn Butler Archive, University of Pennsylvania.

Blau, J. (1989). Theories of the welfare state. *Social Service Review, 63*(1), 26–38.

Blau, J. (1992). *The visible poor: Homelessness in the United States.* New York: Oxford University Press.

Block, F., Cloward, R. A., Ehrenreich, B., & Piven, F. F. (1987). *The mean season: The attack on the welfare state.* New York: Pantheon.

Blumberg, D. (1966). *Florence Kelley: The making of a social pioneer.* New York: Augustus M. Kelley.

Bolin, W. W. (1973, July). *Feminism, reform and social service: A history of women in social work.* Minneapolis: Minnesota Resource Center for Social Work Education.

Bombyk, M. (1995). Progressive social work. In R. Edwards (Ed.), *Encyclopedia of social work* (19th ed.). Washington, DC: National Association of Social Workers.

Boris, E. (1993). The power of motherhood: Black and white activist women redefine the "political." In S. Koven & S. Michel (Eds.), *Mothers of a new world: Maternalist politics and the origins of welfare states* (pp. 213–245). New York: Routledge.

Boyer, M. (1935, December). [Editorial]. *Social Work Today*, 7–8.

Boyer, P. (1978). *Urban masses and moral order in America, 1820-1920.* Cambridge, MA: Harvard University Press.

Brackett, J. (1909). *Social work.* Jeffrey Richardson Brackett Papers (MS 8), Simmons College Archives, Boston.

Brager, G., & Purcell, F. (Eds.). (1967). *Community action against poverty: Readings from the mobilization experience.* New Haven, CT: College and University Press.

Brake, M., & Bailey, R. (Eds.). (1980). *Radical social work and practice.* Beverly Hills, CA: Sage.

Branch, T. (1988). *Parting the waters: America in the King years, 1954–1963.* New York: Simon and Schuster.

Branch, T. (1998). *Pillar of fire: America in the King years, 1963–1965.* New York: Simon and Schuster.

Braverman, H. (1974). *Labor and monopoly capital.* New York: Monthly Review.

Brenden, M. E. (1993). Mary van Kleeck: Social worker and leader. In J. Andrews (Ed.), *From vision to action: Social workers of the second generation* (pp. 75–88). St. Paul, MN: University of St. Thomas.

Bricker-Jenkins, M., & Hooyman, N. (Eds.). (1986). *Not for women only: Feminist practice for a feminist future.* Silver Spring, MD: National Association of Social Workers.

Bricker-Jenkins, M., & Lockett, P. (1995). Women: Direct practice. In R. Edwards (Ed.), *Encyclopedia of social work* (19th ed., pp. 2529–2539). Washington, DC: National Association of Social Workers.

Brilliant, E. (1990). *The United Way: Dilemmas of organized charity.* New York: Columbia University Press.

Brindle, J. (1962, April 4). *The union as a factor in social welfare in America.* Paper presented at the University of Pennsylvania School of Social Work. Evelyn Butler Archive, Box 55, University of Pennsylvania.

Brody, S. J. (1969, May 28). *The coalition as a tool for social action and social change.* New York: National Conference on Social Welfare.

Brooks, J. G. (1894, July). The future problem of charity and the unemployed. *Annals of the American Academy of Political and Social Science, 5,* 1–27.

Brown, A. (1991). A social work leader in the struggle for racial equality: Lester Blackwell Granger. *Social Service Review, 65*(2), 266–280.

Brown, B. S. (1968, June 4). Social change: A professional challenge, Convocation Address, Baltimore: University of Maryland School of Social Work. Evelyn Butler Archive, University of Pennsylvania.

Brown, L. (1948). The great teacher that teaches nothing. *The Survey, 87*(4), 469–471.

Bruno, F. (1957). *Trends in social work, 1874–1956.* New York: Columbia University Press.

Buhle, M. J. (1981). *Women and American socialism, 1870–1920.* Urbana, IL: University of Illinois Press.

Burghardt, S. (1982). *The other side of organizing.* Cambridge, MA: Schenkman.

Burt, M. (1992). *Over the edge: The growth of homelessness in the 1980s,* New York: Russell Sage Foundation.

Bussey, G. C. (1965). *The Women's International League for Peace and Freedom, 1915–1965: A record of fifty years' work.* London: Allen and Unwin.

Bussiere, E. (1997). *(Dis)entitling the poor: The Warren court, welfare rights, and the American political tradition.* New York: MacMillan.

Calkins, C. (1930). *Some folks won't work.* New York: Harcourt, Brace & Co.

Carlton-Laney, I. (1993). George Edmund Haynes' impact on social work education. In J. Andrews (Ed.), *From vision to action: Social workers of the second generation* (pp. 21–42). St. Paul, MN: University of St. Thomas.

Carlton-Laney, I. (1999, September). African American social work pioneers' response to need. *Social Work, 44*(4), 311–321.

Carlton-Laney, I., & Burwell, Y. (Eds.). (1996). *African American community practice: Models, history, and contemporary responses.* Binghamton, NY: Haworth.

Carner, L. P. (1945, April 3). *Why new settlements?* Paper presented at meeting of Chicago Settlements and Neighborhood Houses, Chicago. Evelyn Butler Archive, Box 43, University of Pennsylvania.

Carniol, B. (1992). Structural social work: Maurice Moreau's challenge to social work practice. *Journal of Progressive Human Services, 3*(1), 1–20.

Caudill, H. (1963). *Night comes to the Cumberlands: A biography of a depressed area.* Boston: Little Brown.

Caute, D. (1973). *The fellow travellers: A postscript to the enlightenment.* New York: MacMillan.

Caute, D. (1978). *The great fear: The anti-Communist purge under Truman and Eisenhower.* New York: Simon and Schuster.

Caute, D. (1988). *The year of the barricades: A journey through 1968.* New York: Harper and Row.

Cazenave, N. (1993). Chicago influences on the war on poverty. In M. V. Melosi (Ed.), *Urban public policy: Historical modes and methods.* College Park, PA: Pennsylvania State University Press.

Cazenave, N. (1999). Ironies of urban reform: Professional turf battles in the planning of the mobilization for youth program, precursor to the war on poverty, *Journal of Urban History, 26*(1), 22–43.

Center on Budget and Policy Priorities. (1984). *End results: The impact of federal policies since 1980 on low income Americans.* Washington, DC: Author.

Chafe, W. (1977). *Women and equality: Changing patterns in American culture.* New York: Oxford University Press.

Chambers, C. (1956). Social service and social reform: A historical essay. *Social Service Review 30*(2), 158–167.

Chambers, C. (1963). *Seedtime of reform: American social service and social action, 1918–1933.* Minneapolis: University of Minnesota Press.

Chambers, C. (1971). *Paul Kellogg and the survey.* Minneapolis: University of Minnesota Press.

Chambers, C. (1986). Women in the creation of the profession of social work. *Social Service Review, 60*(1), 1–31.

Chambers, C., & Hinding, A. (1968). Charity workers, the settlements and the poor. *Social Casework, 99*(1), 96–101.

Chandler, S. K. (1994). "Almost a partnership:" African-Americans, segregation, and the Young Men's Christian Association. *Journal of Sociology and Social Welfare, 21*(1), 97–111.

Chandler, S. K. (1995). "That biting, sting thing which ever shadows us": African-American social workers in France during World War I. *Social Service Review, 69*(4), 498–514.

Chandler, S. K. (1996). Industrial social work: African American origins. *Journal of Progressive Human Services, 7*(1), 3–22.

Chernin, K. (1983). *In my mother's house.* New Haven, CT: Ticknor and Fields.

Clague, E., & Couper, W. J. (1931, February). When shutdown came. *Survey Graphic,* 3–7.

Clark, C. (1970, March). Religious beliefs and social reforms in the Gilded Age. *New England Quarterly.*

Clendenin, M. (1969, May 26). Students and clients stage raid on social workers. *New York Daily News.*

Close, K. (1949, July). Bread, freedom, and interdependence. *The Survey, 85,* 373–385.

Cloutier, A. (n.d.). *Free to disagree: YMCA response to the challenge of McCarthyism.* Unpublished manuscript, YMCA Archives, St. Paul, MN.

Cloward, R. A. (1990). Foreword. In A. Epstein & Reeses (Eds.), *Professionalization and activism in social work* (pp. ??–??).

Cloward, R. A., & Elman, R. M. (1965). Advocacy in the ghetto, *Transaction, 27*(4). Reprinted in F. M. Cox et al. (Eds.). (1970). *Strategies of community organization* (pp. 209–215). Itasca, IL: F.E. Peacock.

Cloward, R. A., & Elman, R. M. (1966, February 28). Poverty, injustice and the welfare state: Part 1—An ombudsman for the poor? *The Nation,* 230–235.

Cloward, R. A., & Epstein, I. (1965). *Private social work's disengagement from the poor: The case of family adjustment agencies.* Buffalo: State University of New York at Buffalo School of Social Work.

Cloward, R. A., & Ohlin, L. (1960). *Delinquency and opportunity: A theory of delinquent gangs.* Glencoe, IL: Free Press.

Cloward, R. A., & Piven, F. F. (1964, April). *Low income people and political process.* New York: Mobilization for Youth, Evelyn Butler Archive, Box 28, University of Pennsylvania.

Cloward, R. A., & Piven, F. F.(1968, October 7). Finessing the poor. *The Nation*, 332–333.

Cloward, R. A., & Piven, F. F. (1975). Notes toward a radical social work. In R. Bailey & M. Brake (Eds.), *Radical social work* (pp. vii–xlvii). New York: Pantheon.

Cloward, R. A., & Piven, F. F. (1984). How students and faculty can help save the human services. *Social Work Education Reporter*, 11–15.

Coalition on Women and the Budget. (1984). *Inequality of sacrifice: The impact of the Reagan budget on women*. Washington: Author.

Cohen, M. (1973). Letter to National Association of Social Workers. NASW Archive, Social Welfare History Archives, University of Minnesota.

Cohen, N. (1947, October). Social action and reaction. *The Group, 10*(1), 7–11.

Cohen, N. (1955). Implications of the present scene for social group work practice. *The Social Welfare Forum*. New York: Columbia University Press, pp. 48–60.

Cohen, W. (1966, July). What every social worker should know about political action. *Social Work, 11*(3), 3–9.

Cohn, F. M. (1943). *Workers' education in war and peace*. New York: Workers' Education Bureau of America, Inc. Evelyn Butler Archive, Box 55, University of Pennsylvania.

Collins, B. G., & Whalen, M. B. (1989). The rape crisis movement: Radical or reformist? *Social Work 34*(1), 61–63.

Commager, H. (1947, September). Who is loyal to America? *Harper's Magazine* [Reprint], n.p.Verne Weed Collection for Progressive Social Work, Social Welfare History Archives, University of Minnesota.

Commission on Interracial Cooperation. (n.d.). *Southern white women on lynching and mob violence*. Atlanta: YWCA.

Conway, J. (1971–1972). Women reformers and American culture, 1870–1930. *Journal of Social Work, 5*, 166ff.

Cook, B. W. (1978). Female support networks and political action: Lillian Walk, Crystal Eastman, and Emma Goldman. In N. Coit & E. Pleck (Eds.), *A heritage of her own: A new social history of American women*. New York: Simon and Schuster.

Coss, Clare (Ed.). (1989). *Lillian Wald: Progressive activist*. New York: Feminist Press at the City University of New York.

Costin, L. B. (1989). Reflections on the1915 international congress of women for peace. *Swords and Ploughshares, 3*(4), 8–10.

Cott, N. (1987). *The grounding of modern feminism*. New Haven, CT: Yale University Press.

ouncil on Social Work Education. (1959). *Curriculum study*. New York: Author.

Council on Social Work Education. (1995). *Curriculum policy statement*. Alexandria, VA: Author.

Coyle, G. (1937, May). Social workers and social action. *Survey, 73*, 138–139.

Coyle, G. (1947). Group work as a method in recreation. *The Group 9*(1), 16–21.

Coyle, G. (1958). *Social science in the professional education of social workers*. New York: Council on Social Work Education.

Crocker, L. (1968). *Rousseau's social contract: An interpretive essay*. Cleveland, OH: Press of Case Western Reserve University.

Crocker, R. (1992). *Social work and social order: The settlement movement in two industrial cities, 1889–1930*. Urbana, IL: University of Illinois Press.

Crosby, A. L. (1952). How they wrecked the welfare department. [12 part series] *The Daily Compass*. Evelyn Butler Archive, University of Pennsylvania.

Curti, M. (1967). *Spearheads for reform: The social settlements and the progressive movement, 1890–1914*. New York: Oxford University Press.

Cushman, R. (1947). The President's loyalty oath. *Survey Graphic 36*(5), 283–287, 313.

Daniels, D. (1989). *Always a sister: The feminism of Lillian D. Wald*. New York: Feminist Press.

Danziger, S.(1991). Relearning lessons of the war on poverty. *Challenge*, September–October, 53–54.

Danziger, S., & Gottschalk, P. (1995). *America unequal*. Cambridge: Harvard University Press.

Danziger, S., & Weinberg, D. (1994). The historical record: Trends in family income, inequality, and poverty. In S. Danziger, G. D. Sandefur, & D. H. Weinberg (Eds.), *Confronting poverty: Prescriptions for change*. Cambridge, MA: Harvard University Press.

Davis, A. (1964). Settlement workers in politics, 1890–1914. *Review of Politics, 26*(4), 505–517.

Davis, A. (1967). *Spearheads for reform: The social settlements and the progressive move-

ment, 1890–1914. New York: Oxford University Press.

Davis, A. (1973). *American heroine: The life and legend of Jane Addams.* New York: Oxford University Press.

Davis, W. A. (1970, July 11). Domestic "war room" ready. *Boston Globe,* pp.1, 4.

Day, P. (1997). *A new history of social welfare* (2nd ed.). Englewood Cliffs, NJ: Prentice-Hall.

Day, P. (2000). *A new history of social welfare* (3rd ed.). Englewood Cliffs, NJ: Prentice-Hall.

de Alvarado, C. R. (1973, June). *Social work: A profession at the crossroads.* Paper presented at the 1st Venezuelan Congress of Social Work, Caracas.

De Anda, D. (Ed.). (1997). *Controversial issues in multiculturalism.* Boston: Allyn and Bacon.

Deckard, B. (1979). *The women's movement: Political, socioeconomic, and psychological perspectives.* New York: Harper and Row.

De Maria, W. (1992). Alive on the street, dead in the classroom: The return of radical social work and the manufacture of activism. *Journal of Sociology and Social Welfare,* 137–158.

De Maria, W. (1992). On the trail of a radical pedagogy for social work education. *British Journal of Social Work, 22*(3), 231–252.

De Maria, W. (1993). Exploring radical social work teaching in Australia. *Journal of Progressive Human Services, 4*(2), 45–63.

Dennis, P. (1981, October). Memories of the witchhunts. *The Progressive,* 21–25.

Denny, G. V. (1950). What is the difference between socialism and social welfare? *Town Hall 15*(39), 3–16. New York: Town Hall, Inc. Evelyn Butler Archive, University of Pennsylvania.

Derthick, M. (1975). *Uncontrollable spending for social services grants.* Washington, DC: Brookings Institution.

De Schweinitz, K. (1956, January 27). *Social values and social action—The intellectual base as illustrated in the study of history.* Paper presented at the Annual Program Meeting of the Council on Social Work Education, San Francisco.

Deutsch, A. (1941, November). Let's face facts this time. *Social Work Today,* 3–6.

Devine, E. (1908, December). The new view of charity. *Atlantic Monthly,* 102.

Devine, J., & Wright, J. (1993), *The greatest of evils: Urban poverty and the American underclass.* Hawthorne, NY: Aldine de Gruyter.

Dewey, J. (1935). *Liberalism and social action.* New York: G.P. Putnam & Sons.

Diliberto, G. (1997). *A useful woman: The early life of Jane Addams.* New York: Scribners.

Dore, M. (1990, September). Functional theory: Its history and influence on contemporary social work practice. *Social Service Review 64*(3), 358–374.

Douglas, P. H. (1937, December 1). Foreword. In H. Seymour (Ed.), *When clients organize.* Chicago: American Public Welfare Association.

Dover, M. A. (1997, Spring). Activism, professionalization and the future of the BCRS: Another view. *BCR Reports, 9,* 5–7.

Duffus, R. L. (1939). *Lillian Wald: Neighbor and crusader.* New York: MacMillan.

Dunbar, E. R. (1976, January). *Organizational change and the politics of bureaucracy.* College Park, MD: American Correctional Association.

Dunham, A. (1948, April 19). *What is the job of the community organization worker?* Address to the National Conference of Social Work, Atlantic City, NJ. Evelyn Butler Archive, University of Pennsylvania.

Dunn, C. (1952, April). When the pot calls the kettle black. *The Survey, 88,* 177–179.

Dutton, E. P. (1984, March). *A case study of four voluntary organizations involved in social change with farm workers prior to the grape strike of 1965.* Presented at the 1984 Annual Program Meeting of the Council on Social Work Education, Detroit.

Dykema, C. (1978). Toward a new age of social services: Lessons to be learned from our history. *Catalyst 1*(1), 57–75.

Edsall, T. (1991). *Chain reaction: The impact of race, rights, and taxes on American politics.* New York: Norton.

Edsforth, R. (2000). *The new deal: America's response to the great depression.* Malden MA: Blackwell.

Edstrom, E. (1970, April 12). A contempt for welfare. *Washington Post,* p. A-1.

Edwards, R. (Ed.). (1995). *Encyclopedia of social work* (19th ed.). Washington, DC: National Association of Social Workers.

Edwards-Orr, M. T. (1986). Robert Hunter. In

W. Trattner (Ed.), *Biographical dictionary of social welfare in America* (pp. 413–415). Westport, CT: Greenwood Press.

Ehrenreich, J. (1985). *The altruistic imagination: A history of social policy and social work in the U.S.* Ithaca, NY: Cornell University Press.

Elshtain, J. B. (1988).

Ephross, P., & Reisch, M. (1982). The ideology of some social work textbooks. *Social Service Review 56*(2), 273–291.

Epstein, A. (1934). Social Security: Fiction or fact? *American Mercury, 33*(130), 129–138.

Epstein, A. (1937, May). *Social Security.* New York: League for Industrial Democracy. Evelyn Butler Archive, Box 41, University of Pennsylvania.

Epstein, I. (1970). Organizational careers, professionalization, and social worker radicalism. *Social Service Review, 44*(2), 123–131.

Epstein, W. M. (1985). *The alliance between organized labor and the voluntary social service sector: A case study.* Unpublished manuscript. Shatin, N.T., Hong Kong.

Epstein, W. M. (1991, March). *Community organization education and American labor unions: An opportunity.* Paper presented at the Annual Program Meeting of the Council on Social Work Education, New Orleans, LA.

Epstein, W. M. (1995, Spring/Summer). Social work in the university. *Journal of Social Work Education, 31*(3), 281–292.

Evans, S. (1989). *Born for liberty: A history of women in America.* New York: Free Press.

Fabricant, M., & Burghardt, S. (1992). *The welfare state crisis and the transformation of social service work.* Armonk, NY: M.E. Sharpe.

Fabricant, M., & Epstein, I. (1986). Legal and welfare rights advocacy: Complementary approaches in organizing on behalf of the homeless. *Urban and Social Change Review, 19,* 15–19.

Faludi, S. (1991). *Backlash: The undeclared war against American women.* New York: Crown.

Farrell, J. C. (1967). *Beloved lady: A history of Jane Addams' ideas on reform and peace.* Baltimore: Johns Hopkins University Press.

Finkel, H., Galper, J., Lichtenberg, P., & Sternbach, J. (1973, May 31). *Social work practice as collective experience.* Paper pre-

sented at National Conference on Social Welfare, Atlantic City, NJ.

Finnerty, D. (1971). *Getting paid to be a radical.* Unpublished manuscript. Graduate School of Social Work and Social Research, Bryn Mawr College, Bryn Mawr, PA.

Fisher, J. (1934). Social work and liberalism. *Social Work Today, 1*(2), 9–12.

Fisher, J. (1936). *The rank and file movement in social work, 1931–1936.* New York: New York School of Social Work.

Fisher, J. (1943). Obituary for Lillian Wald. *New York Times.*

Fisher, J. (1980a). *The response of social work to the depression.* Boston: G.K. Hall.

Fisher, J. (1980b). *Social Work Today,* 1934–1942, and the dissenting left for which it spoke. *Catalyst, 3*(1), 3–22.

Fisher, J. (1986). *Security risk.* Sarasota, FL: Piney Branch.

Fisher, J. (1987). *The postwar purge of Federal employees: The world that made it and the government's loyalty-security program today.* Unpublished typescript, Social Welfare History Archives, University of Minnesota.

Fisher, J. (1990), The rank and file movement 1930-1936. *Journal of Progressive Human Services, 1*(1), 95–99

Fisher, R. (1994). *Let the people decide: A history of neighborhood organizing in America* (rev. ed.). New York: Twayne.

Fisher, R., & Karger, H. J. (1997). *Social work and community in a private world: Getting out in public.* New York: Longman.

Fisher, R., & Kling, J. (Eds.). (1994). *Mobilizing the community: Local politics in the era of the global city.* Newbury Park, CA: Sage.

Fitch, J. (1938, September). *Security in social work.* New York: United Office and Professional Workers of America, C.I.O. Evelyn Butler Archive, Box 29, University of Pennsylvania.

Fitch, J. (1949). The CIO and its Communists, *The Survey, 85*(12), 642–647.

Fitzpatrick, E. (1990). *Endless crusade: Women social scientists and progressive reform.* New York: Oxford University Press.

Flaherty, F. J. (1988, February). The Feds prepare a blacklist. *The Progressive,* 15–17.

Flexner, A. (1915). Is social work a profession? *Proceedings of the National Conference on Charities and Corrections* (pp. 576–590). Chicago: Hildmann Printing Company.

Folks, H. (1898). *Democracy as a factor of civilization*. Homer Folks Archives, Columbia University.

Folks, H. (1934). *Making relief respectable: A radical reconstruction of our conception of public relief*. New York: State Charities Aid Association, Evelyn Butler Archive, Box 56, University of Pennsylvania.

Follett, M. P. (1920). *The new state: Group organization, the solution of popular government*. New York: Longmans, Green.

Fondi, M., Hay, J. Kincaid, M. B., & O'Connell, K. (1977, February). *Feminist therapy: A working definition*. Philadelphia: Feminist Therapy Referrals Committee.

Foner, P. (1982). *Women and the American labor movement: From the first trade unions to the present*, New York: Free Press.

Fook, J. (1993). *Radical casework: A theory of practice*. St. Leonards, New South Wales, Australia: Allen & Unwin.

Forbes, J. V. G. (1943). The American friends in Spain, 1937–1939. In D. Howard (Ed.), *Administration of relief abroad* (pp. 3–21). New York: Russell Sage.

Fox, G. M. (1920). *An idea that grew: From a little cooperative store to a world-wide movement*. New York: YWCA.

Fraenkel, O. K. (1937). *The supreme court and civil liberties: How far has the court protected the bill of rights?* New York: American Civil Liberties Union. Evelyn Butler Archive, Box 58, University of Pennsylvania.

Franklin, D. (1990). The cycles of social work practice: Social action vs. individual interest. *Journal of Progressive Human Services, 1*(2), 59–80.

Frazier, E. F. (1924, April). Social work in race relations. *The Crisis, 27.*

Freedberg, S. (1986, March). Religion, profession and politics: Bertha Capen Reynolds' Challenge to Social Work. *Smith College Studies in Social Work, 56*(2), 95–110.

Freedman, E. B. (1995). Separatism revisited: Women's institutions, social reform, and the career of Miriam Van Waters. In L. K. Kerber, A. Kessler-Harris, & K. K. Sklar (Eds.), *U.S. history as women's history: New feminist essays* (pp. 170–188). Chapel Hill, NC: University of North Carolina Press.

Freeman, J. (1975). *The politics of women's liberation*. New York: Longman.

Freire, P. (1970). *Pedagogy of the oppressed*. New York: Continuum.

Freire, P. (1990). A critical understanding of social work. *Journal of Progressive Human Services 1*(1), 3–9.

Friedman, T. (2000). *The Lexus and the olive tree*. New York: Anchor Books.

Fukuyama, F. (1992). *The end of history and the last man*. New York: Free Press.

Furniss, N., & Tilton, T. (1978). Do we really live in a welfare state? *Dissent 25*(2), 143–146.

Gailmor, W. (1951a, May 28). What's behind the purge in the welfare department? *Compass*, Evelyn Butler Archive, Box 30, University of Pennsylvania.

Gailmor, W. (1951b, October 5). Dewey backs states' rights to stigmatize people on relief. *Compass*. Evelyn Butler Archive, Box 30, University of Pennsylvania.

Gailmor, W. (1952a, February 12).

Gailmor, W. (1952b, April 9). Indiana's insecurity act sets a dangerous pattern. *Compass*. Evelyn Butler Archive, Box 30, University of Pennsylvania.

Galbraith, J. K. (1958). *The affluent society*. Boston: Houghton Mifflin.

Galper, J. (1975). *The politics of the social services*. Englewood Cliffs, NJ: Prentice Hall.

Galper, J. (1980). *Social work practice: A radical perspective*. Englewood Cliffs, NJ: Prentice Hall.

Garcia, B., & Van Soest, D. (1997). Changing perceptions of diversity and oppression: MSW students discuss the effects of a required course. *Journal of Social Work Education, 33*(1), 119–129.

Garrow, D. (1986, December). *FBI surveillance of the civil rights movement, 1955–1970*. Presented at the annual meeting of the American Historical Association, Chicago.

Gelb, J., & Sardell, A. (1974). Strategies for the powerless: The welfare rights movement in New York City. *American Behavioral Scientist, 17*(4), 507–530.

George, V., & Wilding, P. (1976, 1985). *Ideology and social welfare* (1st and 2nd eds.). London: Routledge.

George, V., & Wilding, P. (1994). *Welfare and ideology*. London: Routledge.

Gessner, R. (Ed.). (1956). *The democratic man: Selected writings of Eduard Lindemann*. Boston: Beacon Press.

Gettleman, M. E.(1963). Charity and social classes in the U.S., 1874–1900, I. *American Journal of Economics and Society, 22*(3), 313–329.

Gettleman, M. E. (1974). The whig interpretation of social welfare history. *Smith College Studies in Social Work, 44*(3), 149–156.

Gettleman, M. E. (1975, Winter). Philanthropy as social control in late nineteenth-century America: Some hypotheses and data on the rise of social work. *Societas, 5*(1), 49–59.

Gettleman, M. E. (1982a, March 10–16). Anticommunist purges on campuses recalled. *In These Times*, 18.

Gettleman, M. E. (1982b, December 28). *Rehearsal for McCarthyism: The New York State Rapp-Coudert Committee and academic freedom, 1940–1941*. Paper presented at the Annual Meeting of the American Historical Association, Washington, DC.

Gil, D. (1976a). *The challenge of social equality: Essays on social policy, social development and political practice*. Cambridge: Schenkman.

Gil, D. (1976b, March 3). *Resolving issues of "social" provision in our society: The role of social work education*. Paper presented at the Annual Program Meeting of the Council on Social Work Education, Philadelphia.

Gil, D. (1998). *Confronting injustice and oppression: Concepts and strategies for social workers*. New York: Columbia University Press.

Gilbert, N. (1977). The transformation of social services. *Social Service Review, 53*(3), 75–91.

Gilbert, N. (1983). *Capitalism and the welfare state: Dilemmas of social benevolence*. New Haven, CT: Yale University Press.

Gillette, M. (1996). *Launching the war on poverty: An oral history*. New York: Twayne.

Gilligan, C. (1982). *In a different voice*. Cambridge, MA: Harvard University Press.

Ginsberg, & Miller (1957).

Ginzberg, E., & Solow, R. M. (Eds.). (1974). *The great society: Lessons for the future*. New York: Basic Books.

Gitlin, T. (1980). *The whole world is watching: Mass media in the making and unmaking of the new left*. Berkeley: University of California Press.

Gitlin, T. (1987). *The Sixties: Years of hope, days of rage*. New York: Bantam Books.

Gitlin, T. (1995). *The twilight of common dreams: Why America is wracked by culture wars*. New York: Metropolitan Books.

Glazer, N. (1961). *The social basis of American Communism*. New York: Harcourt Brace and Co.

Goldberg, G. S., & Kremen, E. (Eds.). (1990). *The feminization of poverty: Only in America?* New York: Greenwood.

Goldin, C. (1990). *Understanding the gender gap: An economic history of American women*. New York: Oxford University Press.

Goldmark, J. (1953). *Impatient crusader: Florence Kelley's life story*. Chicago: University of Chicago Press.

Goldstein, R. (1978). *Political repression in modern America*. Boston: G.K. Hall & Co.

Gordon, L. (1988). *Heroes of their own lives: The politics and history of family violence*. New York: Penguin.

Gordon, L. (Ed.). (1990), *Women, the state and welfare*, Madison: University of Wisconsin Press.

Gordon, L. (1994). *Pitied but not entitled: Single mothers and the history of welfare, 1890–1935*. New York: Free Press.

Gordon, L. (1995). Putting children first: Women, maternalism, and welfare in the early twentieth century. In L. K. Kerber, A. Kessler-Harris, & K. K. Sklar (Eds.), *U.S. History as Women's History: New Feminist Essays* (pp. 63–86). Chapel Hill, NC: University of North Carolina Press.

Gordon, L. (1998). How welfare became a dirty word. *New Global Development, 14*, 1–14.

Gordon, S. (1983, October). Impaired faculties. *The Progressive*, 18-21.

Goroff, N. (1988, May). *Helping overcome family violence: A social group work approach*. Unpublished paper. Toronto.

Goroff, N. N. (n.d.a). *Clinical social work practice and issues of social justice*. Unpublished paper. West Hartford, CT.

Goroff, N. N. (n.d.b). *Feelings of personal inadequacy: Social group work as antidote*. Unpublished paper. West Hartford, CT.

Goroff, N. N. (n.d.c). *Never good enough! The consequence of competition and comparison: Source of emotional pain*. Unpublished paper. West Hartford, CT.

Goroff, N. N. (n.d.d). *A pedagogy for radical social work practice*. Unpublished paper. West Hartford, CT: University of Connecticut.

Goroff, N. N. (n.d.e). *The social construction of the feeling of personal inadequacy: An aspect of social control*. Unpublished paper. West Hartford, CT.

Goroff, N. N. (n.d.f). *Social group work: Helping to heal the hurt*. Unpublished paper. West Hartford, CT.

Gramsci, A. (1971). *Selections from the prison notebooks of Antonio Gramsci*. London: Lawrence and Wishart.

Granger, L. (1944). *To the unfinished struggle: Three addresses to American college youth*. New York: Astoria Press, Evelyn Butler Archive, Box 40, University of Pennsylvania.

Granger, L. (1949). Testimony before the U.S. House of Representatives Un-American Activities Committee.

Granger, L. (1952). Social work's response to democracy's challenge. *The Social Welfare Forum* (pp. 3–18). New York: Columbia University Press.

Grayson, V. S. (1980). *NASW oral history project*. New York: Columbia University Press.

Green, J. (1999). *Cultural awareness in the human services* (3rd ed.). Needham Heights, MA: Allyn and Bacon.

Green, W. (1936). *The thirty-hour week*. Washington, DC: American Federation of Labor. Evelyn Butler Archive, University of Pennsylvania.

Greenwood, E. (1957). Attributes of a profession. *Social Work* 2(2), 45–55.

Griffin, E. (1949, April 7). Three universities listed as hives of communism. *Chicago Daily Tribune*, p. 6.

Groneman, C., & Norton, M. B. (Eds.). (1987). *"To toil the livelong day": America's women at work, 1780–1980*. Ithaca, NY: Cornell University Press.

Gross, E. R.(1995). Deconstructing politically correct practice literature: The American Indian case. *Social Work, 40*(2), 206–213.

Guild, J. P. (1933). The social worker and the depression. *The Nation, 136*(3545), 667–668.

Guinther, J. (1999). Heart of the red scare [review of S. Labovitz, *Being red in Philadelphia*. Philadelphia: Camino Books]. *Philadelphia Inquirer*, pp. 1, 5.

Gunther, B. (1949, May 5). The united seniors of America. *Pittsburgh Post Gazette*. Marion T. Hathway Papers, Folder 52, Social Welfare History Archives, University of Minnesota.

Gutierrez, L. (1998). Macro practice for the 21st century: An empowerment perspective. In D. Tucker, C. Garvin, & R. Sarri (Eds.), *Social work and social science: An integration*, Westview Press.

Gutierrez, L. (1997). Multicultural community organizing, In M. Reisch & E. Gambrill (Eds.), *Social work in the 21st century* (pp. 249–259). Thousand Oaks, CA: Pine Forge Press.

Gutierrez, L. (1990). Working with women of color: An empowerment perspective. *Social Work, 35*(2), 149–154.

Gutierrez, L., Parsons, R., & Cox, E. (Eds.). (1998). *Empowerment in social work: A sourcebook*. Pacific Grove, CA: Brooks/Cole.

Hacker, A. (1992). *The two nations: Black and wWhite, separate, hostile, unequal*. New York: Ballantine.

Hagen, J. (1986). Mary van Kleeck. In W. Trattner (Ed.), *Biorgraphical dictionary of social welfare in America* (pp. 725–728). Westport, CT: Greenwood.

Hall, H. (1971). *Unfinished business in neighborhood and nation*. New York: MacMillan.

Hammond, L. H. (1917). *Southern women and racial adjustment*. Charlottesville, VA: John F. Slater Fund.

Hammond, L.H. (1920). Interracial cooperation, in *Interracial cooperation: Helpful suggestions concerning relations of white and colored citizens*. New York: National Board of the YWCA.

Harkavy, I., & Puckett, J. (1994). Lessons from Hull House for the contemporary urban university. *Social Service Review, 68*(3), 299–321.

Harrington, M. (1981), *The other America: Poverty in the United States* (rev. ed.). New York: MacMillan.

Harris, B. (1978). *Beyond her sphere: Women and the professions in American history*. Westport, CT: Greenwood.

Harvey, A., & Coleman, A. (1997). An Afrocentric program for African American males in the juvenile justice system. *Child Welfare,* 76(1), 197–211.

Harvey, A., & Rauch, J. (1997). A comprehensive Afrocentric rites of passage program for black male adolescents. *Health and Social Work,* 22(1), 30–37.

Hathway, M. T. (1939) *Trade unions and professional workers*. New York: United Office and Professional Workers, C.I.O. Evelyn Butler Archive, Box 29, University of Pennsylvania.

Hathway, M. T. (1941). Introduction. In M. van

Kleeck, B. C. Reynolds, R. Hetzel Jr., R., & F. C. Bancroft, *Social work, peace and the people's well-being*. New York: Astoria Press. *Social Work Today*, pamphlet no. 7, 2.

Hathway, M. T.(1942, June). The primary responsibilities of social workers in the United States. *The Compass*, 13–18.

Hathway, M. T. (1948, March). *Our responsibility—1948: Preparation for social responsibility*. Paper presented at the annual meeting of the American Association of Schools of Social Work, Minneapolis, MN. Evelyn Butler Archive, Box 50, University of Pennsylvania.

Haynes, J. E. (1975, Winter). The 'rank and file movement' in private social work. *Labor History, 16*, 78–98.

Haynes, K., & Mickelson, J. (2000). *Affecting change: Social work in the political arena* (4th ed.). Boston: Allyn and Bacon.

Heale, M. J. (1999). *Franklin Delano Roosevelt: The new deal and war*. New York: Routledge.

Heale, M. J. (1998). *McCarthy's Americans: Red scare politics in state and nation, 1935–1965*. Athens: University of Georgia Press.

Healey, D., & Isserman, M. (1993). *California red: A life with the American Communist Party*. Urbana, IL: University of Illinois Press.

Hellman, L. (1976). *Scoundrel time*. Boston: Little Brown.

Herbers, J. (1969, March 9). Rights groups' split reducing influence with white house. *New York Times*, reprinted by the National Welfare Rights Organization, New York.

Hertz, S. (1981). *The welfare mothers' movement: A decade of change for poor women*. Washington: University Press of America.

Hill, S. (1934). *Housing under capitalism*. International Pamphlets no. 46, New York: International Publishers.

Himmelstein, D. (1969, May 16). Lindsay & co. backed bigger cuts in p.a. grants than Rockefeller. *SSEU News*, reprint.

Hirschfeld, G. (1943, March 22, 29). Cost of an American Beveridge plan. *Barron's, The National Business and Financial Weekly*, reprint. Evelyn Butler Archive, Box 41, University of Pennsylvania.

Hoffman, P. (1951, November). The tyranny of fear. *The Survey, 87*(4), 480.

Hoover, H. (1935–1936). *American ideals versus the new deal*. New York: The Scribner Press.

Hooyman, N., & Bricker-Jenkins, M. (Eds.). (1984). *Not for women only: Social work practice for a feminist future*. Silver Spring, MD: National Association of Social Workers.

Hopkins, C. H. (1940). *The rise of the social gospel in American Protestantism, 1865–1915*. New Haven, CT: Yale University Press.

Horchow, F. (1970). New York to Chicago: An observer's comment, 165–167. *The Social Welfare Forum*, New York: Columbia University Press.

Hunter, R. (1904). *Poverty: Social Conscience in the Progressive Era*. New York: Russell Sage Foundation.

Hunter, R. (1901). *Tenement conditions in Chicago*. Chicago: City Homes Association.

Hunter, R. W. (1999). *Voices of our past: The rank and file movement in social work, 1931–1950*. Unpublished dissertation, Ann Arbor, MI: University Microfilms, Inc.

Hyde, C., Fisher, R., & Reisch, M. (1995). *A panel on empowerment-based curriculum design that builds towards social change*. Annual program meeting of the Council on Social Work Education, San Diego, CA.

Hymowitz, C., & Weissman, M. (1978). *A history of women in America*. New York: Bantam.

Iglehart, A., & Becerra, R. (1995). *Social services and the ethnic community*. Needham Heights, MA: Allyn and Bacon.

Imre, R. (1989, March 5). *Caring about justice: A philosophical inquiry*. Paper presented at the Annual Program Meeting, Council on Social Work Education, Chicago.

Isserman, M. (1987). *If I had a hammer: The death of the old left and the birth of the new left*. New York: Basic Books.

Jackson, L., & Johnson, W. (1974). *Protest by the poor: The welfare rights movement in New York City*. Lexington, MA: D.C. Heath.

Jackson, N. C. (1957). Building community understanding of racial problems. *Social Work, 2*(3), 9–15.

Jansson, B. (1993). *The reluctant welfare state: A history of American social welfare policies* (1st ed.). Pacific Grove, CA: Brooks/Cole.

Jansson, B. (1994). *Social policy: From theory to policy practice* (2nd ed.). Pacific Grove, CA: Brooks/Cole.

Jansson, B. (1997). *The reluctant welfare state: Past, present, and future*. Pacific Grove, CA: Books/Cole.

Jencks, C., & Peterson, P. (Eds.). (1991), *The urban underclass*. Washington, DC: The Brookings Institution.

Johnson, A. (1947). Science and social work. *The Social Welfare Forum* (pp. 3–18). New York: Columbia University Press.

Johnson. Y. M. (1999). Indirect social work: Social work's uncelebrated strength. *Social Work, 44*(4), 323–334.

Jones, J. (1992). *The dispossessed: America's underclasses from the civil war to the present*. New York: Basic Books.

Joseph, B. L. (1975). Radical perspectives in our field. *Social Service Alternative View, 1*(4).

Joseph, B. R. (1986). Taking organizing back to the people. *Smith College Studies in Social Work, 56*(2), 122–131.

Joyce, J. (1951). Liberty or fear . . . the final choice. *The Survey, 87*(1), 7–10.

Kahn, A. J. (1998). *Themes for a history: The origins of the American social work profession, with special reference to its professional education*, 11th Annual Robert J. O'Leary Memorial Lecture. Columbus, OH: Ohio State University College of Social Work.

Kahn, D. C. (1934, May 14). *Philadelphia in 1950*. Paper presented at the annual conference of the Community Council of Philadelphia. Evelyn Butler Archive, University of Pennsylvania.

Kalberg, S. (1975). The commitment to career reform: The settlement movement leaders. *Social Service Review, 49*(4), 608–628.

Kampelman, M. (1957). *The Communist party and the C.I.O.* New York: Praeger.

Karger, H. (1988). *Social workers and labor unions*. Westport, CT: Greenwood.

Kasson, J. (1976). *Civilizing the machine: Technology and republican values in America, 1776–1900*. New York: Penguin Books.

Katz, M. (1986), *In the shadow of the poorhouse: A history of public welfare in America*. New York: Pantheon.

Katz, M. (1989). *The undeserving poor: From the war on poverty to the war on welfare*. New York: Pantheon.

Katz, M. (1993). *The "underclass" debate: Views from history*. Princeton, NJ: Princeton University Press.

Kaus, M. (1992), *The end of equality*. New York: Basic Books.

Kayser, J. A. (1996, August). *The impact of nineteenth-century Europe on twentieth American social work: Tracing the tradition of social justice through the biography and autobiography of Jane Addams*. Paper presented at the Fifth Conference of the International Society for the Study of European Ideas, Utrecht, The Netherlands.

Keefe, T. (1978a). Beyond radicalism: An historical-materialist framework for the social policy curriculum. *Journal of Education for Social Work, 14*(2), 60–65.

Keefe, T. (1978b, March). *Radical change and solidarity: The future of practice*. Paper presented at the Iowa NASW Symposium, Waterloo, Iowa.

Keefe, T. (1978c, September). The transition: An historical-materialist perspective on social welfare and social work practice. *Journal of Sociology and Social Welfare, 5*(5), 627–643.

Keefe, T. (1980, September). Empathy skill and critical consciousness, *Social Casework, 61*(3) 387-393.

Keefe, T. (1984, March). Alienation and social work practice. *Social Casework, 65*(1), 145–153.

Keisling, P. (1984, December). Lessons of the great society. *The Washington Monthly*, 50–53.

Keith-Lucas, A. (1967, Fall). *Social work values and their development*. Paper prepared for the Integrated Methods Beginning, School of Social Work, University of North Carolina, Chapel Hill.

Kelley, F. (1905). *Some ethical gains through legislation*. New York: MacMillan.

Kelley, F. (1922). *Twenty questions about the equal rights amendment*. Florence Kelley papers, Sophia Smith Collection, Smith College, Northampton, MA.

Kelley, F. (1924). *Equality or protection?* Florence Kelley papers, Sophia Smith Collection, Smith College, Northampton, MA.

Kellogg, D. O. (1880). The objectives, principles and advantages of association in charities. *Journal of Social Science, 12*.

Kellogg, P. (1924). Supplementary statement. *Proceedings of the National Conference of Social Work, 51*, 378–379.

Kendall, K. A. (1989, May). Jane Addams, pacifist. *Swords and Plowshares, 3*(4), 2–3.

Kennedy, J. C. (1933). *Unemployment and its problems*. New York: The Affiliated Schools for Workers, Inc. Evelyn Butler Archive, Box 56, University of Pennsylvania.

Kerber, L. B., Kessler-Harris, A., & Sklar, K. K. (Eds.). (1995). *U.S. history as women's history: New feminist essays*. Chapel Hill, NC: University of North Carolina Press.

Kidneigh, J. (1969). The New York conference story. *The Social Welfare Forum* (pp. 178–184). New York: Columbia University Press.

King, C. (1946, January). Should social workers organize? *The Woman's Press*, reprinted by the United Office and Professional Workers of America, C.I.O. Evelyn Butler Archive, Box 55, University of Pennsylvania.

Kirk, W. T. (1936). *Lobbying for social legislation*. New York: Social Work Publicity Council, Evelyn Butler Archive, Box 48, University of Pennsylvania.

Klehr, H. (1984). *The heyday of American Communism: The depression decade*. New York: Basic Books.

Klehr, H., & Haynes, J. (1995). *The secret world of American Communism*. New Haven, CT: Yale University Press.

Klehr, H., Haynes, J., & Anderson, K. (1998). *The Soviet world of American Communism*. New Haven, CT: Yale University Press.

Knickmeyer, R. (1972). A Marxist approach to social work. *Social Work, 18*(1), 58–65.

Kolko, G. (1963). *The triumph of conservatism*. Chicago: Quadrangle.

Konopka, G. (1958). *Eduard Lindemann and social work philosophy*. Minneapolis: University of Minnesota Press.

Kornbluh, F. (1997). To fulfill their 'rightly needs': Consumerism and the national welfare rights movement. *Radical History Review, 69*, 76–113.

Kornweibel, T. (1975). *No crystal stair: Black life and the Messenger, 1917–1928*. Westport, CT: Greenwood.

Kornweibel, T. (1998). *Seeing red: Federal campaigns against Black militancy, 1919–1925*. Bloomington, IN: Indiana University Press.

Kotz, N., & Kotz. M. (1977), *A passion for equality: George A. Wiley and the movement*. New York: Norton.

Kraft, B. S. (1978). *The peace ship*. New York: MacMillan.

Kurzman, P. A. (Ed.). (1971). *The Mississippi experience: Strategies for welfare rights action*. New York: Association Press.

Kurzman, P. A., & Solomon, J. R. (1970). Beyond advocacy: A new model for community organization. 65–73.

Kusmer, K. L. (1973). The functions of organized charity in the progressive era: Chicago as a case study. *The Journal of American History, 60*(3), 657–678.

Kutzik, A. (1986). The poverty index and two decades of neglect. *Political Affairs, 65*(3), 31–34.

Labovitz, S. (1997). *Being red in Philadelphia: A memoir of the McCarthy era*. Philadelphia: Camino.

Lacerte, J. (1976, December). If only Jane Addams had been a feminist. *Social Casework*.

Lasch, C. (Ed.). (1965). *The social thought of Jane Addams*. New York: Bobbs-Merrill.

Lasch, C. (1977), *Haven in a heartless world: The family besieged*. New York: Basic Books.

Lasch-Quinn, E. (1993). *Black neighbors: Race and the limits of reform in the American settlement house movement, 1880–1945*. Chapel Hill, NC: University of North Carolina Press.

Latham, E. (1965). *The meaning of McCarthyism*. Lexington, MA: D.C. Heath.

Lazarus, R. (1965, January). *Progress, poverty and social change*. Philadelphia: Citizens Conference on Community Planning. Evelyn Butler Archive, Box 28, University of Pennsylvania.

League for Industrial Democracy. (1935). *Looking forward: Discussion outlines, 1936*. M. W. Hillyer (Ed.), New York: League for Industrial Democracy. Evelyn Butler Archive, University of Pennsylvania.

Lee, P. (1937). *Social work as cause and function and other papers*. New York: Columbia University Press.

Lehman, H. H. (1950, November 20). *Freedom and the general welfare*. Address at the 45th Anniversary of the League for Industrial Democracy. New York, Evelyn Butler Archive, University of Pennsylvania.

Leiby, J. (1994, Fall). The early years. *Social Welfare at Berkeley*, 11–13.

Leighninger, L. (1986). Bertha Reynolds and Edith Abbott: Contrasting images of professionalism in social work. *Smith College Studies in Social Work, 56*(2).

Leighninger, L. (1999, March 12). *Missed opportunities: Social work and the public social service, 1930–1970*. Paper presented at the Annual Program Meeting of the Council on Social Work Education, San Francisco.

Leighninger, L., & Knickmeyer, R. (1976), The

rank and file movement: The relevance of radical social work traditions to modern social work practice. *Journal of Sociology and Social Welfare, 4*(2), 166–177.

Lemann. N. (1988–1989). The unfinished war, Parts I & II. *Atlantic Monthly*, December–January, 37–56, 53–68.

Lemann, N. (1991). *The promised land: The great black migration and how it changed America.* New York: Alfred Knopf.

Lemons, J. S. (1975). *The woman citizen: Social feminism in the 1920s.* Urbana, Illinois: University of Illinois Press.

Leonard, P. (1995). Postmodernism, socialism, and social welfare. Journal of *Progressive Human Services* 6(2), 3–19.

Leonard, P. (1975). Towards a paradigm for radical practice. In R. Bailey & M. Brake (Eds.), *Radical social work* (pp. 36–61). New York: Vintage Press.

Lerner, M. (1946). Toward an American society. *The Social Welfare Forum* (pp. 55–64). New York: Columbia University Press.

Levenstein, H. (1981). *Communism, anticommunism and the C.I.O.* Westport, CT: Greenwood.

Levine, D. (1971). *Jane Addams and the liberal tradition.* Madison: Wisconsin Historical Society.

Levine, J. A. (1968, August 17). National welfare unit tells what it wants. *Christian Science Monitor*, reprint.

Levy, J. (1934). New forms of organization among social workers. *The Social Welfare Forum.* Chicago: University of Chicago Press.

Lewis, H. (1976-1977). The cause in function. *Journal of the Otto Rank Society, 2*(2), 17–25.

Lewis, H. (1966). The functional approach to social work practice: A restatement of assumptions and principles. *Journal of Social Work Process. 15.*

Lewis, H. (1969a, May). *Social work education: Preparation for practice in 1970.* Keynote address, alumni day program, University of Pennsylvania, Philadelphia. Evelyn Butler Archive, University of Pennsylvania.

Lewis, H. (1969b, January). *Societal crises—Strategies for social work education.* Paper presented at the CSWE/APM, Cleveland.

Lewis, H. (1972, April). *Values, knowledge and practice—Issues facing the profession in the '70s.* Paper presented at the Ruth E. Smalley Colloquium, University of Pennsylvania, Philadelphia.

Lewis, H. (1982). *The intellectual base of social work practice: Tools for thought in a helping profession.* New York: Haworth.

Lewis, H. (1983). The social work service commodity in the inflationary '80s. In M. Reisch & S. Wenocur (Eds.), *The political economy of social work.* Hartford, CT: *Journal of Sociology and Social Welfare,* 550–562.

Lewis, H. (1992). Some thoughts on my forty years in social work education. *Journal of Progressive Human Services.* 3(1), 39–51.

Libros, H. (1962, December 21). Gray area project: New frontiers in social change. *Pennsylvania Guardian*, pp. 6–8. Evelyn Butler Archive, Box 34, University of Pennsylvania.

Lichtenberg, P. (1976, November). Radicalism in casework. *Journal of Sociology and Social Welfare, 4*, 258–276.

Lichtenberg, P. (1990). *Undoing the clinch of oppression.* American University Studies, Series VIII, Psychology V21: P. Lang.

Lichtenberg, P., & Roman, C. (1990), Psychological contributions to social struggle. *Journal of Progressive Human Services, 1*(2), 1–16.

Lindeman, E. (1921). *The community.* New York: Association.

Lindeman, E. (1948, January). *Educating youth for social responsibility.* New York: Community Chests and Councils, Inc. Evelyn Butler Archive, Box 50, University of Pennsylvania.

Lindeman, E. (1955). ????. In H. Trecker (Ed.), *Group work: Foundations and frontier* (pp. ??–??). New York: William Morrow.

Lindsay, I. (1980). Interview. In V. S. Grayson (Ed.), *NASW oral history project.* New York: Columbia University Press.

Linn, J. (1975). *Jane Addams: A biography.* New York: Appleton Century Croft.

Lissak,. R. S. (1989). *Pluralism and progressives: Hull House and the new immigrants, 1890–1919.* Chicago: University of Chicago Press.

Livingston, D. (1951, January 6). *Report to the general council.* United Office and Professional Workers of America, C.I.O. Evelyn Butler Archive, Box 55, University of Pennsylvania.

Longres, J. (1997). The impact and implications of multiculturalism. In M. Reisch &

E. Gambrill (Eds.), *Social work in the twenty-first century* (pp. 39–47). Thousand Oaks, CA: Pine Forge Press.

Longres, J. (1977). *Radical social casework.* Paper presented at the Annual Program Meeting of the Council on Social Work Education, Phoenix, AZ.

Longres, J. (1986). Marxian theory and social work practice. *Catalyst: A Socialist Journal of the Social Services, 5*(4), 14–34.

Longres, J. (1996). Radical social work: Is there a future?In P. Raffoul & C. A. McNeece (Eds.), *Future issues for social work practice* (pp. 229–239). Needham Heights, MA: Allyn and Bacon.

Lourie, N., & Smalley, R. (1961). *Statement to U.S. Congress on behalf of the National Association of Social Workers.* Evelyn Butler Archive, Box 34, University of Pennsylvania.

Lourie, N., & Vasey, W. (1962, February 13). *Statements to the Committee on Ways and Means of the U.S. House of Representatives on HR 10032—the Public Welfare Amendments of 1962.* Evelyn Butler Archive, Box 34, University of Pennsylvania.

Lovejoy, O. (1912). Remarks. *Proceedings, National Conference of Charities and Corrections.*

Lowe, G. R. (1987). Social work's professional mistake: Confusing status for control and losing both. *Journal of Sociology and Social Welfare, 14*(2), 187–206.

Lowe, J. I. (1997). A social-health model: A paradigm for social work in health care. In M. Reisch & E. Gambrill (Eds.), *Social work in the twenty-first century* (pp. 209–218). Thousand Oaks, CA: Pine Forge.

Lowe, J. I., & Reisch, M. (1998). Bringing the community into the classroom: Applying the experiences of social work education to service-learning courses in sociology. *Teaching Sociology, 26*(4), 292–298.

Lowenstein, S. (1938). General address. *The Conference Bulletin, 42*(4). Chicago: National Conference of Social Work.

Lubove, R. (1965), *The professional altruist: The emergence of social work as a career, 1880–1930.* Cambridge, MA: Harvard University Press.

Lubove, R. (1968). *The struggle for Social Security, 1900–1935.* Cambridge: Harvard University Press.

Lum, D. (1986, 1992, 2000). *Social work practice with people of color: A process stage approach* (1st, 2nd, 3rd eds.). Monterey, Belmont, Pacific Grove, CA: Brooks/Cole.

Lundblad, K. S. (1995, September). Jane Addams and social feform: A fole model for the 1990s. *Social Work, 40*(5), 661–669.

Lundblad, K. S. (1996, March 10). *Jane Addams: Pacifist social worker.* Unpublished manuscript. Philadelphia, PA.

Lurie, H. L. (1935, October). The dilemma of the case worker. *Social Work Today, 3*(October), 13–15

Lush, G. H. (1950, May 23). Reds ineligible for state relief, Chidsey rules. *Philadelphia Inquirer.* Evelyn Butler Archive, Box 30, University of Pennsylvania.

Lynd, S. (1961, July). Jane Addams and the radical impulse. *Commentary.*

MacDonald, ?? (1951, March 5). National meeting closed to red-led social work unit. *World Telegram.* Marion T. Hathway Papers, Social Welfare History Archives, University of Minnesota.

MacDonald, D. (1963, January 19). Our invisible poor. *The New Yorker*, 82–132.

MacLeish, A. (1961). Jane Addams and the future. *Social Service Review, 35*(1), 1–5.

Mahaffey, M. (1981, March). Orchestrating mass support for social change. Paper presented at a symposium on Community Organization for the 1980s, Louisville, KY.

Malin, P. M. (1953). Civil liberties and social responsibilities in social work. *The Social Welfare Forum* (pp. 321–356). New York: Columbia University Press.

Mandell, B. R. (1996). Women and welfare, parts I & II. *NWSA Journal, 8*(2), 107–116, 8(3), 129–143.

Mandell, B. R. (1997). Downsizing the welfare state. *New Politics*, Winter, 33–46.

Marcus, G. (1948a). *Discussion of Mr. Bigge's paper on "Looking ahead in public assistance."* Evelyn Butler Archive, Box 30, University of Pennsylvania.

Marcus, G. (1948b, June 21). *A social work platform in 1948.* Paper presented at a Social Work Forum of the Social Welfare Division of the National Council of Arts, Sciences and Professions, New York. Evelyn Butler Archive, Box 41, University of Pennsylvania.

Marris, P., & Rein, M. (1967). *Dilemmas of social reform: Poverty and community action in the United States.* New York: Atherton.

Martin, G. W. (1976), *Madame Secretary, Frances Perkins*. Boston: Houghton Mifflin.

Martin, P. M. (1934). *Prohibiting poverty: Suggestions for a method of obtaining economic security*. New York: Farrar and Rinehart, Inc.

Mathis, T. P. (1977, April 7). *Race, class, and inequality: Implications for Black liberation*. Paper presented at the Annual Conference of the National Association of Black Social Workers.

Matusow, A. J. (1984). *The unraveling of America: A history of liberalism in the 1960s*. New York: Harper and Row.

McCarthy, K. D. (Ed.). (1989). *Lady bountiful revisited: Women, philanthropy and power*. New Brunswick, NJ: Rutgers University Press.

McElvaine, R. S. (1993). *The great depression, 1929–1941* (rev. ed.). New York: Times Books.

Meacham, S. (1987). *Toynbee Hall and social reform, 1880–1911: The search for community*. New Haven, CT: Yale University Press.

Meeropol, R., & Meeropol, M. (1975). *We are your sons: The legacy of Ethel and Julius Rosenberg*. Boston: Houghton Mifflin.

Mencher, S. (1962, December 4). *Perspectives on recent welfare legislation, fore and aft*. Evelyn Butler Archive, Box 34, University of Pennsylvania.

Mendes, R. (1964, May). *On conservatism in social work*. Unpublished manuscript. New York.

Meyer, C. (1970). *Social work practice: A response to the urban crisis*. New York: Free Press.

Meyer, C. (Ed.). (1983). *Clinical social work in the eco-systems perspective*. New York: Columbia University Press.

Meyer, C. (1998). *The foundations of social work practice: A graduate text*. Washington: National Association of Social Workers.

Midgley, J. (1992). Society, social policy and the ideology of Reaganism. *Journal of Sociology and Social Welfare, 19*(1), 13–28.

Midgley, J. (1997). *Social welfare in a global context*. Thousand Oaks, CA: Sage.

Miller, D. (1990). *Women and social welfare: A feminist analysis*. New York: Praeger.

Miller, H. (1994). The school of social welfare in the 1960s: A personal reminiscence. *Social Welfare at Berkeley*, (Fall), 38–41.

Miller, D., & Nowak, M. (1975). *The Fifties: The way we really were*. Garden City, NY: Doubleday.

Mills, C. W. (1956). *The power elite*. New York: Oxford University Press.

Mills, C. W. (1959). *The sociological imagination*. New York: Oxford University Press.

Mohl, R. (1988). *The making of urban America*. Wilmington, DE: Scholarly Resources.

Moore, D. (1970, May 6). Letter to the editor. *Hotch Pot*, 3.

Moreau, M. (1979). A structural approach to social work practice. *Canadian Journal of Social Work Education, 5*(1), 78–94.

Morell, C. (1987). Cause is function: Toward a feminist model of integration for social work. *Social Service Review, 61*(1), 144–155.

Morell, C. (1996). Radicalizing recovery: Addiction, spirituality, and politics. *Social Work, 41*(2), 306–312.

Morris, A. (1984). *The origins of the civil rights movement: Black communities organizing for change*. New York: Free Press.

Moynihan, D. P. (1969). *Maximum feasible misunderstanding*. New York: Random House.

Moynihan, D. P. (1973). *The politics of a guaranteed income: The Nixon administration and the family assistance plan*. New York: Random House

Mullaly, R. (1997). *Structural social work: Ideology, theory, and practice* (2nd ed.). Toronto: Oxford University Press.

Mullaly, R. P., & Keating, E. F. (1991), Similarities, differences and dialectics of radical social work. *Journal of Progressive Human Services, 2*(2), 49–78.

Muncy, R. (1991). *Creating a Female Dominion in American Reform, 1890–1935*. New York: Oxford University Press.

Murray, C. (1984). *Losing ground: American social policy, 1950–1980*. New York: Basic Books.

Murray, C. E. (1944). *New horizons for the settlement movement*. New York: National Federation of Settlements. Evelyn Butler Archive, Box 43, University of Pennsylvania.

Myrdal, G. (1944). *The Negro in America*. New York: Public Affairs Committee.

Myrdal, G. (1964). *An American dilemma*. New York: McGraw-Hill.

Naison, M. (1983). *Communists in Harlem during the depression*. Urbana, IL: University of Illinois Press.

National Association of Social Workers

(NASW). (1984, 1988). *Social work speaks.* Silver Springs: Author.

National Association of Social Workers (NASW). (1996). *Code of ethics* (rev. ed.). Washington, DC: Author.

Navarro, V. (1976). *Medicine under capitalism.* New York: Prodist.

Navasky, V. (1980). *Naming names.* New York: Viking.

Needleman, M., & Needleman, C. (1974). *Guerrillas in the bureaucracy: The community planning experiment in the U.S.* New York: Wiley.

Nes, J. A., & Iadicola, P. (1989). Toward a definition of feminist social work: A comparison of liberal, radical, and socialist models. *Social Work, 35*(1), 12–21.

Newdom, F. (1993). Beyond hard times. *Journal of Progressive Human Services, 4*(2), 65–77.

Newdom, F. (1997). Guilty, your honor, but not guilty enough. *BCR Reports, 9*(1), 1.

Newdom, F. (1996). Progressive and professional: A contradiction in terms? *BCR Reports, 8*(1), 1.

Newman, D. K. (1969). Changing attitudes about the poor. *Monthly Labor Review*, Reprint No. 2604, 32–49.

Norris, D., & Thompson, L. (Eds.). (1995). *The politics of welfare reform.* Thousand Oaks, CA: Sage.

Northen, H. (1994). Historical trends. *Tulane Studies in Social Welfare, 19*, 13–38.

O'Brien, F. S. (1968). The "Communist-dominated" unions in the United States since 1950. *Labor History, 9*, 184–209.

O'Brien, J. C. (1951, October 3). Governors hit relief meddling. *Philadelphia Inquirer.* Evelyn Butler Archive, Box 30, University of Pennsylvania.

O'Connor, J. (1973). *The fiscal crisis of the state.* New York: St. Martin's.

Ohlin, L. (1957). *Sociology and the field of corrections.* New York: Russell Sage.

Olsen, T. L. (1972). *Unfinished business: American social work in pursuit of reform, community and world peace, 1939–1950.* Unpublished doctoral dissertation. Minneapolis: University of Minnesota.

O'Neill, W. (1969). *Everyone was brave: The rise and fall of feminism in America.* Chicago: Quadrangle Books.

O'Neill, W. (1971). *The woman movement: Feminism in the U.S. and England.* Chicago: Quadrangle Books.

Orleck, A. (1987, December). *"We were a unified working class community"—Women's neighborhood organizing in the 1920s and 1930s.* Paper presented at the Annual Meeting of the American Historical Association.

Ottanelli, F. M. (1991). *The Communist party of the United States: From the depression to World War II.* New Brunswick, NJ: Rutgers University Press.

Parenti, M. (1988). *Democracy for the few.* New York: St. Martin's.

Patterson, J. (1994). *America's struggle against poverty, 1990–1994* (2nd ed.). Cambridge, MA: Harvard University Press.

Perkins, F. (1954). My recollections of Florence Kelley. *Social Service Review, 28*(1), 12–19.

Perlmutter, E. (1969, May 16). Albany closes; welfare dies. *SSEU News.*

Perlmutter, F. (1994). *Women and social change: Nonprofits and social policy.* Washington: National Association of Social Workers.

Pincus, A., & Minahan, A. (1973). *Social work practice: Model and method.* Itasca, IL: F.E. Peacock.

Pinderhughes, E. (1989). *Understanding race, ethnicity and power: The key to efficacy in clinical practice.* New York: Free Press.

Piven, F. F., & Cloward, R. A. (1971). *Regulating the poor: The functions of public welfare.* New York: Vintage.

Piven, F. F., & Cloward, R. (1977). *Poor people's movements: How they succeed, why they fail.* New York: Vintage.

Piven, F. F., & Cloward, R. (1982). *The new class war: Reagan's attack on the welfare state and its consequences.* New York: Pantheon.

Piven, F. F., & Cloward, R. A. (1988). *Why Americans don't vote.* New York: Pantheon.

Piven, F. F., & Cloward, R. (1995). *Regulating the poor: The functions of public welfare* (rev. ed.). New York: Vintage Books.

Platt, T., & Chandler, S. K. (1988). Constant struggle: E. Franklin Frazier and Black social work in the 1920s. *Social Work, 34*(4), 293–297.

Plotkin, W. (1996, August 6). [On-line]. Available: COMM-ORG.

Polansky, N. et al. (1953). Social workers in society: Results of a sampling study. *Social Work Journal, 34*(2), 74–80.

Pomerantz, C. (1963). *Un-Americana*. New York: Marzani & Mansell.

Pope, J. (1990). Women in the welfare rights struggle: The Brooklyn welfare action council. In G. West & R. Blumberg (Eds.), *Women and social protest* (pp. 57–73). New York: Oxford University Press.

Popple, P. R., & Leighninger, L. (1998). *Social work, social welfare, and American society* (3rd ed.). Needham Heights, MA: Allyn and Bacon.

Posner, W. (1995). Common human needs: The story of the prehistory of government by special interest. *Social Service Review*, 69(2),

Pray, K. L. M. (1933, March). A plan for the treatment of unemployment. *The Survey*. reprint in Evelyn Butler Archive, Box 56, University of Pennsylvania.

Pray, K. L. M. (1937). *Public funds in public hands?* Paper presented to the National Conference of Social Work. Indianapolis, Evelyn Butler Archive, Box 33, University of Pennsylvania.

Pray, K. L. M. (1940, October 28). *To an undecided voter.* Evelyn Butler Archive, Box 28, University of Pennsylvania.

Pray, K. L. M. (1945). Social work and social action. *Proceedings of the National Conference of Social Work*, 349–354.

Pray, K. L. M. (1946, May 19). *Social work in a revolutionary age.* Presidential address to the National Conference of Social Work, Buffalo, NY. Evelyn Butler Archive, Box 48, University of Pennsylvania.

Pray, K. L. M. (1947a, April 14). *When is community organization social work practice?* Paper presented at the National Conference of Social Work, San Francisco. Evelyn Butler Archive, University of Pennsylvania.

Pray, K. L. M. (1947b, October 21). *A philosophy of change in the community of social work.* Paper presented to the Massachusetts State Conference, Boston. Evelyn Butler Archive, Box 44, University of Pennsylvania.

Preston, (1989). In C. Belfrage (Ed.), *The American Inquisition, 1945–1960.* New York: Thunder Mouth.

Prigoff, A. (1987, July). *Progressive strategies: Worker-client relationships.* First Annual Meeting of the Bertha Capen Reynolds Society, Northampton, MA.

Prigoff, A. (1996). *Economic development policies: Institutional forms of violence against women.* Paper presented at the pre-Congress Women's Symposium, International Federation of Social Work-International Association of Schools of Social Work.

Prigoff, A. (1999, March 13). *Economic globalization: Impact on social welfare around the world.* Paper presented at the Annual Program Meeting of the Council on Social Work Education, San Francisco.

Prichard, D. (1998). Where have all the radicals gone? *Journal of Progressive Human Services*, 9(2), 1–6.

Prunty, H. E. (1970). Chicago scene II: Report from a participant. *The Social Work Forum* (pp. 156–160). New York: Columbia University Press.

Prunty, H. E. (1969). The New York story: A participant's viewpoint. *The Social Work Forum* (pp. 185–192). New York: Columbia University Press.

Quadagno, J. (1994). *The color of welfare: How racism undermined the war on poverty.* New York: Oxford University Press.

Quirion, H. (1972). Community organization and political action in Montreal. *Social Work*, 18(4), 85–90.

Rabinoff, G., & King, C. (1940, April 4). *Memo on qualifications and training for c.o.* New York: New York City Group for Study of C.O. Evelyn Butler Archive, University of Pennsylvania.

Radical Social Work Collective. (1975). *A statement of radical social work practice.* West Hartford, CT: University of Connecticut.

Rauch, J. (1975). Women in social work: Friendly visitors in Philadelphia, 1880. *Social Service Review*, 49(2), 241–259.

Rawls, J. (1971). *A theory of justice.* Cambridge: Harvard University Press.

Reamer, F. (1993). *The philosophical foundations of social work.* New York: Columbia University Press.

Reamer, F. (1995). *Social work values and ethics/* New York: Columbia University Press.

Record, W. (1951). *The Negro and the Communist Party: Studies in American Negro life.* Chapel Hill, NC: University of North Carolina Press.

Reeser, L. C. (1988, Fall). Women and social work activism in the 1980s. *Affilia*, 3(3), 51–62.

Reeser, L. C., & Epstein, I. (1990). *Professionalization and activism in social work: The sixties, the eighties, and the future.* New York: Columbia University Press.

Rein, M. (1970). Social work in search of a radical profession. *Social Work, 15*(2), 13–28.

Reisch, M. (1987a). From cause to case and back again: The reemergence of advocacy in social work. *Urban and Social Change Review, 19*, 20–24.

Reisch, M. (1987, November). *The changing nature of social service work: Implications for the post-Reagan era*. Paper presented at the West Coast Marxist Scholars Conference, Berkeley, CA.

Reisch, M. (1988). The uses of history in teaching social work. *Journal of Teaching in Social Work, 2*(1), 3–16.

Reisch, M. (1991). *The future of social work in an era of change*. Keynote address at the 1991 Annual State Conference of the National Association of Social Workers, California Chapter, San Jose.

Reisch, M. (1993a, March). *The future of social work in a world without socialism*. Paper presented at the Annual Meeting of the Council on Social Work Education, New York.

Reisch, M. (1993b). Linking client and community: The impact of Bertha Reynolds on social work. In J. Andrews (Ed.), *From Vision to Action: Social Workers of the Second Generation* (pp. 58–74). St. Paul, MN: University of St. Thomas.

Reisch, M. (1996). Urbanisation et politique sociale aux Etats-Unis. *Revue M, 85–86,* 9–14.

Reisch, M. (1997). The political context of social work. In M. Reisch & E. Gambrill (Eds.), *Social work in the twenty-first century* (pp. 80–92). Thousand Oaks, CA: Pine Forge.

Reisch, M. (1998). The socio-political context and social work method, 1890–1950. *Social Service Review, 72*(2), 161–181.

Reisch, M., & Andrews, J. (1999). Uncovering a silent betrayal: Using oral history to explore the impact of McCarthyism on the profession of social work in the United States. *Oral History Review, 26*(2), 87–106.

Reisch, M., Wenocur, S., & Sherman, W. (1981). Empowerment, conscientization, and animation as core social work skills. *Social Development Issues, 5*(2–3), 108–120.

Reisch, M., & Wenocur, S. (1983). Professionalization and voluntarism in social welfare: Changing roles and functions. *Journal of Voluntary Action Research, 11*(2–3), 11–31.

Reisch, M., & Wenocur, S. (1986). The future of community organization in social work: Social activism and the politics of profession-building. *Social Service Review, 60*(1), 70–91.

Reynolds, B. C. (1924). The mental hygiene of children. *The Social Welfare Forum.* Toronto, Canada.

Reynolds, B. C. (1932). An experiment in short contact interviewing. *Smith College Studies in Social Work, 3*(1).

Reynolds, B. C. (1934). Between client and community. *Smith College Studies in Social Work, 5*(1).

Reynolds, B. C. (1935, May), Whom do social workers serve? *Social Work Today, 2*(8), 5–8.

Reynolds, B. C. (1938). Rethinking social casework. *Social Work Today, 5*(2), 5–8.

Reynolds, B. C. (1941, February). Social workers and civil rights. In M. van Kleec et al. (Eds.), *Social work, peace and the people's well-being* (pp. 19–26). New York: Astoria.

Reynolds, B.C. (1951). *Social work and social living.* New York: NASW (reprint 1968).

Reynolds, B. C. (1953). *Fear in our culture.* Paper presented at the Cleveland Council of Arts, Sciences, and Professions.

Reynolds, B. C. (1963). *An uncharted journey.* New York: The Citadel Press.

Rice, (1948). Marian Hathway Papers, Folder 53, Social Welfare History Archives, University of Minnesota.

Richan, W. (1973). The social work profession and organized social welfare. In A. J. Kahn (Ed.), *Shaping the new social work* (pp. 147–168). New York: Columbia University Press.

Richan, W., & Mendlesohn, A. (1973). *Social work: The unloved profession.* New York: New Viewpoints/Franklin Watts.

Richmond, M. E. (1896, February). Criticism and reform in charity. *Charities Review, 5*(4).

Richmond, M. E. (1906, December 10). *Industrial conditions and the charity worker.* Mary Richmond Collection, Columbia University.

Rifkin, J. (1995). *The end of work: The decline of the global labor force and the dawn of a post-market era.* New York: G.P. Putnam & Sons.

Rittenhouse, M. W. (1937, November 17). *Trade unionism and professionalism.* Philadelphia: Young Men's Hebrew Association. Evelyn Butler Archive, Box 29, University of Pennsylvania.

Rivera, F., & Erlich, J. (1998). *Community organizing in a diverse society* (3rd ed.). Needham Heights, MA: Allyn & Bacon.

Robinson, V. (1937, June 12). *Is unionization compatible with social work?* Paper presented at a forum conducted under the auspices of the National Coordinating Committee of Social Service Employees, Philadelphia. Evelyn Butler Archive, Box 29, University of Pennsylvania.

Rogers, M., & Fitzgerald, E. J. (1934, July). Social work is futile. *The American Mercury*, 265–273.

Rose, N. E. (1989). Work relief in the 1930s and the origins of the Social Security Act. *Social Service Review, 63*(1), 63–91.

Rose, N. E. (1995). *Workfare or fair work: Women, welfare, and government work programs*. New Brunswick, NJ: Rutgers University Press.

Rose, S. J. (2000, March 5). Death of the helping professions. *Sacramento Bee*.

Rose, S. M. (1972). *The betrayal of the poor: The transformation of community action*. Cambridge, MA: Schenkman.

Rose, S. M., & Black, B. (1985). *Advocacy and empowerment: Mental health care in the community*. Boston: Routledge and Kegan Paul.

Rosen, E. K. (1950, January 26). *Public assistance under attack*. Paper presented at a meeting sponsored by the Philadelphia chapter of the American Association of Social Workers and the Pennsylvania Citizens Association for Health and Welfare, Philadelphia. Evelyn Butler Archive, Box 30, University of Pennsylvania.

Rosenberg, R. (1992). *Divided lives: American women in the 20th century*. New York: Hill and Wang.

Rosengard, B. (1986). In memoriam: Verne Weed, 1909–1986. *Catalyst: A Socialist Journal of the Social Services, 5*(4), 3–4.

Rosenthal, B. S. (1993). Graduate social work students' beliefs about poverty and attitudes toward the poor. *Journal of Teaching in Social Work, 7*(1), 107–121.

Ross, E. (1978). *Black heritage in social welfare, 1870–1930*. Metuchen, NJ: Scarecrow.

Ross, M. G. (1949). A share is yours. *The Social Welfare Forum*. New York: Columbia University Press, 382–385.

Ross, M. G. (1954, July 3). *Community development for health and welfare and its implications for professional social work*. Paper presented at the International Congress of Schools of Social Work, Toronto, Canada. Evelyn Butler Archive, University of Pennsylvania.

Rothman, G. (1985). *Philanthropists, therapists and activists: A century of ideological conflict in social work*. Cambridge, MA: Schenkman.

Rothman, S. (1978), *Women's proper place: A history of changing ideas and practices, 1870 to Present*. New York: Basic Books.

Rovere, R. H. (1959). *Senator Joe McCarthy*. New York: Harcourt Brace.

Rubin, L. G., Iberg, L., Silverstein, M., & Vincent, H. P. (1935, May). *A paper to indicate some of the trends in community attitudes as they have affected public relief policy in Philadelphia*. Philadelphia: Department of Public Welfare, Evelyn Butler Archive, University of Pennsylvania.

Ryan, M. (1979). *Womanhood in America: From colonial times to the present* (2nd ed.). New York: Franklin Watts.

Ryan, W. (1971). *Blaming the victim*. New York: Vintage.

Sale, K. (1976). *Power shift: The rise of the Southern rim and the challenge to the Eastern establishment*. New York: Random House.

Saleeby, D. (1997). *The strengths perspective in social work practice* (2nd ed.).

Salvatore, N. (1982). *Eugene Debs: Citizen and Socialist*. Urbana, IL: University of Illinois Press.

Sampson, T. (1976). Welfare advocacy: Part of the problem? San Francisco: Author.

Sanders, D. S. (1989, May). Social work values, nonviolence, peace, and development. *Swords and Ploughshares, 3*(4), 4–7.

Sanders, I. T. (1964). Professional roles in planned change. In M. Morris (Ed.), *Centrally planned change* (pp. 102–116). New York: National Association of Social Workers.

Sands, R. G., & Nuccio, K. (1992). Postmodern feminist theory and social work. *Social Work, 37*(5), 489–494.

Sarri, R., & Meyer, C. (1992). Is social work inherently conservative—designed to protect the vested interests of dominant power groups? In E. Gambrill & R. Pruger (Eds.), *Controversial issues in social work* (pp. 39–51). Boston: Allyn and Bacon.

Scherr, M. I. (1970, April 9). *Position paper on income maintenance*. Philadelphia.

Evelyn Butler Archive, Box 28, University of Pennsylvania.

Schlesinger, A. (1949). *The vital center: The politics of freedom.* Boston: Houghton Mifflin.

Schorr, A. (1959). The retreat to the technician. *Social Work, 4*(1), 29–33.

Schrecker, E. (1982, December). *An obligation of candor: The academy's response to congressional investigating committees.* Paper presented at the Annual Meeting of the American Historical Association, Washington, DC.

Schrecker, E. (1986). *No ivory tower: McCarthyism and the universities.* New York: Oxford University Press.

Schrecker, E. (1992) McCarthyism and the labor movement: The role of the state. In S. Rosswurm (Ed.), *The CIO's left-led unions* (pp. 139–158). New Brunswick, NJ: Rutgers University Press.

Schrecker, E. (1998). *Many are the crimes: McCarthyism in America.* Boston: Little Brown.

Schreiber, J. (1948). Political implications of mental health. *The Social Welfare Forum* (pp. 189–200). New York: Columbia University Press.

Schreiber, M. (1990). Book review of *Security Risk* by J. Fisher. *Journal of Progressive Human Services, 1*(2), 121–126.

Schreiber, M. (1995). Labeling a social worker a national security risk: A memoir. *Social Work, 40*(5), 656–660.

Schwartz, W. (1959). Group work and the social scene. In A. Kahn (Ed.), *Issues in American social work.* New York: Columbia University Press.

Schwartz, E. (1970). *Towards an alliance for radical change.* Boston: n.p.

Shoemaker, L. (1998, June). Early conflicts in social work education. *Social Service Review, 72*(2), 182–191.

Silverstein, M. (1975, April 19). *Social work and social change.* Paper presented at annual meeting of the Otto Rank Association, Philadelphia. Evelyn Butler Archive, University of Pennsylvania.

Simmons, L. (1996). Dilemmas of progressives in government: Playing Solomon in an age of austerity. *Economic Development Quarterly, 10*(2), 159–171.

Simmons, L. (1997). The battle for city hall: What do we fight over? *New England Journal of Public Policy,* 97–116.

Simmons, L. (1998). A new urban conservatism: The case of Hartford, Connecticut. *Journal of Urban Affairs, 20*(2), 175–198.

Simon, B. L. (1990). Rethinking empowerment. *Journal of Progressive Human Services, 1*(1), 27–39.

Simon, B. L. (1994). *The empowerment tradition in social work practice.* New York: Columbia University Press.

Simon, R. (Ed.). (1969). *As we saw the thirties: Essays on social and political movements of a decade.* Urbana, IL: University of Illinois Press.

Sims, N. (1947). The AAGW and social action. *The Group, 10*(1), 3–6.

Sklar, K. K. (1989). Who funded Hull House? In L. McCarthy (Eds.), *Lady bountiful revisited: Women, philanthropy and power* (pp. 94–115). New Brunswick, NJ: Rutgers University Press.

Sklar, K. K. (1991). Explaining the power of women's political culture in the creation of the American welfare state, 1890–1932. In S. Koven & S. Michel (Eds.), *Gender and the origins of welfare states in Western Europe and North America.* New York: Routledge.

Sklar, K. K. (1992). *Doing the nation's work: Florence Kelley and women's political culture, 1860–1932.* New Haven, CT: Yale University Press.

Sklar, K. K. (1993). The historical foundations of women's power in the creation of the American welfare state, 1830–1930. In S. Koven & S. Michel, S (Eds.), *Mothers of a New World: Maternalist politics and the origins of welfare states* (pp. 43–93). New York: Routledge.

Sklar, K. K. (1995). *Florence Kelley and the nation's work.* New Haven, CT: Yale University Press.

Slobodzian, J. A.(1997, June 1). "Red" recalls landmark Phila. Trial. *Philadelphia Inquirer,* pp. E1, 4.

Smukler, M., McEldowney, C., & Coblentz, S. (1970a). *Social welfare worker as political activist.* Cleveland and New York: Movement for a Democratic Society.

Smukler, M., McEldowney, C., & Coblentz, S. (1970b). *This is social work education or . . . here we go 'round the prickly pear.* Cleveland, OH: Movement for a Democratic Society.

Social Work Action for Welfare Rights (SWAWR). (1969, May). Social workers: "Part of the problem or part of the solution?" *Social Work Action for Welfare Rights News.*

Solender, S. (1957, May 21). *Public social policy and social work practice.* Paper presented at the Session of the National Association of Social Workers, Philadelphia.

Soll, G. (1950, December). Civil liberties and security. *The Survey, 86,* 541–545.

Solomon, B. (1976). *Black empowerment: Social work in oppressed communities.* New York: Columbia University Press.

Spano, R. (1982). *The rank and file movement in social work.* Latham, MD: University Press of America.

Specht, H. (1968, May 29). *Disruptive tactics.* Paper presented at the National Conference on Social Welfare, San Francisco.

Specht, H. (1972, March). The deprofessionalization of social work. *Social Work, 28*(1), 3–15.

Specht, H. (1994). Looking back, looking forward: 50 years of social welfare education at Berkeley. *Social Welfare at Berkeley, Fall,* 4–6.

Specht, H., & Courtney, M. (1994). *Unfaithful angels: How social work abandoned its mission.* New York: Free Press.

Speizman, M. (1968, February). The radicals and the poor. *Social Casework, 99*(1), 102–110.

Staples, M. A. (1983, June 15). A voice for the have-nots. *The Lutheran,* 11–13.

Starr, P. (n.d.). *Why am I a Socialist?* Daily Campaign Edition, Box 19, Folder 273, Sophia Smith Collection.

Starr, P. (1982). *The social transformation of American medicine.* New York: Basic Books.

Statham, D. (1978). *Radicals in social work.* London: Routledge and Kegan Paul.

Stebner, E. (1997). *The women of Hull House: A study in spirituality, vocation and friendship.* Albany: State University of New York Press.

Stern, H. R. (1950, February 23). New York City public assistance budgets. Address presented at midwinter meeting of New York State Public Welfare Association, Albany. Evelyn Butler Archive, Box 30, University of Pennsylvania.

Sternbach, J. (1972a, April 4). *The dialectics of social work.* Faculty colloquium, University of Pennsylvania, Philadelphia.

Sternbach, J. (1972b, November 28). *Organizing behind bars.* Paper presented at 3rd National NASW Professional Symposium, New Orleans.

Stoesz, D. (1981, September). A wake for the welfare state: Social welfare and the neoconservative challenge. *Social Service Review.*

Stoesz, D. (1997). The end of social work. In M. Reisch & E. Gambrill (Eds.), *Social work in the twenty-first century* (pp. 368–375). Thousand Oaks, CA: Pine Forge.

Stoesz, D. (1999). Unraveling welfare reform. *Society, 36*(4), 53–61.

Stoesz, D., & Karger, H. (1992). *Reconstructing the American welfare state.* Lanham, MD: Rowman and Littlefield.

Stoesz, D., & Saunders, D. (1999). Welfare capitalism: A new approach to poverty policy? *Social Service Review, 73*(3), 380–400.

Stouffer, S. (1966). *Communism, conformity and civil liberties.* New York: Wiley.

Strom-Gottfried, K.(1997). The implications of managed care for socia work education. *Journal of Social Work Education, 33*(1), 7–18.

Strong, J. (1898). *The twentieth century.* New York: MacMillan.

Stuart, P. (1989, March). *Philanthropy, voluntarism, and innovation: Settlement houses in twentieth-century America.* Paper presented at the Annual Program Meeting of the Council on Social Work Education, Chicago.

Stuart, P. (1992). The Kingsley House extension program: Racial segregation in a 1940s settlement program. *Social Service Review, 66*(1), 112–120.

Stuart, P. (1996, February). *Social workers and public policy: The 1912 "social standards for industry."* Paper presented at the Annual Program Meeting of the Council on Social Work Education, Washington, DC.

Sumner, W. G. (1884). *What social classes owe each other.* New York: Harper & Bros.

Swensen, C. (1998). Clinical social work's contribution to a social justice perspective. *Social Work, 43*(5), 527–537.

Sylvester, L. (1964, December 7). *Poverty and social change in Pennsylvania,* Harrisburg: Committee on Children and Youth of the Governor's Council for Human Services. Evelyn Butler Archive, Box 28, University of Pennsylvania.

Symes, L., & Clement, T. (1972). *Rebel America: The story of social revolt in the U.S.* New York: Harper and Bros.

Sytz, F. (1947, June 17). Letter to the editor. *New Orleans State.*

Sytz, F. (1957). Desegregation: One view from the deep South. *Social Work, 2*(3), 3–8.

Taft, J. (1939, June). *Function as the basis of development in social work processes.* Paper presented at the meeting of the American Association of Psychiatric Social Workers, National Conference of Social Work. Evelyn Butler Archive, University of Pennsylvania.

Tambor, M. (1973). Unions and voluntary agencies. *Social Work, 19*(1), 41–47.

Tambor, M. (1981). Independent unionism and the politics of self-defeat. *Catalyst, 11,* 23–31.

Taubman, B., & Polster, S. M. (1969, May 26). Militants again raid welfare conference. *New York Post,* p. 5.

Tentler, L. W. (1979). *Wage earning women: Industrial work and family life in the U.S., 1900–1930.* New York: Oxford University Press.

Terrell, P. (Ed.). (1994). *Social welfare at Berkeley, 6*(1), Berkeley: University of California.

Thomas, N. (1936). Speech at Socialist Party rally in New York. Evelyn Butler Archive, University of Pennsylvania.

Thursz, D. (1966). Social action as a professional responsibility. *Social Work, 11*(3), 11–21.

Thursz, D. (1971). The arsenal of social action strategies: Options for social workers. *Social Work, 16*(1), 27–34.

Titmuss, R. (1958). *Essays on the welfare state.* London: Allen & Unwin.

Toll, H. W. (1934, December 31). *Federal-state unemployment insurance.* Chicago: The American Legislators' Association. Evelyn Butler Archive, Box 56, University of Pennsylvania.

Towle, C. (1945). *Common human needs.* Washington, DC: U.S. Department of Health, Education, and Welfare.

Towle, C. (1952). *Common human needs* (rev. ed.). New York: American Association of Social Workers.

Towle, C. (1954). *The learner in education for the professions.* Chicago: University of Chicago Press.

Trattner, W. (1986). *Biographical dictionary of social welfare in America.* Westport, CT: Greenwood.

Trattner, W. (1995). *From poor law to welfare state* (5th ed.). New York: Free Press.

Trecker, H. (1955). *Group work: Foundations and frontiers.* New York: William Morrow.

Trolander, J. (1975). *Settlement houses and the great depression.* Detroit: Wayne State University Press.

Trolander, J. (1987). *Professionalism and social change: From the settlement house movement to neighborhood centers, 1886–present.* New York: Columbia University Press.

Tropman, J. (1989). *American values and social welfare: Cultural contradictions in the welfare state.* Englewood Cliffs, NJ: Prentice-Hall.

Trumbo, D. (1972). *The time of the toad: A study of inquisition in America, and two related pamphlets.* New York: Harper and Row.

Tucker, W. J. (1903). The progress of the social conscience, Boston: South End House Association. Reprint from the *Atlantic Monthly, 116*(3), 289–303..

Tugwell, R. G. (1934, May 21). *Relief and reconstruction.* Address before the National Conference of Social Workers, Kansas City, MO. Evelyn Butler Archive, Box 56, University of Pennsylvania.

United Nations. (1948). *Universal declaration of human rights.* New York: United Nations.

van den Bergh, N. (Ed.). (1995). *Feminist practice in the 21st century.* Washington, DC: National Association of Social Work.

van den Bergh, N., & Cooper, L. B. (Eds.). (1986). *Feminist visions for social work.* Silver Spring, MD: National Association of Social Workers.

van Kleeck, M. (1915). *Facts about wage-earners in the United States census* [instructional materials]. New York: The New York School of Philanthropy.

van Kleeck, M. (1932). *Social research and industry.* Paper presented at the International Conference of Social Work, 4th section, Frankfurt-am-Main, Germany. Evelyn Butler Archive, University of Pennsylvania.

van Kleeck, M. (1934). *Miners and management.* New York: Russell Sage.

van Kleeck, M. (1934). Our illusions regarding government. *The Social Welfare Forum* (pp. 473–485). Chicago: University of Chicago Press.

van Kleeck, M. (1936). *Creative America: Its resources for Social Security*. New York: Covici, Friede.

van Soest, D. (Ed.). (1992). *Incorporating peace and social justice into the social work curriculum*. Washington, DC: Peace and Social Justice Committee, National Association of Social Workers.

Van Soest, D. (1995). Multiculturalism and social work education: The non-debate about competing perspectives. *Journal of Social Work Education, 31*(1), 55–66.

van Soest, D. (1996, Spring/Summer). Impact of social work education on student attitudes and behavior concerning oppression. *Journal of Social Work Education, 32*(2), 191–202.

van Soest, D. (1997). *The global crisis of violence: Common problems, universal causes, shared solutions*. Washington: National Association of Social Workers.

van Soest, D., & Bryant, S. (1995, July). Violence reconceptualized for social work: The urban dilemma. *Social Work, 40*(3), 549–557.

van Wormer, K. (1997). *Social welfare: A world view*. Chicago: Nelson-Hall.

Volk, L. (1921, November 19).

Wagner, D. (1989b, September). Fate of idealism in social work: Alternative experiences of professional careers. *Social Work, 35*(4), 389–395.

Wagner, D. (1989a). Radical movements in the social services: A theoretical framework. *Social Service Review, 63*(2), 264–284.

Wagner, D. (1990). *The quest for a radical profession: Social service careers and political ideology*. New York: University Press of America.

Wagner, D. (1999). Progressive, not . . . , *Journal of Progressive Human Services, 10*(2), 3–6.

Wagner, D. (2000). *What's love got to do with it? A critical look at American charity*. New York: New Press.

Wald, L. (1915a). *The house on Henry Street*. New York: Henry Holt.

Wald, L. (1915b). *Windows on Henry Street*. New York: Russell Sage Foundation.

Walker, S. H. (1924, June). *Impressions of the Toronto conference*. Laura Spellman Rockefeller Memorial Collection, Series III, Subseries 6, Box 62, Folder 672, Rockefeller Archive Center, Tarrytown, New York.

Walker (1968, December 6).

Walkowitz, D. J. (1987, December 29). 'Fudge alone does not work': Work, gender and the mystification of professional workers—social workers at work in the 1920s. Paper presented at the Annual Meeting of the American Historical Association, Washington, DC.

Walkowitz, D. (1988). *Professionalizing social workers: The social and ideological reconstruction of women's work, 1900–1930*. Seattle: University of Washington Press.

Walkowitz, D. (1999). *Working with class: Social workers and the politics of middle class identity*. Chapel Hill, NC: University of North Carolina Press.

Warburg, J. P. (1936, January 15). *What of 1936?* Address presented at the Chicago Association of Commerce, Chicago, Washington, DC: National Liberty League. Evelyn Butler Archive, Box 58, University of Pennsylvania.

Ware, S. (1981). *Beyond suffrage: Women in the New Deal*. Cambridge: Harvard University Press.

Weed, V. (1985). The importance of community organizing. *Catalyst, 5(1)*, 83–85.

Weick, A., & Vandiver, S. (Eds.). (1982). *Women, power, and change*. Washington: National Association of Social Workers.

Weinstein, J. (1968). *The corporate ideal in the liberal state, 1900–1918*. Boston: Beacon Press.

Wenocur, S. (1975, September). The social welfare workers' movement: A case study of new left thought in practice. *Journal of Sociology and Social Welfare, 3(1)*, 3–20.

Wenocur, S., & Reisch, M. (1983). The social work profession and the ideology of professionalization. *Journal of Sociology and Social Welfare, 10*(4), 684–732.

Wenocur, S., & Reisch, M. (1989). *From charity to enterprise: The development of American social work in a market economy*. Urbana, IL: University of Illinois Press.

Wenocur, S., & Weisner, S. (1992). Should community organization be based on a grassroots strategy? In E. Gambrill & R. Pruger (Eds.), *Controversial issues in social work* (pp. 228–300). Boston: Allyn and Bacon.

West, G. (1981). *The national welfare rights movement: The social protest of poor women*. New York: Praeger.

West, G., & Blumberg, R. L. (Eds.). (1990).

Women and social protest. New York: Oxford University Press.

Whitaker, W., & Federico, R. (1990). *Social welfare in today's world* (2nd ed.). New York: McGraw Hill.

White, C. (1953). Social workers in society: Some further evidence. *Social Work Journal, 75*(4), 162–164.

White. G. C. (1959, March). Social settlements and immigrant neighbors, 1889–1914. *Social Service Review, 30*(1), 56-66.

Wickenden, E. (1954). *How to influence public policy: A short manual on social action*. New York: American Association of Social Workers.

Williams, P. (1946, October 15). Preliminary summary of report on *Refugees and displaced persons: An urgent United Nations problem*. New York: Russell Sage, Evelyn Butler Archive, Box 35, University of Pennsylvania.

Williams, W. A. (1968). The great evasion. Chicago: Quadrangle Books.

Wilson, G. (1978). Interview. In V. S. Grayson (Ed.), *NASW oral history project*. New York: Columbia University Press.

Wilson, W. J. (1996). *When work disappears: The world of the new urban poor*. New York: Alfred Knopf.

Wirth, L. (1949). Social goals for America. *The Social Welfare Forum* (pp. 3–20). New York: Columbia University Press.

Withorn, A. (1976). Helping ourselves: The limits and potential of self-help. *Radical America*, 25–39.

Withorn, A. (1984). *Serving the people: Social services and social change*. New York: Columbia University Press.

Withorn, A. (1996, October). "Why do they hate me so much?" A history of welfare and its abandonment in the U.S. *American Journal of Orthopsychiatry, 66*, 496–509.

Withorn, A., & Newdom, F. (1997). "Let's do something": A BCRS national action initiative to move the agenda forward. *BCR Reports, 9*(2), 1–2.

Wolfe, T. (1970). *Radical chic and mau-mauing the flak catchers*. New York: Farrar, Straus and Giroux.

Wolfson, T. (1951, June 23). *Can the middle class work with organized labor?* Presented at the Dinner Meeting of the Ninth Annual Conference of the Philadelphia Labor Education Association, Haverford, PA. Evelyn

Butler Archive, Box 55, University of Pennsylvania.

Woloch, N. (1984). *Women and the American experience*. New York: Alfred Knopf.

Woods, R. A., & Kennedy, A. J. (1922). *The settlement horizon: A national estimate*. New York: Russell Sage Foundation.

Young Men's Christian Association (YMCA). (1934). *Twenty questions on the economic security of the people: A study outline*. New York: YMCA. Evelyn Butler Archive, University of Pennsylvania.

Young, R. E. (1969, November 14). *The peace march to Washington—The first few steps*, Address to the staff of Children's Hospital, Philadelphia. Evelyn Butler Archive, Box 34, University of Pennsylvania.

Young, W. (1970, November 2). *Centennial symposium address*. School of Social Work, Ohio State University.

Young, W., & Lourie, N. (1969, November 3). *Testimony on family assistance and Social Security legislation before the Committee on Ways and Means of the U.S. House of Representatives*. Washington, DC. Evelyn Butler Archive, Box 34, University of Pennsylvania.

Young Women's Christian Association (YWCA). (1920), *Southern white women on lynching and mob violence*. Atlanta: Commission on Interracial Cooperation, YWCA.

Young Women's Christian Association (YWCA). (1932). *Association of Southern women for the prevention of lynching: Beginning of the movement*. Atlanta: Commission on Interracial Cooperation, YWCA. Evelyn Butler Archive, Box 58, University of Pennsylvania.

Young Women's Christian Association. (YWCA). (1946, January 9).

Young Women's Christian Association (YWCA). (1965). *Annual report*. New York: Author.

Young Women's Christian Association (YWCA). (1969–1970). *Annual report*. New York: Author.

Young Women's Christian Association, (YWCA). (1971). *Institutes to eliminate racism*. New York: Author.

Youngdahl, B. (1949, June). Civil rights versus civil strife. *The Social Welfare Forum* (pp. 21–37). New York: Columbia University Press.

Youngdahl, B. (1952). What we believe. *The*

Social Welfare Forum (pp. 29–45). New York: Columbia University Press.

Zaroulis, N. L., & Sullivan, G. (1984). *Who spoke up? American protest against the war in Vietnam, 1963–1975*. Garden City, NY: Doubleday.

Zimbalist, S. (1977). *Historic themes and landmarks in social work research*. New York: Harper and Row.

Zinn, H. (1994). *You can't be neutral on a moving train: A personal history of our times*. Boston: Beacon.

Index